hairdressing

THE FOUNDATIONS

THE OFFICIAL GUIDE TO S/NVQ LEVEL 2   FIFTH EDITION

LEO PALLADINO AND MARTIN GREEN

City & Guilds   habia   DELMAR CENGAGE Learning

Australia • Brazil • Japan • Korea • Mexico • Singapore • Spain • United Kingdom • United States

Hairdressing: The Foundations,
The Official Guide to S/NVQ Level 2
5th edition
Leo Palladino and Martin Green

Publishing Director: John Yates
Publisher: Melody Dawes
Development Editor: Jenny Clapham
Content Project Editor: Fiona Freel
Manufacturing Manager: Helen Mason
Senior Production Controller: Maeve Healy
Marketing Manager: Jason Bennett
Typesetter: Meridian Colour Repro,
Berkshire
Cover design: Vince Cusack, CPI London
Text design: Design Deluxe. Bath, UK
Illustrators: Oxford Designers & Illustrators

For product information and technology assistance, contact **emea.info@cengage.com**.

For permission to use material from this text or product, and for permission queries, email **clsuk.permissions@cengage.com**

British Library Cataloguing-in-Publication Data
A catalogue record for this book is available from the British Library.

ISBN: 978-1-84480-417-7

Cengage Learning EMEA
High Holborn House, 50-51 Bedford Row
London WC1R 4LR

Cengage Learning products are represented in Canada by Nelson Education Ltd.

For your lifelong learning solutions, visit
www.cengage.co.uk

Printed by C&C Offset Printing, China
4 5 6 7 8 9 10 – 10 09 08

contents

part one

part two

foreword

When Habia first began to promote the S/NVQ Level 2 qualification in hairdressing, back in 1989, no one envisaged the phenomenal success that would be achieved. Within five years the S/NVQ established itself as the accepted qualification throughout the hairdressing industry. Fundamental to this achievement was the success of Leo Palladino's book *Hairdressing – The Foundations*.

Ever since my first meeting with Leo and our publishers in 1989, Habia has been an integral part of *Hairdressing – The Foundations*. So much so, that we are now publishing the fifth edition. I am delighted that Leo has actively and consistently updated his original book in keeping with changes to the qualification and to changes within the industry. This edition has the added bonus of being co-written by the respected author Martin Green. Both authors have a great ability to cater to learners at all levels. Martin is also the author of *Begin Hairdressing: The Official Guide for Level 1* and co-author with Leo Palladino for *Professional Hairdressing: The Official Guide for Level 3*.

A Lecturer's Resource Pack by Jane Goldsbro also accompanies this great book.

Alan Goldsbro, Habia CEO

acknowledgements

The author and publishers would like to thank the following.

For providing pictures for the book

Alan Edwards (at the 50th L'Oréal Colour Trophy, London, May 2005)
Alteq
American Dream
Antoinette Beenders (at the 50th L'Oréal Colour Trophy, London, May 2005)
Babyliss
BLM Health
Carol Hayes and Associates
Charles Worthington (at the 50th L'Oréal Colour Trophy, London, May 2005)
Comby
Corbis
Cricket
Denman
Desmond Murray
Dr Andrew Wright
Dr John Gray
Dr M. H. Beck
Ellisons
Getty Images
Ghd hair
Goldwell
HMSO
International PACT Art Team
istockphoto.com
John Carne
L'Oréal Professionnel
Lawrence Anthony
Luster
Mahogany
Mediscan
Michael Balfre
Namasté
National Westminster Bank
Pat Wood
Patrick Cameron
Paul Falltrick for Matrix
Redken
Rush London for Goldwell
Sacha New
Science Photo
Splinters Academy
Stella Lambrou at The Crib, Lytham
The Company Hairdressing
Thornton Howdle
Toni&Guy (at the 50th L'Oréal Colour Trophy, London, May 2005)
Trevor Sorbie (at the 50th L'Oréal Colour Trophy, London, May 2005)
Wella

The publisher would also like to thank Rush London for Goldwell for providing the image used on the front cover of this book.

For their help with the photoshoot

Photoshoot location:
Stroud College
Stratford Road
Gloucestershire GL5 4AH

Models:
Francesca Wegrzyn
Natasha Wegrzyn
Fiona Dean
Sasha Green
Debbie Horsemann
Sarah Turner
Abbie Turner
Samantha Richmond
Nick Pilbury

Stylists:
HQ Hairdressing, Cheltenham

Martin Green
Becci Fincham
Gemma Winrow

Trainee:
Cutting Room, Cirencester

Vicky Powell

Photography:
Xcaret Media
James Oliver

introduction

The perimeter outline formed by the hair in relation to the shape of the face provides a frame that projects the image and personality that it contains within. The impression that a hairstyle gives therefore has an influence on how people perceive you and they often comment about it: 'Love the haircut.' 'I think that really suits you.'

This unique look is based upon the frame that the hair creates for the face; this total aspect is vitally important and produces individuality. How you 'fill in' the detail – the movement, texture, colour and placement – is down to you. It is your interpretation, understanding, technical ability and experience and this special trust is invested in your hands.

Under your stewardship, make it work for both you and your client.

Good luck.

Leo Palladino and Martin Green

hairdressing
NVQ/SVQ Level 2

As our customers' expectations rise, our standards must rise too. This means that our hairdressing industry will need better-trained staff who are more flexible and highly motivated. Over recent years the NVQ/SVQ Level 2 has provided the definitive minimum standard for occupational competence and a foundation level forming the basis of professional excellence.

Many jobs have a similar work focus since all companies need customers in order to exist. You will notice this particularly if you think about those practices that are similar to many different industries or professions. For instance, many of the day-to-day duties performed by a receptionist in a hairdressing salon are similar to the tasks performed by a receptionist in a leisure centre. There is a common denominator and this is primarily concerned with communication. The communication may be carried out in many different ways: on the telephone, face to face, by e-mail or through other electronic means. Similarly if you think about the tasks in retail – stock control, product rotation, the restocking of shelves and till operation – you can see that there are many ways in which people working in different occupations do similar things.

So, bearing these factors in mind, the modern standards have been devised to be far more flexible in their approach. It is now common for one industry sector to use another sector's standards. This principle of stand-alone, reusable material is now widely used. Our Hairdressing Level 2 units have been designed this way and in the next section you will find an outline of the units and the main outcomes that make up the qualification.

NVQ/SVQ – AN INTRODUCTION

National vocational qualifications (NVQs) and Scottish vocational qualifications (SVQs) have a common structure and design. That is to say, they all follow a particular format for all occupations and vocational sectors. Each vocational qualification is structured the same way and is made up from a number of grouped components.

Each grouping or unit will address a specific task or area of work e.g. reception. When a staff member is asked to 'do reception' the work involves many different tasks: handling payments, making appointments, receiving clients and restocking products and stationery materials. These individual tasks are referred to in NVQ/SVQ terms as the 'main outcomes'.

HAIRDRESSING LEVEL 2 NVQ/SVQ STRUCTURE

Nine units must be completed for the full NVQ/SVQ. Each candidate must complete the seven mandatory units plus two optional units.

Mandatory units (all of these must be completed)

Unit code	Unit title	Covered in this chapter of the book
G1	Ensure your own actions reduce risks to health and safety	5 Health and safety in the salon
G5	Give clients a positive impression of yourself and your organisation	2 Client care and communication
G7	Advise and consult with clients	1 Client consultation
H6	Cut hair using basic techniques	6 Cutting hair
H9	Shampoo and condition hair	4 Shampooing and conditioning hair
H10	Style, dress and finish hair using basic techniques	8 Styling hair
H13	Change hair colour using basic techniques	7 Colouring hair

Optional units (two of the following units must be completed)

Unit code	Unit title	Covered in this chapter of the book
H12	Perm and neutralise hair using basic techniques	9 Perming, relaxing and neutralising hair
H15	Perm, relax and neutralise hair	
H16	Perm, relax and neutralise African-Caribbean hair	
G4	Fulfil salon reception duties	3 Salon reception
G6	Promote additional products or services to clients	12 Promoting the business
G8	Develop and maintain effectiveness at work	11 Working effectively
H11	Style hair using basic plaiting techniques and adding hair	8 Styling hair
H18	Provide scalp massage services	4 Shampooing and conditioning hair

Units and main outcomes

The units listed above denote the smallest components of the NVQ/SVQ that can be credited by certificate: they are the smallest parts of a full NVQ/SVQ that can be awarded to a candidate. Each unit comprises a unit title and one or more individual main outcomes and these main outcomes are the smallest meaningful activities in NVQ/SVQs.

Unit code, title and main outcomes (example: health and safety)

Unit code	Unit title	Main outcomes
G1	Ensure your own actions reduce risks to health and safety	G1.1 Identify the hazards and evaluate the risks in your workplace G1.2 Reduce the risks to health and safety in your workplace

The main outcomes

Main outcomes are brief statements that outline the tasks in hand. Their titles are always expressed in 'do this' language, e.g. 'Identify the hazards and evaluate the risks in your workplace'. However, while giving you an idea of what needs to be done, it doesn't say how it's to be done.

The National Occupational Standards cover this in greater detail. Not only do they specify how each task is to be performed (i.e. 'performance criteria'), they also give the circumstances or situations in which these actions must be done (the 'range').

Performance criteria

The performance criteria are a list of the essential actions. Although these may not be necessarily in the order in which they should be done, they do provide a definitive checklist of what needs to be done. During training these performance criteria form the smallest components of method.

Example of performance criteria showing how the task must be done

Main outcome	Performance criteria
G4.3 Make appointments for salon services	● Deal with client requests for appointments promptly and politely ● Find out what the client wants ● Confirm the appointment details back to the client ● Make sure the details are correct and accurately recorded

Range

The range statements provide a number of conditions or applications in which the main outcomes must be performed. Quite simply, they state under what particular circumstances, and on what occasions, or in which special situations, the activity must take place.

Example of range statements – identifying which situations or circumstances need to be included when doing the task

Main outcome	Range
G4.3 Make appointments for salon services	● Appointments are made face-to-face with the client ● Appointments are made remotely by mobile, telephone or e-mail ● The client appointment details – name, contact details, service required, date and timings – are recorded

Knowledge and understanding

NVQs and SVQs are not only about doing. If you do your work properly, you need to understand what you are doing and why you are doing it. The terms 'theory', 'learning' and 'principles' generally refer to essential knowledge and understanding.

Typical knowledge statements covering what you need to know

Main outcome	Knowledge and understanding
G4.3 Make appointments for salon services	● How good communication is conducted with customers ● How to take messages for other people ● How and when to ask questions

At the point where a task's performance criteria and range have been covered and knowledge has been learnt, the task is carried out competently and a skill has been acquired.

Units and main outcomes often share similar components. For example, some of the performance criteria used within the main outcomes are the same e.g. H6.1, Maintain effective and safe methods of working when cutting hair, and H10.1, Maintain effective and safe methods of working when styling hair. Similarly, knowledge that is essential and underpins one main outcome will often occur in another. This duplication may at first seem unnecessary, but it occurs because of the modular, stand-alone design of NVQ/SVQs. This can be useful in terms of speeding up the learning process as sometimes knowledge or skills learnt in one activity are then directly applicable to other tasks. Recording and documenting these learnt experiences is then made even simpler; knowledge learnt in one situation can be quickly cross-referenced to similar activities in your portfolio or work log.

Under assessment

Your competence, your ability to carry out a task to a standard, is measured during **assessment**. Your ability to carry out the task, 'performance evidence', will be observed and measured against the performance criteria. Therefore your assessor will be watching to see how you carry out your work. Sometimes, when it is not possible to cover all the situations that might crop up, your assessor might ask you questions about what you have done and how you might apply that in a different situation. To help you get used to this, the activities that appear throughout the book contain lots of the types of questions that you might be asked.

Your understanding and background knowledge of work tasks is also measured through questions asked by your assessor. Sometimes you might be asked to give a personal account of what you have learned. This could take the form of writing a sequence of events that need to be done to complete the task satisfactorily. Other questions may ask you specifically about particular tasks; more often than not, these types of questions take the form of short-answer questions. Again, the activities covered within this book give plenty of examples and practice.

about this book

The common structure and design that exists within NVQ/SVQs is mirrored in many ways within this text. For the first time in the hairdressing NVQ/SVQ official series, revisions and updates have been totally reworked to both 'target' and 'fit' the needs of the learner and the occupational standards. The navigation to standards, access to information, quick referencing and illustration have been redesigned and reorganised in order to help you accelerate through your Level 2 programme. This uniform format or book style incorporates a number of features:

- a common structure and design throughout the text with explanations of the standards and on how to use this book;
- easy referencing systems to include tables, checklists, activities and tips;
- the same format and unit references as NVQ/SVQs, covering both mandatory and the various option groups.

HOW TO USE THIS BOOK

The format will help you to use and read this book more easily. Each chapter addresses specific units from the NVQ/SVQ Level 2. At the beginning of each chapter a referencing system provides a quick signposting to the information you want, providing a variety of starting and finishing points. In this next example, you can see the variety of features and icons used within the text.

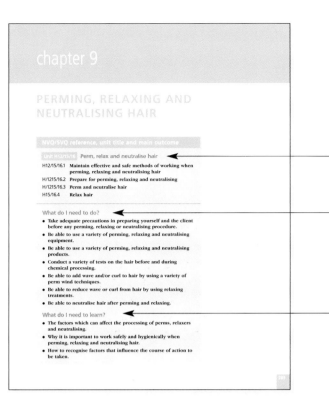

chapter 9

PERMING, RELAXING AND
NEUTRALISING HAIR

NVQ/SVQ reference, unit title and main outcome

UNIT H12/15/16 Perm, relax and neutralise hair

H12/15/16.1 Maintain effective and safe methods of working when perming, relaxing and neutralising hair
H/1215/16.2 Prepare for perming, relaxing and neutralising
H/1215/16.3 Perm and neutralise hair
H15/16.4 Relax hair

What do I need to do?
- Take adequate precautions in preparing yourself and the client before any perming, relaxing or neutralising procedure.
- Be able to use a variety of perming, relaxing and neutralising equipment.
- Be able to use a variety of perming, relaxing and neutralising products.
- Conduct a variety of tests on the hair before and during chemical processing.
- Be able to add wave and/or curl to hair by using a variety of perm wind techniques.
- Be able to reduce wave or curl from hair by using relaxing treatments.
- Be able to neutralise hair after perming and relaxing.

What do I need to learn?
- The factors which can affect the processing of perms, relaxers and neutralising.
- Why it is important to work safely and hygienically when perming, relaxing and neutralising hair.
- How to recognise factors that influence the course of action to be taken.

NVQ/SVQ reference, unit title and main outcome
An at-a-glance diagrammatic overview of the unit and main outcomes covered in the chapter.

What do I need to do?
A brief overview of the activities involved in the unit and customised information telling you what you need to do about practical tasks.

What do I need to learn?
Customised information on what you need to learn and understand in order to complete a task satisfactorily.

Information covered in this chapter
A list of information covered within the chapter.

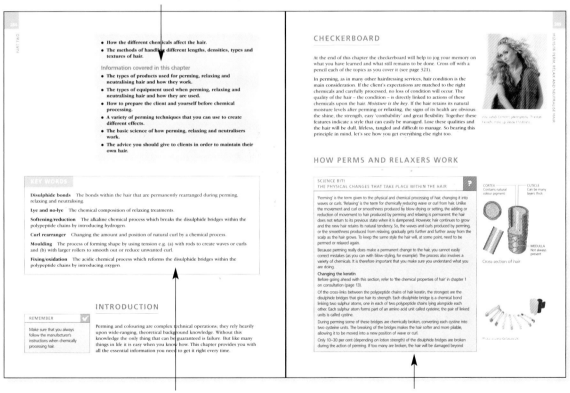

- How the different chemicals affect the hair.
- The methods of handling different lengths, densities, types and textures of hair.

Information covered in this chapter
- The types of products used for perming, relaxing and neutralising hair and how they work.
- The types of equipment used when perming, relaxing and neutralising hair and how they are used.
- How to prepare the client and yourself before chemical processing.
- A variety of perming techniques that you can use to create different effects.
- The basic science of how perming, relaxing and neutralisers work.
- The advice you should give to clients in order to maintain their own hair.

KEY WORDS

Disulphide bonds The bonds within the hair that are permanently rearranged during perming, relaxing and neutralising.

Lye and no-lye The chemical composition of relaxing treatments.

Softening/reduction The alkaline chemical process which breaks the disulphide bridges within the polypeptide chains by introducing hydrogen.

Curl rearranger Changing the amount and position of natural curl by a chemical process.

Moulding The process of forming shape by using tension e.g. (a) with rods to create waves or curls and (b) with larger rollers to smooth out or reduce unwanted curl.

Fixing/oxidation The acidic chemical process which reforms the disulphide bridges within the polypeptide chains by introducing oxygen.

INTRODUCTION

REMEMBER

Make sure that you always follow the manufacturer's instructions when chemically processing hair.

Perming and colouring are complex technical operations, they rely heavily upon wide-ranging, theoretical background knowledge. Without this knowledge the only thing that can be guaranteed is failure. But like many things in life it is easy when you know how. This chapter provides you with all the essential information you need to get it right every time.

CHECKERBOARD

At the end of this chapter the checkerboard will help to jog your memory on what you have learned and what still remains to be done. Cross off with a pencil each of the topics as you cover it (see page 321).

In perming, as in many other hairdressing services, hair condition is the main consideration. If the client's expectations are matched to the right chemicals and carefully processed, no loss of condition will occur. The quality of the hair – the condition – is directly linked to actions of these chemicals upon the hair. *Moisture is the key*. If the hair retains its natural moisture levels after perming or relaxing, the signs of its health are obvious: the shine, the strength, easy 'combability' and great flexibility. Together these features indicate a style that can easily be managed. Lose these qualities and the hair will be dull, lifeless, tangled and difficult to manage. So bearing this principle in mind, let's see how you get everything else right too.

HOW PERMS AND RELAXERS WORK

SCIENCE BIT!
THE PHYSICAL CHANGES THAT TAKE PLACE WITHIN THE HAIR

'Perming' is the term given to the physical and chemical processing of hair, changing it into waves or curls. 'Relaxing' is the term for chemically reducing wave or curl from hair. Unlike the movement and curl or smoothness produced by blow-drying or setting, the adding or reduction of movement to hair produced by perming and relaxing is permanent; the hair does not return to its previous state when it is dampened. However, hair continues to grow and the new hair retains its natural tendency. So, the waves and curls produced by perming, or the smoothness produced from relaxing, gradually gets further and further away from the scalp as the hair grows. To keep the same style the hair will, at some point, need to be permed or relaxed again.

Because perming really does make a permanent change to the hair, you cannot easily correct mistakes (as you can with blow-styling, for example). The process also involves a variety of chemicals. It is therefore important that you make sure you understand what you are doing.

Changing the keratin
Before going ahead with this section, refer to 'the chemical properties of hair' in chapter 1 on consultation (page 13).

Of the cross-links between the polypeptide chains of hair keratin, the strongest are the disulphide bridges that give hair its strength. Each disulphide bridge is a chemical bond linking two sulphur atoms, one in each of two polypeptide chains lying alongside each other. Each sulphur atom forms part of an amino acid unit called cysteine; the pair of linked units is called cystine.

During perming some of these bridges are chemically broken, converting each cystine into two cysteine units. The breaking of the bridges makes the hair softer and more pliable, allowing it to be moved into a new position of wave or curl.

Only 10–30 per cent (depending on lotion strength) of the disulphide bridges are broken during the action of perming. If too many are broken, the hair will be damaged beyond

CORTEX
Contains natural colour pigment

CUTICLE
Can be many layers thick

MEDULLA
Not always present

Cross-section of hair

Key words Special or technical terms.

Science bit Other technical information relevant to the chapter.

Step-by-steps Photo sequences to illustrate procedures

Remember boxes Tips or hints on points to remember.

Checkerboard A self-check system and means of recording progress towards achievement.

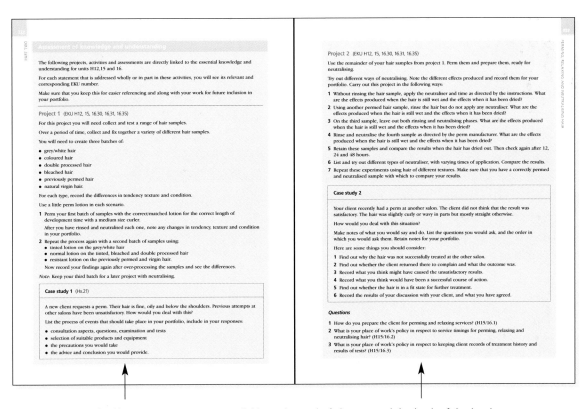

Tests A variety of self-assessment tests are available at the end of chapter and the back of the book.

NVQ/SVQ mapping grid

Mandatory units *(all must be completed)*

	G1	G5	G7	H6	H7	H9	H10	H13
1 Client consultation			X					
2 Client care and communication		X						
3 Salon reception								
4 Shampooing and conditioning hair						X		
5 Health and safety in the salon	X							
6 Cutting hair				X				
7 Colouring hair								X
8 Styling hair							X	
9 Perming, relaxing and neutralising hair								
10 Men's styling					X			
11 Working effectively								
12 Promoting the business								

G1   Ensure your own actions reduce risks to health and safety
G5   Give clients a positive impression of yourself and your organisation
G7   Advise and consult with clients
H6   Cut hair using basic techniques
H7   Cut hair using basic barbering techniques
H9   Shampoo and condition hair and scalp
H10   Style, dress and finish hair using basic techniques
H13   Change hair using basic colour techniques

Optional units *(One must be completed)*

	G4	G6	G8	H11	H12	H15	H16	H18
1 Client consultation								
2 Client care and communication								
3 Salon reception	X							
4 Shampooing and conditioning hair								
5 Health and safety in the salon								
6 Cutting hair								
7 Colouring hair								
8 Styling hair								
9 Perming, relaxing and neutralising hair					X	X	X	
10 Men's styling								
11 Working effectively			X					
12 Promoting the business		X						

G4   Fulfil salon duties
G6   Promote additional products or services to clients
G8   Develop and maintain your effectiveness at work
H11   Style hair using basic plaiting techniques and added hair
H12   Perm and neutralise hair using basic techniques
H15   Perm, relax and neutralise hair
H16   Perm, relax and neutralise African-Caribbean hair
H18   Provide scalp massage services

TONI & GUY AT THE 50TH ANNIVERSARY
L'ORÉAL COLOUR TROPHY, LONDON, MAY 2005.

ANTOINETTE BEENDERS AT THE 50TH ANNIVERSARY
L'ORÉAL COLOUR TROPHY, LONDON, MAY 2005.

TREVOR SORBIE AT THE 50TH ANNIVERSARY
L'ORÉAL COLOUR TROPHY, LONDON, MAY 2005.

CHARLES WORTHINGTON AT THE 50TH ANNIVERSARY
L'ORÉAL COLOUR TROPHY, LONDON, MAY 2005.

M. BALFRE AT THE ALTERNATIVE HAIR SHOW, 2005.

part one

chapter 1

CLIENT CONSULTATION

NVQ/SVQ reference, unit title and main outcome

Unit G7 Advise and consult with clients

G7.1 Identify what the client wants

G7.2 Analyse the hair, skin and scalp

G7.3 Advise your client and agree services and products

What do I need to do?

- You need to find out by using a combination of questions and visual aids what the client wants.
- You need to look for physical factors that will affect the options for following services and treatments.
- You need to provide advice based upon those factors that you have found before proceeding with any services and treatments.
- You need to then agree with the client a suitable course of action(s) that will produce the desired outcome.

What do I need to learn?

You need to know and understand:

- how to communicate positively, professionally and confidently
- how to recognise the types of hair and skin conditions that affect hairdressing services and treatments
- how to recognise the physical features and aspects that affect hairdressing services and treatments
- how to solve problems and provide suitable courses of action and advice
- a range of hair, skin and scalp conditions and characteristics at a basic, scientific level.

Information covered in this chapter

- **The client consultation processes of analysis, negotiation and professional advice.**
- **The physical and chemical properties of hair and the skin.**
- **Hair: textures, types, colour, conditions and growth.**
- **What to look for when examining the hair and scalp.**
- **Head shapes and facial features.**
- **Hair and scalp problems and diseases.**
- **Hair and scalp tests.**

KEY WORDS

Communication   Listening, hearing and responding to the client.

Body language   The *visual* communication of feelings, emotions and views.

Client care   Maintaining goodwill while developing a regular, repeated business.

Professional advise   Providing information based upon experience and knowledge.

INTRODUCTION

Consultation is the primary 'cornerstone' of hairdressing services. If this part isn't done correctly, all of your efforts will be wasted! Consultation is the starting point; the way that you conduct this service will show to the client the depth and breadth of your experience, your abilities in communicating professionally and, if it is done correctly, it will make the client confident that anything that follows will turn out fine.

REMEMBER

You don't get a second chance to create a good first impression.

CHECKERBOARD

At the end of this chapter the checkerboard will help to jog your memory on what you have learned and what still remains to be done. Cross off with a pencil each of the topics as you cover it (see page 36).

THE IMPORTANCE OF CONSULTATION

Client consultation is the most important service provided in the hairdressing salon. Unfortunately, though, it is usually provided as a sort of 'loss leader', given away freely in the hope of attracting a sale. Because of this, it is often given little time and lacks the thoroughness needed in its execution.

M. Balfre

M. Balfre

M. Balfre

Alan Edwards at the 50th Anniversary L'Oréal
Colour Trophy, London, May 2005

Never underestimate the value of consultation. If it is done properly it will:

1 provide the client with the confidence that you are the right person to do their hair;

2 give you the opportunity to create a mutually beneficial relationship that could last for years;

3 be the catalyst in building your professional profile, business and standing within the locality.

The communication and relationship between the stylist and client is quite different during the consultation process. When the client wants to know if a new style is going to be right, they are asking you for advice. In this formal relationship, they quickly learn about the breadth and depth of your technical knowledge and hairdressing expertise. Compare this to the type of conversation that takes place during routine visits: a lighter and less formal bond exists and the topics for conversation relate to families, friends and social activities.

So, by comparing the nature of these two roles that you need to take on, you can see that different opportunities arise. Even if your regular customers are totally happy with the service you provide, at least take the opportunity from time to time to redress the professional balance by treating them to the occasional consultation review. By doing this you will ensure that the customer never falls in to the trap of doing the 'same old thing' with their hair time after time. At the point where you routinely keep doing the same hairstyle, *your days as 'my hairdresser' are numbered*!

ACTIVITY

Role play is a way of acting out and testing what happens in a variety of situations. It is a mock-up or simulation of what would take place in a real live context.

Client consultation lends itself to role play very well and it can be practised with your colleagues. You can develop your communication and analytical skills further by putting them to the test in conducting consultation techniques and scenarios upon each other.

For example, conduct a role play consultation for the following hairdressing services:

- providing a client with home care advice
- recommending and advising suitable retail products to clients
- colour selection
- handling a complaint about a perm.

THE PURPOSE OF CONSULTATION

A consultation is a meeting in which advice is given and taken. It consists of talking to the client, listening to them so you can establish their needs and jointly negotiating a suitable course of action. You will be expected to exchange views and to discuss with them what is to be done with their hair. You, the professional, already know a lot about hair generally, but your client is more familiar than you are with their own hair and how it behaves.

Listen to what your client tells you and find out what they have in mind. They may ask for something that you know just won't work. Consultation will always lead to change and change is something that, although often desired, isn't always easy. You will need to help your client make that change, particularly if it means having a new look. Recommending a course of action, agreeing a new effect and doing it isn't necessarily going to ensure that the client will be totally comfortable with the outcome.

People will naturally develop routines within their lives and this relates to hairdressing as well as everything else. When you restyle a client's hair, you change its appearance from how it was. This means that your client must change their hair routine. This sounds simple, but in actual fact the hardest thing to do is break a habit!

In order for your client to be totally satisfied with the effect that you have created you need to get them to take on board the necessary change.

> **REMEMBER** ✓
>
> Consultation precedes any other service. Always find out what your client wants before they are shampooed at the basin, even if it's only a blow dry!

M. Balfre

ACTIVITY ⇆

Find out exactly what your client's previous routine was.

Here are typical questions on which you will need to give consideration and advice.

Question	Consideration and advice
What products does the client use to wash and condition their hair?	Are these still suitable, will the benefits from using these still be the same?
Is their hair normally left to dry in a towel for a while whilst they are getting on with other things?	Is this satisfactory? Will they still be able to achieve the same result if they do this?
What styling tools do they use?	Are these still applicable or are new tools now required?
What hairdressing skills do they possess?	Have they the ability to achieve the same results as you? Would they be prepared to learn new skills?
What styling and finishing products do they use?	Are these still valid or are new products an essential part of this new routine?
How often do they revisit the salon? Does their lifestyle, work, social or family commitments present any problems?	Are they prepared to maintain and look after this style as often as it is needed?

Consultation includes:

- finding out exactly what a client wants before any hairdressing services are carried out;
- questioning and making observations, possibly with visual aids such as magazines, pictures and colour charts to select the correct course of action, services and products;
- conducting tests to ensure safe working practice or to find out how the hair will respond in certain situations;
- accurately recording the findings of these tests;
- referral to others: this could be in relation to special technical requirements to other salon staff, or for medical, remedial treatment to a doctor or **trichologist**;
- negotiating a mutually beneficial conclusion

REMEMBER

Personal requirements
Take into consideration any factors that could affect the ways in which you might need to modify any service or treatment to accommodate your client's particular needs.

For example, if your client has been previously involved in an accident will they be able to sit for a long period of time in one position?

Similarly, if they have had some previous injury that has affected their back, spine or neck muscles, will they be able to sit at a back washbasin?

Britt Erlanson/Getty Images

- explaining the costs and benefits to the client before any process is started
- maintaining the client's goodwill for the business.

In order to achieve all these things, you will need to be able to communicate on a professional level. If professional communication is new to you, see Chapter 2, on client care and communication.

HAIR AND SKIN

Every client entering a salon is different, with a combination unique to them, of hair type and colour, skin and scalp conditions, past treatment history and current requirements. It is your job as a professional responsible for giving good client care to examine the hair and scalp, to assess what state they are in, to ask questions and listen to your client's responses, to decide what treatment is necessary and to agree a course of action.

Just as a doctor needs knowledge of medicine and a reassuring bedside manner, so you need knowledge of the hair, **scalp** and the skin, and the ability to discuss these with your clients clearly, confidently and tactfully. You also need to be able to recognise any problems and know how to deal with them. For this you need to have a basic understanding of the shape of the bones that make up the physical structure of the head. This chapter includes detailed information about all these aspects.

The structure of skin

The skin is the outer covering of the body. It is a complex organ, made up of different layers and containing many parts: oil and sweat glands, hair muscles, blood and lymph vessels, nerves and sensory organs.

SCIENCE BIT!
DID YOU KNOW

The skin has four main functions: protection, temperature control, secretion and excretion, and sensation.

- *Protection* – The skin forms a tough flexible, physical barrier. It keeps excess water out, and body fluids in. The oil and sweat it produces are acidic, helping to prevent bacterial growth. Melanin pigments in skin help to filter out harmful rays of the sun. In the presence of sunlight vitamin D is produced in the skin, which helps to maintain body health.

- *Temperature control* – The hair muscle (arrector pili) and sweat glands help to maintain the normal body temperature of 37°C. In cold weather the arrector pili contracts, making the hair stand on end and trapping an insulating layer of warm air over the surface of the skin. In hot weather sweat glands excrete water which evaporates from the skin, cooling the body.

- *Secretion and excretion* – Oil or 'sebum', to use its proper name, is used as a protective covering, waterproofing and lubricating the skin and hair. Waste products such as water and salt are passed out of the body as sweat.

- *Sensation* – Beneath the top layer of the skin are nerve endings. These are responsible for feeling heat, cold, pain and textures. These sensations protect the body from harm by informing the brain of what the body is coming into contact with.

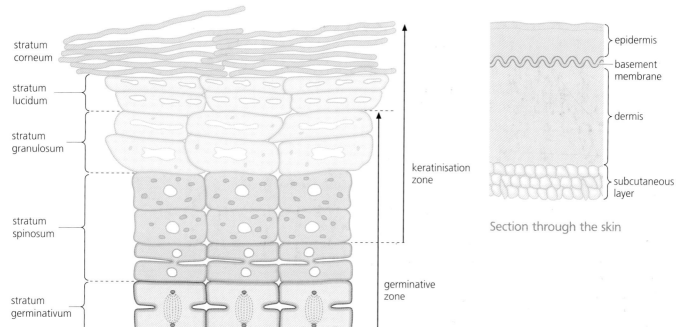

The layers of the epidermis

Section through the skin

The dermis

The **dermis** is the thickest layer of the skin. It is here that the hair follicle is formed. The dermis is made up of elastic and connective tissue, and is well supplied via the blood capillary network. The skin receives its nutrient supply from this area. The upper part of the dermis, the papillary layer, contains the organs of touch, heat and cold, and pain. The lower part of the dermis, the reticular layer, forms a looser network of cells.

The subcutaneous layer

The subcutaneous fat lies below the dermis. It is also known as the 'subcutis', or occasionally as the 'hypodermis'. It is composed of loose cell tissue and contains stores of fat. The base of the hair follicle is situated just above this area, or sometimes in it. This fatty subcutaneous tissue gives fullness and roundness to the shape of the body, whilst providing protection for the internal organs and insulation against the cold.

The epidermis

Above the dermis and the extending to the surface of the skin, the **epidermis** provides protection for the body. It is made up from five separate layers of skin.

SCIENCE BIT!
DID YOU KNOW

?

That skin consists of several layers of different cell tissue. The outermost layer is called the 'epidermis'. It has five distinct layers:

● The 'horny layer' (stratum corneum) is the hard, cornified top layer of skin. It is constantly being worn away and shedded, it is then replaced by the underlying tissue.

● A lower, 'clear layer' (stratum lucidum) is transparent. It allows the colour from below to be seen, there is no melanin present, but the cells contain keratin, the principle protein of hair.

● The 'granular layer' (stratum granulosum) lies between the softer living cells below and the harder dead cells above. It is made up of a granular-like tissue.

● The 'mixed layer' (stratum spinosum) is made up from prickle cells, which are softer, active and alive, and Malpighian cells, containing melanin which colours the skin.

● The 'germinating layer' (stratum germinativum) is at the lowest part of the epidermis. The most active skin cells are present and they have a softer and fuller i.e. 'fattier' consistency.

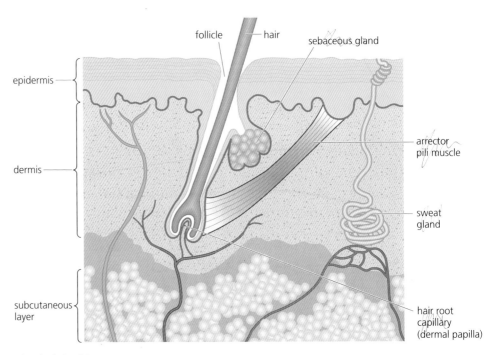

The hair in skin

The hair follicle

Hair grows from a thin, 'tube-like' space in the skin called a hair **follicle**.

● At the bottom of the follicles are areas well supplied with nerves and blood vessels, which nourish the cellular activity. These are called hair papillae.

● Immediately surrounding each papilla is the germinal matrix which consists of actively forming hair cells.

● As the new hair cells develop the lowest part of the hair is shaped into the hair bulb.

ACTIVITY

Example questions	Model answers
What types of questions should you ask during consultation?	I would ask the client about the style that they wanted. I would ask if there has been any recent technical services on the hair. I would ask the client about how they will manage a new style themself. I would ask the client about the types of products used on hair.
Why is consultation so important?	Because if it is not done properly, the client may not get the result they expect, or something might go wrong in the process.
What are the limiting factors affecting consultation decisions?	The factors could be to do with lifestyle, physical features such as shape and size, hair and scalp problems, or the results of any tests I carry out.
What should you do if you find that the client has head lice?	I will discreetly tell the client (or the parent) about the infestation and explain what needs to be done next. I will not be able to carry out any service on the premises, because I need to ensure that there is no risk of **cross-infection** within the salon.

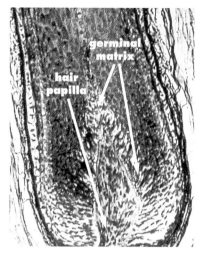

The hair papilla and germinal matrix

- The cells continue to take shape and form as they push along the follicle until they appear at the skin surface as hair fibres.
- The cells gradually harden and die. The hair is formed of dead tissue. It retains its elasticity due to its chemical structure and keratin content.

Oil

The oil gland, or sebaceous gland, is situated in the skin and opens out into the upper third of the follicle. From it sebum is secreted into the follicle and on to the hair and skin surface. Sebum helps to prevent the skin and hair from drying. By retaining moisture it helps the hair and skin to stay flexible and elastic. Sebum is slightly acid – about pH 5.6 – and forms a protective antibacterial covering for the skin.

Sweat

Sweat glands lie beside each hair follicle. These are appendages of the skin. They secrete sweat which passes out through the sweat ducts. The ends of these ducts can be seen at the surface of the skin as sweat pores.

There are two types of sweat gland: the larger, associated closely with the hair follicles, are the apocrine glands; the smaller, found over most of the skin's surface, are the eccrine glands.

Sweat is mainly water with salt, and other minerals may be present. In abnormal conditions sweat contains larger amounts of waste material. Evaporation of sweat cools the skin. The function of sweat, and thus the sweat glands, is to protect the body by helping to maintain its normal temperature.

Mahogany

Hair: Stella Lambrou, The Crib, Lytham; make-up: Lynsey Alexander; photography: Emma Hughes; styling: Stuart Well

The hair muscle

The hair muscle or arrector pili is attached at one end to the hair follicle, and at the other to the underlying tissue of the epidermis. When it contracts it pulls the hair and follicle upright. Upright hairs trap a warm layer of air around the skin. This contraction by the hair muscle acts as a warning system: it reacts to shock, fear and excitement as well as the cold.

Structure of hair

Hairs are fine protrusions of protein above the skin's surface. They cover the majority of the body, except for the eyelids, palms of the hands and soles of the feet. There are three different types.

- *Lanugo hair* – fine downy hair that covers the body of the unborn child.
- *Vellus hair* – fine, short, fluffy hair which contains little or no colour pigment and covers most of the body.
- *Terminal hair* – longer, coarser hair, found on the head, on the faces of men, in ears and eyebrows, on the arms, legs and chest and around the genitals.

The cross-section taken through the hair lengthways shown in the diagram provides us with a microscopic view of the three specific layers.

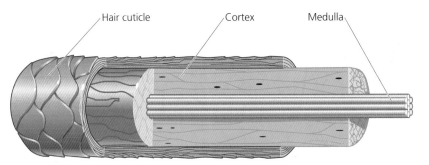

The hair shaft

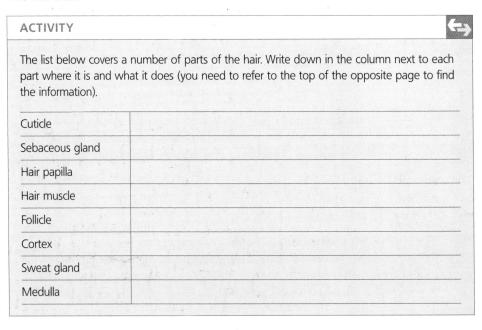

ACTIVITY

The list below covers a number of parts of the hair. Write down in the column next to each part where it is and what it does (you need to refer to the top of the opposite page to find the information).

Cuticle	
Sebaceous gland	
Hair papilla	
Hair muscle	
Follicle	
Cortex	
Sweat gland	
Medulla	

The **cuticle** is the outer layer of colourless cells, which forms a protective surface to the hair. It regulates the chemicals entering and damaging the hair, and protects the hair from excessive heat and drying. The cells overlap, like the tiles on a roof, with the free edges pointing towards the tips of the hair. The amount of layers is proportional to hair texture; hair with fewer layers of cuticle is finer than coarser hair types which have several layers.

Hair in good condition has a cuticle that is tightly closed, limiting the ingress of moisture and chemicals. Conversely, **dry hair** or **porous hair** has damaged or partially missing cuticle layers. One simple indicator of cuticle condition relates to the time taken to blow-dry hair. Hair in good condition will dry quickly in proportion to the amount of hair on the head (the hair's 'density'); if the cuticle is closely packed the hairdryer is allowed to 'chase' the water from the hair shaft. Porous hair absorbs moisture. It therefore takes far longer to dry and unfortunately is subjected to more heat, which exacerbates the problem.

The **cortex** is the middle and largest layer; it is made up of a long fibrous material which has the appearance of rope. If you look at them more closely, you will see that each of the fibres are made up of even smaller chains of fibres. The quality and condition of these bundles of fibres will determine the hair's strength; the way in which the fibres are bonded together has direct effect upon curl and ability to stretch ('hair elasticity'). It is within this part of the hair that the natural hair colour is distributed. The pigments are diffused throughout the cortex and their colour(s) and rate of distribution will determine the colour that we can see. It is also in this layer that both synthetic colours and perming make the permanent chemical changes.

The medulla is the central, most inner part of the hair. It only exists in medium to coarser hair types and is often intermittent throughout the hair's length. The medulla does not play any useful part in hairdressing processes and treatments.

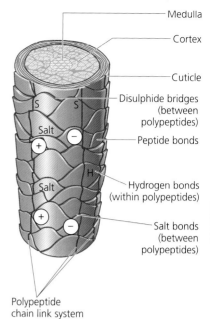

Medulla
Cortex
Cuticle
Disulphide bridges (between polypeptides)
Peptide bonds
Hydrogen bonds (within polypeptides)
Salt bonds (between polypeptides)

Polypeptide chain link system

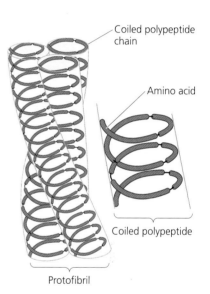

Coiled polypeptide chain
Amino acid
Coiled polypeptide
Protofibril

Cross-links within the hair

Chemical properties of hair

The bundles of fibres found in the cortex are made from molecules of amino acids. There are about 22 amino acids in hair, and the molecules of each contain atoms of elements in different proportions. Overall, the elements in hair are in approximately these proportions:

carbon 50%	hydrogen 7%	nitrogen 18%
oxygen 21%	sulphur 4%	

The amino acids combine to form larger molecules, long chains of amino acids called polypeptides or, if they are long enough, proteins. One of the most important of these is keratin. Keratin is an important component of nails, skin and hair: it is this protein that makes them flexible and elastic. Because of the keratin it contains, hair can be stretched and compressed, curled and waved. In hair, keratin forms long chains that coil up like springs. They are held in this shape by cross-links between chains. The three kinds of link are **disulphide bonds** or bridges (sulphur bonds), salt bonds and hydrogen bonds. Salt bonds and hydrogen bonds are relatively weak and are easily broken, allowing the springs to be stretched out: this is what happens in curling. The normal, coiled form of keratin is called **alpha keratin**; when it has been stretched, set and dried it is called **beta keratin**. The change is only temporary. Once the hair has been made wet, or has gradually absorbed moisture from the air, it relaxes back to the alpha state. Disulphide bridges are much stronger, but these too can be altered, as in perming.

Physical properties of hair

Hair naturally contains a certain amount of water, which lubricates it, allowing it to stretch and recoil. Hair that is dry and in poor condition is less elastic.

Hair is 'hygroscopic': it absorbs water from the surrounding air. How much water is taken up depends on the dryness of the hair and the moistness of the atmosphere. Hair is also porous: there are tiny tube-like spaces within the hair structure and the water flows into these by 'capillary action', rather like blotting paper absorbing ink. Drying hair in the ordinary way evaporates only the surface moisture, but drying over long periods or at too high a temperature removes water from *within* the hair, leaving it brittle and in poor condition. Damaged hair is more porous than healthy hair and easily loses any water: this makes it hard to stretch and mould.

Curled hair returns to its former shape as it takes up water, so the drier the atmosphere, the longer the curl or set lasts. Similarly, curling dry hair is most effective just after the hair has been washed, because although the surface is dry the hair will have absorbed water internally. Blow-styling and curling with hot irons, heated rollers, hot combs and hot brushes all have similar temporary effects.

REMEMBER ✔

Hair grows at a rate of 12.5mm (nearly $\frac{1}{2}$ inch) per month. Hairdressers recommend that their clients return on a six-weekly basis: this is the maximum growth that a hairstyle will sustain before the extra weight and length will make it difficult to handle.

Hair growth

Hair is constantly growing. Over a period of between one and six years an individual hair actively grows, then stops, rests and degenerates, and finally falls out. Before the hair leaves the follicle the new hair is normally ready to replace it. If a hair is not replaced within the follicle, then an area of baldness results.

The lives of individual hairs vary and are subject to variations in the body. Some are actively growing while others are resting. Hairs on the head are at different stages of growth.

Stages of hair growth

The life cycle of hair is as follows.

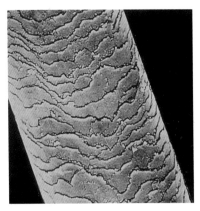

The hair cuticle

- *Anagen* – the active growing stage of the hair, a period of activity of the papilla and germinal matrix. This stage may last from a few months to several years although on average it is around three years. It is at this stage of formation at the base of the follicle that the hair's thickness is determined. Hair colour too is formed in the early part of anagen.

- *Catagen* – A short period lasting a couple of weeks, when the hair stops growing but cellular activity continues at the papilla. The hair bulb gradually separates from the papilla and moves further up the follicle.

- *Telogen* – The final stage, when there is no further growth or activity at the papilla. The follicle begins to shrink and completely separates itself from the papilla area. Around 15 per cent of the hair is in this stage at any one time. It lasts between four and six months: then towards the end of the telogen stage, cells begin to activate in preparation for the new anagen stage of regrowth.

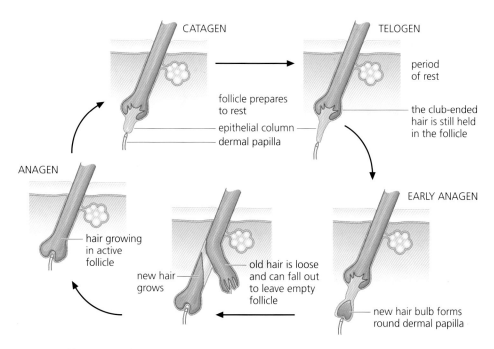

Stages of hair growth

The new anagen period involves the hair follicle beginning to grow down again. Vigorous papilla activity generates a new hair at the germinal matrix. At the same time the old hair is slowly making its way up and out of the follicle. Often the old and new hair can be seen at the same time in the follicle.

In some animals most of the hairs follow their life cycle 'in step', passing through anagen, catagen and telogen together. This results in moulting. Human hair, however, develops at an uneven rate and few follicles shed their hair at the same time. (If all hairs fell out at the same time we would have periods of baldness!)

REMEMBER

The more layers of cuticle that the hair has, the greater its resistance to absorbing moisture and chemicals. Therefore, coarse hair in good condition can often take longer to perm than finer hair types.

ACTIVITY

The list below has a number of hair and scalp problems. Write down in the column next to it the type of problem it is, what it looks like and how it is treated. You will need to refer to pages 27–32 to find the information you will need to complete this.

Head lice	
Nits	
Impetigo	
Split ends	
Porous hair	
Scalp ringworm	
Monilethrix	

Hair texture

Individual hair thickness is referred to as **hair texture**. The main types are

- very fine hair
- fine hair
- medium hair
- coarse hair.

The main differences between the hair textures relate to the number of layers of cuticle. Human hair types are grouped into the following types:

- *Caucasian (European)* – normally straight or loosely waved
- *black (African Caribbean)* – tightly curled hair
- *Mongoloid (Eastern Asia)* – coarse, straight hair.

Curly	W avy	Straight
Flat ribbon-like	Less oval	Round

Hair types

Hair colour

The natural colour of hair and skin depends on the amount and diffusion of melanin (natural pigments). Two types of pigment are found in hair: eumelanin and pheomelanin. These pigments are created in the lower dermis at areas called 'melanocytes'; at these points natural pigments are deposited into the skin.

- Eumelanin gives black and brown colours in hair. Dark ash-brown hair contains a lot of eumelanin.
- Pheomelanin gives red and yellow colours in hair.

Weathering, colouring, bleaching and neutralising processes can change these pigments and make hair lighter in colour.

Indicators of hair in good condition

Moisture levels within the hair are essential for maintaining good condition. We can see the evidence of this moisture from the shine that we associate with great looking hair. 'Bad hair' denotes poor condition; the lack of shine is due to the unevenness of the hair's surface, i.e. the cuticle. A roughened cuticle surface is an indicator of either physical or chemical damage. Either

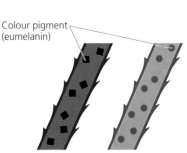

Colour pigment (eumelanin)

Black   Brown

Colour pigment (pheomelanin)

Hair cuticle

Cortex

Red   Yellow

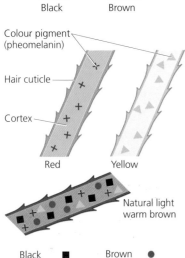

Natural light warm brown

| Black | ■ | Brown | ● |
| Red | + | Yellow | ▲ |

Hair pigments

of these states is difficult to correct. In mild cases of dryness, treatments can be applied to improve the hair's manageability and handling. In more serious situations of porous hair, the hair's ability to resist the ingress of chemicals and moisture is severely impaired. There are no long-lasting remedies for this, so regular reconditioning treatments must be used.

WHAT TO LOOK FOR WHEN EXAMINING THE HAIR

There are many factors that you must consider when conducting a consultation. Previously in this chapter the structure of hair and skin has given you the background aspects of what is taking place under and around the skin. These are things that you need to know, but are out of your control.

What takes place next depends upon what you see and how you act on your assessment. During consultation you will be drawing conclusions from a number of different aspects. The course of action that you take is dependant upon:

- client expectations
- hair health and condition
- hair growth, type and texture
- previous services and treatments
- physiognomy and style suitability
- lifestyle, personality and age
- hair and scalp diseases, conditions and defects
- hair and scalp tests.

Client expectations

The aim of consultation is to arrive at a suitable hairstyle or **hair colour** which is pleasing to the client. It should be done in a way that gives the client confidence in both the salon and you. The process should be inspiring.

It is necessary to look at the 'complete picture' when you first meet the client, this makes sure that you have enough information to advise properly. During discussion this may highlight aspects or areas which you feel are wrong or unnecessary, so you need to be able to express your views back to the client in a clear and simple way, avoiding any confusion. Avoid technical terms and break hairdressing language down into understandable English. Clients will often respond to things they have seen in magazines or on TV and in doing so often pick up on the latest 'buzz' words. These terms may have nothing to do with the work in hand so clarify misconceptions.

Facial expression is an important part of communication. Even if your client looks disgruntled or is scowling, you will need to use a friendly, pleasant expression to encourage them to relax. Facial expression reflects the client's mood or how they are feeling. You need to pick up on these expressions and react to them appropriately; they will help you to understand the client's needs and aspirations.

REMEMBER

Always make and maintain eye contact with your client. Be aware of your client's expressions and react appropriately.

REMEMBER

- Look at the amount and quality of your client's hair.
- Remember that clients with fine hair want volume.
- Look at the proportion, partings and distribution of the hair.
- How much natural movement has the hair got? Will it impede the styling plan?
- Are there any strong growth patterns to contend with?

Hair is the frame for the face; its length, quantity, quality and texture all contribute to the total image. Fine hair often lacks body; most clients want fullness and volume that will last. Cutting techniques can help this problem.

You could also consider proportioning the hair weight: by setting hair or using light **perms**, you can create bulk and volume, which gives a foundation to shape and style.

Hair fashion is constantly changing and the client who wears a hairstyle which is of the moment, wants to give the impression of being in touch with trends. Sometimes clients want up-to-the minute hairstyles to keep a youthful image or to make them feel confident. Others will often choose a particular image that complements their career and lifestyle.

Hair health and condition

The health and the condition of the hair is your starting point. Whatever happens next should be a process of improving what went on before. A client will expect the service or treatment that you advise to be a step in the right direction. You will need to look for each of the following properties and aspects:

Features of hair in good condition

- Shine and lustre.
- Smooth outer cuticle surface.
- Strength and resistance.
- Good elasticity.
- Good natural moisture levels.

Features of hair in poor condition

- Raised or open cuticle.
- Damaged torn hair shaft.
- Split ends.
- Low strength and resistance.
- Over-elastic/stretchy.
- Dry, porous lengths or ends.

Physical hair damage is caused by

- harsh, or incorrect usage of brushes and/or combs
- excessive heat from styling equipment.

Chemical hair damage is caused by

- incorrect over-timing of all colouring and perming treatments
- strengths of hydrogen peroxide
- over-bleaching and highlighting services

- excessive overuse of colouring/tinting products
- perm products that are too strong or over-processing
- chlorine from swimming pools.

Weathering

- Hair is also damaged by excesses of sunlight.

And generally speaking

- The normal and abnormal working of the body has a direct effect on the hair and scalp. Good health is reflected in good hair and skin. A balanced diet with plenty of fresh foods contributes to good health.
- Disease and drugs used in the treatment of disease take their toll on the hair and skin.
- Genetic factors affecting hair growth determine hair strength and texture.
- The hair of women is usually at its best during pregnancy.
- Deterioration of the hair and skin after giving birth is usually due to stress and tiredness.

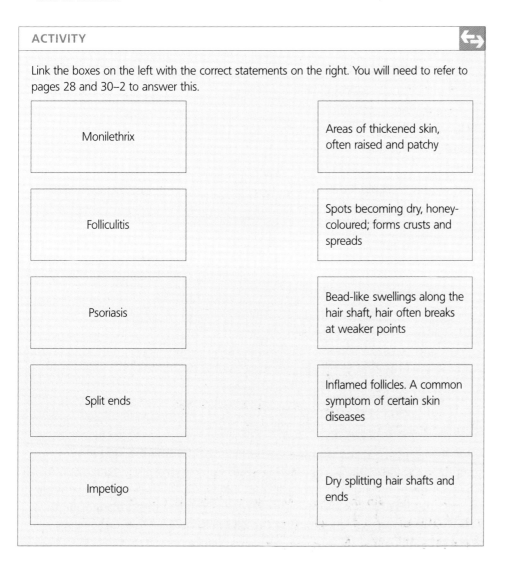

ACTIVITY

Link the boxes on the left with the correct statements on the right. You will need to refer to pages 28 and 30–2 to answer this.

Monilethrix	Areas of thickened skin, often raised and patchy
Folliculitis	Spots becoming dry, honey-coloured; forms crusts and spreads
Psoriasis	Bead-like swellings along the hair shaft, hair often breaks at weaker points
Split ends	Inflamed follicles. A common symptom of certain skin diseases
Impetigo	Dry splitting hair shafts and ends

Corbis

Corbis

Corbis

Hair growth patterns

(see also types and textures)

The hair's 'movement' is the amount of curl or wave within the hair lengths. However, its growth pattern denotes the direction from which it protrudes from the scalp. Natural hair fall can be seen on wet and dry hair and strong directional growth will have a major impact on the lie of the hair when it is styled. So it is essential that it is taken into account during consultation.

Double crown

The client with a double crown will benefit if you leave sufficient length in the hair to over-fall the whole area. If it is cut too short the hair will stick up and will not lie flat.

Nape whorl

A nape whorl can occur at either or both sides of the nape. It can make the hair difficult to cut into a straight neckline or tight 'head-hugging' graduations – often the hair naturally forms a V-shape. Tapered neckline shapes may be more suitable, but sometimes the hair is best left long so that the weight of the hair over-falls the nape whorl directions.

Cowlick

A cowlick appears at the hairline at the front of the head. It makes cutting a straight fringe difficult, particularly on fine hair, because the hair often forms a natural parting. The strong movement can often be improved by moving the parting over so that the weight over-falls the growth pattern. Sometimes a fringe can be achieved by leaving the layers longer so that they weigh down the hair.

Widow's peak

The widow's peak growth pattern appears at the centre of the front hairline. The hair grows upward and forward, forming a strong peak. It is often better to cut the hair into styles that are dressed back from the face, as any 'light fringes' will be likely to separate and stick up.

Hair: Pat Wood; photography: Thornton Howdle; make-up: Leanne Shaw

Previous services and treatments

The client's previous history has a large bearing on what can be done with their hair in the future. If the client is a regular visitor to the salon, then you should have plenty of information at hand relating to what has happened before. For example, if the client had previously had highlights in her hair and she now wanted to have it chemically straightened, you would be able to see if the two chemical processes were realistically a good idea.

On the other hand, if the client is new to the salon, you will be 'filling in a lot of blanks'. Your understanding will rely heavily on the questions you ask, the responses you get and, most importantly, what you can see.

Hair: Pat Wood; photography: Thornton Howdle; make-up: Leanne Shaw

Faces and head shapes

The basic, natural shape of the head, face and features are what form the underlying structure in styling. The proportions of the hair mass and its distribution in relation to the face and head are vital in choosing a style. The outer hair shape should fit the face shape if a suitable hairstyle is to be achieved.

The contours of the head are its focal points. Those on the side of the head are formed by the parietal and temporal bones. Those on the back of the head and the nape are formed by the occipital bones, which can be concave or convex: curving inwards or outwards. The frontal bone forms the forehead shape. It is the beginning of the profile, which follows along the nose to the lips and chin. This can vary in shape and may also be concave or convex.

The face shape is made up of straight or curved lines, and sometimes a mixture of the two. Straight fine shapes appear angular, chiselled or firm and solid. They can be triangular, rectangular, square or diamond shaped. Curved-line shapes appear soft and may be round, oval, pear shaped or oblong. Shapes that have some straight and some curved lines are defined as heart shaped or soft square shaped.

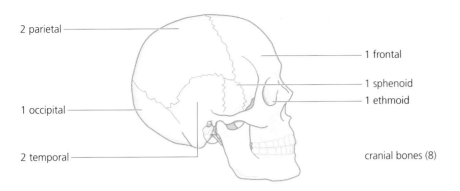

2 parietal

1 frontal

1 sphenoid

1 ethmoid

1 occipital

2 temporal

cranial bones (8)

The head and cranial bones

To create a pleasant balance, the hairstyle and face shape need to be compatible. An angular haircut will not suit a soft rounded face. A soft hair shape will not complement a chiselled face. Hair-shape outlines can be made to look quite different from the front by simply changing a parting from side to centre. Side partings tend to make the face appear wider, whilst centre partings close down the width of a wide forehead.

Ears, nose and mouth

Often ears are out of balance, which can affect the cut if you use them as a guide. Generally, large ears or even large lobes are accentuated by hair cut short or dressed away from the face. It is often better to leave hair longer over the ears unless it is an essential part of the style's impact.

Your client may wear a hearing aid, and this may be a sensitive issue. Some clients wish to have all signs of an aid hidden, but others do not mind and even display it. You should discuss this with your clients carefully and with sensitivity: they may feel too embarrassed to bring the subject up themselves. The size of the aid will need careful consideration when completing the total image.

The position, shape, size and colour of the nose and mouth are very important in the facial expression. The angles that they create can be softening or harsh, and must not be ignored when the image is being planned. Hair shape and make-up can contribute to the required effect.

> **REMEMBER** ✔
>
> - What is the shape, position and size of the client's ears?
> - What is the shape and size of the client's nose and mouth?
> - Are these features a major concern to the client?
> - What are your client's facial and head shapes?
> - Are there any significant features that need to be accounted for?
> - Smaller faces need opening up whilst larger ones need narrower, framing effects.

Oval face shape

An oval-shaped face suits any hairstyle, so these facial types present the fewest problems and style selection limitations.

Round face shape

Generally speaking, round face shapes need height to compensate for the width of the face. Hairstyles that are cut to a level just below the ears tend to draw a focus to that point and therefore longer lengths at the side are a better option.

Long facial shape

Shorter profile lengths improve longer facial shapes with added width as opposed to added height.

Square face shape

Squarer face shapes need rounder styled edges with texture on to the face to soften the corners or heavier jawlines. Longer lengths also are favourable; these tend to create a frame focus elsewhere.

Triangular face shape

The width of the face can be compensated for with height. However, the triangular face tends to be accompanied by a pointed chin. Avoid short perimeters with solid angles, as this will exacerbate the problem. Compensate with longer lengths at the sides with fullness and movement.

Facial shapes

REMEMBER

- The eyes are the focal point of the face. Use them within the style's construction.
- What colour and shape are your client's eyes?
- What are the eyebrows like?
- Does your client normally wear spectacles?

REMEMBER

- How long or short is your client's neck?
- How wide or narrow is your client's neck?
- Have you taken these features into consideration?

Body shape

The body shape needs to be considered too. You need to carefully balance the amount, density and overall shape of the hair to your client's physical body shape. This is particularly important if your client considers their shape or size a particularly important factor. A small, clinging hairstyle would look wrong on a large body shape, for example.

REMEMBER

Strong images in magazines always use eye contact in order to sell everything from clothes to hairdressing. Your client will be drawn to strong images, but are they wearable in everyday life? The majority of 'hair shots' sweep hair across the eye line to partially obscure the eyes; this creates a stronger artistic impact and emphasises body language. These snapshots of 'still life' are stimulating but not feasible in everyday life. You must make this point during your consultation.

Mahogany

Mahogany

Mahogany

Lifestyle, personality and age

Remember that people are constrained by what they do for a living or what they like to do in their spare time. Usually, people who work in environments where they have face-to-face contact with clients have to be more particular about the image they portray. This is a very important factor in style selection. From a leisure point of view, you should consider whether the client does a lot of sport or exercise. If so, the hairstyle will have to be versatile and able to withstand a lot of washing. Also, think about how the style could be handled to create a number of different effects when the client is going out. If you are styling for a special occasion, it is worth asking what dress will be worn. A beautiful gown needs to be accompanied by an elegant hairstyle. However, this style will need to be altered for normal wear.

- Many clients want practical and manageable styles for work.
- Nurses, doctors and caterers, among others, may require styles which keep the hair off the face, or they may have to wear face and head coverings at work.
- Dancers, athletes and skaters, among others, need hairstyles that will not get in their eyes and obscure their vision.
- Fashion models may require elaborate styles for special photographic or modelling sessions or displays.

Character and personality can often override physical features when you are choosing a style for your client. A self-confident client will be able to wear looks that a self-conscious client cannot. Make sure you take this into account so that mistakes are not made. Is your client confident and outgoing or shy, timid and retiring, not wishing to stand out in a crowd? Is the client professional and businesslike? And what age group does your client fall into? There are basic rules that apply to people at certain ages:

- children – simple, practical shapes
- teenager – something slightly different, especially from older styles, fashionable
- young married – something suitable for work, attractive styles
- parents – practical and attractive styles, often shorter styles
- middle aged – softening shapes to disguise wrinkles
- senior age – softening shapes
- young businessmen – fashionable cuts
- older men – simple, practical styles.

Manageability

Different styles need different amounts of commitment from the client once they leave the salon. You need to take these factors on board when consulting with the client to make sure that they will carry on being happy with the style you both choose until it is time for the next visit.

Using visual aids in consultation

Pictures are an immensely important visual aid. They are another form of language that hairdressers understand very well. One reason for this is their good understanding of visual/spatial imagery; however, there is a vast difference in terms of aesthetics between what the client sees in a photo and what the hairdresser will see.

A simple picture is an ideal way of conveying what is wanted. Lengths, colours, shapes, textures and movement are instantly made clear. It works both ways too. Clients will often bring in a visual of what they want, but you

M. Balfre

> **REMEMBER**
>
> - What is the purpose of the style: fashion, special occasion?
> - Work, social and leisure pursuits are all factors to be considered in choosing a hairstyle.
> - Different styles suit certain age groups.
> - Will the final effect suit the client's lifestyle requirements?

can also use pictures with them to show possible and achievable outcomes. A picture says much more than words can in the same time. As time is always an issue, style magazines or salon collections are an essential tool.

Colour charts

Colour charts are extremely useful for hairdressers: we rely on them every day. However, they are not always a brilliant medium for the client. We tend to treat others as we would want to be treated ourselves. This is a good philosophy; however, there are times when our expectation of others is a little over-optimistic. Clients, generally speaking, have very little ability for visualising styles on themselves. An example will illustrate this clearly. Think about shopping: how often do women shop in pairs? Other people's comments, assistance and point of view are very important. The reason is obvious: if we need reassurance for what we are doing we have to involve someone else, ideally someone who knows us, our likes, dislikes and, most important of all, who can objectively comment about our purchasing decisions.

The colour chart is a useful tool for hairdressers and a nice colouring book for clients. When you do use it remember that the colour swatches are small and therefore difficult to visualise over a larger area or with the intensity that a final colour effect will look all over.

Checklist for consultation

✓ Listen carefully to what is requested.

✓ Use visual aids to assist the consultation process.

✓ Communicate the possible effects.

✓ Explain why certain effects are not possible.

✓ Give good reasons for suggested actions.

✓ Ensure that the client understands what is being said.

✓ Agree on a final and suitable course of action.

✓ Make clear the full cost of services and products needed.

✓ Make it clear if follow-up appointments are necessary.

✓ Carry out the agreed service or treatment.

✓ Encourage the client to rebook the next visit before she leaves.

✓ Maintain the client's goodwill and safety throughout the appointment.

✓ Record the details for future reference.

HAIR AND SCALP DISEASES, CONDITIONS AND DEFECTS

We all carry large numbers of micro-organisms on our skin, in our hair and inside our bodies. These are small living things that include bacteria, fungi, parasites and viruses. Many micro-organisms are harmless, but some can cause disease. Infectious diseases can be passed from one person to another and from a health and safety point of view the risk of cross-infection within the salon must be minimised. This section covers a wide variety of hair and skin problems that you could come into contact with.

Diseases of the hair and scalp may be caused by a variety of infectious organisms. Signs or symptoms are presented which enable us to recognise them. Initial examination, during consultation, should be carried out before any hairdressing procedure is applied. If this precaution is not taken, there is a danger of cross-infection where both hairdresser and clients may contract and spread disease. Other hair and scalp conditions or defects may be due to abnormal formation or the result of a variety of chemical and physical causes. They are not infectious.

ACTIVITY

Link the boxes on the left with the correct statements on the right. You will need to refer to pages 28–9 to find the answers.

Furunculosis

Herpes simplex

Scabies

Tinea capitis

Head lice

Head lice bite the scalp, feeding on the victim's blood

Circular bald areas of grey or whitish skin

Raised, inflamed, pus-filled spots; irritation, swelling and pain

Fluid-filled blisters, usually on the lips and surrounding areas

The itch mite burrows under the skin where it lays eggs

REMEMBER

A warm, humid salon can provide the perfect home for germs; they will spread rapidly in these conditions. Therefore it is essential that the salon, including work clothing, equipment, surfaces and tools, is kept clean at all times. A tidy salon is easier to maintain so get into the habit of clearing up as you go. See Chapter 5 on health and safety for more information.

REMEMBER

Head lice are particularly prevalent among younger children. Make sure that you check for infestations of either the parasites or their eggs before inadvertently carrying out any hairdressing service.

Infectious diseases

	Condition	Symptoms	Cause	Treatment	Infectious
 ©Mediscan	**Folliculitis** Inflammation of the hair follicles	Inflamed follicles. A common symptom of certain skin diseases	A contact bacterial infection, or due to chemical or physical action	Medical referral	Yes
 Dr M H Beck	**Impetigo** A bacterial infection of the upper skin layers	At first a burning sensation, followed by spots becoming dry, honey-coloured, forms crusts and spreads	A staphylococcal or streptococcal infection	Medical referral	Yes
 Dr Andrew Wright	**Sycosis** A bacterial infection of the hairy parts of the face	Small, yellow spots around the follicle mouth; burning, irritation and general inflammation	Bacteria attack the upper part of the hair follicle, spreading to the lower follicle	Medical referral	Yes
 Dr Andrew Wright	**Furunculosis** Boils or abscesses	Raised, inflamed, pus-filled spots; irritation, swelling and pain	An infection of the hair follicles by staphylococcal bacteria	Medical referral	Yes

	Condition	Symptoms	Cause	Treatment	Infectious
 Dr M H Beck	**Herpes simplex** (cold sore) A viral infection of the skin	Burning, irritation, swelling and inflammation precede the appearance of fluid-filled blisters, usually on the lips and surrounding areas	Possibly exposure to extreme heat or cold, or a reaction to food or drugs; the skin may carry the virus for years without exhibiting any symptoms	Medical referral	Yes
 ©Mediscan	**Warts** (Verrucae) A viral infection of the skin.	Raised, roughened skin, often brown or discoloured. There may be irritation and soreness. Common on the hands and face	The lower epidermis is attacked by the virus, which causes the skin to harden and skin cells to multiply	Medical referral	Yes

SCIENCE BIT!
ANIMAL PARASITES

John Burbidge/Science Photo Library

A nit (the egg of a louse)
BLM Health

Dr M H Beck

	Condition	Symptoms	Cause	Treatment	Infectious
	Head lice (Pediculosis capitis) Infestation of the hair and scalp by head lice	An itchy reaction to the biting head louse; 'peppering' on pillow cases and minute egg cases (nits) attached to the upper hair shaft close to the scalp	The head louse bites the scalp, feeding on the victim's blood. Breeding produces eggs, which are laid and cemented onto the hair shaft for incubation until the immature louse emerges	Referral to pharmacist	Yes
	Scabies An allergic reaction to the Itch mite	A rash in the skin folds, around the midriff and on the inside of the thighs. Extremely itchy at night	The itch mite burrows under the skin where it lays eggs	Medical referral	Yes

SCIENCE BIT!
FUNGAL DISEASES

	Condition	Symptoms	Cause	Treatment	Infectious
	Tinea capitis Ringworm of the head	Circular bald areas of grey or whitish skin, surrounded by red, active rings; hairs broken close to the skin, which looks dull and rough. The fungus lives off the keratin in the skin and hair. This disease is common in children	Fungal infection of the skin or hair	Medical referral	Yes

Dr John Gray

Non-infectious diseases

SCIENCE BIT!
DID YOU KNOW?

Dr M H Beck

CNRI/Science Photo Library

©Mediscan

Condition	Symptoms	Cause	Treatment	Infectious
Acne vulgaris Disorder affecting the hair follicles and sebaceous glands	Raised spots and bumps within the skin, commonly upon the face in adolescents	Increased sebum and other secretions block the follicle and a skin reaction occurs	Medical treatment required	No
Eczema and dermatitis In its simplest form a reddening of the skin	Ranging from slightly inflamed areas of the skin to severe splitting and weeping areas with irritation and soreness	Many possible causes: eczema often associated with internal factors i.e. allergies or stress. Dermatitis is a reaction or allergy to external factors	Medical treatment required see RIDDOR page 140	No
Psoriasis An inflamed, abnormal thickening of the skin	Areas of thickened skin, often raised and patchy. Often on the scalp and also at the joints (arms and legs)	Unknown	Medical treatment required	No

SCIENCE BIT!
CONDITIONS OF THE HAIR AND SKIN

Dr P Marazzi/Science Photo Library

Condition	Symptoms	Cause	Treatment	Infectious
Dandruff (Pityriasis capitis) Dry scaling scalp	Dry, small, irritating flakes of skin. If moist and greasy it sticks to the skin and the condition 'scurf' results.	Fungal (yeast-like) infection, or physical or chemical irritants	Anti-dandruff treatments	No
Seborrhoea Excessive greasiness of the skin exuding on to the hair	Very greasy, lank hair and greasy skin, making styling difficult	Over-production of sebum	Astringent shampoos	No

SCIENCE BIT!
ALOPECIA OR HAIR LOSS

Dr Andrew Wright

Dr P Marazzi/Science Photo Library

©Mediscan

Condition	Descripton	Treatment
Alopecia areata	The name given to balding patches over the scalp. Often starts around or above the ears, circular in pattern ranging from 1 to 2.5cm in diameter	Trichological referral
Traction alopecia	Hair loss as a result of excessive pulling at the roots from brushing, curling and straightening. Very often seen with younger girls, tying, plaiting or braiding long hair	None needed, hair will grow back if tension is removed
Alopecia totalis	Complete hair loss sometimes as a result of Alopecia areata spreading and joining up across the scalp	Trichological referral
Ciatrical alopecia	Baldness due to scarring of the skin arising from chemical or physical injury. The hair follicle is damaged and permanent baldness results.	
Male pattern alopecia	Male baldness or thinning of hair occurring in teens or early twenties. Hair recedes at the hairline or loss at the crown area. Condition is hereditary (passed on in families)	Remedies currently being developed

SCIENCE BIT!
DEFECTS OF THE HAIR

Dr John Gray

Condition	Symptoms	Cause	Treatment
Split ends (fragilitis crinium) Fragile, poorly conditioned hair	Dry splitting hair ends	Harsh physical or chemical treatments	Cutting off, or special treatment conditioners

	Condition	Symptoms	Cause	Treatment
Redken	Monilethrix Beaded hair	Bead-like swellings along the hair shaft, hair often breaks at weaker points	Irregular development of the hair forming during cellular production	None (and because of the weakness to the hair shaft chemical services are not advisable)
Dr John Gray	Trichorrhexis nodosa Nodules forming on the hairshaft	Areas of swelling along the hair shaft. Splitting and rupturing the cuticle layer	Harsh physical or chemical processing	None, cutting and conditioning may help
©Mediscan	Sebaceous cyst Swelling of the oil gland	Bumps, lumps and swellings on the scalp containing fluid, soft to the touch	Sebaceous gland becomes blocked allowing a build-up of fluid to take place	Medical referral
Eye of Science/Science Photo Library	Damaged cuticle Broken, split, torn hair	Rough raised, missing areas of cuticle; hair loses its moisture and becomes dry and porous	Harsh physical or chemical processes	None, cutting and conditioning may help

REMEMBER

Always create a record when you carry out any tests on your client's hair. This will serve as a useful reminder in the future and provide a record for others to refer to.

TESTING THE HAIR AND SKIN

During consultation there are a number of tests that you can make to help you diagnose the condition of your client's hair. The tests will help you to decide an appropriate course of action before any service is carried out.

Skin or patch test

A sensitivity test is used to assess the reaction of the skin to chemicals or chemical products. In the salon it is mainly carried out before **colouring**. Some people are allergic to external contact of chemicals such as PPD (found in permanent tints). This can cause dermatitis or, in even more severe cases, permanent scarring of skin tissue and hair loss. Some people are allergic to irritants reacting internally; these are conditions such as asthma and hay fever. Others may be allergic to both internal and external irritants. To find out whether a client's skin reacts to chemicals in permanent tints, carry out the following test at least 24 hours prior to the chemical process.

Carrying out a skin test

1 Mix a little of the tint to be used with the correct amount of hydrogen peroxide – as recommended by the manufacturer.

2 Clean an area of skin about 8mm square, behind the ear. Use a little spirit on cotton wool to remove the grease from the skin.

3 Apply a little of the colour mixture to skin.

4 Ask your client to report any discomfort or irritation that occurs over the next 24 hours. Arrange to see your client at the end of this time so that you can check for signs of reaction.

5 If there is a positive response – i.e. a skin reaction such as inflammation, soreness, swelling, irritation or discomfort – do not carry out the intended service. Never ignore the result of a skin test. If a skin test showed a reaction and you carried on anyway, there might be a more serious reaction which could affect the whole body!

6 If there is a negative response i.e. no reaction to the chemicals, then carry out the treatment as proposed.

Skin test   L'Oréal Professionnel

Skin test   L'Oréal Professionnel

> **REMEMBER**
>
> - Always examine the client's hair and scalp before starting any hairdressing process. Part the hair in several areas around the top, sides and back so that you can see the scalp and its condition.
>
> - If you find signs of disease, infection or infestation, do not proceed with any service but discreetly seek assistance from a senior member of staff for further confirmation or directions.
>
> - If you have started and notice infection after, finish what you are doing and seek assistance from a senior member of staff for further confirmation or directions.

> **REMEMBER**
>
> **Warning**
> In recent years there have been a growing number of successful personal injury claims made against salons where they have not taken the necessary precautions!

> **REMEMBER**
>
> **Incompatibility test**
> Henna is still widely used throughout the world as a hair- and skin-dyeing compound. In the UK people using natural henna will often add other ingredients such as coffee, wine or lemon juice to intensify the final colour. However, people in other countries also add compounds to henna; for instance in India and Turkey they sometimes add iron ore deposits; these are crushed into the powder to increase the 'reddening' effect. If this subsequently comes into contact with hydrogen peroxide (either through colouring or perming) a chemical reaction occurs. In the exchange that takes place permanent damage and breakage will occur! (Other incompatibles include glitter sprays and some men's hair colourants which are metallic salt-based.)

	When is it done	How is it done
Strand test Most colouring products just require the time recommended by the manufacturer – check their instructions.	A **strand test** or hair strand colour test is used to assess the resultant colour on a strand or section of hair after colour has been processed and developed.	1. Rub a strand of hair lightly with the back of a comb to remove the surplus tint. 2. Check whether the colour remaining is evenly distributed throughout the hair's length. If it is even, remove the rest of the colour. If it is uneven, allow processing to continue, if necessary applying more colour. If any of the hair on the head is not being treated, you can compare the evenness of colour in the tinted hair with that in the untinted hair.
Test cutting This can test the amount of chemical processing needed and the effect it will have upon the hair.	It precedes colouring, perms, straightening, relaxers and bleaching services.	Cut a small section of hair from the lower back of the head. Apply the chemicals e.g. colour and apply it to the test cutting. Check the development of the curl, colour etc. and make a record of the results.
Pre-perm test curl This test determines the size of rod, lotion strength and development time to be used when perming a client's hair.	Before a perm is carried out.	Wind, process and neutralise one or more sections of hair. Choose areas that are easily covered with the remaining hair.
Development test curl This test determines the development of the curl or 'S' wave whilst a perm is still processing.	During the perm process at various times prior to neutralising.	Unwind a perm rod a couple of revolutions at various points of the wound head. Push the hair back to check the 'S' shape development. When sufficient movement is evident the process is complete and neutralising should be started.
Incompatibility test This will show if there are any chemicals present within the hair that will react against any new proposed services.	Carried out prior to colouring, highlighting and perming treatments.	Place a small sample of hair in a mixture of 20 parts hydrogen peroxide (6%) and one part ammonium-based compound from perm solution. If the mixture bubbles, heats up or discolours do not carry out the service.
Elasticity test This will determine how much the hair will stretch and return to its original length. Overstretched hair will not return to the same length and remains permanently damaged.	Prior to chemical treatments and services. (Ideal for hair that has impaired elasticity such as bleached and tinted.)	Take a couple of strands of hair between your fingers, holding them at the roots and the ends. Gently pull the hair between the two points to see if the hair will stretch and return to its original length. (If the hair breaks easily it may indicate that the cortex is damaged and will be unable to sustain any further chemical treatment.)

	When is it done	*How is it done*
Porosity test This tests the hair's ability to absorb or resist moisture from liquids. (Hair in good condition has a tightly packed cuticle layer which will resist the ingress of products.) Hair that is very porous holds on to moisture. This is particularly evident when you try to blow dry it. The hair takes a long time to dry.	Before chemical services. If the cuticle is torn or damaged, the absorption of moisture is quicker therefore the processing time will be shorter.	Rub strands of hair between your finger tips to feel how rough or smooth it is. If it feels roughened, as opposed to coarse, it is likely that the hair is porous.

REMEMBER ✔

Sensitivity Test and PPD
A test used to assess the client's tolerance of chemicals introduced to the skin. PPD is the abbreviation for paraphenylenediamine, the main ingredient within permanent colour that can cause an allergic reaction. It is a known irritant to skin and eyes.

Porosity test   L'Oréal Professionnel

Porosity test   L'Oréal Professionnel

REMEMBER ✔

The natural moisture levels in hair play a significant part in the way that hair responds to treatments and styling. If the natural levels can be retained following perming, colouring and bleaching the client's hair will remain manageable, easier to detangle, and be able to hold thermal styling effects for far longer.

Deplete those natural levels and the hair becomes porous and will tangle easily; it is less manageable and will not be able to hold a set for long.

Pre-chemical treatments help to reduce the hair's moisture reduction.

Photo courtesy Goldwell UK

Started it	I know and understand the principles of positive communication	I can communicate positively and professionally with the clients	I know that lifestyle is an important factor when choosing the right style for clients
☐	☐	☐	☐
I can identify the range of hair and scalp problems: which may be bacterial, fungal or animal infestations	I know how to negotiate, reaching a mutually beneficial conclusion	I always explain technical terms eliminating ambiguity and false beliefs	I know when and to whom to refer clients in situations where external assistance is required
☐	☐	☐	☐
I understand the necessity of personal hygiene and presentation	I know how to carry out a range of tests on the client's hair and why they must be done		CHECKER BOARD ✓
☐	☐		

Assessment of knowledge and understanding

The following projects, activities and assessments are directly linked to the essential knowledge and understanding for unit G7.

For each statement that is addressed wholly or in part in these activities, you will see its relevant and corresponding EKU number.

Make sure that you keep this for easier referencing and along with your work for future inclusion in your **portfolio**.

Project (EKU G7.5 and G7.6)

For this project you will need to gather information from a variety of sources.

List the services, treatments and products that are available in your salon.

Then for each one listed explain:

(a) what the features and benefits are to the client

(b) how you would go about explaining these to clients

(c) the costs of each of these.

Case study (G7.18, G7.22)

Carol Clark is a regular customer of John's. She has a standing appointment on Saturdays at 11.00 a.m. John knows that her hair doesn't take long so always marks out half an hour in the appointment book for her blow-dry.

Last Saturday, Carol arrived a little late but, as normal, John was over-running so it didn't seem to matter. He asked Jane the junior to sit Carol at the basin and shampoo her right away.

As Jane was shampooing Carol, John was finishing off his client. On his showing her the back in the mirror, John's client told him that she really needed the perimeter length above the collar. So John carefully sectioned off the back to remove another couple of centimetres. On realising that he was now going to be another five or ten minutes, he turned to Jane and said, 'I think we need to put a treatment on Carol's hair. Use this and leave it to soak in for ten minutes.'

When John finished the client, Jane rinsed off the excess product and sat Carol at a spare workstation. John finally got round to attending to Carol.

This week Carol cancelled her appointment and told the receptionist that she won't be returning again.

John is really surprised by this. Where did he go wrong?

Write down why you think Carol has stopped coming to the salon.

Questions

1 How does the Data Protection Act affect you at work? (G7.1). See page 58.

2 What is your place of work's policy in respect of conducting tests? (G7.3)

3 What is your place of work's policy in respect of maintaining confidentiality? (G7.4)

4 Which hair and scalp conditions require medical referral? (G7.10)

5 When is it necessary to carry out tests upon a client's hair? What could happen if they are not done? (G7.12)

6 What factors can have an adverse affect on the general healthiness of hair? (G7.16)

7 Why does the client's lifestyle have an impact on the choice of style? (G7.9)

8 What sorts of things have a critical impact on carrying out services for clients? (G7.8)

Preparing for assessment checklist

Remember to:

- communicate effectively in the salon
- listen to clients and show them that you care
- listen to the client's requirements and discuss suitable courses of action
- adhere to the safety factors when working on clients' hair
- use positive body language and the reasons why it plays such an important part in good customer service
- acknowledge the legal rights of clients and what might happen if they were breached
- identify the factors that affect the variety of choices available to the client
- identify any limitations or adverse problems that affect styling choices
- promote the range of services, products and treatments with the salon
- recognise the adverse conditions that prevent salon services
- conduct the tests that are needed and avoid the risks of not taking appropriate actions
- record the outcomes of the tests for future purposes.

chapter 2

CLIENT CARE AND COMMUNICATION

NVQ/SVQ reference, unit title and main outcome

Unit G5 Give clients a positive impression of yourself and your organisation

G5.1 **Establish effective relationships with clients**

G5.2 **Respond appropriately to clients**

G5.3 **Communicate information to clients**

What do I need to do?

- Always make sure your appearance is suitable for personal service.
- Provide services to clients in the way in which you would expect to be handled and made to feel valued.
- Listen and respond to clients' needs.
- Provide accurate, up-to-date information to clients.

What do I need to learn?

- How to communicate positively and effectively.
- How to recognise the customer's body language.
- A variety of legal rights that clients have.
- How to respond to customer needs.

Information covered in this chapter

- Making the most of yourself in the job.
- Good customer service.
- Written and spoken communication.
- Body language.

INTRODUCTION

Good customer care or, specifically, good **client care** is a fundamental part of your continued success as a hairdresser. We all know when we have been served well and particularly when the person serving us has been really trying to create the right impression.

As hairdressers we are always on show. Every detail of our behaviour when we deal with clients is plain to see. How we conduct ourselves affects the impression that the clients form of the service they receive. *Excellent client service can only be provided by people who are good with people* and the key word here is **communication**, in particular professional communication.

CHECKERBOARD

At the end of this chapter the checkerboard will help to jog your memory on what you have learned and what still remains to be done. Cross off with a pencil each of the topics as you cover it (see page 59).

PERSONAL HEALTH, HYGIENE AND APPEARANCE

Hairdressing, beauty therapy and nail craft are personal services, and as such are very different to trades such as retail, joinery or engineering in the way that practitioners communicate with and handle their clients. Salon staff and their clients can have quite a close relationship, which has both advantages and disadvantages. Your clients will judge your personal and professional standards by your **personal presentation**, the way in which you present yourself. Remember, hairdressing is an image-conscious industry. We strive to provide a high-quality service that gives clients well-cut, well-styled and well-groomed hair, so that they feel pleased and confident and have greater self-esteem. Would you give clients confidence if you turned up for appointments with stained overalls, unkempt hair and dirty hands and nails?

Mahogany

Hands and nails

Your hands should always be perfectly clean. Dirt on your hands and under your nails will harbour bacteria, and by spreading germs you could infect other people. Your hands need washing not only before going to work, but several times throughout the day. When you are shampooing and conditioning, your hands could lose moisture and become dry and cracked. Broken skin allows germs to enter and infection may follow. To prevent this from happening, you should use a barrier cream. Barrier creams cover the skin with an invisible barrier that greatly reduces the penetration of hairdressing washing and conditioning chemicals. (Many trainees have had to give up hairdressing after developing the skin condition called contact dermatitis, in which the hands become sore, cracked, itchy and red. It is described in Chapter 1.)

> **REMEMBER**
>
> Remember, hairdressing is an image-conscious industry. Would you give clients confidence if you turned up for appointments with stained overalls, unkempt hair and dirty hands and nails?

> **REMEMBER**
>
> Always wear gloves.
> *When*? On any occasion where you come into contact with chemicals.
> *Why*? Because gloves are a protective barrier against infection.
>
> Always wash your hands.
> *When*? Before work, after eating, after using the toilet and after coughing, sneezing or blowing your nose.
> *Why*? Because your hands are one of the main sources for spreading infection.
>
> Always wear protective clothing/equipment.
> *When*? Always wear a plastic apron for any salon procedure involving chemicals.
> *Why*? This will prevent spillages onto your clothes, particularly when tinting and perming.

Your body

Human skin contains sweat glands that secrete waste in the form of sweat. Skin in areas such as the armpits, feet and genitals have more sweat glands than elsewhere and the warm, moist conditions provide an ideal breeding ground for bacteria. Decaying bacteria causes body odour or BO, so it is essential to take a shower/bath daily to remove the build-up of sweat, dead skin cells and surface bacteria.

Mouth

Unpleasant breath is offensive to clients. Bad breath (halitosis) can result from digestive troubles, stomach upsets, smoking and strong foods, for example onions, garlic, curries and some cheeses. Frequent brushing will help to eliminate bad breath and maintains good, personal oral hygiene by removing particles of food from between the teeth that can cause a build-up of plaque and even start tooth decay!

Personal appearance

Your personal appearance is as important as your personal cleanliness. The effort you put into getting ready for work reflects your pride in the job. Your own individual look is OK as long as you appreciate and accept that there are professional standards of dress and appearance that must be followed.

Clothes

It's far easier to wear a uniform at work than your own clothes. Uniforms are created specifically with work in mind; they are an easy option for cleaning, maintenance and eliminating difficult 'what to wear' choices.

If you do wear your own clothes they should be clean, well ironed and made from fabrics that are suitable not only for your intended work, but also for the time of year. Less restrictive or tight clothes will allow air to circulate around your body and will keep you cool and fresh, avoiding uncomfortable perspiration or possibly BO. Also, clothes revealing too much of your body could be considered unprofessional and possibly provocative!

Hair: Charlotte Cole at Lawrence Anthony; photography: Roberto Aguilar/Wolfgang Mustain; make-up: Amelia Pruen

Shoes

Hairdressing involves a lot of standing and your feet can get tired, hot, sweaty and even sore, so wear sensible shoes with low heels and make sure the shoe will protect your feet from any falling objects.

It is also better to wear shoes that allow your feet to 'breathe', as ventilated feet remain cool and comfortable throughout the working day. Many modern materials can combine comfort with contemporary style. Trainers are great but check that your workplace permits them before turning up at work in them.

Hair

When working in a salon, it is important to maintain a professional appearance and your hair needs to be clean and well presented. Long hair should be kept away from your face to allow eye contact with clients and display positive **body language**.

Jewellery

It is better not to wear to much jewellery because it harbours germs. Rings, bracelets and long necklaces can get in the way of everyday tasks such as washing hair. Moisture and shampooing products may get trapped under rings and this can cause dermatitis. Jewellery will also cause discomfort to clients if it gets caught in their hair.

Posture

It is important that you adopt the correct posture whilst working, as bad posture can lead to clinical fatigue – symptoms include impaired coordination – aches, pains, an accident, or even longer-term skeletal injury. An incorrect standing position will put undue strain on your back, shoulders and neck muscles.

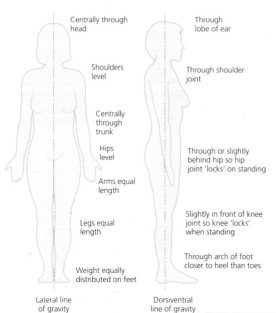

Centrally through head

Shoulders level

Centrally through trunk

Hips level

Arms equal length

Legs equal length

Weight equally distributed on feet

Lateral line of gravity

Through lobe of ear

Through shoulder joint

Through or slightly behind hip so hip joint 'locks' on standing

Slightly in front of knee joint so knee 'locks' when standing

Through arch of foot closer to heel than toes

Dorsiventral line of gravity

Good posture

As we have already said, hairdressing involves a lot of standing and this may come as rather a shock to new recruits as a busy stylist can be on their feet for up to six or seven hours a day. If you watch a stylist cutting their client's hair you will see that they need to hold the hair in many different ways, often bending their bodies and lifting their arms to achieve the precise cutting positions.

Professional posture is derived from standing correctly. Their shoulders are level, their head upright and their body weight distributed evenly over their legs with their feet slightly apart. Any other standing position – dropped shoulder, hip pushed forwards or sideways – looks unprofessional. Slouching is not only uncomfortable; it is dangerous and is an example of poor body language: it communicates to customers and colleagues an uncaring attitude.

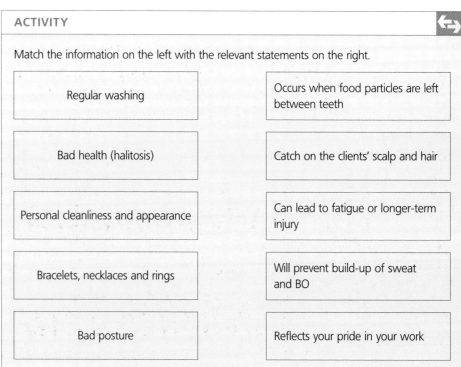

ACTIVITY

Match the information on the left with the relevant statements on the right.

Regular washing	Occurs when food particles are left between teeth
Bad health (halitosis)	Catch on the clients' scalp and hair
Personal cleanliness and appearance	Can lead to fatigue or longer-term injury
Bracelets, necklaces and rings	Will prevent build-up of sweat and BO
Bad posture	Reflects your pride in your work

ACTIVITY

Now find the expected standards at your place of work in relation to the following aspects.

Standards

Your personal hygiene	
Your jewellery	
Your work shoes	
Your work clothing	

What is your company's policy if you fail to meet these standards?

Typical questions with model answers.

Q1 How do you prevent BO? A1 By taking daily showers/baths.

Q2 Why is your choice of footwear important at work? A2 Hairdressing involves a lot of standing and therefore you need shoes that are comfortable and protective to the wearer.

Q3 Why is a uniform a good idea for salon workwear? A3 Uniforms are easy to clean and maintain. They eliminate having to choose what to wear and they avoid competition between staff. They give a professional team look for the salon.

PREPARING THE CLIENT

So far in this chapter we have covered the preparation that you should take before starting work. Now you are ready to receive and prepare clients.

Once a client has arrived for an appointment and you have taken their coat and belongings, find out what services have been requested or booked in advance and prepare the client accordingly.

M. Balfre

Gowning and protecting

- Remember to check that the hair is clean.
- Place a clean, fresh gown around the client, making sure that it covers their clothes and collar, and then fasten it so it doesn't fall away when the client stands up to go to the basins.

If the client is only having a dry cut you can:

- place a clean, dry cutting collar around the shoulders so that any clippings fall to the floor and do not go down the neck. Hair down the neck can be quite an irritation for the rest of the day, particularly if the client has to return to work etc.

If the client is about to have a colouring service:

- put a clean, fresh colour-resistant colouring gown around the client, making sure that all of the clothes are covered
- then put a suitably clean colouring towel around the client and fix it into position by using a plastic clip at the front.

If the client is having their hair washed:

- put a dry, clean, freshly laundered towel around their shoulders.

REMEMBER

All towels and ideally all gowns should be freshly laundered. Where gowns are reused for clients, make sure that there are no stains or any odours on it. This includes perfume too!

REMEMBER

If a client's clothes are stained, make sure that this is noted before they leave. Clothes may be returned to the salon for cleaning. It's one thing having an accident occur in the salon, for which the salon is responsible, but quite another if the client has done this herself and blamed the salon for it!

REMEMBER

Do not tuck absorbent materials like cotton wool around the neckline. When the client has their hair washed such materials will draw moisture to this area and make the clothes wet. This is both uncomfortable and unprofessional.

Saks, Covent Garden

Preparing the hair

Hair has to be free of tangles, knots, hairspray and other materials before it can be worked on. Prepare the client's hair as follows:

- Loosen longer hair first by running your fingers down through to the ends. If there are any loose tangles they will fall away. Tighter tangles can be located and this will avoid unpleasant tugging when you come to brush it.
- Using a wide-toothed 'paddle' brush start brushing the hair from nearer the ends and working back up the hair closer to the scalp.
- Remove the tangles lightly, without pulling or using any firm tension.
- Once the hair is free from tangles, brush the hair in different directions to ensure all the knotting has been removed.

Combs

There are many types of plastic combs. They come in different qualities and many shapes and sizes and they all have a different purpose.

Good-quality combs are well moulded. They are firm and rigid, but remain flexible in use and regardless of how narrow the teeth are; they have smooth points that will not scratch the scalp or tear the hair.

Poor-quality combs are easily recognised, even by the client! Their teeth are often sharper and they are made from an inferior plastic that bends and will not re-straighten with prolonged use.

The larger, wider-toothed combs are used for the application of treatments, conditioners and chemical hair straighteners. They have a large handle and are easy to control. The smaller, straight combs have two different tooth patterns. These combs are for cutting hair and the length of comb is relative to the size of your hands. In normal cutting situations the wider-toothed end of the comb is used. When more tension is needed, say on finer hair or in precision cutting, then the narrower-toothed end is used.

Brushes and brushing

The majority of brushes are made from plastics. They are durable and are easy to maintain; some even have removable teeth or cushioned bases. The design and shape of a brush depends on what it used for. Some are for general grooming and will have a larger brush head with teeth that are widely spaced. Brushes that you use for styling hair are curved or circular depending on the movement or curl needed. The narrower the curve radius the tighter the finished curl will be. The circular or radial brush has closely packed teeth and these tend to be made of plastic or pure bristle.

When you initially brush your client's hair to remove the tangles before washing, you need to use a brush that is larger and has firm but widely spaced teeth. You always start brushing out towards the ends of the hair and then work back up the hair lengths nearer to the scalp. This makes brushing easier and is far more comfortable for the client.

For delicate finer hair, use a brush with longer more flexible teeth. This is kinder on the hair and will not damage it. The action of brushing will stimulate and distribute the natural oils and, providing there isn't an excess of oil, it will lubricate and stimulate shine. Hair styling requires a variety of brushes, but the personal choice of brush is determined by a brush's weight, length, size and comfort in use.

> **REMEMBER** ✓
>
> Brushing should always a smoothing, stroking action. It should be a comfortable, pleasurable experience – so never use a harsh scrubbing technique.

Brushes   Denman

> **REMEMBER** ✓
>
> Make sure that you only use professional-quality combs and brushes. These will not damage or tear your client's hair, as their design and manufacture creates products that are far superior to general-purpose equipment.

WHAT IS GOOD CUSTOMER CARE?

Good customer care means making the client your number one priority. Quite simply, it is looking after their individual needs and making sure that their visit to the salon is both a pleasurable and enjoyable experience. This begins from the point that the client makes contact with or enters into the salon, and continues until they leave. Helping the client to manage their own hair between visits too extends the service they receive from you further. This after-care is based upon the advice that you give whilst they are in the salon and is invaluable to them, so that they can keep that 'just been to the salon' effect.

How can I demonstrate good customer care?

- Check that all the salon's protective clothing is clean, fresh and properly worn.
- Prepare the work area with all the equipment you need so that the client's services and treatments are not continually disrupted.
- Look after the client's belongings whilst they are in the salon's care.
- Explain practices and procedures as you go along.
- Provide feedback on the progress of these practices and procedures so that the client knows what is happening.
- Don't forget to offer the client style books or magazines as well as the drinks that are available at your salon.

Maintaining client goodwill

The client's trust and goodwill are enhanced by clear communication and in the ways that you communicate with them. Leaving misunderstandings unexplained can undermine a great deal of hard work. So, while you are working, make sure that you:

- Tell the client the reasons for any delays or disruptions in services. Give them reassurance in what is taking place, particularly if it involves a new service or a different look.
- Learn to recognise the needs of your clients. Everyone is different with differing requirements.
- Remember your clients; even the simplest of things can make all the difference – whether a client prefers coffee to tea, or if they take sugar in hot drinks. Little things like this show that you have listened and learned and, what's more, you have taken an interest in them.
- Tell your client about the services that your salon provides, the special techniques and promotions that are currently on offer.
- Get help from your team. If there is something that you are not sure about or something unexpected is happening, get a senior's opinion and avoid something going wrong.

And after services:

- Make sure that the client's clothes are not stained or covered with loose clippings.
- Complete the client's records for future reference.
- Make sure that the client doesn't leave behind any belongings and that includes earrings and glasses as well as hats, scarves, bags or coats.

ACTIVITY ⟷

In your own words, write in the space provided what the words mean:

Goodwill

Client care

Positive communication

Body language

Good service

M. Balfre

- Offer to make the next appointment before the client leaves, complete all the details and provide them with an appointment card before they go.

COMMUNICATION

Good communication between you and your client is one of the most important aspects that will determine your success as a hairdresser.

Most hairdressers are good communicators. The relationship between stylist and client is built on quality of service, **professional advice**, trust, support and a listening ear. Good communication ensures productive and effective action. On the other hand poor communication can lead to misunderstandings, misinterpretation and mistakes.

ACTIVITY ⟷

With a colleague, take turns at being the client or hairdresser in a consultation scenario. Notice the kinds of remarks that gain most information. Note also how listening, and then the responses it generates, tend to lead a series of questions.

M. Balfre

There is a number of different ways in which we communicate:

Oral communication

Speech is used to pass on information and to ask questions. There are two types of questioning:

- *Open questions* – These are a better type of question to use when you want the client to give you information. Examples are: 'What products do you use when you wash your hair at home?' 'How do you apply the colour when you do it at home?' 'Which way do you style the front of your hair?' 'When was the last time that you had a full set of highlights?'

● *Closed questions* – This type of question should be avoided. Closed questions lead the client to give only simple yes or no responses and yield very little information. Examples are: 'Have you washed your hair with anything different lately?' 'Do you find the colour application at home is easy?' 'Have you always had a centre parting?' 'Did you have your highlights done recently?'

You will have informal conversations chatting with your client during the service and more formal, structured conversations greeting your client and in a consultation situation.

Talking and listening to your client is one of the most important parts of the hairdressing service. It will enable you to find out what the client wants and if they have any problems with their hair. You need to listen closely to what they are saying and ask questions to clarify any areas you are not sure about. You also need to ask open questions about their hair to ensure that you get enough information to make a choice, explore ideas and give opinions, such as:

● Would you like to change anything about your hairstyle?

● What products do you use on your hair?

● How much time do you have to style your hair?

ACTIVITY

With a colleague, practise asking different types of questions. Ask your supervisor to explain the difference between open and closed questions. Notice the difference in the amount of information offered when you do ask open questions.

Written communication

Most day-to-day communication between staff or clients is spoken. However, there are times when information has to be recorded. Client records, taking messages and stock procedures are typical examples of this.

Client records can be manual or computerised; in either event they will contain similar information:

● client name and title

● address and contact information

● previous service, treatment, tests and product information

● date, costs and timings of previous visits

● stylist/operator details and any other additional memos.

REMEMBER

Always make sure that your written records are accurate. Incorrect or incomplete client information could result in a future disaster.

The client record is normally used during consultation; this will give you detailed background information relating to their previous visits and allows you a more informed basis for planning a suitable course of action. When completing the client's record whether on computer or manually make sure that the information is clear. A shortage of time between clients tends to make the recording process a rushed or hurried exercise. If you have to put

CLIENT RECORD CARD

Name:	Address:	
Telephone numbers: Home: Work:	Date first registered: Stylist:	Age group ☐ 5–15 ☐ 16–30 ☐ 31–50 ☐ 50+
Hair condition:	Scalp:	Skin type:

Date	Services and products used	Remarks/price charged	Stylist

A client record card

it off until later make a quick note of what has taken place and keep it with you until you have sufficient time to do the job properly. The information needn't be too long; as long as you have covered the essential aspects that will do.

Taking messages

A memo (memorandum) is a quick and easy way of recording information rather than trying to remember and pass on messages later. In most cases we don't remember or if we do it's too late to do anything about it.

Memorandum

TO: John
FROM: Linda
DATE: 1/10
SUBJECT: Staff absence

Jayne will not be in for the rest of the week as she has a virus. Please could you reschedule her appointments, and advise all clients accordingly

Thanks.

Written communication: a memorandum

An effective memo is clear and includes the following:

- for whom it is intended
- who took the message
- the date and time
- its purpose
- clear details or instructions.

Good communication

Good communicators use a mixture of skills in their daily routines. They have:

- *Excellent listening skills* – This is the ability to hear and understand what the client is saying. This can be particularly useful as sometimes the person prompting the change may not be the client in the chair! Other people can have a strong influence on our clients, so you need to find out if the proposed changes are realistic, suitable, practical or even possible.

- *Good speaking skills* – Long silent pauses can often be uncomfortable. Knowing when it is right to speak or when to keep quiet is an invaluable interpersonal skill. During normal consultation, you the hairdresser will be taking the lead. You will be asking questions, i.e. trying to elicit enough information in the time span available to make the right judgements. You will be weighing up what the client wants and balancing it against the limitations arising from the analysis. You will be getting the client to agree on the various possible options and planning the necessary course of action.

- In day-to-day, routine communication with a client the balance can change. More often than not, the client will have plenty to say, particularly when you ask them about what has happened since their last visit.

- *'Reading' skills* – The ability to read situations, to understand what has been said or not said, is exceptionally useful. There are times when your client will take on a certain facial expression, or say something that makes you think. In these situations, your ability to read the situation, your perceptiveness in picking this up and responding appropriately, may have a crucial impact on your long-term relationship.

Body language

As well as using words we show our interest, attitude and feelings by bodily expressions. Non-verbal communication, or body language to put it more simply, is especially important. It can truly show what we are feeling, even if our mouths are saying something quite different!

In the animal world the main form of communication and interaction from one creature to another is through body language. The cat that is alarmed when it is confronted by a dog on the street turns sideways on and hunches up. This makes him look larger than he actually is. Size means everything. You pull away sharply and when you get home the dog sulks; he gets right in your view and turns his back to you. Animals' positioning, posturing and mannerisms all mean something; they all convey a very clear and strong message.

We too, express our interest and attitudes via non-verbal communication through eye contact, posture and general body positioning. So it is very important that we send the right message, particularly when dealing with clients and potential customers.

Eye contact

The first rule of good communication is always maintain eye contact when talking to the client. Where possible, maintain eye level as well. For example if you are carrying out a consultation, sit down with your client; never stand over them or talk to them through the mirror. Standing over or above your client and looking down conveys a feeling of authority, as if you were trying to assert control.

Body zones

People have a comfort zone. This is the space around the body within which they feel at ease. Obviously the extent of this space varies from person to person. Within a close, intimate relationship, shared proximity may be welcome, but an uninvited invasion of this space is at best, very uncomfortable and at worst – menacing or threatening!

Posture, body position and gestures

Much has been written on the subject of body language and the psychological effects that it has on those reading it. It is far too complex a subject to address in a few simple paragraphs. Posture, or composure of the body, is a form of body language in this context. Reading the message of this form of communication is a skill that develops over time and once learnt is never forgotten. However, there are few obvious rules that can help to convey the right message and create a right impression.

- Slouching in the salon or at reception looks very unprofessional.
- Folded arms and the crossing of arms on the chest is a protective gesture that portrays a closed mind or shows defensiveness.
- Open palms, as a gesture supporting explanation or information, with hands at waist height and palms upward, indicates that the person has nothing to hide. This is interpreted as openness or honesty.
- Scratching behind the ear or the back of the neck whilst listening indicate that the listener is uncertain or doesn't understand. Rubbing the nose whilst listening can indicates that you don't believe what you are hearing.
- Talking with your hand in front your mouth may lead the listener to believe you are not being honest. You're hiding yourself by your gestures.

These forms of communication are only an indication of feelings and emotions. In isolation they may not mean anything at all. However, taken together they can convey a very clear message. Make sure that you send the appropriate signals and look interested, keen, ready to help and positive. And above all show that you can listen.

> **REMEMBER**
>
> **Body zones**
> Do not crowd or appear over-familiar with your client. Imagine how you would feel if someone came up to you and got a little too close. What do you do? Immediately back off and go onto the defensive.

During your break ask your fellow staff members to identify a range of body language gestures. Create a table to record this information. Then later, collectively deliberate on the meaning of each gesture. Is everyone getting the same message?

Confidential information

M. Balfre

Throughout all of your dealings with your clients you must remain professional. This is particularly true when it comes to handling confidential information. There are more clients lost by stylists through careless talk than through poor hairdressing!

- Make sure that your discussions with clients remain discreet. Private information should remain private.

- You should never repeat to another person what has been said to you in confidence. Even if it is true!

- Recorded or documented information is personal to the clients. The **Data Protection Act** protects you and your clients from unlawful disclosure of information to others.

REMEMBER

The Data Protection Act 1998 exists to ensure that personal information held on record is not mishandled, mismanaged or used inappropriately. It requires every data controller who is processing personal data to make notification of disclosure unless they are exempt e.g. a data bureau.

DEALING WITH DIFFICULT CLIENTS

As discussed above, good communication is vital. It will help you deal with many situations. However, not all clients are easy to get along with or to extract information from. Some clients may be angry because they have been made to wait or may be unhappy with the finished style. Some clients may find it difficult to explain what they want or may not understand what you are asking. As a stylist it is your job to remain calm and deal with the situation in a supportive, concerned and caring way.

Angry clients

Photo courtesy Goldwell

Stay calm, listen to the client, let them explain why they are angry, use open, friendly body language and maintain eye contact. Keep your speech clear and low when asking questions or giving information to clarify the situation. If you are not in a position to deal with the problem make sure that you get someone who can – this may be a senior stylist or the manager. Never ignore the client; they are angry for a reason and usually the situation can be easily rectified.

Confused clients

Not all clients know what they want when they book for an appointment or what you are suggesting for their hairstyle. Make sure that you give the client time to talk and ask questions. Listen to them again, maintain eye contact, use open body language and gestures such as nodding your head or open palms to confirm your honesty in listening and being ready to support your client. Use simple explanations and questions to extract information. Use visual aids such as style books or colour charts to confirm the requirements.

M. Balfre

Dealing with complaints

Dealing with a dissatisfied client is not easy – you will need a great deal of tact and diplomacy. The client has every right to expect the services that were agreed and paid for, so an unexpected conclusion may result in a showdown.

When a complaint is made it is very difficult to rationalise what is right or wrong, reasonable or unreasonable. Whatever your personal feelings, try to remain calm, polite and understanding. Arguing back will definitely make the client 'dig their heels in' even more. It is not good for your reputation or the salon's image!

If you notice a mistake, don't try to cover it up or pretend it hasn't happened. Put the situation right then and there, before the client leaves the salon. Only a satisfied client promotes a good business!

If a client approaches you with a complaint you should:

- move your client away to a quieter area of the salon
- find out exactly what the problem is
- assess the validity of the complaint supportively and sympathetically

- relay the discussion to a senior member of staff
- mutually agree on a suitable course of action
- carry out any corrective work
- record the occurrence and the remedial action that you took.

If the complaint is serious – such as hair breakage or discolouration – it may be difficult to rectify. Give a complete account to the manager and seek their assistance. The client has a legal right to pursue acts of gross negligence and recently this has proved a popular route to compensation. If a client does follow this course of action, the salon's insurers will need to be notified sooner rather than later.

ACTIVITY

The only way of preparing for the unexpected is to trial the situation beforehand. Role play is one way that you can explore the different scenarios that might occur during client complaint.

Simple misunderstandings do occur during consultation and this can be due to many different reasons. Unfortunately, the result will be not what the client was prepared for. Take it in turns to play client and stylist to see if you can improve your client-handling skills before it happens to you!

Photo courtesy Goldwell

RELEVANT CONSUMER LEGISLATION

See Chapter 5 on Health and Safety for the Health and Safety At Work Act.

Equal opportunities

The Equal Opportunities Commission (EOC) has the statutory duty to

- work towards the elimination of discrimination
- promote equality of opportunity between men and women (and in relation to persons undergoing gender reassignment)
- keep the relevant legislation under review.

The legislation within the remit of the EOC is wide ranging; however, the main considerations are:

- equal pay
- sex discrimination
- disability discrimination (summary below).

In general, the Sex Discrimination Act (SDA) requires goods, facilities and services, whether for payment or not, which are offered to the public to be provided on the same basis for both sexes. The SDA prohibits direct and indirect sex discrimination.

Direct sex discrimination is treating a woman less favourably than a man (or vice versa) because of her sex.

Indirect sex discrimination occurs when a condition or requirement is applied equally to both women and men but, in fact, it affects more women than men (or vice versa) and is not justifiable on objective grounds unrelated to sex. The Act provides for exceptions but unless a relevant exception to the requirements of the SDA can be used, facilities and services should be open to both sexes in the same way.

For more information visit www.eoc.org.uk/index.asp.

Disability Discrimination Act 2005 (DDA 2005)

The Act makes it unlawful to discriminate against disabled persons in connection with employment, the provision of goods, facilities and services or the disposal or management of premises; to make provision about the employment of disabled persons; and to establish a National Disability Council.

The Act protects the rights of disabled people and new revisions in 2005 have particular relevance to the business proprietor. For more information on this or accessibility issues visit www.disability.gov.uk/legislation.

Data Protection Act

Your clients have the following rights which can be enforced through any county court:

- *Right of subject access* – This is the right to find out what information about them is held on computer and in some paper records.

- Correcting inaccurate data – They have the right to have inaccurate personal data rectified, blocked, erased, or destroyed. If your client believes that they have suffered damage or distress as a result of the processing of inaccurate data they can ask the court to award compensation.

- Preventing junk mail (from salons that market to their customer base) – Your client has the right to request in writing that a data controller does not use your personal data for direct marketing by post (sometimes known as 'junk mail'), by telephone or by fax.

For more information on consumer rights in relation to the Data Protection Act visit www.informationcommissioner.gov.uk/

I always explain technical terms eliminating ambiguity and false beliefs ☐	I know and understand the principles of positive communication ☐	I can communicate professionally and know the benefits of good body language ☐	I understand the necessity of personal hygiene and presentation ☐
I know when and to whom to refer clients, in situations where external assistance is required ☐	I know how to negotiate, reaching a mutually beneficial conclusion ☐	I always carry out working practices according to the salon's policy ☐	I know and respect the client's rights; data protection, equal opportunities, discrimination, consumer legislation ☐
			CHECKER BOARD ✓

Assessment of knowledge and understanding

The following projects, activities and assessments are directly linked to the essential knowledge and understanding for unit G5.

For each statement that is addressed wholly or in part in these activities, you will see its relevant and corresponding EKU number.

Make sure that you keep this for easier referencing and along with your work for future inclusion in your portfolio.

Project (EKU G5.1 and G6.1 part)

For this project you will need to gather information from a variety of sources.

For the following legislation find out how:

(a) the Disability and Discrimination Act

(b) the Consumer Protection Act

affect the way that services can be provided to clients.

In your project pay particular attention to the aspects that would have impact on a business and the implications if this legislation were not considered.

Case study (G5.11, G5.12 and G5.13)

Body language is a form of communication that crosses the barriers of language. The messages sent between people in the way that they:

(a) position their bodies

(b) make hand gestures

(c) maintain eye contact or otherwise

all mean different things.

For this activity watch what happens during the day-to-day situations where stylists are dealing with their clients.

Make a record of the most significant occurrences when body language is used to communicate and what is meant by the messages being sent. Check with the stylists after the event to see if your evaluations concur.

Questions

1 How does the Data Protection Act affect the way that client information is held? (G5.1 part)

2 What is your place of work's policy in respect to your personal conduct and appearance? (G5.6)

3 What is your place of work's policy in respect to the provision of services to clients? (G5.2)

4 In what ways (if any) does your salon's service policy differ from that of the local supermarket? (in particular think about the ways that clients' needs are dealt with.) (G5.7 and G5.11)

5 How can you tell if a client is:

(a) not happy with the service being provided

(b) angry? (G5.13)

Preparing for assessment checklist

Remember to:

- communicate positively and effectively in the salon at all times

- be polite, but confident in carrying out communications with clients

- maintain confidentiality and the consequences of failing to keep things private

- listen to clients and show them that you care

- use positive body language and the reasons why it plays such an important part in good customer service

- acknowledge the legal rights of clients and what might happen if they were breached

- promote the range of services, products and treatments available within the salon

- work towards personal targets and know why they should be achieved.

chapter 3

SALON RECEPTION

Unit G4   Fulfil salon reception duties

G4.1 **Maintain the reception area**

G4.2 **Attend to clients and enquiries**

G4.3 **Make appointments for salon services**

G4.4 **Handle payments from clients**

What do I need to do?

- Always keep the salon reception area clean and tidy.
- Greet people entering the salon and attend to their enquiries.
- Listen and respond to client's needs.
- Make appointments carefully and without mistakes.
- Accurately handle payments from clients for salon services.

What do I need to learn?

- How to communicate positively and effectively.
- How to process a range of payment types.
- How to recognise valid and invalid payments.
- The salon's range of services, treatment and retail products.
- The salon's system for making appointments for clients.

Information covered in this chapter

- Reception maintenance and organisation.
- Good customer service.
- Manual and electronic payment systems.
- Appointment systems.

Appointment system   The efficient way of organising the salon work.

Confidentiality   The professional way of handling client information.

Client care   Maintaining goodwill whilst developing a regular, repeated business.

Valid and invalid payment   The differences between the honest and dishonest attempts for payment.

INTRODUCTION

The reception is the most important area of the salon. It is here that clients make their initial contact with the business; clients are greeted as they arrive, incoming calls are handled and appointments and payments are made. It is a busy place. It is also the first impression that clients get of the salon and its staff. Therefore the waiting area, retail displays and reception desk should always be clean, organised and welcoming. It is the job of reception staff to maintain the area and deal with clients in a friendly, relaxed, yet professional manner.

CHECKERBOARD

At the end of this chapter the checkerboard will help to jog your memory on what you have learned and what still remains to be done. Cross off with a pencil each of the topics as you cover it (see page 86).

Wella

SALON RECEPTION

MAINTAINING THE RECEPTION AREA

Hairdressing is a personal service industry and if we are going to keep our clients happy, we have to provide a complete and professional service. This service is not just focused around the stylist's abilities – cutting, styling, perming or colouring – though, it has to be right from the point of entry and exit from the salon. It's the first and the last impression of the salon.

The total service experienced by salon customers involves all of the people within the salon. It is both what is done in the salon and how it is done, and you play a vital role. The first impression clients get when they arrive at reception is a lasting one. It doesn't matter whether the visitor is new to the salon or a long-standing regular client, the overall impression, i.e. image of the salon, is created by what they see and hear.

ACTIVITY

Match the following operations to the tasks. We have already done the first for you.

Retail products should be dusted daily	because handling information correctly is so important
Hairstyle books and magazines are useful	because people don't buy or handle dirty items
Offer clients a drink or magazines	because we must convey a professional image and service
Appointment books are essential	because they help people describe a new look
Good communication is essential	because sometimes they have to wait for a while
Messages should always be passed on to the right person	because they organise the stylist's day

The reception area is the hub of the salon; clients arrive, calls are received, visitors arrive, bills are paid and appointments are made. As part of your duties as the receptionist you will be responsible for making sure that the client waiting area is kept clean and tidy; that magazines are regularly checked for condition and currency and that the style books are replaced after use. A client who has had to wait will feel less angry if they have been attended to, offered something to drink or at least had something at hand to pass the time.

Make sure that the retail displays are regularly cleaned and refilled, that retail products are checked for condition and that price labels are clearly visible. The retail products must look attractive: we want the clients to be encouraged to draw closer, pick them up and handle them. Part of creating the right selling ambience is making products accessible. People are already used to shopping in supermarkets, picking up things that they have an interest in and finding out more about the product they are holding in their hands.

The reception area is always busy with clients arriving or wanting to pay their bill, the telephone is often ringing with clients wanting to make appointments. Therefore the desk must be well organised. Stationery, such as memo pads, pens and payment processing items, should be checked each morning before the salon opens, making sure that there is enough to last throughout the day. The receptionist is also responsible for the till; there should also be enough change and card processing materials to last all day.

REMEMBER

Always make sure that product shelves and retail items are clean and tidy. Nobody will want to handle products that are dusty or on murky shelves!

REMEMBER

Clients' expectations of service are high. Always offer a prompt, welcoming, efficient service, be attentive and helpful.

ACTIVITY

What is your salon's policy in respect to dealing with clients and enquiries? What is the procedure for receiving clients? (Write your answers in the space below.)

Reception checklist

Salon tidiness is essential and maintenance in reception is equally important: make sure that each of these is done every day.

✓ 1. Desk dusted and tidied before clients arrive

✓ 2. Appointment diary close to hand and ready for use

✓ 3. Card payment receipt rolls and till rolls replenished and spares available

✓ 4. Stationery stocks checked and replenished

✓ 5. Shelves and retail products dusted or wiped

✓ 6. Missing items or low stock levels replaced or reordered

✓ 7. Damaged or faulty product packaging removed and reported to the manager

✓ 8. Products rearranged and gaps in product lines removed from displays

✓ 9. Product information and pricing relevant, up to date, close at hand and easy to read

GETTING ORGANISED

The same tabulated system is used in all salons for organising work, although the way that it appears and the way in which it is completed changes from salon to salon. If the reception is the hub of the salon, then the **appointment system** is the most important business process within the salon. It provides:

- a snapshot of expected levels of business
- a detailed action plan of work for staff
- a minute-by-minute schedule of business activities
- a record of client visits, creating a pattern of repeat business.

From this information you can:

- plan the salon **resources**, e.g. people, time, stock and equipment
- organise client records, contact details and treatment history
- prepare the till and electronic payment processes.

From this it is easy to see that the appointment system is the centre of an efficiently run business. The information it contains must be clear, accurate and up to date. However, maintaining the appointment system doesn't always guarantee the smooth running of the salon. You will always need to be prepared for the unexpected, to cover for the following:

Late arrivals

Hardly a day will go by where there isn't someone who is late for their appointment. People are not deliberately late, it's just one of those things put down to modern living, transportation hold-ups, last-minute duties and trying to fit too much into a busy day. All have an impact on time. Unfortunately it's not your time they are using: in most cases it's the next client's! In a situation where the client has arrived late above all you do need to be sympathetic and understanding. The first thing to do is find out if there is still enough time to complete the service without over-running throughout the rest of the day? If there isn't enough time left, see if one of the other stylists can help out: often a bit of 'juggling' will put things back on track.

Will the client have to wait? Is there going to be a delay? Tell the client immediately, let them choose between staying and waiting, coming back a little later or, if there is no other option, rebooking for another appointment at some other time.

Unscheduled arrivals and 'walk ins'

The client who arrives without an appointment should always be accommodated. If you think about the situation from their point of view, they have made the decision to come into your salon. Why? Is it because they have been recommended by someone else? Did they like the look of the salon from the outside? Or did they just happen to be in the area at the time? Whatever the reason, it's all good business.

Double bookings

Overbooking, or **double booking**, does occur, but shouldn't do too often. It is usually the result of either a staff member or the client making a mistake, or through poor communication. Don't try to beat the appointment system; you may upset clients, colleagues or both. Providing a high-quality service includes making sure people know the expected timescales and duration of services and if there will be any waiting.

Deliberate overbooking is only done by the over-optimistic staff member. (This could be likened to the large airlines: they gamble on the premise that something will crop up and some of the passengers will not turn up.) It doesn't work, it only causes bad feelings and disappointment, and make sure you don't do it.

> **REMEMBER**
>
> Never attempt to carry out any hairdressing service without the client's consent.

ACTIVITY

What is your salon's procedure for handling telephone enquires? Write in the space provided what you are supposed to say when you answer a call.

Hair: Pat Wood; photography: Thornton Howdle; make-up: Leanne Shaw

Changes to booked services

There will often be occasions where a client has booked for one service, but by the time they reach the salon they have changed their mind and want something else totally different. People change their minds all the time. Don't worry, this could be good business – a client may come in expecting a restyle, cut and finish, and go out with highlights too. In fact many salons set incentives around this very activity; for example, staff performances and commissions may be based on 'up selling' or 'client conversion'.

Staff absences

Staff absences will always stretch the salon's resources to its limits but your salon should have a contingency plan to cover this situation. Generally this will involve:

- checking to see if other salon staff can or have provided services to the client before
- rearranging appointments to accommodate the disruption
- if all else fails – contact the client before they set out to schedule a reappointment.

M. Balfre

ACTIVITY

Typical assessment questions and model answers: when clients arrive at the salon…

Q1 What's the first thing you should do when a client arrives?
A1 Check the client's name, appointment time, what they are having done and who it is with.

Q2 What should you do next?
A2 Take their coat and any shopping etc. and put them away carefully and safely.

Q3 The stylist is not quite ready for the client. What should you do next?
A3 Ask the client to take a seat and offer them a drink and something to look at for the time being.

Dealing with people

Every salon needs clients to exist. The clients come because they know what the salon has to offer; this includes the salon ambience, the services and treatments provided and most of all the people with whom they feel comfortable.

Good technical skills are achieved through patience and hard work. Good customer communication is achieved in exactly the same way and the realisation of this simple formula and how you handle it is your key to success. Poor communication, bad manners and disagreements have no place in a successful business and therefore they must be eliminated or resolved.

M. Balfre

Greeting people and handling enquiries

We want visitors to become clients and there are ways to make this happen. An important part of this process and one that effects the conscious decisions people make about us, is communication. We want people to see us as professional communicators. Professional communication occurs when we handle or anticipate the needs of others in a prompt and businesslike manner.

Effective communication takes place in the following ways:

- speech, in what we say to others and the way in which we say it;
- listening, by hearing the requests of others properly;
- writing, by recording information accurately and clearly;
- body language – the way we communicate our feelings and attitude to situations by posture, expression and mannerisms.

Enquiries made by a client either in person (i.e. face-to-face) or on the telephone should be handled in the same way. In both instances, we need to respond promptly and politely. If you don't know the answer to a question, ask someone who does: accurate information is essential. So stop! Listen to what is being said, hear the request and act on the information. Misinterpreting what has been said will lead to giving or recording the wrong information. As we saw earlier, wrong information is a disaster when making appointments or in those situations where the client turns up on the wrong day and can't be done because her stylist is too busy!

On the telephone

Making the right impression is even more difficult on the telephone, when callers gain an impression of the salon from the person that they are speaking to. This person becomes the salon's sole representative, acting on behalf of the business and their ability to listen, speak clearly, respond to requests and act upon information is vital.

Smile when you answer the telephone: people will 'hear' the friendliness in your voice. At the same time speak clearly so that the caller can understand everything you say. After listening to the caller's request, confirm the main points back to them. This summarises the information and ensures that all details are correct. Keep in mind the length of the call: calls cost money and waste valuable salon time.

Face to face

When clients arrive in person, they should be attended to promptly, their appointment and time should be checked before they are directed to a seat. Always make a point of making them feel welcome; perhaps offer a magazine or a drink before informing the stylist that their client has arrived. This is important as it will avoid any unnecessary waiting or possible embarrassment when the stylist realises (perhaps much later) that their client has actually arrived.

There will be occasions when you need to seek assistance or advice from others. Being able to recognise situations where you are unable to help is not a failure, it is all part of professional communication. There will be situations that require the attention of someone else, perhaps when the window cleaner arrives and says 'Shall I just get on with it?' or when stock arrives and the signature of a person responsible for taking delivery and accepting condition of goods is required.

The visual impressions made from a person's body language are equally important (see Chapter 2 on client care and communication).

Confidentiality

Certain circumstances need special care and attention and probably the most important aspect of professional communication is confidentiality. During our day-to-day work it is possible that we come into contact with information that others consider private. It is important that you recognise these situations and handle them accordingly. This **confidential information** will be disclosed in numerous ways: during routine conversation between staff or clients and from business contacts and enquirers. Whatever the source, it is vitally important that you do not divulge personal or potentially sensitive information to anyone.

M. Balfre

REMEMBER ✔

Always keep a pad for notes handy at reception. It will provide a far more useful aid than writing over the appointment page!

ACTIVITY

In the space provided explain why taking messages and passing them on to the correct person is so important.

MAKING APPOINTMENTS

The appointment system is the very centre, the 'hub' of the whole salon operation. Without an appointment system the business would stop! So it is essential that appointments are made accurately and promptly, every time, whether a client makes an appointment over the telephone or in person.

Before you can schedule appointments you must have an idea of the services available. Each salon provides a unique 'menu' of services. Different stylists will have different abilities and skills, and so might be available for certain services at certain levels. You need to know the variety of services available, their timings and relevant costs.

Making appointments needn't be difficult. It's about matching client requests with the time available. We want to help the customer make the booking, while bearing in mind the time that it will take and who will be providing the service. When clients are contacting the salon by telephone you should always speak first saying, 'Good morning/afternoon, this is Head Masters hair salon. This is xxxxx speaking, how may I help you?' This friendly but positive approach will immediately give a professional image of both the salon and yourself.

Each salon has its own system for making appointments but, generally speaking, appointment scheduling maximises the time available with appropriate staff members. Bearing this in mind, we should always remain ready, prompt and polite in attending to the client's requests.

Make sure that when the booking is made that you record the information accurately and clearly and that you have considered all the factors:

- date and time
- service required
- stylist required
- the client's name
- client contact details.

Record the client's name clearly in the appointment system, alongside the service, and check that it is scheduled for the correct day and time with the appropriate stylist. As a matter of customer service it is also useful to give the client an approximate idea of service cost and length of appointment time. At the end, summarise all the information back to the client, thus ensuring that all the details are correct.

If in doubt

There may be situations where you are not sure. It is always better to ask someone else than to make an incorrect booking. When unsure always ask someone for help. There is nothing worse than a stylist who is running late, particularly if this is the result of someone else's booking error. The situation will be stressful for the stylist but, more importantly, we do not want any clients waiting longer than absolutely necessary, whatever the reason.

> **REMEMBER**
>
> Always introduce yourself when handling calls. People like to speak to people with whom they can associate, not strangers or machines!

> **REMEMBER**
>
> When making appointments ensure you have a contact number for the client.

Appointments page   L'Oréal Professionnel

Service abbreviations

Cut and blow-dry	**CBD**
Blow-dry	**BD**
Shampoo and set	S/S
Ladies' wet cut	**W/C**
Gents' wet cut	G W/C
Gents' cut and blow dry	G CBD
Highlights T section	**H/L T**
Highlights full head	**H/L** fh
Highlights half head	H/L$^1/_2$
Retouch colour	**Col rt**
Full head colour	**Col fh**
Permanent wave	**PW**
Chemical straightening	Strght

ACTIVITY

In this exercise you need to read the following service information and then complete the blank appointment sheet accordingly with the appropriate abbreviations.

A salon employs three experienced hairstylists:

Jane	A stylist who works part-time 1 pm to 5.30 pm
Samantha	A stylist who works full-time 9 am to 5.30 pm and has an hour for lunch
Tina	A colourist who works mornings only 9 am to 12 noon

Service		Duration
Cut and blow-dry	(CBD)	45 mins
Blow-dry	(BD)	30 mins
Wet cut only	(WC)	30 mins
Dry trim	(DT)	15 mins
Highlights T section	(HLT)	30 mins (plus 30 mins' development)
Highlights full head	(HL fh)	45 mins (plus 30 mins' development)
Retouch colour	(Col rt)	30 mins (plus 45 mins' development)

Add the name of each stylist at the top of the appropriate column. Now read the following service information and complete the blank appointment page.

- Miss Cooper and her daughter would like full head highlights at the same time as each other with a cut and blow-dry back with Samantha later.

- Mrs Ford wants the earliest appointment available with Jane for a cut and blow-dry and would like to bring her two children for dry trims with whoever is available at the same time.

- Miss Jones would like a mid-morning cut and blow-dry appointment with Samantha.

- A Miss Collins telephones to ask if there is an appointment for retouch colour and then a cut and blow-dry back with Samantha after 10.30 am.

- Mark out time for Samantha's lunch.

- Two college girls, Miss Green and Miss Dorkin, call in and ask if there are any appointments for cut and blow-drys, after lectures and as near to 2.00 pm as possible. They don't mind who they have, but they would like it at the same time.

● Someone telephones at 1.00 pm and asks for their children, Paula and Cheryl Tombs to have a wet cut and a dry trim respectively, before 3.00 pm. Where can they be fitted in?

Appointment sheet

Date:			
Time			
9.00			
9.15			
9.30			
9.45			
10.00			
10.15			
10.30			
10.45			
11.00			
11.15			
11.30			
11.45			
12.00			
12.15			
12.30			
12.45			
1.00			
1.15			
1.30			
1.45			
2.00			
2.15			
2.30			
2.45			

Date:			
3.00			
3.15			
3.30			
3.45			
4.00			
4.15			
4.30			
4.45			
5.00			

HANDLING PAYMENTS AND PAYMENT TYPES

When the hairdressing services have been completed and the client is satisfied with the result, the last thing that takes place before leaving the salon is the payment. The payment is made and kept in either a manual or automatic till.

- The manual till is a lockable drawer, often attached or built in to the reception desk. At the end of the day the money is cashed up and manually recorded onto the salon's accounting system.

- The electronic till has a freestanding cash drawer that is built in to the till's body; this automatically opens when the payment process is complete. The till sits upon the desk or (because these tend to be quite bulky) sits in a specially shaped reveal that makes it less conspicuous. During daily use, the till records the payments and allocates them to individuals automatically. Electronic tills can be programmed for a number of functions. Each person may be given a department key which identifies their takings; this code can be used to calculate commission payments. On an automatic till, a turnkey system can display X and Z totals. These readings when printed out are used to check the amounts registered against the actual amount in the till.

  X readings may be used to provide subtotals throughout the day: this is particularly useful in larger companies where it may be helpful to check takings when the cashier or receptionist leaves the till, removes cash etc. from the till, or leaves the reception for break or for lunch. The Z reading is a figure taken at the close of business at the end of day. This provides a breakdown of the payment types, the times that payments were made and the allocations of sales against individuals.

Computerised till

- The computerised till like the electronic till has a built-in cash drawer and sits upon the reception desk. The advantage of this type of till over the others is its ability to provide a better analysis of salon sales as well as keeping a central point of access to all the clients' records and treatment history. During daily use they will monitor the individual sales, client repeat patterns and stocks sold or used; they will also provide a range of management reports.

> **REMEMBER**
>
> Any tips given by clients should always be kept separately from the money in the till.

Sales-related equipment

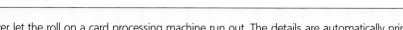

- *Calculator* – Always a useful and necessary item to be kept somewhere handy on the desk for totalling large bills or during end-of-day summaries.
- *Till rolls and spare rolls for card processing machines* – These provide records of sales and provide the client with a receipt for payment. Always keep spares handy just in case they run out in daily use. As the rolls get close to running out you will notice a red continuous marking, indicating that the roll must be changed at the earliest possible moment.

> **REMEMBER**
>
> Never let the roll on a card processing machine run out. The details are automatically printed on the receipt roll when the machine is being used, and when it starts a transaction it can't be stopped. If it runs out during a payment neither the client nor the salon will have a copy of the record of payment.

> **REMEMBER** ✔
>
> Always close the cash drawer firmly; do not leave the key in the drawer or the till open.

> **REMEMBER** ✔
>
> Fraud is happening all the time! Find out what your salon's policy is in relation to fraudulent or attempted fraudulent transactions.

- *Credit card equipment* – If the business accepts payment by cards you will have an electronic terminal which processes payments automatically, through a telephone connection (e.g. 'Chip and Pin'). The machine is loaded with a two-ply receipt roll and the details of the sale are automatically printed onto the receipt. However, in the event of breakdown, i.e. power outage or telephone communication breakdown, a manual imprinter is used as a back-up system. The manual imprinter is a system whereby the client's embossed credit card details are transferred to a self-carbonating sales voucher. The details of the sale are written on to the voucher and the client checks all the details and provides a signature to confirm.
- *Cash float* – At the start of the day a small sum of money, low denomination notes and smaller coins, is put in the till in order to provide change to clients paying in cash. This float is removed at the end of the day before any of the rest of the money is tallied. (A typical float, say £50.00, would be made up of the following: 1 × ten-pound note, 2 × five-pound notes, 5 × two-pound coins, 10 × one-pound coins, 10 × fifty-pence coins, 10 × twenty-pence coins, 20 × ten-pence coins, 20 × five-pence coins.)
- *Cash book* – Used as a way of accounting for sales by manually writing up the day's totals.

Mahogany

Mahogany

Methods of payment

Cash payment

When taking cash from clients make sure that you follow these simple steps:

1 Carefully 'ring up' all the services and products provided to the client into the till and press 'subtotal'.
2 Inform the client of the amount to be paid.
3 Look carefully but not suspiciously to make sure that the money offered is legal tender (you should check that the notes are still valid, not out of date and not counterfeit i.e. fake!).
4 Place the money tendered to you on the ledge at the top of the till drawer, so that it can be seen by the client too.
5 Press the numeric keys of the till to equal the amount tendered by the client.
6 Press the total button. The till will automatically show the amount of change to be given and the till drawer will open.
7 Take out and count back this amount into the client's hand.
8 Tear off the till receipt and don't forget to thank them as well as asking, 'Would you like to make your next appointment now?'.
9 If the amount given back to the client is disputed, ask how much is missing. It is quite simple to make a genuine mistake, but if you are in any doubt call for a senior member of staff to assist. (If there is any dispute the till will need to be cashed up there and then to check for discrepancies.)

REMEMBER

Checking the validity of notes
Hold the note in front of you with the Queen's head uppermost and on the right. You are looking for:

1 a clear, detailed watermark of the Queen (facing to the right) in the lower centre of any denomination note
2 a continuous metal strip through the note on the left which, if looked at from the back, appears to be a woven and an intermittently shiny foil
3 a hologram decal in the mid-left section of the note. When this is turned in the light it will disclose the denomination, matching the face value above it.

The note should feel crisp and fine without any distortion even if it has been accidentally washed.

The note should be intact without tears or sign of tampering, (A torn note can be accepted providing that the note remains in one piece – a damaged note is discretional and can be refused. However, damaged notes can easily be exchanged at a bank or post office.)

Cheques

Some clients still prefer to pay their bill by cheque. Cheques must be accompanied by a cheque guarantee card. These are normally a debit card and denote a spending limit which is etched into a hologram on the back of the card; normally this limit is set at £100, although limits up to £250 are available on credit cards which can also be used for cheque guarantees in certain situations. It is not advisable to accept cheques drawn for amounts above the guarantee limit, even if the client is a regular.

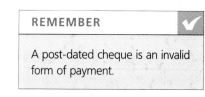

REMEMBER ✔

A post-dated cheque is an invalid form of payment.

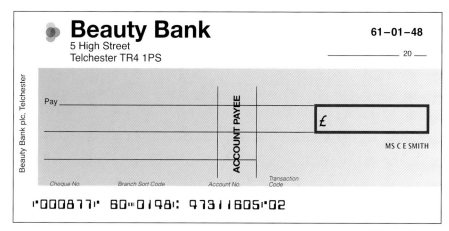

A cheque

A credit card   Courtesy Barclays PLC

When receiving payment by cheque follow these steps:

1 The cheque must have the correct date in the top right-hand corner.
2 The cheque must be payable to the firm or company (you may have a pre-printed stamp for this).
3 The amount in figures must match the amount written in words.
4 Any mistakes or errors made must be initialled by the client.
5 The cheque must be signed and must match the signature on the back of the cheque guarantee card.
6 The sort code and account number on the cheque must match those on the guarantee card.
7 The payment date must be within the valid from and to dates on the cheque guarantee card.
8 The cheque cannot exceed the guarantee limit.

Payments by card

Payment by card is the most popular form of payment and there are a number of reasons why clients prefer to use this type of payment.

- *Cash availability* – Most people are paid directly into their bank accounts, therefore it is easier to draw down on these funds by debit card than to queue at an ATM (automated teller machine) to get cash out.
- *Cost of drawing out cash* – Many competing banking organisations will charge for withdrawing cash. If you can't find a branch of the bank with

which you have an account, you could be charged for withdrawing from another bank's ATM.

- *Easier to account for expenditure* – It is simpler to keep a tally on the bank account as each amount drawn will be itemised on a monthly statement.
- *Different types of card* – There are many different types of card, so people can make choices on how they pay. Therefore people can manage their money easier by opting to pay by debit card, credit card or charge card.

Card types

There are three basic types of card:

- debit card
- credit card
- charge card.

- *Debit cards* – Switch/Maestro and SOLO cards all act as an automated cheque: the transaction process is the same as for a cheque or credit card, but once processed the salon's account is electronically credited and the client's bank account is debited. The card processing company applies a nominal fixed fee to the salon for each card transaction made.
- *Credit cards* – These are accepted as a method of payment at the discretion of the salon. When a card has been accepted as the method of payment, a fixed percentage of the total bill is charged by the card processing company for the use of this facility. A list of cards that are accepted by the salon for payment should be clearly displayed on the door or front window as well as the reception desk. Clients tend to assume that payment by card will be acceptable so failing to inform them otherwise could cause an embarrassing situation to arise. Card payments are given a 'floor limit' by the card company: payment will be honoured up to a specific amount; for large amounts prior authorisation by telephone is required. Thorough training needs to be given if staff are to understand these procedures.
- *Charge cards* – These provide another payment alternative. Many businesses now accept charge card payments too – American Express is the main operator in this field. Charge card payments are made in a similar way to credit or debit cards and therefore can be treated the same way. The difference is more for the card holder, they are often used as business cards, for travel, accommodation and business expenses. Each month the card holder receives a statement for the purchases made on the card over the period. This statement is a request for settlement and the bill must be paid.

> **REMEMBER** ✔
>
> Card-issuing companies believe that customer spend is greater on credit cards and that is why they charge a percentage of the total bill as opposed to a fixed charge per transaction.

Card authenticity

The use of cards as a means of payment simplifies till transactions, but as an increasing number of cards are made available it is essential that precautions are taken to guard against card theft and fraud. The latest system, 'Chip and

Pin' (i.e. where the client uses their own personal pin number instead of a signature to verify authenticity), is expected to reduce this problem, but you should be on your guard anyway.

The card processing company provides full support for the services it offers. This includes:

1 training materials and regular updates of information to staff

2 24/7 telephone support help lines

3 accounting and management information

4 advertising support and in salon promotional materials.

Before you except a card payment you should make sure that the card is genuine and valid. Within the salon information pack you will find a card recognition guide for each card that is permitted. The guide provides the following information:

1 *Card symbol* – This is a logo (Visa, MasterCard) which will appear at the front lower right corner of the card. For charge cards i.e. American Express the Centurion head is printed across the centre of the card.

2 *Card hologram* – The card hologram service mark is in the centre right-hand edge of the card. This service mark is etched on to a foil decal which is superimposed on the card's printed background. The service mark on the holographic service mark (e.g. Visa) appears as a dove ascending when angled in the light, the hologram changes according to the angle from which it is viewed.

3 *Card member number* – The card member's number will be embossed on to the surface and across the width of the card. When you use an electronic terminal, always ensure that the card member number matches that which is printed on your terminal receipt.

4 *Card validity dates* – The card will show a 'valid from' date as well as an 'expires end' date. If the card is not in date it can not be accepted.

5 *Card member's name* – Check that the name on the card and the title of the card member, if it is embossed, match the person presenting it.

Card type identification

There are many cards now in force – some advertise charities or sponsorships but all will show the service provider's international trademark(s) and hologram(s). Look for these features, also apparent upon the back of the card (debit cards such as Maestro or Delta will also contain clearly defined logos and may be used as cheque guarantee cards, but only up to the value shown on the hologram at the back of the card):

1 *Magnetic strip and metal foil chip* – this incorporates the data which can be read when the card is used via an electronic terminal

2 *Signature strip* – check that the signature strip has not been tampered with and that it is flush with the surface of the card

3 *Card member's signature* – the card should be signed on the signature strip

Extra security features continue to be added to credit and charge cards and most cards are used as 'Chip and Pin'.

Processing manual payments by card

Different cards have different sales vouchers. Receipt for payment by Visa or MasterCard cannot be transacted upon an American Express voucher and vice versa. Similarly Switch, Delta and Electron cannot be transacted on a manual imprinter as these are debit cards and require electronic means in order to draw down on the account funds.

Procedure for manual transactions

1 Place the card face up on the imprinter.
2 Place the correct sales voucher face up over the card and operate the imprinter by drawing the rollers (using the handle) across to the right and then back to the left.
3 Check that the details from the card and the merchant's stamped plate are imprinted through all the parts of the voucher.
4 Remove the sales voucher and the card from the imprinter. Write all the necessary sales details, including the date, the amount and a brief description of the sale, on the sales voucher using a ballpoint pen. Make sure that any space boxes for the total amount are struck through if you are not going to enter figures into them.
5 Ask the cardholder to sign the sales voucher. Hold the card and watch the cardholder sign in the box indicated. While holding the card lightly rub your thumb over the signature strip. It should be smooth and flush with surface of the card.
6 Check that the signature on the voucher matches that on the card.
7 Check that the spelling of the surname of the signature corresponds with that embossed on the card and also that the card is in date.
8 Check that the card is not in any 'Hot card' warnings.
9 Check that the card has not been subjected to any damage or tampering.

If the total value of sales exceeds your agreed 'floor limit' (that is a predetermined sum for manual transactions) or in any way you are suspicious of either the card or the circumstances, you must telephone for authorisation.

If you are satisfied that all the procedures have been completed and that all checks have been made, you can detach the cardholder copy of the voucher and hand it to the customer with the card.

Processing payments electronically

Payments made by debit, charge and credit card by electronic terminals are authorised during the transaction process and provide funds which are deposited into the business current account on either a daily or weekly basis. This excludes transactions carried out in fraudulent circumstances, which might include theft, tampered and damaged cards and mail order when the customer is not present at the point of sale.

The electronic terminal is a rented unit which consists of a customer keypad, terminal keypad, card swipe and chip reader input, with LED display recording each step of the transaction procedure. In addition there is a carbonless two-ply receipt roll which is connected to the power supply and the card companies via a telephone link.

Procedure for electronic payment systems (Chip and Pin)

1 Check that the terminal is in sale ready mode.

2 Insert the card into the chip reader.

3 Enter the amount by using the key pad (if you make a mistake you can clear the figures using the 'clear' button).

4 Press 'enter', which will connect the terminal to the card processing company.

5 The customer details are automatically accessed and after a few moments, a message will prompt for 'Enter customer pin'. The customer can enter their four-digit pin to the customer keypad and press enter. The payment is authorised or declined automatically.

6 Separate the receipts. Pass the bottom copy back to the client and retain the top copy for the till.

Seeking authorisation

If the total value of services and/or goods exceeds the pre-arranged floor limit, or if you are in any way suspicious of the card, its presenter or the circumstances of the sale, you must seek authorisation.

Having ensured that no goods are within the customer's reach, take the card and the completed sales voucher, with a ballpoint pen, to the telephone. Dial the authorisation number and you will be connected to the authorisation operator. Be ready to provide the following information:

- the number embossed on the client's card
- the salon's merchant number (a unique registration number allocated by the card processing company)
- the amount of the transaction.

Occasionally you may be asked to obtain some form of positive identification from the customer presenting the card.

When the sale is authorised you will be given a code which may include numbers and letters. You must write this code in the authorisation code box on the sales voucher. If the card is declined, no reason will be given. You should return the card to the customer and ask for some other form of payment.

REMEMBER

All information regarding clients should be handled in strict confidence. This safeguards all concerned and helps to reduce the possibility of embarrassment and loss of clients.

Code 10 authorisation calls

There are times when it is necessary to seek authorisation for a transaction where it is not possible to speak freely over the telephone – particularly if you are suspicious of the circumstances surrounding the transaction. To avoid any difficulties, when it is not possible to speak freely you simply state that it is a Code 10 call. The operator will understand your predicament and will deal with your call sympathetically. If you are able to speak freely and are suspicious of the circumstances surrounding the transaction, let the operator know immediately.

Hot card warnings

From time to time notification will be sent to the salon about cards that cannot be accepted. If a customer attempts to purchase goods on a hot card you should retain the card and telephone authorisation. The full instructions on how to handle hot cards will be sent with each hot card warning to the salon.

Retaining a suspicious card

There are occasions when the authorisation operator will require you to retain a card. When this is so politely inform the customer without causing embarrassment or putting yourself at risk. Preserve the evidence for further action and take the following steps:

- cut off the bottom left-hand corner from the front of the card
- preserve intact the signature panel and magnetic strip
- handle the card by its edges to preserve fingerprints and other forensic evidence
- return both pieces back to the card company along with any receipts or sales vouchers
- claim your reward! All card companies want to stamp out card fraud and pay generous rewards for the recovery of wanted cards.

Other payment types

- *Accounts* – Your salon may provide an account facility for regular clients, and a formal arrangement whereby all bills for an individual or a family are paid at agreed intervals. It is advisable to ask the client to sign the bill at the time of service. It should be clear to the stylist when the commission will be paid – either at the time of service or at the time of the account payment.
- *Traveller's cheques* – These are often accepted as payment by companies who operate in tourist locations. However, to avoid losing out in currency conversions, traveller's cheques for the moment should only be accepted in pounds sterling. As these are not normally used by regular clients they should be checked against the bearer's passport for proof of identity.

- *Gift vouchers* – These may be sold by the salon for payment against hairdressing and beauty services or retail sales. When the salon is operating as a concession, gift vouchers may be available for purchase from the host company. You in turn will require reimbursement from the source of the voucher. Company policy should outline procedures for issuing and receiving gift vouchers.

ACTIVITY

Make a list of all the different card types that may be used for payment in your salon, and the differences between them.

Discrepancies

Inconsistencies, disagreements or differences – invalid currencies being tendered, out-of-date cheque cards or unsigned cheques – should be dealt with as soon as possible. Where a payment card is being fraudulently used or there is a payment dispute, such as a bill totalling more than was previously agreed, then a senior member of staff should be referred to. Should an illegal transaction or even one suspected of being illegal be attempted, it may be decided to refer the matter to the police. This decision should always be made by the manager alone; however, in these circumstances you must act discreetly as serious allegations must be backed up with a formal statement and or evidence.

Discrepancies within the till where the sales don't balance with the money in the till could be a genuine mistake or, alternatively, indicate dishonesty. The till should be neither up nor down at the end of the day and your salon will have a procedure for looking into 'unders' or 'overs' more closely.

Theft

Theft is a crime. If someone is caught in the act of theft or if it is proven that a previous theft has taken place, then it should be reported to the police.

Police strongly urge businesses to prosecute staff who have stolen from the business. Theft is an act of gross misconduct and any person found guilty of it will be dismissed immediately without any justifiable recourse.

Computers

As more people come into contact with computers and the Internet as part of their daily life, computer-based salon solutions are now a fixture in all forward-thinking modern salons. And there are a number of purpose-built applications for running and operating a salon system to choose from.

Most of these **database** applications provide a very comprehensive package and have features that address the following business aspects:

- appointment booking system
- client records: patterns of repeat business and history, as well as contact information
- product usage, stock control and retail sales
- staff details: sales, commissions, hours of work, sickness, holidays etc.
- sales functions: sales audits, tracking and VAT, as well as normal till operation
- management information: reports, accounting, financial breakdowns, trading patterns.

The individual features of particular products are usually very similar; however, the main difference between systems is more to do with look and functionality. Some systems tend to go for a more graphical front end (pictorial information depicted upon the screen) whilst others go for a more business-type look that is more like a typical (Microsoft Office™) application.

As more clients do their business, accounts and shopping online, a growing number of salons communicate to their customer base either through their website or by e-mail. Its just as easy to make an appointment online as it is on the telephone, so there will be a big take-up over the next few years in hairdressing and beauty therapy online booking systems.

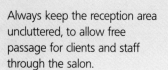

REMEMBER

Always keep the reception area uncluttered, to allow free passage for clients and staff through the salon.

ACTIVITY

Collect information about the different types of computer-based systems available. When you have information on say two or three make a comparison between the software products. See what features and benefits each one has to offer.

Hair: Desmond Murray; make-up: Xavier; photography: Thornton Howdle; assistant: Gemma Adams

RECEPTION SECURITY

The reception is the first part of the salon that people walk into off the street, so this area must maintain a high level of security. All monies must be kept safely locked away and products should be monitored so that they are not maliciously removed. Records relating to the business, client details, accounts books etc. should never be left unattended. If a client were to see these things left around that would be bad enough. But if an unknown viewed them, then the salon's security measures would have been breached and personal information disclosed. In order to avoid these situations:

- the salon reception should be manned at all times;
- don't keep any money on the premises when the salon is shut and keep cash in the till during working hours to an absolute minimum;
- never leave the till drawer open when it is not in use;
- check all notes that have been handed over in payment to avoid counterfeits;
- always leave the cash drawer, or at least the chassis that it fits into, open overnight: this discourages forced entries;
- large amounts of money should be regularly transferred to the company safe or banked;
- never make regular visits to the bank at the same times;
- receipts should be given for all payments;
- never use the cash in the till for petty cash purchases;
- any other money removed for whatever reason must always be recorded;
- follow the salon's safety and security procedures at all times.

Mahogany

I understand my job position and the impact of not keeping information confidential ☐	I know how to record accurate information for messages and appointments ☐	I always follow the salon's policy in respect to client care and customer service ☐	I know how to maintain the reception area and retail displays ☐
I know how to do the reception duties ☐	I know how to attend to clients when they arrive at reception ☐	I always carry out working practices according to the salon's policy ☐	I know how to communicate effectively with staff and customers ☐
I understand the implications of poor client communications ☐	I know how to work the till, handle payments and process payment by card ☐	I know the salon's appointment system and how to make appointments for clients ☐	I know the salon's services; how long they take and how much they cost ☐
I know what to look for in relation to stationery shortages and product imperfections ☐	I understand the extent to which the Data Protection Act affects what I do at work ☐	I understand the necessity of personal presentation when dealing with clients ☐	CHECKER BOARD ✓

Assessment of knowledge and understanding

The following projects, activities and assessments are directly linked to the essential knowledge and understanding for unit G4.

For each statement that is addressed wholly or in part in these activities, you will see its relevant and corresponding EKU number.

Make sure that you keep this for easier referencing and along with your work for future inclusion in your portfolio.

Project (EKU G4.9, G4.12, G4.13, G4.14)

With two of your colleagues you can practise and document the different scenarios that occur in a hairdressing salon.

Let one person take the place of the client and another the receptionist. The third acts as an observer and takes notes for the others. Take it in turns to cover the following salon situations:

1 An angry client who is not happy with their hair.

2 A client who needs assistance with buying retail products.

2 A client who wants to make several bookings for her daughter's wedding.

In your notes you need to cover how the client was handled, how if at all the service could be improved and what information needs to be recorded in each of the different scenarios.

Case study (G4.5, G4.8 and G4.11)

A client has asked for an appointment with a stylist who longer works at the salon.

Describe your salon procedures for:

- what you say to the client
- the questions you would ask
- the alternatives that you would offer the client
- what you would do if you could not deal with the situation.

Questions

1 What is your salon's policy in respect to confidentiality? (G4.1)

2 What is your place of work's policy in respect to taking messages? (G4.1, G4.7)

3 What is your place of work's policy in respect to making and recording appointments? (G4.1)

4 In what ways (if any) does your client reception policy differ from that of your local supermarket? (In particular think about the ways that clients needs are dealt with.) (G4.1, G4.2)

5 What is the salon's policy in respect to damaged goods? (G4.17)

Preparing for assessment checklist

Remember to:

- promote the range of services available in the salon and know what they cost
- promote the range of products available in the salon and know what they cost
- keep the reception area clean and tidy at all times
- keep stationery stocks handy at reception and know where to find replacements
- cover all the salon's payment types and methods
- always make appointments correctly, according to the salon's policy
- take messages and pass them on to the right person promptly
- give the right change when payment is made by cash
- recognise the current and valid forms of payment that the salon accepts
- keep the reception area and the till secure at all times.

TONI & GUY AT THE 50TH ANNIVERSARY
L'ORÉAL COLOUR TROPHY, LONDON, MAY 2005.

ANTOINETTE BEENDERS AT THE 50TH ANNIVERSARY
L'ORÉAL COLOUR TROPHY, LONDON, MAY 2005.

TREVOR SORBIE AT THE 50TH ANNIVERSARY
L'ORÉAL COLOUR TROPHY, LONDON, MAY 2005.

CHARLES WORTHINGTON AT THE 50TH ANNIVERSARY
L'ORÉAL COLOUR TROPHY, LONDON, MAY 2005.

M. BALFRE AT THE ALTERNATIVE HAIR SHOW, 2005.

part two

chapter 4

SHAMPOOING AND CONDITIONING HAIR

NVQ/SVQ reference, unit title and main outcome

Unit H9 Shampoo and condition the hair and scalp

H9.1 **Maintain effective and safe methods of working when shampooing and conditioning the hair and scalp**

H9.2 **Shampoo the hair and scalp**

H9.3 **Condition the hair and scalp**

What do I need to do?

- Take adequate precautions in preparing yourself and the client before any backwash procedure.
- Prepare the backwash area ready for work.
- Be able to handle different hair types and lengths.
- Be able to make the backwash procedures a pleasurable experience.

What do I need to learn?

You need to know and understand:

- why it is important to take care when carrying out backwash procedures
- how to recognise types of hair conditions and select appropriate products to use
- a range of backwash products, their purposes and applications
- the different massage techniques used in backwash operations.

Information covered in this chapter

- The types of products used and how they work.
- The range of hair types that you will need to cover.
- How shampoos and conditioning treatments work.
- What is dermatitis?
- What is barrier cream?

KEY WORDS

Effleurage   A gentle stroking movement used in shampooing.

Rotary   A quicker and firmer circular movement used in shampooing.

Friction   A vigorous rubbing movement used when shampooing on the scalp areas.

Petrissage   A slower circulatory kneading movement generally used for scalp massage when applying conditioner.

INTRODUCTION

The process of shampooing and conditioning has an impact on the overall satisfaction of the client's visit to the salon. If done properly these services are a personal, invigorating and stimulating therapeutic experience. If not, the client is left feeling that they are part of an inferior production line, in a salon where staff take no interest in their jobs. This chapter covers everything that you need to know in order to get it right every time.

CHECKERBOARD

At the end of this chapter the checkerboard will help to jog your memory on what you have learned and what still remains to be done. Cross off with a pencil each of the topics as you cover it (see page 114).

REMEMBER

Shampooing and conditioning can be a relaxing, enjoyable experience when it is done well; conversely, if it is done badly, it will imply something else about the other **salon services** that will follow.

Gio Barto/Getty Images

Cuticle

Cortex

Deposits

Dirt on the hair cuticle

The backwash or wash point
Courtesy of Alteq

WHY SHAMPOO?

The action of shampooing cleans the hair by removing dirt, grease, skin scale and sweat, plus any hairspray, gel, mousse, wax etc. Water alone cannot dissolve and rinse out all these substances or leave the hair ready for blow-drying, setting or perming.

Using large amounts of shampoo is unnecessary, expensive and wasteful. A small amount thoroughly spread and massaged into the scalp will do just as well. Thorough shampooing is an essential preparation for other services: if any deposits or product build-up remain on the hair after shampooing, they will affect the next service being carried out – for example they could block perm chemicals or leave the hair too greasy to blow-dry.

Good shampooing is physically soothing, psychologically calming and, overall, an enjoyable experience. A poor shampoo has the opposite effects!

PREPARING TO SHAMPOO

- Prepare a clean fresh gown and towel.
- Look at the client's hair and scalp to see what condition they are in.
- Ask questions such as: 'What products do you use at home?' 'How often do you have to shampoo your hair?' 'How often do you style your hair?'
- Look for any signs of infection, infestation or injury that would stop you from carrying out any other hairdressing processes.
- If you recommend any treatments, confirm them with the client before you apply them and advise the client of any additional time and costs involved.

Choosing a shampoo

Shampoos come in a variety of forms, including creams, semi-liquids and gels, and a range of different sizes too. The products that salons buy to resell to clients tend to be small in quantity and handy, whereas the salon's backwash products are in larger containers with pumps for easier dispensing. The backwash containers are in continual use and will run down quickly, so you need to make sure that they are replaced or refilled daily before work starts.

There are many different types of shampoo bases (the substances that form the bulk of the shampoo) and some are kinder and gentler on the skin than others. The balance of these various shampoo ingredients is important; for example, the detergent content in shampoos for **greasy hair** is higher than those for normal and dry hair. So too is their ability to deal with different hair types and conditions.

Shampoos are named after the ingredients or essences within them: henna, camomile, rosemary, jojoba, aloe vera and mint are just a few typical varieties available in the supermarkets today. Choosing the right shampoo for the hair condition or following service is important. If the wrong choice is made the hair may become difficult to manage afterwards: it may become

ACTIVITY

See if you can match the shampoos on the right with their appropriate applications on the left.

Moisturising shampoo	Dandruff
Medicated shampoo	Fine, lank hair
Volumising shampoo	Dry or porous hair
Colour-protecting shampoo	Tinted or highlighted hair

brittle, flyaway, static, greasy or even dry. If the shampoo doesn't remove all of the styling products that have been previously applied, they could block the next service that you want to carry out. For example, hair wax that is applied on a daily basis adheres to the hair and creates a product build-up. This must be removed in order to achieve a final satisfactory result.

Shampoos   M. Balfre

Shampoo types

Type	Effects on the hair
Aloe vera	A popular, mild natural base ideal for healthy hair and scalps that can be used on a frequent basis
Camomile	Better on greasy hair; has a natural lightening effect
Clarifying	Strong, deep acting often used prior to chemical services to remove build-up of styling products and dirt
Coconut	Contains an emollient which helps dry hair to regain its smoothness and elasticity
Jojoba	A natural base better on normal to dryer hair types
Lemon	Contains citric acid; ideal for greasy hair types or for removing product build-up
Medicated	Helps to maintain the normal state of the hair and scalp; contains antiseptics such as juniper or tea tree oil
Mint	A natural base suited to normal to slightly greasy hair, often used as a frequent use shampoo
Oil	Can contain a range of natural bases such as pine, palm and almond; these are used to smooth and soften dryer hair and scalps
Soya	Helps to lock in moisture for the hair and scalp
Tea tree oil	A natural essential oil, which is like an antiseptic which will fight infections on the scalp

Photo courtesy Goldwell UK

L'Oréal Professionnel Volume
Extreme Shampoo   *L'Oréal*

Wella

Wella

Wella

Making the right choice of shampoo

The right choice of shampoo depends on the following factors:

- *Type, texture and condition of hair* – Fine hair requires a shampoo that will not degrease it or make it too fluffy. Choose a shampoo that will add body and volume. Coarse hair requires a shampoo that will tend to soften it and make it more pliable. Thick hair requires a shampoo that will penetrate and make good contact with all the hair and scalp.

ACTIVITY

Shampooing is a process that can differ between salons: what is the preferred process for shampooing in your salon and how long should it take? Write down your response in the space provided.

1

2

3

4

- *Frequency of shampooing* – If hair is washed once or more daily, choose a shampoo specially designed for frequent use.
- *Water quality* – If the water in the salon is in a hard water area, more shampoo is needed to form a good lather. In soft water areas shampoos foam more easily, so less product is required to do the job.
- *Shampoo purpose* – Is the shampoo intended just for cleaning or is it to condition, tone or colour the hair?
- *Planned services* – What are you going to do with the hair later? Some shampoo ingredients (Pro V or dimethicone) produce a flexible coating on the hair shaft. This could be beneficial in adding protection and locking in moisture or, conversely, in the case of conditioning-type shampoos and most conditioners, it could prevent or prolong the processing of some treatments such as perms.

Answer the following questions in the space provided:

Q1 Who manufactures your salon's backwash products and what different types of products are available?

Q2 What shampoo would you use for dry or porous hair in the salon?

Q3 What shampoo would you use for fine or lank hair in the salon?

Q4 What shampoo would you use for greasy hair in the salon?

Mahogany

WHAT IS SHAMPOO?

Modern shampoos contain the following base ingredients: natural essences, smoothing agents or emollients and a cleanser, together with a foaming agent. They are effective in both hard and soft water areas and they do not leave any scum deposits. Earlier versions of shampoo were harsh, they stripped the hair of moisture. Now, research has made shampoo one of the most diverse chemical products on the supermarket shelves. The cleansing agent within the chemical make-up of shampoo is a detergent. Because of this you must take care to protect your hands: detergents are chemicals and if you continually come into contact with them, you could get contact dermatitis.

What is dermatitis?

Dermatitis is a painful, itchy condition that affects the skin. Generally speaking, when hairdressers have this condition, it appears as a sore, sometimes moist reddening of the skin between and along the fingers and hands. The skin takes on this condition due to frequent contact with chemicals: shampoos, hair colourants, **perm solutions** and **neutraliser**. You must take adequate precautions to prevent this from happening. Always wear gloves for technical processes and, if this is not suitable for shampooing, apply barrier creams regularly throughout the day.

Carol Hayes and Associates

REMEMBER ✔

If you look at the ingredients on the packaging of shampoos you will find somewhere the term SLS or TLS. These are the common chemical terms for the detergents Sodium Lauryl Sulphate or Triethanolamine Lauryl Sulphate. Detergent in shampoo will, with prolonged use, cause contact dermatitis. You must take adequate precautions to avoid this happening. Barrier creams are an effective way to do this. They should always be applied to clean dry hands before any backwash activity takes place. They will need regular reapplication throughout the day to get maximum protection.

Detergents – how do they work?

Water by itself will not spread easily over the hair and scalp. This is because water molecules are attracted together by small electrical forces. These have their greatest effect at the water's surface, creating the effect called 'surface tension'. On hair, water by itself would form droplets. The detergent in shampoo reduces surface tension, allowing the water to spread easily over the hair and scalp, wetting them. Detergents are therefore 'wetting agents' and shampoos are detergents.

Each detergent molecule has two ends similar to a magnet. The 'hydrophilic' end is attracted to water molecules; the other 'hydrophobic' end repels water and is attracted to dirt and grease instead.

Detergent molecules lift the grease off the hair and suspend it in the water. This suspension is called is called an 'emulsion'. The grease holds the dirt, so as the grease is removed, the dirt loosens too. The emulsion containing the dirt can be rinsed away with water leaving the hair clean.

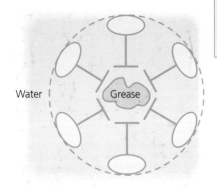

Detergent molecules surrounding grease

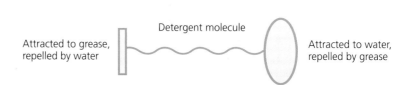

A detergent molecule

SHAMPOOING TECHNIQUE

Step-by-step: Shampooing

1 Sit the client at the basin and put on a clean fresh gown.

2 Place a freshly laundered towel around the client's neck and across their shoulders.

3 Adjust the basin so that when the client's head is tilted back their position is comfortable with the minimum of towel supporting their neck.

4 When working on longer hair carefully disentangle the hair by initially working the fingers through the lengths and then by brushing with a wide-toothed comb.

5 Turn on the water and control the mixture of hot and cold. Test the temperature on the back of your hand to ensure the temperature is neither too hot nor too cold.

6 Carefully place your hand across the client's hairline, 'damming' the water from splashing forward onto the face. Start rinsing the hair from the forehead, down either side, cupping the ears and through to the lengths.

7 Check the flow of water pressure and temperature throughout.

8 After the hair is thoroughly wet, apply a small amount of the correct shampoo to the palms of the hand. Lightly rub together then apply evenly to the client's hair.

9 With your fingers clawed, massage the scalp with the correct massage technique. Cover the whole scalp ensuring that no part is missed.

10 Rinse the hair thoroughly, checking water temperature and pressure.

11 Finally rinse all traces of shampoo lather away from the hair and lightly squeeze out the excess water. Repeat steps 5–11 if a second shampoo is needed.

Step 5: Checking the water temperature.

Step 6: Carefully dampening the hair.

Step 8: Using the dispenser to meter the correct amount of shampoo.

Step 9: An even and balanced shampoo massage technique.

Step 11: Rinsing away the lather.

Massage techniques

There are three types of shampooing massage techniques:

- Begin shampooing with **effleurage**, gentle stroking movements that help to spread the products evenly.
- Continue with firm but gentle **rotary massage**, circular movements. Let the fingertips glide over the scalp, whilst moving your hands towards each other in the centre (up from the sides, over the top and down into the nape). Move your hands in decreasing circles around the head to make sure you cover the scalp fully.
- Occasionally change the rotary massage to **friction**, the quick rubbing techniques used to deep clean any difficult areas.
- Finally, use soothing effleurage movements again to complete the shampoo process.

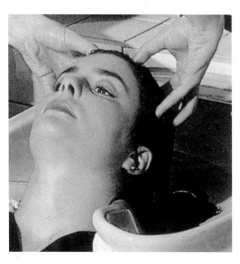

Shampooing: finger positions

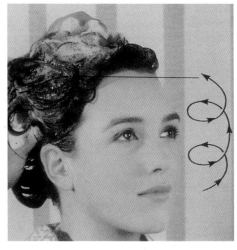

Shampooing: finger movements

REMEMBER

While shampooing
- Make sure the client is comfortable at all times.
- Be careful, especially with your hand positioning and massage technique, water flow and temperature, and client's head and neck positioning throughout the process.
- Work in a clean, methodical and hygienic way.

After shampooing
- Make sure the water is turned off and replace the shower head back in its place.
- Apply suitable conditioning treatment (see conditioning process later in this chapter).
- Lift the hair away from the face and basin and carefully wrap in a towel. Place either side of the towel up and around the hairline, overlapping, and the remainder at the back, up and balanced evenly on the top.
- Lead the client from the basin area back to the work point.
- Remove the towel and comb the client's hair through.

REMEMBER

Shampooing do's and don'ts
- Always use clean, fresh towels and gowns.
- Make sure that your hands and nails are hygienic and clean.
- Avoid splashing water or shampoo lather onto the client's face or near their eyes as the chemicals will cause discomfort if not injury.
- Always keep your hand in contact with the water whilst rinsing so that you can detect any sudden change in its temperature.
- Always direct the water spray away from the hairlines and into the basin.
- Carefully comb the hair after shampooing to remove any tangles.
- After using the basin, always clear and clean the area before it is used again.
- Turn off the water in between shampoos and conditioning to avoid wastage.
- Rinse and dry your hands afterwards to remove any shampoo or conditioning chemicals and reapply a barrier cream.

REMEMBER

Wet hair can tangle very easily which makes it very painful to comb through. So when you comb through your client's wet hair, you should always disentangle the ends first, then work back up through the lengths getting closer to the scalp. This makes the process simpler, it takes less time and it doesn't hurt either!

REMEMBER

Health and safety
- Raising the client too quickly from the basin can be dangerous; for some, it may make them feel dizzy when they try to stand up and, for others, if they have had any neck problems, it could cause injury.
- Make sure that you do not apply to much pressure on the back of the neck or 'joggle' the client's head around by wrongly applying uneven pressure on either side.
- Always test the water temperature on the back of your hands before transferring the flow to the client's head. Look out for changes and fluctuations in water temperatures and pressures.

REMEMBER

Hard, linear and circulatory massage movements are uncomfortable for the client. Practise the right pressure with your colleagues at the salon.

REMEMBER

Always record the products that you have used on the client's record card so that they can be charged for and used again in the future.

Mahogany

ACTIVITY

You can always find out if your own shampooing practices are acceptable if you shampoo your colleagues' hair at work. Ask each other in what ways you need to modify or change your techniques.

WATER AND WASTE

Water is essential to all the salon's services and shampooing alone can take 10–20 litres for each wash. So it is vitally important that this valuable and expensive resource is not unnecessarily wasted. Always use water sparingly and never leave the taps running between shampoos, even if it is just the cold water!

Many hairdressing procedures create potential blockages and for this reason salons are very careful about the materials put down the drain. Beneath each basin is a waste trap. This fitting serves two purposes:

1 it stops vapours and smells coming back from the sewerage system

2 it provides a safeguard for stopping hair, tint and debris from entering into the sewerage system.

In addition, if a client loses an earring during shampooing it can be retrieved by undoing the waste trap. But, since this procedure could be difficult and is certainly disruptive during opening hours, salons now also use plastic hair traps which are inserted from above. These are ideal for stopping any small items from penetrating further below. Make sure that they are regularly cleaned and free of tangled hair. This will keep the drainage clear and stop water backing up in the basin!

REMEMBER

Always wear gloves when handling chemicals. This will avoid the risk of contact dermatitis.

SCIENCE BIT!
DID YOU KNOW

Acidity and alkalinity
Like many other chemicals, shampooing can affect the surface of the skin. This changes its natural pH balance and removes essential moisture.

The pH scale measures acidity or alkalinity. It ranges from pH1 to pH14. Acid compounds have pH values 1 to 6 and alkalis have pH values of 8 to 14. A compound with a value of 7 is neither acidic nor alkaline and is therefore neutral.

Approximate values of substances

Substance	pH value
Acid	0.1–6.9
Alkali	7.1–14.0
Neutral solutions	7.0
Normal hair and scalp	5.5
Pre-perm shampoo	7.0
pH balanced shampoo/conditioner	5.5

The normal pH of the hair and the skin's surface is 5.5. This is referred to as the skin's 'acid mantle'. The acidity is due in part to the sebum, the natural oil produced by the skin. Sebum production is an important skin function. Skin protects the underlying tissue, acting as a barrier; it prevents liquid loss from inside and keeps excess liquid outside the body. It also protects the body from infection. An acid skin surface inhibits, i.e. slows down, the growth of bacteria and makes them less likely to enter the skin. If the acidity of the skin is reduced and rises above pH 5.5 infection is more likely to occur.

Hairdressing procedures can affect this natural equilibrium, so pH-balancing products are used after perming and straightening, to return the skin to the natural acid mantle.

The pH of solutions is measured using pH (litmus) papers or universal indicator. Either pink or blue litmus papers are used to indicate the strength of the solutions. Pink litmus paper used in alkali substances will turn mauve/blue. Conversely, blue litmus paper used in acid solutions will turn red.

If hairs are placed in an alkaline solution above pH 8.5 they swell and the cuticle lifts. In slightly acid solutions the cuticle is smooth and the hair is soft; in strong solutions of either acid or alkali the hair will break down and is destroyed.

Acids and alkalis are used in this way for high lift tints. High lift colours have added ammonia and this alkaline compound helps to swell the hair, enabling the tint to penetrate deep into the cortex of the hair.

Stronger alkaline compounds are available as hair removing creams; these are applied to areas where the skin contains unwanted hair. The application is left for the prescribed time and is then wiped away, removing the hair with it. The skin is then rinsed and an acid balancing skin conditioner is then applied.

> **REMEMBER**
>
> Always report blocked pipes or basins immediately. Standing waste water is quickly contaminated by bacteria and it has an unpleasant smell too!

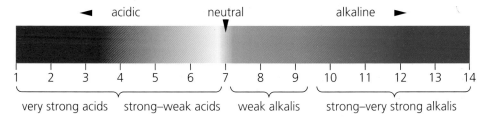

The pH scale

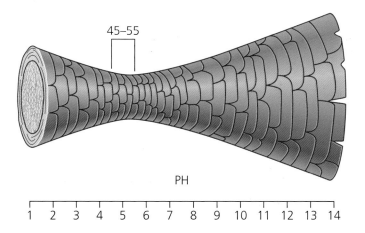

How pH affects the hair

ACTIVITY

Example questions and model answers

Q1 How long should it take to complete the shampoo and conditioning service at work?
A1 *We are allowed to take up to X minutes for the whole process.*

Q2 What is dermatitis and how do you avoid contracting it?
A2 *Dermatitis is a skin condition that arises from direct contact with chemical substances. It has patchy red areas, often between the fingers or over the hands. The areas are itchy and the surface of the skin can break. It can be avoided by wearing barrier creams or thin vinyl gloves.*

Q3 What types of protective wear are available for clients while they are in the salon?
A3 *The salon provides gowns, towels and protective capes, which are worn whilst the services and treatments are provided.*

Q4 How would you advise your clients about choosing a shampoo?
A4 *I would look at the hair and scalp before I took my client to the basin to see the natural condition.*

ACTIVITY

Answer the following questions in the spaces provided:

Q1 Why is your posture important when you are shampooing and conditioning?

Q2 What safety considerations do you have to think about whilst the client is at the basin?

Q3 Why do you have to rinse the hair well after shampooing or conditioning?

Q4 Why do you need to keep the wash area clean and tidy?

CONDITIONING – THE PRINCIPLES

One of our primary roles as hairdressers is to improve and maintain the condition of our client's hair. If the cuticle surface of the hair is roughened or damaged the appearance will be dull. Clients want their hair to shine; therefore we have to improve the cuticle surface to make it as smooth as possible. We do this with the help from conditioners and that way their hair will be easier to manage, easier to comb and easier to brush.

REMEMBER

Conditioner or treatment?
If your client does not routinely condition their hair, then the problem of dull hair is made worse. In a case like this, deeper-acting and longer-lasting treatments will be needed.

The principle of seeing shine can be thought of like this.

If you walk down the street, stop outside a shop window and look in, you will see your own reflection in the glass. The image of yourself is bounced back to your eyes from the smooth, flat surface of the glass. If the surface was roughened and uneven the image would be distorted and you will not be able to see a clear reflected image.

Now think of this in hair terms. The smoother the surface of the hair the better the shine. The duller the hair, the more roughened the surface is.

Corbis

Conditioning: what do you do?

Question	First of all ask the client what has been previously done and what has been used upon the hair. If this is a regular client in the salon check out the treatment history on their records.
Look	Examine the hair and scalp closely. What condition is the hair in now? Look at the tell-tale signs – porous lengths and ends; loss of natural moisture and elasticity; dry, split or damaged ends.
Advise	From what you see and feel, what would be the best course of action? A simple surface conditioning treatment? A salon-based deep-acting treatment? A prescribed course of treatment at home? Or a combination?
Agree	From the course of action you advise, get your client to see the benefits too. Explain how long the process will take, and also the costs involved.
Reassurance	Tell the client when to expect to see any marked changes and improvements. Explain that maintenance at home is just as important.
Maintenance	Prescribe any follow-ups. Explain how the hair should be managed at home or if products are needed to support the whole process.

Corbis

What will conditioners do?

Professional products are formulated to protect and improve a range of different hair types and disorders. The main benefits are:

- smoothing the cuticle edges
- improving the handling and combing when the hair is both wet and dry
- repairing and filling damaged or missing areas of the cuticle or cortex
- providing shine, lustre and sheen
- creating flexibility and movement by locking in moisture
- balancing the pH value back to a slightly acid 5.5.

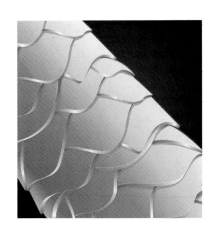

Why is it easier to comb hair downwards?

If you have ever attempted to backcomb dry hair, you may have noticed some resistance. This is because the cuticles' free edges all point towards the ends of the hair. So when you push against them they will tangle together.

But that makes combing hair out much simpler. When we comb through conditioners we always detangle the ends first, working back up the lengths. This helps the cuticle edges to slip over one another making the whole process far less painful.

ACTIVITY

What is your salon's policy in respect of the following and what products would you use on each occasion?

1 Shampooing and conditioning hair prior to a cut and blow-dry?

2 Shampooing and conditioning hair prior to a perm?

3 Shampooing and conditioning hair after a highlighting service?

How do conditioners work?

Conditioners use a combination of chemical and electrical (ionic) properties to achieve their effects. They can balance and counteract the effects that the chemical services and physical processes have upon the hair. There are two ways in which they bond with the hair.

- *Absorption* – This relies upon the natural state of the hair. Dry and porous hair has many tiny spaces within the hair's internal structure. These areas suck in the conditioning agents by capillary action, just as water is drawn into a sponge.

- *Attraction* – This occurs after the hair has been shampooed. The action of the detergent on the hair during shampooing ensures that all product, dirt and dust is removed. When these particles are removed it leaves the surface of the hair in a 'charged' state. This prepares the hair for the conditioner which is now attracted to the sites upon the hair that have been electrically charged.

(This ionic attraction principle can be explained another way. Do you remember how you stick balloons to the wall or ceiling at a birthday party? After blowing the balloons up, you rub them vigorously on the sleeve of your jumper. This removes electrical particles and now makes the balloon stick to anything it comes into contact with, just like a magnet!)

TYPES OF CONDITIONER

There are three different types of hair conditioners:

- surface conditioners
- penetrating conditioners
- scalp treatments.

Surface conditioners

These conditioners do not enter the hair but remain on the cuticle surface. Their main purpose is to coat the hair and improve the look and feel by adding shine and moisture. Some of these conditioning rinses are used after perms and chemical straighteners to return the hair back to its natural pH balance. This group of conditioners would normally contain:

- vegetable and mineral oils
- lanolin
- fats and waxes
- mild acidic compounds which could be citric or acetic-based.

Conditioning treatments
Photographs courtesy Goldwell UK

Penetrating conditioners

Penetrating conditioners have deeper-acting benefits. They enter the hair shaft through the cuticle layer and are deposited into the cortex by capillary action. This suction of the product is like a natural magnetism, drawing the product in to the cellular spaces within the hair. These penetrating conditioners, often called 'restructurants', are designed to repair the physical structure of the fibres within the cortex and damaged areas within the cuticle layers. Apart from smoothing the hair and adding shine, they tend to make the whole hair structure much stronger. (Examples are hair strengtheners e.g. L'Oréal's Kerastase Ciment Anti-Usure or Wella's Liquid Hair.)

> **REMEMBER**
>
> A protective conditioner is used before chemical processes to prepare the hair and even out the porosity of the hair before the process is carried out.

REMEMBER

A corrective conditioner is used after chemical processes to replenish moisture and shine or to return the hair back to its natural pH balanced state.

Their composition is more chemically complex. They are based on:

- quaternary ammonium compounds
- proteins – amino acids
- humectants, which lock in moisture to the hair
- emollients, which soften, smooth and moisturise the hair.

Before and after chemical services

Where the cuticle has been damaged, the hair cortex becomes too porous, like a sponge soaking up any chemicals applied to the hair. Older hair is more likely to be damaged than newer growth. The porosity must be reduced before hair can be successfully permed or coloured. Pre-straightener or **pre-perm treatments** will balance the porosity evenly through the hair. This enables the chemical service to be carried out in the confidence that no parts of the hair will be unduly damaged through the action of additional chemical application.

The pre-colouring treatments have a similar effect. These products will 'fill' the damaged sites along the hair shaft, repairing the cuticle layer and maintaining an even absorption, i.e. 'take-up', of colouring products into the cortex.

After chemical services the hair may need rebalancing. The normal state of hair is slightly acidic (pH 5.5) and many of the processes use caustic – ammonium-based compounds – or corrosive – acid-based compounds. In these situations it is always advisable to use an acid balancing conditioner. Acid balancing conditioners will act either as an anti-oxidant to remove unwanted 'free oxygen' which may be residual in operations using hydrogen peroxide (e.g. neutralising, colouring and bleaching) or reduce the alkaline state of hair with mild acidic compounds following perming and straightening.

Scalp treatments

Other than improving the look, feel and condition of hair, the final group of conditioners are designed to remedy a variety of skin problems. These scalp-active treatments are chemical preparations that are developed to target specific disorders. Therefore, your correct analysis of the client's scalp condition is essential. You will need to be able to identify and distinguish between:

- dry scalp conditions
- dandruff problems
- excessively oily scalp conditions.

Dry scalps

Dry scalps can often be mistaken for dandruff. A dry scalp has some of the symptoms of dandruff, such as epidermal skin shedding, but if this is wrongly diagnosed, the corrective treatment may make the problem worse. A dry scalp can occur for a number of reasons. It may be:

- a natural moisture imbalance, within the client's skin
- a reaction to shampoo, conditioning and styling products
- a reaction following a chemical service.

If the client has a natural imbalance of moisture levels within the scalp, it would be normal to expect this problem to arise somewhere else as well, and this is your clue. Dry, Caucasian scalps tend to look 'whiter' than a natural, healthy 'pinkish' scalp. What you are seeing is the symptoms of an epidermal inability for the skin to retain moisture. Your first approach would be to ask if the client has a tendency towards dry skin elsewhere; you might have noted this yourself if it were on the face, but it may be somewhere else on the body or arms or legs.

A dry skin condition is often a chronic or long-term problem; you should recommend a scalp-active treatment that will nourish and moisturise the scalp, whilst getting an agreement with the client that this is followed up at home as well. The type of treatment will depend upon the condition of the hair too. If the client has a dry scalp it doesn't necessarily follow that the hair will be dry too. This will have a bearing on how the treatment is to be applied. If the hair is normal and healthy you would not want to overload it with heavy moisturisers and emollients, so a more 'topical', carefully applied solution is required. Your client will also need to learn that not all products are the same. An application that is generally applied and combed through will have little effect! The product must target the problem and therefore the hair will need to be divided and the application should be made directly to the scalp.

Dry scalps can occur from intolerance to hairdressing products. A client can get a reaction when they use something different on their hair. Ask them whether they have tried something new. A typical cause would be newly introduced styling and finishing products such as 'root lift' mousse or heavy definition waxes. However, even a simple change of shampoo can cause dryness.

A dry scalp can also occur after chemical treatments. Many of the solutions we use in hairdressing have a quenching effect upon the skin. Alkaline solutions create this continual drying 'thirst' upon the scalp, so this is particularly relevant to perming and chemical straighteners. However, a reaction can be caused by any exposure to chemicals and you can prevent this by taking particular care when you apply any chemical service to the client.

M. Balfre

M. Balfre

> **REMEMBER** ✓
>
> Always use balancing conditioners after any chemical processes.

Dandruff

Dandruff can sometimes in its simplest form be mistaken for a dry scalp. Unfortunately, if you wrongly diagnose this condition; you will either make the problem worse or have no effect at all.

Normally, the skin cells produced in the lower dermis take up to 35–45 days to work up through to the surface of the epidermis. Once there, the cells are shed daily in the form of a fine visible dust. In the case of dandruff, though, this process becomes erratic.

In the diagram you can see that, as the layers of dermal cells work up towards the surface of the epidermis, they eventually 'lift' and come away as

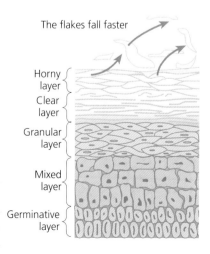

The flakes fall faster

Horny layer
Clear layer
Granular layer
Mixed layer
Germinative layer

Flaking scalp

'shedding'. This is commonly noticeable as 'scurf', white skin cells, when you brush or comb the client's hair. More often, it is deposited onto their clothes.

Dandruff or Pityriasis capitis is caused by the overproduction of skin cells. It initially appears as small white flakes that loosen and continually shed from the scalp, rather as is the case with dry skin. A secondary condition occurs if the problem isn't rectified: the scalp becomes infected by bacteria and larger yellowier, waxy flakes now appear that usually stick to the scalp. When dandruff has progressed this far you often smell it too! This condition is often more prevalent in people with oilier scalps.

In tackling this problem in its earliest stages, you should ask the client if they have or have had a dry skin condition. If they say no, then the scurf is probably due to this skin production imbalance. This can be rectified over a period of time by regular home use of the correct shampoos and conditioners.

If the dandruff has progressed to the second stage, it must be treated initially in the salon, and then with a follow-up at home over a longer period in time. The first objective would be to combat the bacterial infection, then to clear the scalp of the scaly build-up. This degree of infection cannot be rectified by one scalp-active application. It will usually involve a course of treatments often in liquid forms applied onto pre-sectioned hair, directly onto the infected areas.

Greasy scalps

Greasy scalps, or 'seborrhoea', is caused by overproduction of natural oil (sebum) from the skin. The sebaceous gland in a normal state produces moderate amounts of oil, which is generally, sufficient to lubricate the hair shaft and create natural moisture for the skin. This moisture, in turn, keeps the skin supple and helps to 'lock in' flexibility and elasticity. When the glands work overtime, then the imbalance of moisture becomes a nuisance. This is seen as excessively greasy hair and scalps that require frequent washing to give lank hair volume and body.

The normal approach to combatting greasy hair is to shampoo it every day. When a client is asked how often they wash their hair and they give the answer 'at least once a day', there is a strong likelihood that there's a reason behind it. Sometimes people wash their hair every day because they fall into the routine of doing it when they take a shower. This is particularly obvious if they have easy-to-manage hairstyles, their lifestyle dictates it or they just have short hair.

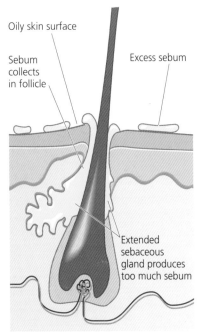

Oily skin surface

Sebum collects in follicle

Excess sebum

Extended sebaceous gland produces too much sebum

Greasy scalp

REMEMBER

When treating conditions of very greasy scalps or dandruff, it is best to try one product at a time, giving it the full opportunity to do its job. It is all too easy to give up on a new introduction before it has had time to make a significant difference.

However, when you do notice that the frequency of washing is more than just a habit and a problem exists, then there are a number of medicated preparations that are designed to sort it out.

These astringent-type lotions will cause the skin to contract slightly; this will temporarily constrict the glands and reduce the production of oil. A treatment like this could initially be undertaken in the salon but, to have any long-lasting effect, it will have to be followed up at home.

Photo courtesy Goldwell UK

> **REMEMBER** ✔
>
> When disentangling long hair, always work from the points of the hair first, working backwards up the hair, towards the roots. This:
>
> 1 makes combing far easier and quicker
> 2 eliminates harsh, painful pulling
> 3 reduces tearing and further damage to the hair
> 4 minimises any discomfort to the client.

APPLICATION TECHNIQUES

Step-by-step: Conditioning

Wella

Each conditioning treatment is specific to the task in hand. It is therefore extremely important to follow the **manufacturer's instructions** so that the product can do its job. Some (like a retouch colour) require the hair to be divided and lotions to be applied directly to the scalp. Others require heat activation and careful timings.

The following sequence provides guidelines for applying more general surface-type conditioners.

1 After shampooing, squeeze out excess moisture from the hair.

2 Apply a small amount of conditioner into the palm of the hand and gently rub your hands together, applying the conditioner evenly to a wider surface area.

3 On longer hair, apply the conditioner to mid-lengths and ends first, working through the hair with the fingers, seprating the lengths, or

4 On short hair, evenly apply the conditioner to all of the hair.

5 Then start the petrissage movements over the scalp from the frontal area, over the top and down through to the nape. Repeat this circular process several times.

6 On longer hair that is in poorer condition, you may need to comb the conditioner through whilst still at the basin. Using a wide-toothed conditioning comb, start disentangling the hair, working at the points of the hair first, then gradually working a little further up the hair, until the hair can be combed easily from roots to ends.

7 Finally rinse all traces of conditioner away from the hair and lightly squeeze out the excess water.

8 Place the towel around the hair, secure into place and move the client to a styling section.

9 Place another fresh towel around the client's shoulders and remove the damp one squeezing out the excess moisture from the lengths.

10 Disentangle the hair with a wide-toothed comb until all tangles are free from the hair.

Steps 1–4: Using the dispenser to meter the correct amount of conditioner.

Step 5: An even and balanced conditioning massage technique.

Steps 8–10: Securing a towel around the head before leaving the basin.

MASSAGE SERVICES

Massage is a therapeutic method of manipulating the skin and muscles by either hand or machine. The effects of this may be:

- improved blood flow and the removal of fatty or bodily waste congestions
- stimulation, re-energising and invigoration
- soothing relaxation
- improved muscle tone.

Scalp massage has been a normal part of hairdressing services throughout history. It is common throughout Asia and has now become a beneficial supplement to the Western range of hairdressing services. There are several different types but the most popular used in Britain are Indian head massage and Oriental Shiatsu massage. Many salons view this as a major area for improvements to their service tariffs and offerings and there are several courses and texts available on the subject.

> **REMEMBER** ✔
>
> Effleurage is a smooth, soothing stroking action, performed with firm but gentle movements of the hands and fingertips. You should use it before and after the more vigorous movements. It improves skin functions, soothes and stimulates nerves and relaxes tensed muscles.

Pre-shampooing scalp massage

Scalp massage stimulates grease production and loosens dead skin cells and dirt from the pores. Given before shampooing, it provides a wonderful prelude to the other salon services. The time taken to do this depends really on you and the client. Some people can stand more stimulation than others. Older clients, for example, may have more sensitive scalps and will not benefit from ten minutes of manipulation. Conversely, other clients may find it more beneficial than the other services offered. It's a very personal thing.

> **REMEMBER** ✔
>
> **Petrissage** is a deeper, circular, kneading movement. It assists the removal of waste build-up and promotes the flow of nutrients to the skin and is normally used in conditioning and hand scalp massage.

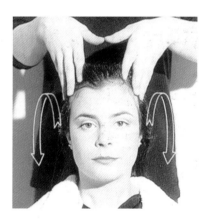

Effleurage

Providing hand massage

1   Seat your client comfortably, with a clean fresh towel and gown.

2   Using effleurage first, draw your fingertips firmly but not too hard over the head. Your hands should move from the front hairline in an even pressure down to the nape several times.

3   Next use petrissage. Apply this lightly but firmly. With the fingertips, feel through the hair to the scalp and gently rotate on the scalp all over the head. Maintain an even pressure and balance throughout the process, covering all areas, slowly but in the same rhythmic momentum without exerting to much pressure.

4   Finally, use effleurage again to release the pressure of blood stimulated around the scalp during the previous movements.

5   Allow the client to sit quietly for a while to enjoy the benefits of the massage process.

Petrissage

I know how to prepare the client correctly for shampooing and conditioning treatments ☐	I know how to check the stock levels of backwash products and how to refill them ☐	I can always shampoo and condition any client's hair within ten minutes ☐	I know the different massage techniques and when they are used ☐
I know how contact dermatitis can occur and how it can be avoided ☐	I understand the implications of backwash product in relation to personal health and safety ☐	I always make sure that the client is comfortable throughout the process of shampooing and conditioning hair ☐	I know how to communicate effectively with staff and customers ☐
I understand the implications of poor posture, cleaning and personal hygiene ☐	I know how to shampoo and condition a wide range of hair lengths correctly ☐	I always follow the stylist's instructions ☐	I know what surface conditioning is, the application techniques and the benefits to the client's hair ☐
I know why the wastage of salon resources should be minimised ☐	I know what deeper-acting conditioners are, their applications and their benefits to the client's hair ☐		CHECKER BOARD ✓

Assessment of knowledge and understanding

The following projects, activities and assessments are directly linked to the essential knowledge and understanding for unit H9.

For each statement that is addressed wholly or in part in these activities, you will see its relevant and corresponding EKU number.

Make sure that you keep this for easier referencing and along with your work for future inclusion in your portfolio.

Project (EKU H9.4, H9.24, H9.26, H9.32, H9.35)

For this project you will need to gather information from a variety of sources.

How long does shampoo and conditioning stock last?

In order to complete this project you will need to monitor the day-to-day usage of stock, how it is replenished and when it is reordered.

In your work you need to cover:

- the variety of shampoo and conditioning products that are available in your salon
- how often each type gets used
- how each product is replaced or replenished
- the salon's own policy in how they should be used
- the time allowed to provide shampoo and conditioning services
- how long the products last in relation to time in use, and averaged out per customer.

Case study (H9.22, H9.23, H9.28)

On Friday afternoon at 2.30 pm Mrs Jackman arrived to have a perm. Sally had arrived back early from lunch so that she could make herself ready before Mrs Jackman arrived. She got the previous treatment history out; she prepared the trolley with the correct curlers along with the perming chemicals.

The new junior Clare was asked to shampoo Mrs Jackman's hair ready for perming. While Clare carried on, Sally got a plastic cape and fresh towels ready.

Sally did not need to cut Mrs Jackman's hair as she had already done this the previous week. After winding, the lotion was applied to Mrs Jackman's hair and allowed to develop fully. When Sally checked the perm it seemed a bit limp, but because it had had full development, she moved her client to the basin and asked Clare to neutralise.

After neutralising, Sally noticed that the curl seemed limp. She set it a bit more firmly and combed it out as usual. Mrs Jackman paid her bill, left a tip for Sally and left the salon.

On Tuesday morning Mrs Jackman called the salon to say that she wasn't happy with her perm; it was too soft in places and wouldn't last. She asked to speak to the manager Paul.

After speaking to Mrs Jackman, Paul asked Sally into the office to give her account.

- What has happened here?
- What are the possible reasons why the perm went wrong?

Write down all the possible reasons why Mrs Jackman's hair has failed to perm. What should Sally have done beforehand to make sure that the service was successful?

Questions

1 What is the salon's policy in respect to protecting clients during services? (H9.1, H9.9,)

2 What is your place of work's policy in respect to cleanliness and working safely, hygienically and methodically? (H9.12, H9.13)

3 What is your place of work's policy in respect to the checking and safe use of electrical equipment? (H9.6)

4 Why is personal hygiene important in the salon? (H9.14)

5 How and when are the following techniques used? (H9.30, H9.31)
- Effleurage
- Petrissage
- Rotary
- Friction.

Preparing for assessment checklist

Remember to:

prepare clients correctly for the services you are going to carry out

shampoo and condition hair correctly, prior to all salon services

'brush up' on the science of how shampoos work on the hair to make it clean

adhere to the safety factors when working on a client's hair

wear **personal protective equipment** (PPE) to avoid contact dermatitis

keep the work areas clean, hygienic and free from hazards

work carefully and methodically through the processes of shampooing and conditioning the hair

use positive body language as it plays such an important part in good customer service

use only the correct shampooing and conditioning products appropriate to the task

use good posture and avoid the consequences of poor posture.

chapter 5

HEALTH AND SAFETY IN THE SALON

NVQ/SVQ reference, unit title and main outcome

Unit G1 Ensure your own actions reduce risks to health and safety

G1.1 Identify hazards and evaluate the risks in your workplace

G1.2 Reduce the risks to health and safety in your workplace

What do I need to do?

- Ensure that your actions at work do not create any risks to health and safety.
- Do not ignore any significant risks within the working environment.
- Make sure that you report any potential hazards with salon equipment or in connection with staff, clients and other people.

What do I need to learn?

You need to know and understand:

- your expected duties, legal responsibilities and key contacts for health and safety at your salon
- the types of hazards that exist in your salon and how you could deal with them
- safe working practices and your salon's health and safety policy and procedures.

Information covered in this chapter

- General salon hygiene.
- Safe and hygienic use of salon equipment.
- Dealing with emergencies.
- Health and safety regulations.

KEY WORDS

Hazard   Something with a potential to cause harm.

Risk   The likelihood of the hazard's potential actually occurring.

INTRODUCTION

REMEMBER

Health and safety laws are being continually reviewed and updated. Make sure you are aware of the latest information.

Health and safety laws are designed to protect you, the clients and your fellow staff members. So your personal health and safety and safe methods of work are absolutely essential. This chapter will explain how you can help in maintaining a healthy and safe working environment for everyone.

ACTIVITY

The Health and Safety at Work Act 1974 is continually being reviewed and updated, it covers many smaller component regulations. See if you can match the individual legal regulations on the left with the appropriate health and safety issues on the right. (Tip: look at the regulation wording to work out its appropriate link.)

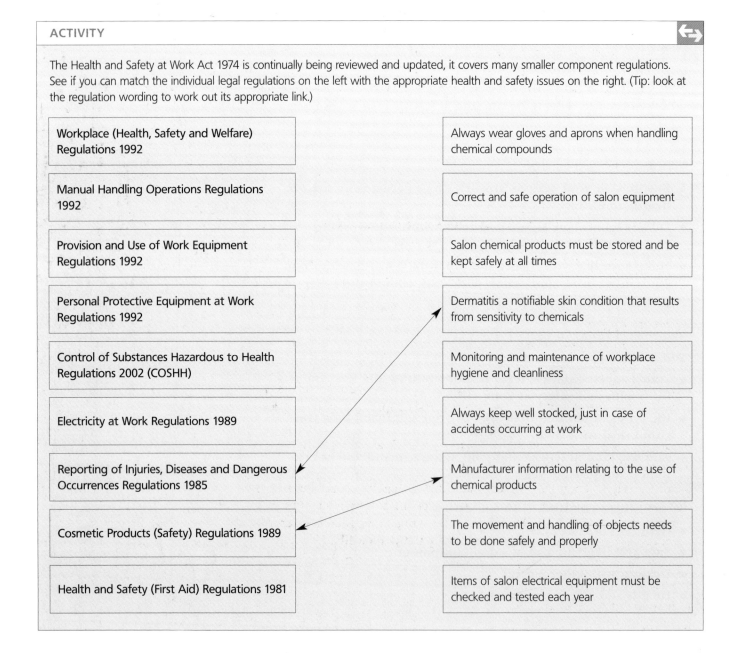

Regulations	Health and safety issues
Workplace (Health, Safety and Welfare) Regulations 1992	Always wear gloves and aprons when handling chemical compounds
Manual Handling Operations Regulations 1992	Correct and safe operation of salon equipment
Provision and Use of Work Equipment Regulations 1992	Salon chemical products must be stored and be kept safely at all times
Personal Protective Equipment at Work Regulations 1992	Dermatitis a notifiable skin condition that results from sensitivity to chemicals
Control of Substances Hazardous to Health Regulations 2002 (COSHH)	Monitoring and maintenance of workplace hygiene and cleanliness
Electricity at Work Regulations 1989	Always keep well stocked, just in case of accidents occurring at work
Reporting of Injuries, Diseases and Dangerous Occurrences Regulations 1985	Manufacturer information relating to the use of chemical products
Cosmetic Products (Safety) Regulations 1989	The movement and handling of objects needs to be done safely and properly
Health and Safety (First Aid) Regulations 1981	Items of salon electrical equipment must be checked and tested each year

CHECKERBOARD

At the end of this chapter the checkerboard will help to jog your memory on what you have learned and what still remains to be done. Cross off with a pencil each of the topics as you cover it (see page 141).

You will need to show that you understand the health and safety requirements in the workplace. This includes monitoring your own work routines and workspace, so that hazards are quickly identified and that the potential risk to others in being harmed is minimised.

The Health and Safety at Work Act 1974 is the main, all-encompassing umbrella of legislation under which all other regulations are made. Although the Act contains many individual regulations the responsibility for maintaining these falls upon you and your employer. In short:

- Employers have a legal duty under this Act to ensure the health, safety and welfare at work of all people for whom they are responsible.

- Employees must take reasonable care of themselves or others who may be affected by their working practices and must support their employer in fulfilling their obligations in the compliance of current health and safety requirements.

M. Balfre

HAZARD AND RISK

Almost anything can be a **hazard**, but it needn't become a **risk**. You share a responsibility with your work colleagues for the safety of all the people within the salon (clients, visitors and staff) so you need to be aware of the types of hazards that could exist. You need to be aware of:

1 environmental hazards, such as:

- wet or slippery floors

- cluttered passageways or corridors

- rearranged furniture

- electrical flexes: a trailing electric cable is a hazard – if it lies across a passageway there is a high risk of somebody tripping over it, if it lies along a wall the risk is much less;

2 hazards to do with equipment and materials, such as:

- worn or faulty electrical equipment

- incorrectly labelled substances, such as cleaning fluids, and leaking or damaged containers: toxic or flammable chemicals are a hazard and may present a high risk. However, if they are properly kept, securely stored and correctly handled the risk is greatly reduced;

3 hazards connected with people, such as:

- visitors to the salon

- handling procedures

- intruders.

Spot the hazards in this hairdressing salon

Simply being aware of potential hazards is not enough. You also have a responsibility to contribute to a safe working environment, so you must take steps to check and deal with any sources of risk. You can fulfil your role in two ways:

1 Deal directly with the hazard, which means that you have taken individual responsibility. This will probably apply to obvious hazards such as:

- *trailing flexes* – roll them up and store them safely
- *cluttered doorways and corridors* – remove objects and store them safely or dispose of them appropriately
- *fire* – follow the correct procedures to raise the alarm and assist with the evacuation.

2 Inform your manager or supervisor of the hazard, which means that it becomes an organisational responsibility. This applies to hazards which are beyond your responsibility to deal with, such as:

- faulty equipment, such as dryers, tongs, straightening irons, kettles, computers, etc.
- worn floor coverings or broken tiles
- loose or damaged fittings, such as mirrors, shelves or backwashes
- obstructions too heavy for you to move safely
- fire.

REMEMBER

Being aware of potential hazards is not enough: you can minimise risks by taking prompt action.

ACTIVITY

Find out the following information from your place of work, then complete the details in the space provided.

Q1 Who has overall responsibility for health and safety?

A1 Name _____

Q2 What is this person's role in the workplace?

A2 Job role _____

Q3 If you found something that you felt was not safe at work, who would you report to?

A3 Name _____

Q4 What sort of unsafe things do you think you might find? (List as many as you can.)

A4 _____

_____

_____

Q5 In relation to product use, why are manufacturer's instructions important?

A5 _____

Q6 What is the salon's policy in respect to maintaining a healthy and safe work environment?

A6 _____

Hair: Lawrence Anthony Team; photography: Pat Mascolo; make-up: Pat Mascolo

A SAFE WORKING ENVIRONMENT

You play an important part in spotting potential hazards and preventing accidents and therefore helping to avoid any emergency situations arising.

So how can you make a difference?

Suppose, for example, that someone had carelessly blocked a fire door with recently delivered stock. You could take the initiative and move the box to a safe and secure location.

If you notice a potential hazard that you cannot easily rectify yourself, tell your supervisor immediately. Imagine, for instance, that the lower, adjustable cutting blade on a pair of clippers became loose. If this was unnoticed by one of the stylists they might pick the clippers up and use them on a client!

Hair: Lawrence Anthony Team; photography: Pat Mascolo; make-up: Pat Mascolo

ACTIVITY

Example questions and model assessment answers

Q1 Why are you responsible for your own actions regarding health and safety at work?
A1 *I need to take care in the way that I carry out my work, so that I don't have any accidents.*

Q2 Why do you have to look out for others at work?
A2 *The things I do at work could have a direct effect on the health and safety of others in the workplace.*

Obstructions

> **REMEMBER** ✓
>
> Always read manufacturer's instructions before using their equipment or products.

Obstructed thoroughfares are dangerous, regardless of whether the obstruction is in doorways or a corridor, on stairs or in a fire exit. In an emergency, people might have to leave the salon in a hurry – perhaps even in the dark if the electricity has gone off. It could be disastrous if someone injured themselves or fell. So:

- always be on the lookout for any obstruction in these areas;
- if you see something that could present a risk, move it away as quickly as you can.

COSHH leaflet HMSO

ACTIVITY

Find out your salon's policy in respect of the following procedures:

1 What would be considered to be safe working practices?
2 How should hazardous substances be stored, dispensed and used?
3 What are the salon's rules regarding smoking, consuming food and drink on the premises and policy in respect to alcohol and other drugs?
4 What is the salon's policy in the event of an emergency occurring?
5 What are the salon's expectations in respect to personal presentation and hygiene?

Spillage and breakages

You do need to act quickly but stop and think before doing anything.

- First of all, what has been spilled or dropped?
- Do you know what it is?
- Is this something that needs special care and attention when handling?
- Should you report the situation to someone else, or can you handle the situation yourself?
- If you can, should you be wearing gloves?
- What else do you need to get to rectify the situation safely without creating another hazard?

Disposal of waste

General salon waste

Everyday items of salon waste should be placed in an enclosed waste bin fitted with a suitably resistant polyethylene bin liner. When the bin is full, the liner can be sealed using a wire tie and placed ready for refuse collection. If for any reason the bin liner punctures, put the damaged liner and waste inside a second bin liner. Wash out the inside of the bin itself with hot water and detergent.

Covered bins   Courtesy of Ellisons

Disposal of sharp items

Used razor blades and similar items should be placed into a safe container ('**sharps** box'). When the container is full it can be discarded. This type of salon waste should be kept away from general salon waste as special disposal arrangements may be provided by your local authority. Contact your local council offices' environmental health department for more information.

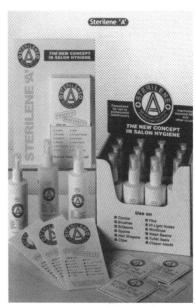

REMEMBER	✔
Hazards	**Check for**
Floors	✔ Are they slippery or wet?
Doorways	✔ Are they clear of obstacles?
Electrical flexes	✔ Are they loose or trailing?
Chemicals	✔ Are they labelled and stored correctly?
Equipment	✔ Is it worn or in need of attention?

Salon hygiene equipment   Comby

ACTIVITY

- List the things that staff use in the salon that could be unsafe if not used the right way.
- Find out what things could be a danger in areas where staff work.
- Find out what types of waste are generated within your salon and how each is disposed of.

GENERAL SALON HYGIENE AND ROUTINE MAINTENANCE

The salon

It is important you develop an awareness of health and safety risks and that you are always aware of any risks in any situation. Quite simply, a tidy salon is easier to clean so get into the habit of clearing up your work as you go.

Sharps box   SP Services

M. Balfre

Floors and seating

Floors should be kept clean at all times. This means that they will need regular mopping, sweeping or vacuuming. When working areas are damp-mopped during normal working hours, make sure that adequate warning signs are provided close to the wet areas. The salon's seating will be made of material that is easily cleaned. It should be washed regularly with hot water and detergent. After they have dried, the seats can be wiped over with disinfectant or an antiseptic lotion.

Working surfaces

All surfaces within the salon, including the reception, staff and stock preparation areas, should be washed down at least once each day. Most salons now use easily maintained wipe-clean surfaces, usually some form of plastic laminate. They can be cleaned with hot water and detergent, and after the surfaces are dry they can be wiped over with a spirit-based antiseptic which will not smear. Don't use scourers or abrasives as these will scratch plastic surfaces. Scratched surfaces look dull and unattractive as well as containing minute crevices in which bacteria will develop.

> **REMEMBER**
>
> Take all precautions to avoid occupational contact dermatitis – use barrier creams and protective vinyl gloves where possible.

Mirrors

Glass mirrors should be cleaned every morning before clients arrive. Never try to style a client's hair while they sit in front of a murky, dusty or smeary mirror. Glass surfaces should be cleaned and polished using either hot water and detergent or a spirit-based lotion that evaporates quickly without smearing.

> **REMEMBER**
>
> You have a duty to your work colleagues and clients to minimise the possible spread of infection or disease. Hairdressers are by the nature of their work in constant close contact with their customers and therefore need to pay particular attention to healthy, hygienic and safe working practices.

Hair: Lawrence Anthony Team; Photography: Pat Mascolo; Make-up: Pat Mascolo

Salon equipment

Towels and gowns

Each client must have a fresh, clean towel and gown. These should be washed in hot soapy water to remove any soiling or staining and to prevent the spread of infection by killing any bacteria. Fabric conditioners may be used to provide a luxurious softness and freshness.

Photo courtesy Goldwell UK

Styling tools

Most pieces of salon equipment, such as combs, brushes and curlers, are made from plastics. These materials are relatively easy to keep hygienically safe, if they are used and cleaned properly.

Combs should be washed daily. When not in use they should be immersed into an antibacterial solution. When they are then needed they can be rinsed and dried and are then ready for use.

If any styling tools are accidentally dropped on to the floor, do not use them until they have been adequately cleaned. Don't put contaminated items onto work surfaces as they could spread infection and disease.

Handle non-plastic items, such as scissors and clipper blades, with care. When they need cleaning, the flat edges can be wiped over after spraying with a disinfectant or surgical spirit and then wiping carefully with a cotton wool swab. Although most of these items are made of special steels, don't immerse them in sterilising fluids. Many of them contain chemicals that will corrode the precision-made surfaces of the blades.

Regularly used clippers in the hairdressing salon will require frequent routine checks for both safety and efficiency. Hair will get trapped between the blades, this reduces cutting performance and constant vibration may loosen the cutting edges. The macerated hair between the blades will increase friction between the cutting surfaces and reduce the amount of movement of the upper, cutting edge. This will need routine checking and lubricating.

General health and safety checklist	Yes	No
Has your salon got a written health and safety policy?		
Who is in charge of health and safety in your salon?		
Has your salon done a risk assessment?		
Do you know what COSHH means?		
Do you know where the first aid kit is?		
Do you know where the accident book is?		
Do you know the emergency procedures?		
Do you carry out routine checks/inspections?		

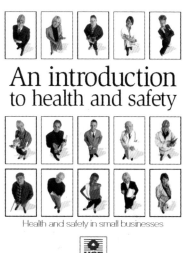

An introduction
to health and safety

Health and safety in small businesses

HSE

What you should know about – where to get more information

HSE leaflet HMSO

HSE leaflet   HMSO

ACTIVITY

The column of the left lists items of personal protective equipment (PPE) that your salon provides for staff and client safety. Complete the information in the space provided

PPE	When is it used	Why it is used
Disposable vinyl gloves		
Gowns and towels		
Stylists waterproof apron		
Barrier cream		
Cotton 'neck' wool		

PREVENTING INFECTION

A warm, humid salon can offer a perfect home for disease-carrying bacteria. If they can find food in the form of dust and dirt, they may reproduce rapidly. Good ventilation, however, provides a circulating air current that will help to prevent their growth. This is why it is important to keep the salon clean, dry and well aired at all times – and this includes clothing, work areas, tools and all equipment.

Some salons use sterilising devices as a means of providing hygienically safe work implements. 'Sterilisation' means the complete eradication of living organisms. Different devices use different sterilisation methods, which may be based on the use of heat, radiation or chemicals.

REMEMBER

On every occasion, before using clippers, make sure you check the alignment and positioning of the blades. Frequent use will not only impair their effectiveness, the constant vibration may also loosen the blades!

SCIENCE BIT!
DID YOU KNOW

Preventing infection and disease
We all carry large numbers of micro-organisms inside us, on our skin and in our hair. These organisms, such as bacteria, fungi and viruses, are too small to be seen with the naked eye. Bacteria and fungi can be seen through a microscope, but viruses are too small even for that.

Many micro-organisms are quite harmless, but some can cause disease. Those that are harmful to people are called 'pathogens'. Flu, for example, is caused by a virus, thrush by a fungus and bronchitis often by bacteria. Conditions like these, which can be transmitted from one person to another, are said to be infectious.

The body is naturally resistant to infection; it can fight most pathogens using its inbuilt immunity system. So it is possible to be infected with pathogenic organisms without contracting the disease. When you have a disease, the 'symptoms' are the visible signs that something is wrong. They are the results of the infection and of the reactions of the body to that infection. Symptoms help you to recognise the disease.

Infectious diseases should always be treated by a doctor. Non-infectious conditions and defects can often be treated in the salon or with products available from the chemist.

Ultraviolet (UV) radiation provides an alternative sterilising option. The items for sterilisation are placed in wall- or worktop-mounted cabinets fitted with UV-emitting light bulbs, and exposed to the radiation for at least 15 minutes. Penetration of UV radiation is low, so sterilisation by this method is not guaranteed.

Chemical sterilisation

Chemical sterilisers are widely used within salons and you should only handle them when wearing gloves. These solutions are hazardous to health and should not come into contact with the skin. The most effective form of sterilisation is achieved by the total immersion of the contaminated implements into a bath of fluid. This is how babies' feeding utensils are usually sterilised.

Disinfectants reduce the probability of infection and are widely used in general day-to-day hygienic salon maintenance. Antiseptics are used specifically for treating wounds. Many pre-packaged first-aid dressings are impregnated with antiseptic fluids.

REMEMBER

All salons carry out a risk assessment of the substances they use. Any substances that have been identified as potentially hazardous to health will have special handling instructions. These instructions, along with any necessary PPE, must be 'publicly' available within the salon.

REMEMBER

Always wear vinyl gloves.

When? On any occasion where you come into contact with chemicals

Why? Because vinyl gloves are a protective barrier against infection and are the only type recommended by the HSE (see www.hse.gov.uk).

Always wash hands.

When? Before work, after eating or using the toilet, and after coughing, sneezing or blowing your nose.

Why? Because your hands are one of the main sources for spreading infection.

Always wear protective clothing.

When? Always wear a plastic apron for any salon procedure involving chemicals.

Why? This will prevent spillages on to your clothes, particularly when tinting and perming.

Courtesy of Ellisons

Courtesy of Ellisons

ACTIVITY

Example questions and model assessment answers:

Q1 Who has overall responsibility for your health and safety at work?

A1 Mr, Mrs, Ms, Miss_____ has overall responsibility.

Q2 Who is directly responsible for your health and safety at work?

A2 Mr, Mrs, Ms, Miss_____ is the person I should take up any health and safety issues that I have on a day-to-day basis.

Q3 What hazards might exist in the salon you work in?

A3 (You should be able to list anything specific to the salon you work in)

Q4 If you found a hazard that you could not put right yourself, who would you report it to?

A4 Mr, Mrs, Ms, Miss_____ (the same person as A1 above).

REMEMBER

Always wear the gloves provided by the salon for clearing up spilt chemicals or cleaning products. Never attempt to do it without them.

Special note: salon stylists tend to use disposable vinyl gloves in their work as these are more hygienic and provide a better barrier against contracting occupational contact dermititis.

Barbicide   Courtesy of Ellisons

Protective apron   Courtesy of Ellisons

ACTIVITY

Do it or report it? Write down the action you should take in the appropriate column.

Sort it out myself	Hazard	Report it immediately
Yes no	Unsafe stacking of boxes in the stock room?	Yes no
Yes no	Faulty kettle in the kitchen?	Yes no
Yes no	Failed bulb in the corridor?	Yes no
Yes no	Spillages on the salon floor?	Yes no
Yes no	A broken glass in the kitchen?	Yes no
Yes no	Smoke appearing around the door of a closed room?	Yes no
Yes no	Bare cable showing on a hand-dryer flex	Yes no

SCIENCE BIT!
DID YOU KNOW

Antiperspirants reduce underarm sweating. These products contain astringents, which narrow the pores that emit the sweat and cool down the skin. Alternatively, deodorants can be used. These products will not reduce the amount of sweating but can mask any odour by killing the surface bacteria with antiseptic ingredients.

ACCIDENTS AND EMERGENCIES

ACTIVITY

Your salon's policy for health and safety: find out the answers to the following questions.

Q1   What would be considered as safe working practice at your salon?

Q2a Where is the salon's first aid box?

Q2b What items are kept in it?

Q3   What are the salon rules regarding smoking, consuming food and drink on the premises and policy in respect to alcohol and other drugs?

Q4   What are the salon's emergency **evacuation procedures**?

Q5   What are the salon's expectations in respect to your personal presentation and hygiene?

Fire

Fires occurring in salons are more likely to arise from electrical faults, gas leaks, or smoking. Faulty or badly maintained electrical equipment, such as hand dryers or hood dryers, may malfunction and overheat, and even ignite! Gas appliances, such as ovens or hobs, present a possible risk if they are left unattended. Staff cooking facilities need to be closely monitored to prevent gas being left on, whether lit or not. Smoking can cause fires when lit cigarettes are dropped, discarded or left unattended to smoulder in ashtrays.

Your salon will have set fire safety procedures, which must always be followed.

Raising the alarm

In the event of fire breaking out, your main priorities are:

- *Raise the alarm* – Staff and customers must be warned, and the premises must be evacuated.
- *Call the fire brigade* – Do this even if you believe that someone else has already phoned. Dial 999, ask the operator for the fire service, and give the telephone number from where you are calling. Wait for the transfer to the fire service and then tell them your name and the address of the premises that are on fire.

> **REMEMBER**
>
> All pieces of salon electrical equipment require annual testing. This must carried out by a competent person who provides the salon with a certificate and itemised list of tested items.

> **REMEMBER**
>
> There are four classifications of fire:
>
> Class A: Fires involving solid material such as paper, wood, hair etc.
>
> Class B: Fires involving liquids such as petrol, paraffin etc.
>
> Class C: Fires involving gases such as propane, butane.
>
> Class D: Fires which involve metals (not normally encountered in salons).

Firefighting equipment   Chubb Fire Ltd

Firefighting blanket   Chubb Fire Ltd

Firefighting symbols

Firefighting

If the fire is small, you may tackle it with an extinguisher or fire blanket. Under the Fire Precautions Act 1971, all premises are required to have fire-fighting equipment, which must be suitably maintained in good working order. Different types of fire require different types of fire extinguisher:

1 *Water* – These are RED with a label to indicate its type and can only be used for Class A fires. The standard size is nine litres (two gallons). (The main problem with this type of extinguisher is the subsequent damage caused by the water and that it can not be used on electrical fires.)

2 *Foam* – These used to be CREAM/BUFF, but are now RED with a CREAM/BUFF LABEL and are used for Class B fires and small Class A fires. The standard capacity is nine litres (two gallons). (This type of extinguisher has the same problems as water extinguishers.)

3 *Carbon dioxide (CO_2)* – These used to be BLACK, but are now RED with a BLACK LABEL and can be used on all fires but are particularly suitable for Class B and electrical fires. They are available in a range of sizes depending on the weight of CO_2 contained.

4 *Dry powder* – These used to be BLUE, but are now RED with a BLUE LABEL and can be used on all classes of fire but are particularly suitable for Class B, C and electrical fires. They are available in a range of sizes from 0.75 kg to 4 kg. The main disadvantage is that the residual powder has to be cleaned up and the powder can cause damage to electronic equipment.

Fire escape

All premises must have a designated means of escape from fire. This route must be kept clear of obstructions at all times and during working hours the fire doors must remain unlocked. The escape route must be easily identifiable, with clearly visible signs. In buildings with fire certificates, emergency lighting must be installed. These lighting systems automatically illuminate the escape route in the event of a power failure and are operated by an independent battery back-up.

Fire safety training

It is essential for staff to know the following fire procedures:

- fire prevention
- raising the alarm
- evacuation during a fire
- assembly points following evacuation.

Training is given to new members of staff during their induction period. This training must be regularly updated for all staff, and fire drills must be held at regular intervals.

REMEMBER

Your workplace will have its own fire safety procedures. Find out where the information is displayed and what action should be taken.

ACTIVITY

If you weren't shown how to use an extinguisher during your induction, ask your manager to demonstrate how to use it. Remember that all extinguishers are noisy when they are discharged and this can be quite a shock! So be careful not to drop it.

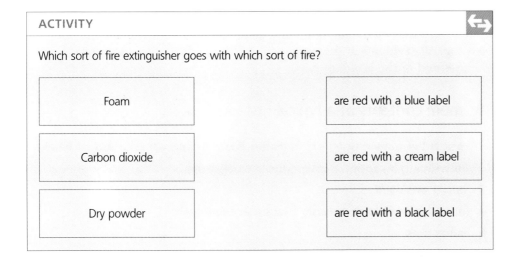

ACTIVITY

Which sort of fire extinguisher goes with which sort of fire?

Foam		are red with a blue label
Carbon dioxide		are red with a cream label
Dry powder		are red with a black label

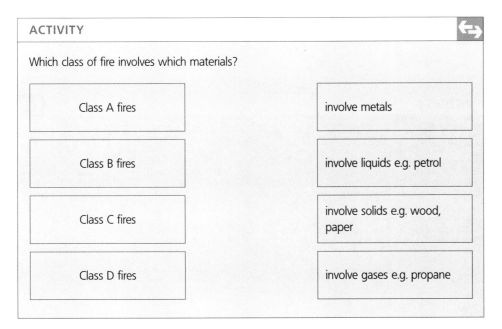

ACTIVITY

Which class of fire involves which materials?

Class A fires		involve metals
Class B fires		involve liquids e.g. petrol
Class C fires		involve solids e.g. wood, paper
Class D fires		involve gases e.g. propane

Dealing with accidents (first aid)

The Health and Safety (First Aid) Regulations 1981 require the employer to provide equipment and facilities which are adequate and appropriate for providing first aid. In the event of an accident occurring the 'Appointed Person' should be notified. This person takes control in these situations and will, if necessary, call an ambulance. There is also an appointed first aider who is qualified to administer first aid within the salon.

What is an Appointed Person?

An Appointed Person is someone who:

- takes charge if someone is injured or falls ill including calling an ambulance if required
- looks after the first aid equipment; e.g. restocking the first-aid box.

They should not attempt to provide first aid unless they have received appropriate training.

A first-aid kit

Every salon must have a first-aid kit in accordance with the regulations and, in the event that materials have been used, they must be replaced as soon as possible. All accidents and emergency aid given within the salon must be documented in the accident book.

Minimum contents of a typical first-aid box

1   First-aid guidance notes (HSE leaflet *Basic Advice on First Aid at Work*)
20 Individually wrapped sterile adhesive dressings
2   Sterile eye pads
4   Individually wrapped sterile triangular bandages
6   Safety pins
6   Medium size (12 cm × 12 cm approx) sterile unmedicated dressings
2   Large size (18 cm × 18 cm approx) sterile unmedicated dressings
1   Pair of disposable gloves

ACTIVITY

Q1a What type of container is liquid or creme hydrogen peroxide kept in?

Q1b Why is hydrogen peroxide hazardous to health?

Q2a **Permanent tints** (hair dyes) are packaged in what sort of container?

Q2b What chemicals are found in permanent hair dyes?

Q3a How should hair bleaching powder be stored?

Q3b Why is hair bleaching powder hazardous to health?

Q4a How are shampoos and conditioners stored ready for use at the backwash?

Q4b How are they dispensed when they are used on clients?

Q5a What type of container is perm solution kept in?

Q5b What hazard to health does perm solution present?

Recording accidents and illness

All accidents must be recorded in the accident book. The recording system should always be kept readily available for use and inspection. When you are recording accidents, you will need to document following details:

- date, time and place of incident or treatment
- name, and job of injured or ill person
- details of the injury/of ill person and the treatment given
- what happened to the person immediately afterwards (e.g. went home, or went to hospital)
- name and signature of the person providing the treatment and entry.

General guidance on first aid

The following basic information is available in leaflet form from HSE, ISBN 0 7176 1070 5 in priced packs of 20.

REMEMBER: YOU SHOULD NOT ATTEMPT TO GIVE ANYTHING MORE THAN BASIC FIRST AID!

When giving first aid it is vital that you assess the situation and that you:

- take care not to become a casualty yourself while administering first aid (use protective clothing and equipment where necessary)
- send for help where necessary
- follow the advice from the HSE.

First Aid leaflet   HMSO

What to do in an emergency

Check whether the casualty is conscious. If the casualty is unconscious or semi-conscious:

- Check the mouth for any obstruction.
- Open the airway by tilting the head back and lifting the chin using the tips of two fingers.
- If the casualty has stopped breathing and you are competent to give artificial ventilation, do so. Otherwise send for help without delay.

First Aid leaflet   HMSO

Unconsciousness

In most workplaces expert help should be available fairly quickly, but if you have an unconscious casualty it is vital that their airway is kept clear. If you cannot keep the airway open as described above, you may need to move the casualty into the recovery position. *The priority is an open airway*.

Wounds and bleeding

Open wounds should be covered – *after putting on sterile gloves*. Apply a dressing from the first-aid box over the wound and press firmly on top of it with your hands or fingers. The pad should be tied firmly in place. If bleeding continues another dressing should be applied on top. *Do not remove the original dressing.* Seek appropriate help.

What is a first aider?

A first aider is someone who has undergone a training course in administering first aid and holds a current first aid at work certificate. The training has to be approved by the HSE.

Minor injuries

Minor injuries, of the sort which the injured person would treat themselves at home, can be treated from the contents of the first-aid box. The casualty should wash their hands and apply a dressing to protect the wound and prevent infection. In the workplace special metallic and/or coloured or waterproof dressings may be supplied according to the circumstances. Wounds should be kept dry and clean.

Suspected broken bones

If a broken bone is suspected obtain expert help. Do not move casualties unless they are in a position which exposes them to immediate danger.

Burns

Burns can be serious – if in doubt seek medical help. Cool the part of the body affected with cold water until the pain is relieved. Thorough cooling may take ten minutes or more, but this must not delay taking the casualty to hospital. Certain chemicals may irritate or damage the skin, some seriously. Treat in the same way as for other burns. It is important that irrigation continues, even on the way to the hospital if necessary. Remove any contaminated clothing which is not stuck to the skin. Make sure that you *avoid contaminating yourself* with the chemical.

Eye injuries

Eye injuries are potentially serious. The casualty will be experiencing intense pain in the affected eye, with spasms of the eyelids. Before attempting to treat, wash your hands.

If there is something in the eye, irrigate the eye with clean, cool water or sterile fluid from a sealed container to remove loose material. Do not attempt to remove anything that is embedded.

If chemicals are involved, flush the open eye with water or sterile fluid for at least 10 to 15 minutes. Apply an eye pad and send the casualty to hospital.

Suggested numbers of first aid personnel

Category of risk	Number employed at one location	Suggested number of first aid personnel
Low risk: shops, offices	Fewer than 50	At least one Appointed Person
	50–100	At least one first aider
	100+	One additional first aider for every 100 people employed

Special hazards

Electrical and gassing accidents can occur in the workplace. You must assess the danger to yourself and not attempt assistance until you are sure it is safe to do so. If the casualty has stopped breathing and you are competent to give artificial ventilation and cardiac resuscitation, do so. Otherwise send for help without delay.

HEALTH AND SAFETY LEGISLATION

This section will provide you with an outline of the main health and safety regulations that affect hairdressers and their work. The Health and Safety at Work Act 1974 is the legislation that covers a variety of safe working practices and associated regulations. You do not need to know the contents of this Act, but you should at least be aware of the existence of relevant regulations made under its provisions. They cover the following aspects at work:

- management of safety at work (assessing risk in the workplace)
- safe equipment and systems of work
- protective equipment
- handling chemicals and substances
- electricity
- first aid
- handling and moving objects
- fire precautions.

HSE information
Go online for more information at www.hse.gov.uk and www.hsedirect.gov.uk

HSE information

COSHH: A brief guide to the regulations
What you need to know about the Control of Substances Hazardous to Health Regulations
2002 (COSHH) INDG136(rev3) is available free as a single copy (from HSE books and on
the www.hse.gov.uk website), or in priced packs of ten (ISBN 0 7176 2982 1) for £5.00.

The Management of Health and Safety at Work Regulations 1999

The main regulation requires the employer to appoint competent personnel to conduct risk assessments for the health and safety of all staff working on the premises as well as other visitors to the business premises. Staff must be adequately trained to take appropriate action, eliminate or minimise any risks. Other regulations cover the necessity to set up procedures for emergency situations, reviewing the risk assessment processes. In salons where five or more people are employed, there is the added obligation to set up a system for monitoring health surveillance, should the risk assessments identify a need.

The main requirements for management of health and safety are:

- identify any potential hazards
- assessing the risks which could arise from these hazards
- identifying who is at risk
- eliminating or minimising the risks
- training staff to identify and control risks
- regular reviewing of the assessment processes.

Young workers at risk

There is also a requirement to carry out a risk assessment for young people. Any staff member who is under school-leaving age must have a personalised risk assessment kept on file. This would be applicable for those on work experience or Saturday staff.

Easy online steps to control health risks from chemicals
COSHH Essentials has been developed to help firms comply with the COSHH regulations.
The COSHH Essentials Website is easy to use and is available free as part of hsedirect – a
database of all health and safety legislation and HSE's priced guidance.
http://www.coshhessentials.org.uk/

The Workplace (Health, Safety and Welfare) Regulations 1992

These regulations supersede the Offices, Shops and Railway Premises Act 1963 (OSRPA) and cover the following workplace key points:

- maintenance of the workplace and the equipment in it
- ventilation, temperature and lighting
- cleanliness
- sanitary and washing facilities
- drinking water supply
- rest, eating and changing facilities
- storage of clothing
- glazing
- traffic routes
- work space.

Amendments and additions in this regulation provide new requirements for employers with particular attention for glazed areas such as windows and doors etc. Any transparent and translucent partitions must be made of safe materials and if they could cause injury to anyone, they should be appropriately marked. Other amendments have particular rules for rest rooms and rest areas. These must include suitable alternative arrangements to protect non-smokers from the effects caused by tobacco smoke and suitable rest facilities for any person at work who is either pregnant or a nursing mother.

The Personal Protective Equipment (PPE) at Work Regulations 1992

These relate to the requirement of employers to provide suitable and sufficient protective clothing and equipment for all employees to use.

The PPE Regulations 1992 require managers to make an assessment of the processes and activities carried out at work and to identify where and when special items of clothing should be worn. In hairdressing environments, the potential hazards and dangers revolve around the task of providing hairdressing services – that is, in general, the application of hairdressing treatments and associated products.

Potentially hazardous substances used by hairdressers include:

- acidic solutions of varying strengths
- caustic alkaline solutions of varying strengths
- flammable liquids, which are often in pressurised containers
- vapours and dyeing compounds.

There are also potentially hazardous items of equipment and their individual applications, such as:

- electrical appliances
- heated/heating instruments
- sharp cutting tools.

All these items require correct handling and safe usage procedures, and for several of them this includes the wearing of suitable items of protective equipment.

Control of Substances Hazardous to Health Regulations 2002 (COSHH)

Hairdressing employers are required by law to make an assessment of the exposure to all the substances used in their salon that could be potentially hazardous to themselves, their employees and other salon visitors, who may be affected by the work activity. The purpose of COSHH regulations is to make sure that people are working in the safest possible environment and conditions.

A substance is considered to be hazardous if it can cause harm to the body. It only presents a risk if it is:

- in contact with the skin or eyes
- absorbed through the skin or via the eyes (either directly or from contact from with contaminated surfaces or clothing)
- inhaled (breathed in from the atmosphere)
- ingested via contaminated food or fingers
- injected
- introduced to the body via cuts and abrasions.

Cosmetic Products (Safety) Regulations 1989

These regulations lay down the recommended volumes and percentage strengths of different hydrogen-based products. The strength will vary depending on whether it has been produced for the professional or non-professional use. It is important that the manufacturer's guidance material and current legislation is checked when using or selling products.

Health and Safety (Information for Employees) Regulations 1989

The regulation requires the employer to make available to all employees, notices, posters and leaflets either in the approved format or those actually published by the HSE.

> **REMEMBER** ✓
>
> Your salon will have made a risk assessment of the products held or used in the salon. Make sure you look at this: it will give you specific information on their handling and precautionary requirements.

HSE workplace information poster HMSO

The Health and Safety (Display Screen Equipment) Regulations 1992

These regulations cover the use of computers and similar equipment in the workplace. Although not generally a high risk, prolonged use can lead to eye strain, mental stress and possible muscular pain. As more hairdressing salons use information technology and computers this is becoming a major consideration for hairdressing employees.

It is the employer's duty to assess display screen equipment and reduce the risks that are discovered. They will need to plan the scheduling of work so that there are regular breaks or changes in activity and provide information training for the equipment users. Computer users will also be entitled to eyesight tests which will be paid for by the employer.

Manual Handling Operations Regulations 1992

These regulations apply in all occupations where manual lifting occurs. They require employers to carry out a risk assessment of the work processes and activities that involve lifting. The risk assessment should address detailed aspects of the following:

- any risk of injury
- the manual movement that is involved in the task
- the physical constraints the loads incur
- the work environmental constraints that are incurred
- the worker's individual capabilities
- steps and/or remedial action to take in order to minimise the risk.

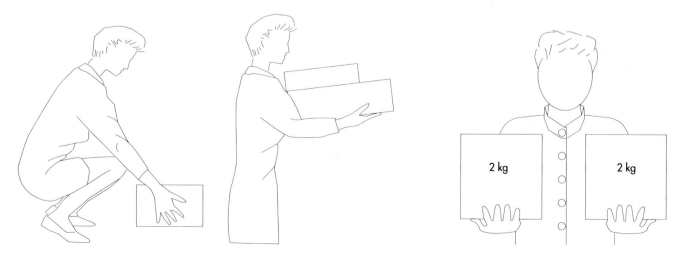

Left: Lifting a box. Centre: Carrying several boxes. Right: Carrying equal weights in both hands

REMEMBER

- Is all salon equipment regularly checked?
- Are maintenance logs kept for items of equipment?
- Has introduced second-hand equipment been checked?
- Have all the staff been trained to use the equipment?

Provision and Use of Work Equipment Regulations (PUWER) 1998

These regulations refer to the regular maintenance and monitoring of work equipment. Any equipment, new or second-hand, must be suitable for the purpose that it is intended. In addition to this they require that anyone using this equipment must be adequately trained.

Electricity at Work Regulations 1989

This requires employers to maintain electrical equipment in a safe condition and to have them checked by a suitably qualified person. A written record of testing must be kept and made available for inspection. It is the employees' responsibility for reporting any known faulty equipment to their employer or supervisor. The following information must be kept:

- the electrician's/contractors name, address, contact details
- an itemised list of salon electrical equipment along with serial number (for individual identification)
- the date of inspection
- the date of purchase/disposal.

The Reporting of Injuries, Diseases and Dangerous Occurrences Regulations 1995 (RIDDOR)

Under these regulations there are certain diseases and groups of infections that, if sustained at work, are noticeable by law. So if any employees suffer a personal injury at work which results in one of the following:

- death
- major injuries including; fractures (not fingers and toes) amputation, dislocation, loss of sight and other eye injuries
- more than 24 hours in hospital
- an incapacity to work for more than three calendar days

they must be reported to the appropriate authority.

I understand my job position and the impact of health and safety responsibilities associated with it ☐	I know who is responsible for health and safety and to whom to report any hazards in the workplace ☐	I always follow the salon's policy in respect to health and safety practices and procedures ☐	I can recognise the hazards and potential risks at work, and take appropriate action ☐
I know the main areas of potential risk for health and safety at work ☐	I understand all of the relevant health and safety regulations applicable to work ☐	I always carry out working practices according to the salon's policy ☐	I know why it is important to be aware of potential risks to personal health and safety ☐
I understand the implications of poor salon hygiene and cross-infecting others ☐	I can handle, use and work with materials, products and equipment safely ☐	I understand the necessity of personal hygiene and presentation ☐	I know the salon's policy and procedures in the event of fire or accidents ☐
I know what would be considered to be unsafe practices at work ☐			CHECKER BOARD ✓

Assessment of knowledge and understanding

The following projects, activities and assessments are directly linked to the essential knowledge and understanding for unit G1.

For each statement that is addressed wholly or in part in these activities, you will see its relevant and corresponding EKU number.

Make sure that you keep this for easier referencing and along with your work for future inclusion in your portfolio.

Project (EKU G.12)

For this project you will need to use the information from the salon's risk assessments and the COSHH salon information booklet.

For each of the following:

- One cold wave perming lotion,
- One tube of permanent tint
- One powder bleaching product

find out:

(a) the chemical composition

(b) how it is used safely

(c) how it should be stored safely

(d) how it is handled

(e) any other special conditions that apply to it.

Case study (G7.18, G7.22)

It was Tuesday morning at Jenny's Hair Salon. Jenny had allocated Karen, one of the juniors, to remain on reception whilst she attended to paperwork in the office. Steve, one of the stylists, had clients booked in. Sharon, the other stylist, had most of the morning free.

A well-dressed woman with short greying hair came in and asked Karen if she would be able to have her hair coloured before she travelled to London that afternoon. Karen said that Sharon could help her.

Sharon greeted the lady, putting her at her ease, and carried out a consultation and colour selection. She asked Claire, another junior, to prepare the client for the service. Claire seated her in the salon, hung up her coat and looked for a colouring gown. There weren't any. 'Use one of the cutting capes then,' said Sharon. 'The others are still at the launderette. I'll mix up the colour and you can apply it while I collect them.'

Claire had applied colours before but tended to be a little careless. Today her application was sloppy, and she did not bother to wear gloves. Ten minutes later Sharon returned. Horrified, she beckoned Claire into reception. 'You've not only coloured her hair, you've got colour on her neck and even on her jacket,' she exclaimed.

'I know,' said Claire. 'I'll change the gowns over now and ask her to take off her jacket so that it won't get creased. Then I'll clean it without her knowing.' 'OK, but keep it to yourself,' said Sharon.

When the hair was finished, the client paid her bill and left.

Two days later, Claire told Jenny that she had visited the doctor because of sore, itching and burning hands. He had diagnosed dermatitis and told her it was an occupational disease and should be reported. He'd signed her off for a week.

On Saturday morning, Jenny received a letter from a firm of solicitors. This is what it said:

Re Ms Cane in pursuance of compensation

Dear Madam

I regret to inform you that my client whilst attending your place of business on Tuesday 11 February did suffer due to the gross negligence of your staff an allergenic reaction following a colouring treatment. There are indications of burns and weeping pustules as well as damage sustained to her attire. We await a comprehensive medical report that we believe will provide the basis for our pursuance in court and recovery of damages. We will be contacting you in due course.

1 List in order the mistakes that were made.

2 What actions should, or could, have been take to avoid the outcomes?

3 Who were to blame and why?

4 What are the possible short- and long-term effects for Jenny, her staff and her business?

5 How do COSHH and RIDDOR apply to this particular scenario?

Questions

1 How does health and safety law affect the way in which you carry out your duties at work? (G1.1)

2 What is your place of work's policy in respect to controlling risks? (G1.3)

3 What types of hazard could occur during your normal working routines? (G1.6)

4 Why is personal presentation at work so important? (G1.14)

5 To what extent are you personally required to minimise the risks to health and safety of others? (G1.16)

6 How are tools sterilised in the salon? (H9.17)

Preparing for assessment checklist

Remember to:

- work safely and hygienically in the salon at all times
- prepare clients correctly for the services you are going to carry out
- put on your personal protective wear when it is appropriate
- get the clients to put on protective wear when it is appropriate
- look out for potential hazards and know what action you should take in rectifying them
- keep the work areas clean, hygienic and free from hazards
- clean and sterilise the tools and equipment before they are used
- dispose of waste items safely and correctly
- adhere to the safety factors when working on clients' hair
- adhere to the salon's emergency procedures at all times
- be aware of the salon's first-aid procedures
- work within the limits of your own authority in the all of the above.

chapter 6

CUTTING HAIR

NVQ/SVQ reference, unit title and main outcome

Unit H6 Cut hair using basic techniques

H6.1 **Maintain effective and safe methods of working when cutting hair**

H6.2 **Cut hair to achieve a variety of looks**

What do I need to do?

- Take adequate precautions in preparing yourself and the client before cutting hair.
- Work safely at all times.
- Be able to cut a range of different hair styles, types and lengths.
- Be able to apply a variety of cutting techniques in different styling situations.

What do I need to learn?

You need to know and understand:

- why it is important to take adequate measures in protecting and preparing your client before cutting their hair
- how to recognise whether a style is suitable for a client, as well as carrying out the appropriate techniques to achieve it
- how to recognise the factors that influence suitable styling choices
- the design aspects of shape, balance and form
- why checking and rechecking shape, balance and form is important.

Information covered in this chapter

- **The principles that influence styling choice and suitability.**
- **The range of hairstyles and techniques that you will need to be able to do.**
- **The principles and design aspects of balance, shape and form.**
- **The range of cutting tools available and the ways in which they are used.**
- **The safe working practices that you must adhere to.**

KEY WORDS

Club cut or clubbing hair   The most basic and most popular way of cutting sections of hair straight across, parallel to the index and middle finger.

Texturising or personalising hair   A variety of cutting techniques that are used to achieve different effects within the cutting scheme of a hairstyle.

Shape, form and balance   The physical and notional aspects that control hair design and hair-styling.

INTRODUCTION

Cutting is the most important aspect of hairdressing, even if it is not considered number one by hairdressers and people within the craft: ask any member of the public. The difference between learning to cut different hairstyles and being *able* to cut different hairstyles automatically doesn't seem much in one sentence, but they are often years apart. Getting to the point where you can *see* people's heads and hairstyles as some sort of wire-frame cutting plan takes time and experience and it is this visualisation that people find intriguing, fascinating and elusive.

> **REMEMBER** ✔
>
> Cutting is the most important and fundamental aspect of hairdressing. It must be done correctly and well if you want to make a living and have a long, successful career!

CHECKERBOARD

At the end of this chapter the checkerboard will help to jog your memory on what you have learned and what still remains to be done. Cross off with a pencil each of the topics as you cover it (see page 183).

Photo: Rush London for Goldwell Styling

REMEMBER ✔

Always find out the underlying reasons why your client is having their hair styled.

REMEMBER ✔

If the client has hair hanging around their face, take this back to see the facial shape. This will help to eliminate some style choices immediately.

Photo courtesy Goldwell UK

HAIR-STYLING CONSIDERATIONS

Good hair-styling is the combination of visualising, designing and then creating a personal and individual look for your client. It is an expression of form and shape that has aesthetic balance, resulting in a suitable style that is both durable and attractive and complements the wearer.

Bad hair-styling is none of the above.

The aim of the style is to enhance the client's appearance; this boosts their confidence and psychologically makes them feel better.

People have hairstyles for different reasons; this can be for work, social or 'just because it grows'. You have to find out the reason as part of the consultation. If you miss this underlying purpose or choose to ignore it you have failed. People having their hair styled for business reasons are trying to find a balance between fashion and professional presentation. Those having it cut for social or lifestyle reasons are trying to find a balance between fashion and style versatility. The last grouping is the least satisfying from a hairdressing and creative point of view: people who have their hair cut just because it grows. They have no self-image awareness and no interest in hair. Fortunately this group is very small and constantly diminishing.

Cutting checklist

✓ Make sure that the client is protected adequately first.

✓ Always gain agreement before attempting anything new or different.

✓ Make sure you consider the reasons and the purpose for the style.

✓ Assess the style limitations, hair problems or physical features.

✓ Avoid technical jargon or style names. If jargon is used, by you or the client, always clarify in simple terms what it means to avoid confusion.

✓ Don't just do the style if you think that it's wrong. If there are reasons why you think it will be unsuitable, you will be doing the client a big favour in the longer term if you tackle the issue straight away.

✓ Always give the client some advice on how to handle the style themselves.

✓ Give the client an idea of how long it will take to do.

Choosing a hairstyle

The hairstyle that you select for your client needs to take account of the following factors:

- head and facial shape
- head, face and body physical features
- reason and purpose for the style
- quality, quantity and distribution of the hair

- hair positioning, type, growth and tendency
- style suitability
- age.

Head and facial shape

The proportions, balance and distribution of the hairstyle will be a frame for the head and face. Therefore you need to examine the head and face carefully. If you look at the outline of your client's face, you will see that it's either round, oval, square, heart-shaped, oblong or triangular. Only an **oval face** suits all hairstyles, so all the others listed present some form of styling limitations; in other words they become a styling choice influencing factor.

Photo: Rush London for Goldwell Styling

General styling limitations

Square and oblong facial shapes	Are accentuated by hair that is smoothed, scraped back or sleek at the sides and top. The lines and angles are made less conspicuous by fullness and softer movement.
Round faces	Are made more conspicuous if the side and front perimeter lengths are short or finish near to the widest part of the face. This is made worse if width is added at these positions too. Generally this facial shape is complemented by length beyond the chin.
Square angular features, jaw, forehead etc.	Is improved with softer perimeter shapes, avoid solid, linear effects around the face. Shattered edges and texturising will help to mask these features.
Flatter heads at the back	Are improved by **graduation**, creating contour and shape that is missing from having a flatter occipital bone.

REMEMBER ✔

Simple mistakes are often made when a hairdresser tries to disguise a prominent feature, e.g. large bushy eyebrows. It is often made worse when too much hair is used, inadvertently compounding the problem and drawing attention to it.

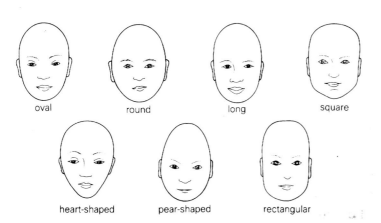

Face and head shapes

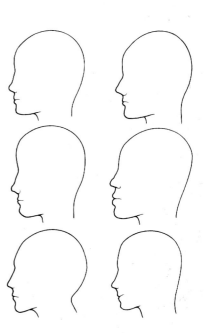

Profiles

ACTIVITY

Explaining the differences between facial shapes and the general styling limitations they impose on paper is one thing. Recognising them on real people is another. For example, how many times do you hear someone say that they have a round face, but when you take a good look at them their face is actually shaped completely differently?

In your class group take turns to look at each colleague closely to find out what general face shape they have. (Sometimes it can be a mixture of two shapes.) When you have created the list, write down next to each in the second column, the general limitations that both their hair and physiognomy imposes. Then finally write down in the last column the ideal styles, lengths and distribution that would be best.

Head, face and body physical features

Physical features

REMEMBER

The more the unwanted features are highlighted, the less suitable the style will be.

Physical feature	How best to work with it
Prominent nose	Hair taken back away from the face accentuates this feature, whilst hair around the face and forehead tends to diminish the feature.
Square jaw line	Is softened by longer perimeter lengths either coming around and on to the face or styled with fullness. Shorter side lengths will have the opposite effect.
Protruding ears	Are better left covered rather than exposed. Sufficient hair should be left to cover and extend beyond their length if at all possible.
Wrinkles around the eyes	Are made more obvious by hair being scraped back at the temples or straighter more angular effects.
Narrow foreheads	Are disguised by softer fringes and side partings, whereas they are made more obvious by hair taken back away from the face.
Larger body shapes	The overall effect is balanced and improved with longer, fuller hair styles; they are made much worse by short, sleek layered shapes.
Small faces	Can be swamped if the hair is left long with a centre parting and no fringe.
Large faces	Are accentuated by short cropped or sculpted hair
Shapes of glasses	There are so many available that they are a fashion accessory. Generally people will have had assistance in the selection and suitability of their frames. Therefore they should not work against the hairstyle that you want to create: they will already suit the shape and size of the face.
The way the head is held	Subtlety and tact are needed as the natural disposition of the client, the way they hold their head, may be for a wide variety of reasons – shyness, uncertainty, illness or an accident.
	Many people tilt their head to one side or forwards. Sometimes this is because they are tall and want subconsciously to reduce their height; sometimes they hide behind their hair because they lack confidence or they think it makes them more alluring.
	You need to look out for this natural posture but not make any comment other than asking whether they have any preference as to finished lengths, fringes and partings.

Reason or purpose for hairstyle

The reason for the hairstyle is a big factor in deciding what is suitable or otherwise.

Photo: Rush London for Goldwell Styling

- A style suitable for a special occasion will differ from one that is selected for work. A ball gown requires an effect that compliments the party theme, whereas an unfussy work style needs to be simpler and versatile. When people think of special events then weddings spring to mind. These are special cases and usually the hairstyle, along with other preparations, is sorted out long before the event. Bridal looks usually involve a lot of work and they should always be trialled several times before the actual day.

- The majority of clients need hairstyles that are easy to manage and that can be dressed up with styling products or accessories for social events. Versatility is definitely the key. People like simple, easy-to-manage effects; they also like the opportunity to look different now and again.

- Some jobs have special conditions about hair lengths and styles, people working in the armed services or police have to wear their hair above the collar whilst at work. For the men, this has been easily accommodated by using clippers for very short styles. For the women they have either had to have short layered styles or hair that is long enough to wear up and out of the way.

REMEMBER

The success of any hairstyle is based on the information that you get during the consultation. Be thorough: an extra five minutes spent discussing the final effect could make all the difference!

Photo courtesy Goldwell UK

Photo courtesy Goldwell UK

The quality, quantity and distribution of hair

- Good hair condition is an essential prerequisite for great hairstyling. It doesn't matter how much work has gone into the thought and design of a hairstyle, *if the hair is in poor condition to start with it still will be afterwards*. Some aspects cannot be altered by cutting, for instance, if the hair is dry, dull and porous cutting it will not change this. The problem should be tackled from the outset. One mistake that hairdressers often try to cover up is the way that they blow-dry the finished style. Dry, porous hair lacks moisture content and moisture is an essential part of condition, flexibility and shine. There is nothing worse than seeing someone blasting a client's hair dry and forcing movement into the hair as if they were using a blow torch!

> **REMEMBER** ✔
>
> **Walk the talk!**
> The answer to sorting out the quality issue about hair is to:
> 1 attack the hair condition problem first
> 2 give advice on how it should be handled at home
> 3 finally demonstrate, by styling it carefully there and then.

Mahogany

- Regular salon clients, the ones you see more often than the others, tend to have something in common. Difficult hair. It can be difficult for a number of reasons; it can be fine and unmanageable or lank and lacking volume, or it may just be that the client has an inability to do their own hair. Thin sparsely distributed hair is always a problem. If there isn't enough hair to get coverage over the scalp, then there is not a lot you can do about it. One thing that you should remember though is not to put too much volume into this sort of hair as it will only make the problem more noticeable. Fine hair presents many problems too. Very fine hair is affected by dampness and quickly loses its shape. This type of hair always benefits from styling products, so get your client used to using them.

- Dry thick hair needs to be tamed. Most clients with hair like this would like their hair to look smoother and shinier. Again this is a conditioning issue and you need to attack the problem before tackling the style. Sometimes this type of hair benefits from finishing products so put them on as you finish and define the hairstyle.

Mahogany

- Very tight curly hair can be difficult too, particularly if your client wants it to appear straight. It is possible to smooth and straighten hair, particularly when you use ceramic straighteners. But keeping it straight is another matter and you may want to consider a chemical straightener instead.

- Cutting wavy hair presents some problems but not if it is looked at carefully before it's wet. Avoid cutting across the crests of the waves. You can't change the natural movement in the hair so try to work with it.

- Straight hair, particularly if it is fine textured, can be difficult to cut. Cutting marks or lines can easily form if the cutting sections and angles are not right. Make sure that you only take small sections of hair and remember to cross-check after at 90° to the angle in which you first cut, to avoid this happening to you.

Photo courtesy Goldwell

Hair positioning, type, growth and tendency

The perimeter outline formed by the hair in relation to the shape of the face is the first thing most people see. It is this effect that people make comments about: 'That's a beautiful haircut.' 'I think that really suits you.' The complete hairstyle is based upon the frame that the hair creates for the face. How you 'fill in' the detail – the movement, direction, colour and placement – is down to your interpretation, understanding, technical ability and experience.

Hair growth direction and distribution should be a major consideration in terms of what is achievable within a hairstyle. You need to make allowances for strong movement, high or low hairlines, natural partings, hair whorls, cowlicks, widow's peaks and double crowns. Look for these before shampooing. The client cannot compensate for these themselves, so when the hair is in need of washing, they will be plain to see. After the hair is washed the degree and strength of the feature can be seen and then you can reconsider how you will tackle it.

Photo: Rush London for Goldwell Styling

REMEMBER

When you choose a suitable hairstyle always allow for the natural fall of the hair.

Style suitability

Style suitability refers to the effect of the hair shape on the face, and on the features of the head and body. Quite simply, a hairstyle is suitable when it 'looks right'. But this is a difficult or certainly a subjective thing to quantify.

Aesthetically speaking, hair 'looks right' when the moulded hair shapes either:

- fits the shape of the face and head – and is therefore in harmony with the overall image, or
- accentuates features of the face and head – when it is in contrast and is therefore projecting the overall image.

For example, a line of the face created by the underlying bone structure can be accentuated when the hair lines are continuous with it. Conversely, it can be softened when they are angled away. A young fashionable hairstyle on an older woman may be totally inappropriate and unattractive. This is because the lines of the face, eyes and forehead are accentuated by the harder style lines of younger styles. Most fashion styles designed for younger women must be adapted if they are going to be suitable for older women.

- **Balance** – Balance is the effect produced by the amount, fullness and weight distribution of hair throughout the style. The opposite, imbalance, is lack of those proportions. Symmetry or symmetrical even balance occurs when the hair is distributed equally as in a mirrored image through a vertical or horizontal plane. Asymmetry or asymmetric effects occur when the overall shape does not have the same distribution on either side. However, both symmetrical and asymmetrical shapes can be balanced: as in the see-saw illustration opposite.

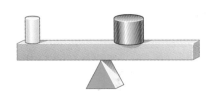

The see-saw effect

- **Style line** – The style line(s) is the direction(s) in which the hair is positioned or appears to flow. This is particularly noticeable on longer hairstyles and long hair that has been put up. In these situations the flow and continuity of the movement is an essential part of the overall effect. When a break occurs within this flow the eye is immediately drawn to it. This break may be a style feature and accentuates what the observer is meant to see, e.g. a hair accessory or a colour feature of the hairstyle. It may be a mistake made by the inexperienced stylist.

- Partings – Partings have a strong effect. A long, straight centre parting will draw attention to the nose. If the nose is prominent it will accentuate the feature further. Conversely, a side parting with a sloping fringe will lessen the effect. Central partings should also be avoided on rounded, fuller faces as this too will make the features more obvious.

- Movement – Movement is the variance of direction within a hairstyle (compare this with style line). The more variety in direction the more movement there will be. Sometimes this movement is because of natural tendency, i.e. curls and waves, sometimes it is artificially created from perming or hairdressing and placement.

- Hard and soft effects – Hard and soft effects occur from the balance or imbalance within a hairstyle or from the movement or lack of movement within it. Subtle colouring enhances softer harmonising effects, whereas stronger, contrasting effects work better in achieving more dramatic results.

The combinations of the above style variables and the way in which they are used will give you the basic rules for which you can create your own original effects. Creating completely new styles requires a great deal of thought and work, and your clients will want to benefit from your creative abilities. The last thing that you should consider is your client's age.

Age

As much as you would like to demonstrate your creative ability on everyone who walks through the salon door, bear in mind that some styles are inappropriate for certain clients. Beyond the physical aspects of style design, age does create some barriers to suitability.

- Younger children are better suited to simpler hairstyles that don't require too much maintenance. More often than not, and certainly from a hair health and hygiene point of view, they are better off with shorter hairstyles.

- Young men and women can get away with anything. Fashion will always dictate, and more often than not, even if there are reasons for not doing a particular style they will insist. This group can enjoy more extreme and dramatic effects. There are more styles applicable to this age group (16–25-year-olds) than to any other. This is because of the diversity of music, TV and social cultures; these people are influenced by the music they buy, the celebrities they follow on TV and the people they mix with.

- Professional men and women tend to go for watered down versions of young fashion. This is similar to the clothing fashion world. The designs that are seen on catwalks in Paris, London and New York are always the precursors of what the high street shops will sell. Dozens of the haute couture fashion houses demonstrate their season's offerings at the pre-season shows, but not all designs are picked up by the fashion buyers, who usually go for the less extreme. People want to appear to be trendy and in touch, but not at the expense of looking ridiculous.

- Older women require greater consideration. Often the signs of ageing in the skin show quite clearly and therefore they must influence the effects that you select as being appropriate and suitable.

> **REMEMBER**
>
> 'Movement' relates to the direction(s) within a hairstyle, whilst 'balance' can relate to movement, positioning, dressing or colour.

Mahogany

Mahogany

See if you can use the salon's old style magazines to do this **project**.

Without making any previous choices;

1 Randomly write down a selection of ten numbers between 1 and say, 150, on a piece of A4 paper, in column 1 of a table with four columns.

2 Now turn to each page of a magazine that corresponds to those numbers and select one style from each of those pages (or the page nearest to them if there is no style shown).

3 In column 2 describe what the haircut is for each of the ten in the list.

4 Now, in column 3, state at which age group this style is aimed: up to ten years, 10–15 years, 16–25 years, 25–35 years, and so on.

5 In the last column try to categorise each one under the following image categories (a) classic (b) natural (c) romantic (d) dramatic.

For each style listed explain in a few words why you think they fall into that category.

Photo: Rush London for Goldwell Styling

REMEMBER

Hairstyles can be grouped into four basic image categories:

1 *Classic* – Timeless hairstyles that involve straight lines and angles that are neither in or out of fashion.

2 *Natural* – Hairstyles that are relatively simple in construction and maintenance, with random movement, soft edges and **texturising**, suited to a busy work or social life.

3 *Romantic* – Hairstyles that incorporate a lot of grooming and finish, probably with products, usually with movement and often exuding sophistication, elegance or chic.

4 *Dramatic* – Straighter more angular or linear effects that are daring and need more confidence on the part of the wearer.

M. Balfre

SAFE PRACTICE FOR CUTTING HAIR AND CUTTING EQUIPMENT

As when performing all other practical services in hairdressing, it is essential that you work safely when cutting hair. In doing this you must take the time to prepare and protect the client adequately. This means that you have:

- pre-selected all the equipment that you are going to use: gowns, towels, combs, scissors and clippers, etc.
- checked that they are prepared for use i.e. freshly laundered or washed, cleaned or sterilised
- got them at hand and ready for use
- ensured that the client is comfortable and in a position where you can work safely.

Mahogany

Gowning

Gowning can take place before or after consultation, it really depends upon the salon's policy, but it must take place before a dry cut is started or, if it is a wet cut, before the client is shampooed.

Dry cutting – Use a clean fresh cutting gown and put it on your client whilst they are seated at the styling location. Make sure that the back is fastened and that any open, free edges are closed together, to keep any loose clippings away from the client's clothes. Place a cutting collar around the neck. Ensure that any bumps or lumps in the client's clothing don't present any false, physical base lines for the haircut and that the collar edges fit snugly against the neck, so that there are no irritating hair fragments that will leave the client itching until they get home.

Wet cutting – Do the same as the gowning above but, when your client is at the basin, place a clean fresh towel around the shoulders before positioning them back carefully and comfortably. Make sure that the client's neck is supported by the basin properly and that the flanged edges of the basin nestle comfortably on to the client's shoulders (which are protected from any moisture by the towel).

Positioning

The positioning of the client in front of the mirror is very important. Any angle of the head other than perpendicular to the mirror and the angle of the head to the seated position will affect the line and balance of the haircut.

Salon workstations have built in foot rests and there are good reasons for this. The foot rest:

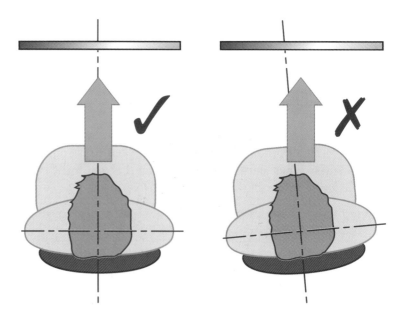

Chair/client angle to mirror

1 is there to improve the comfort for the seated client at any cutting height

2 helps balance the client and encourages them to sit squarely in front of the mirror

3 tries to discourage the client from sitting cross-legged

4 promotes better posture by making the client sit back properly with their back flat against the back of the chair.

All of the above factors are critical for you and the client in ensuring their comfort throughout, and that you are not hindered in doing your task. For example, if your client sits with crossed legs, it will alter the horizontal plane of their shoulders and this will make your job of trying to get even and level baselines more difficult.

Your work position

The client's cutting position and height from the floor have a direct effect on your posture too. You must be able to work in a position where you do not have to bend 'doubled up' to do your work. Cutting involves a lot of arm and hand movements and you need to be able to get your hands and fingers into positions where you can cut the hair without bad posture.

1 You should adjust the seated client's chair height to a position where you can work upright without having to over-reach on the top sections of their head.

2 You should clear trolleys or equipment out of the way so that you get good all-round access (300°) around the client.

> **REMEMBER** ✔
>
> If damp hair is sticking to the client's skin use a small amount of talcum powder dusted onto a neck brush: this will remove it.

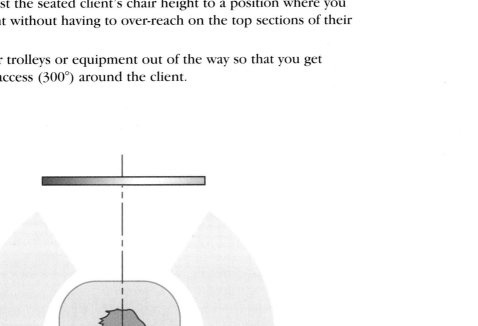

Cutting access

Mahogany

Mahogany

Other health and safety considerations

	What do I do?
Spillages Take care when moving trolleys around in the salon, or when you place products, drinks etc. on the shelves in front of clients.	If you do spill anything on to the floor, mop it up straight away. If the spillage is chemical make sure you know how to handle it. If you don't, tell someone in charge.
Slippery floors Other than spillages the hair clippings are also a potential hazard as people could easily slip on them.	Sweep clippings up immediately and put them into a lined and covered bin.
Tools and equipment Clippers, driers, tongs and straighteners can also be a hazard to clients and staff alike.	Always unplug them and ravel up the trailing leads so that they can be stored safely for next time.
Obstructions Trolleys and moveable equipment, i.e. Rollerballs, Climazones, hood driers and steamers, are potential hazards.	Equipment should always be removed from the work area as soon as it is finished with and put back into its storage area.

Cutting tools

Scissors

Scissors are and will always be the most important piece of hairdressing equipment that you will ever own. Your future income, popularity and success will rely upon this relatively inexpensive item. If you look after them you will be surprised how long a single pair will last. Scissors vary greatly in their design, size and price. There isn't any single way of choosing the correct pair for you; however, there are a number of aspects that you should consider. Scissors should never be too heavy or too long to control; heavy scissors become cumbersome in regular use and if they are too long you will not be able to manipulate them properly for precision, angular work. Long blades are really good for cutting solid baselines on longer hair, but a real nuisance for deft work around hairlines and behind ears!

Paul Falltrick for Matrix

To judge a pair of scissors' balance and length, put your fingers in the handles as if you were about to use them. When the scissors are held correctly the pivotal point should just extend beyond the first finger. This allows the blades to open easily and means that the thumb is in an ideal position to work them.

Cutting comb

Get into the habit of only using quality cutting combs. You will find that by spending only a little more you will get so much more out of them. The design of a cutting comb for hairdressing is different to that of barbering.

Types of scissors   Photo courtesy
Goldwell UK

The hairdressing cutting comb is parallel throughout its length whereas the barbering comb is tapered. There are two sorts of cutting comb. The first and by far the most popular has two sets of teeth, one end to the middle is fine and close together the other end is wider and further apart. This allows you to do fine sections on fine hair and wider sections on coarser hair. The second type of cutting comb has uniform teeth throughout the length of the comb.

The length of cutting combs varies greatly. Again, what's best for you depends on the size of your hands and what you can manage and manipulate quite easily. The normal length of a cutting comb is around 15 cm but longer ones are now very popular and give a better guide for cutting baselines, these can be 2 or 3 cm longer. The quality of combs and the materials they are made from varies greatly. The best-quality combs are made from plastics that have the following properties:

Large cutting comb   Denman

Barbering comb   Denman

- They are very strong but flexible; the teeth do not chip or break in regular use.

- They remain straight in regular use and do not end up looking like a banana after a couple of weeks!

- They are constructed by injection moulding and do not have sharp or poorly formed edges (as opposed to combs that are made from pressings and have flawed seams).

- They are resistant to chemicals making them ideal for cleaning, sterilisation and colouring (as they will not stain).

- They have anti-static finishes that help to control finer hair when dry cutting.

REMEMBER

Use quality combs

The comfort of quality combs and in particular cutting combs is the most important factor. *Your professionalism will be inferred from the comb that you use.* There is nothing worse than using cutting combs on clients when each time you take a section you scrape and scratch the client's scalp!

You will also find that, in regular use, if you persist in using cheap combs your hands will become sore as the teeth will scratch you when you pass the comb into your hand on every section that you take!

Thinning scissors

Thinning scissors have either one or two serrated blades. These will remove bulk or density from the hair depending on the way in which they are used. This has two useful applications for cutting:

1 the tips of finely serrated scissors provide a quick way for texturising the perimeter edges of hairstyles;

2 the whole blades can be used for removing weight from sections of hair but closer to the head.

REMEMBER

Never keep scissors in your pockets: it is unhygienic but, more importantly, it is a dangerous thing to do.

Thinning scissors   Paul Falltrick for Matrix

Scissors with both blades serrated will remove hair more quickly than those with serrations on just one side, and this is more noticeable on scissors that have broader notches in them as opposed to fine teeth.

Razors

Clippers   Wella

The open or 'cut-throat' style razor used to be made out of a single steel blade which was hinged and closed into a protective handle.

The modern counterpart for this has disposable blades which can be removed and discarded after use. (Blades are discarded after each client to avoid cross-infection. They are disposed of safely into the salon's sharps box.) Razor cutting is carried out on wet hair and always with sharp blades. Because of the way in which razors are used, razoring should never be done on dry hair as this it will pull and tear the hair even if the blades are new.

Electric and rechargeable clippers

M. Balfre

Clippers consist of a moulded, easy-to-handle body with a pair of serrated cutting blades. The lower blade has a fixed position whilst the upper blade is adjustable to increase or reduce cutting height and moves left to right and back again several times per second. Generally, these are used for short, graduated styles and can be used on either wet or dry hair. They can be used in a **scissor over comb** technique but more often they are used with plastic attachment grades which enable them to be used safely in cutting hair to a uniform layered length. These attachments vary the cutting depth from grade 1 (extremely short) to grade 8 (around 2 cm), the most popular lengths for men's hairdressing being grades 2–4.

Clippers need to be cleaned, checked and maintained each time they are used. When clippers have been used on wet hair they will often trap small fragments of hair between the blades and teeth. This macerated hair must be removed for hygiene and performance reasons. In addition to cleaning, the blades need to be oiled and maintained regularly otherwise corrosion will set in and impair the blade's ability to glide properly. This causes friction, heat and eventually the blades will seize up and stop working all together!

(With the electric clippers removed from the power supply or rechargeable clippers 'run-down'.)

Knowing how to remove, replace and maintain the clipper blades is an essential part of hairdressing.

Get your supervisor to show you how the lower blade-retaining screws are undone and removed. This will give you access to both cutting blades and the area below the armature (the vibrating arm that works them) for cleaning purposes.

When you have dismantled the blades get used to checking for signs of corrosion. If a rusted area exists it will look like blackened areas around the blade edges. If blades have been allowed to get to this stage they should be replaced by new ones as their ability to cut cleanly without friction has been greatly reduced.

With the blades stripped down, you can now use clipper oil to lubricate the two blades, wiping any excess away. Now you can replace the blades (the right way up) and partially re-tighten then retaining screws.

Finally, readjust the alignment of the blades and tighten the screws. Check the alignment once more: the lower cutting blade should extend around 3 mm further than the upper cutting blade with the clippers adjusted fully forwards to the shortest cutting length.

Hand them back to your supervisor so that your maintenance can be checked.

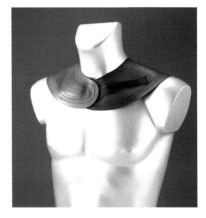

Denman

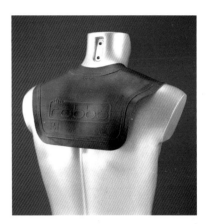

Denman

Neck brushes, water sprays and sectioning clips

Neck brushes will remove loose hair clippings from around the neck and face. Get used to passing the neck brush to your client when you are cutting dry hair as the small fragments are irritating when they fall onto the face. Neck brushes usually have synthetic bristles and these are easily washed and dried before they are used.

Water sprays are used for damping down dry or dried hair, to assist you in controlling the haircut. Stale water is unhygienic, so make sure that the water is emptied out and refilled on a daily basis.

Sectioning clips are usually made from plastic or thin alloys. They are used to divide the hair and keep bulk out of the way whilst you work on other areas. They are sterilised by immersing them into Barbicide solution for the manufacturer's recommended length of time.

Neck brush   Cricket

Safe use of electrical equipment – the dos and don'ts

Do	Don't
Do check the plugs and leads to make sure they are not loose or damaged before they are used	Use electrical equipment with wet hands
Do replace equipment after every time it is used	Use any piece of equipment for any purpose other than that for which it was intended
Do unravel and straighten the leads properly before use	Ravel up leads tightly around the equipment, it could work the connection loose
Do switch off electrical items when they are not in use	

Cleaning plastic and rubber cutting tools

- Never use dirty or damaged tools. Germs can breed in the crevices and corners and can cross-infect other clients.
- Clean or wipe all tools before disinfecting or sterilising.
- Cutting collars should be washed and dried before use.

Cleaning other cutting tools

- Some disinfectants can corrode metal and blunt edges. Check the manufacturer's instructions before using them.
- If corrosion or rusting occurs the equipment is rendered unsafe. Always make sure that this doesn't happen.
- Take special care when cleaning and lubricating scissors.
- All repairs should be carried out by professional people. Do not attempt to undertake them yourself.

Hair: Lawrence Anthony Team; photography: Pat Mascolo; make-up: Pat Mascolo

What you do if you accidentally cut a client

- Put on protective gloves first!
- Apply a small amount of pressure with a sterilised dressing to stem the flow of blood.
- Call for your first aider to attend immediately.
- Complete the details in the accident book explaining fully what has happened.
- Dispose of any blood-contaminated materials safely and hygienically.

ACTIVITY

Scissor cutting can be done on wet hair or dry hair, so what are the benefits?

Q1 List the reasons for choosing to cut dry hair.

Q2 List the reasons for choosing to cut wet hair.

Accurate sectioning

Having made the previous considerations of safety, care and the hair design aspects, you are almost ready to start cutting. The only other thing that you need to consider is how you tackle all that hair, when parts of it can easily get in the way whilst you work. Very short hair doesn't really pose any problem but sectioning isn't just for those with very long hair.

In order for you to be able to manage sizeable amounts of hair at any one time, you must organise and plan the haircut. The planning bit becomes automatic; it's the few moments that you spend thinking:

- How do I go about this?
- Where do I start?
- What is the finish going to be like?

So, if the planning is automatic it's the organisation bit that you have to address. Quite simply, being organised is working in a methodical way. It is the way in which you routinely start at one point; divide all the rest of the hair out of the way, finish that bit, then take down the next part to work on, and so on. Each part or section that you work on should be small enough for you to cope with, without losing your way and continuing on blindly! It seems a strange term to use, but 'blindly' is exactly the right word. If the sections are too deep or too wide you will not be able to see the cutting guide that you need to work to. Accurate sectioning guarantees that every cut is addressed to the same length every time.

CUTTING AND STYLING TECHNIQUES

Club cutting

This is the method of cutting hair bluntly straight across. It systematically cuts all the hair, at an angle parallel to the first and middle finger, to the same length. It is the most popular technique and often forms the basis or first part of a haircut, before other techniques are employed.

Club cutting is used in both layered and **one-length cuts** and is therefore a particularly suitable choice for maintaining or creating bulk and volume. It is an ideal way to cut finer hair types or for use with people who have sparser (less dense) hair.

Freehand cutting

Freehand cutting is mainly used on straighter hair for creating the profile or perimeter shape. The technique is used on straighter hair because curlier hair needs more control, through holding and tensioning, if you are to make

Hair: Stella Lambrou, The Crib, Lytham; make-up: Lynsey Alexander; photography: Emma Hughes; styling: Stuart Well

Mahogany

Holding with an even tension.
Paul Falltrick for Matrix

Cutting with the scissor blades parallel to the fingers.
Paul Falltrick for Matrix

A completed 'club cut' section.
Paul Falltrick for Matrix

an accurate cut. As the name suggests, freehand cutting relies upon one hand holding and combing the hair into position, and the other controlling the scissors to make the cut. More often than not, when cutting longer, one-length hair, the comb is used to create the guide for making the cut.

This technique is more widely used in cutting fringes though. Adults with fringes are particularly cautious about what the exact finished length should be. Therefore it is easier to comb the length into position and create a profile shape that both suits the client and follows or covers the eyebrows. This would be guesswork if the hair were held between the fingers and cut, because the width of your fingers would obscure the exact length and position you are trying to cut.

Freehand cutting using the comb to hold the hair.   Paul Falltrick for Matrix

Rechecking the accuracy of the line.
Paul Falltrick for Matrix

A completed freehand 'club cut' section.   Paul Falltrick for Matrix

Scissor over comb

Hair: Sacha New, Wickham Hair Studio

This technique has been traditionally a barbering technique. In recent years there has been a move in hairdressing generally towards easier-to-manage hairstyles, so therefore this technique is widely used in hairdressing for cutting short styles on both men and women.

Scissor over comb cutting is ideal for producing contoured, layered shapes and close-cut, 'fade-out' perimeters. Faded or graduated perimeters have no set cut length (i.e. baseline); they rely upon the hairline profile and are graduated out from that into the rest of the hairstyle. The technique is used with either wet or dry hair as it uses the comb as a guide instead of the fingers.

Clipper over comb

Clipper over comb involves exactly the same technique as scissor over comb; instead of using scissors the clippers whisk away the hair. Again, this technique enables you to cut hair far closer than you would be able to if you were holding it between your fingers.

REMEMBER	

Cutting combs used for scissor over comb need to be very flexible. You may want to buy a barbering, tapered comb as this makes cutting easier and quicker.

This does not apply to clipper over comb techniques. Because of the weight and bulkiness of electric clippers it is easier to use a standard parallel cutting comb.

Thinning

Thinning is a technique which can done with scissors or a razor and can be used for reducing bulk from thicker hair without reducing the overall length, or as a way of texturising the profile of hairstyles to remove lines and angular shapes to create softer, faded, more ambiguous effects.

Point cutting with thinning scissors.
Paul Falltrick for Matrix

Removing the bulk from the ends.
Paul Falltrick for Matrix

Maintaining the same cutting angle throughout the technique.
Paul Falltrick for Matrix

Finally removing any definition to the previously club cut lengths.
Paul Falltrick for Matrix

Razor tapering.
Paul Falltrick for Matrix

Removing weight from the ends.
Paul Falltrick for Matrix

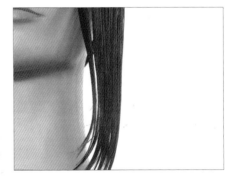

The tapered effect.
Paul Falltrick for Matrix

Pointing/point cutting

Point cutting or pointing is a technique where the angle of the cut changes to become almost parallel with the held hair. It is a way of reducing lines and bulk from the ends (1–2 cm) of the hair in order to create softer, more textured edges. It uses the point ends of the scissors and is more successful on straighter hair than wavy; it does not add any value to curly hairstyles at all. If curlier hair is point cut it can often make it more difficult for the client to manage: the hair would lose perimeter density and the curl would increase, making the hair fluffier.

Note the scissor position, parallel to the held lengths.   Paul Falltrick for Matrix

Point cutting to 'shatter' the club cut lengths.   Paul Falltrick for Matrix

Continue the technique until the weight is removed.   Paul Falltrick for Matrix

Removing mid-length hair with the point of the scissors.   Paul Falltrick for Matrix

Brick cutting

Brick cutting is similar to point cutting in that it only uses the point ends of the scissor blades, but is intended to remove 'fine chunks' of hair from the mid-length and nearer the root of hand-held sections. Its main advantage is when cutting shorter hair to create stiffer sections that support the outer hair perimeter shape. Put another way, it can produce volume whilst creating spikier edges.

Change positions within the length to avoid any cutting lines.

Paul Falltrick for Matrix

Weight reduces quickly.

Paul Falltrick for Matrix

The tapered effect.   Paul Falltrick for Matrix

Slicing

Slicing is a technique for either very sharp scissors or razors. Slicing will produce a tapering effect in a hair section without reducing the overall length. It is always done with the hair held at an angle slightly downwards. The scissors or razor is introduced to the hair nearer the root and then, in one continuous and angled, downward motion, it takes a longer slice out and towards the ends of the held hair.

The finished effects will produce 'shattered' looks with irregular, tousled appearances that can be dressed with product to create texture and definition.

Positioning the scissors safely away from the fingers.   Paul Falltrick for Matrix

Scoop away the hair without totally closing the blades.   Paul Falltrick for Matrix

The final part of the movement.
Paul Falltrick for Matrix

Holding the section.
Paul Falltrick for Matrix

Offer the razor to the hair almost parallel to the angle of the hair.
Paul Falltrick for Matrix

Draw down the razor, through the held section.   Paul Falltrick for Matrix

Continue the action further down the section.   Paul Falltrick for Matrix

The tapered effect achieved by the razor.   Paul Falltrick for Matrix

Hair: Stella Lambrou, The Crib, Lyham; make-up:
Lynsey Alexander; photography: Emma Hughes;
styling: Stuart Well

Controlling the shape

There are only two aspects of cutting that you must get right on every haircut:

- *the holding angle* – the angle at which the hair is held out from the head
- *the cutting angle* – the angle at which the scissors, razor etc. cuts the hair.

That doesn't seem much to guarantee success, but it does take a lot of practice and concentration. Even if you start well in the haircut you cannot afford to lose it in the closing stages.

| REMEMBER | |

The most important factor in cutting hair
Very few people can do two things at the same time! You will have to learn very quickly that you need to hold a conversation with the client without losing your way and concentration on the haircut. This is the biggest single cause of poor quality hairdressing! (If you cannot do this yet, tell your client that you need the time to focus on the task ahead. Believe it or not, they won't mind.)

| ACTIVITY | |

Write down in your portfolio the meanings of the following cutting terms:

Tapering
Texturising
Graduation
Scissor over comb
Reverse graduation
Clubbing

Cutting lines – Or perimeter lines are the outline shape created when layered hair is held directly out (perpendicular) from the head. The curves and the angle in relation to the head, determines the shape of the cut style. The main ones are:

- the contour of the shape from top to bottom
- the contour of the shape around the head, side to side.

Cutting guides – Are prepared sections of hair that control the uniform quality of the haircut. When the cutting guide is taken and first cut, it is to this length and shape that all the other following sections relate. In preparing this cutting guide you need to take all the client's physical features and attributes into consideration, i.e. eyes, eyebrows, nose, bone structure, head shape, neck length, hairlines etc.

Cutting the lines and angles – Comb the hair and hold the sections with an even tension. The position in which you hold and cut the hair determines the position the cut sections take when combed back on the head. The angles and lines of cutting depend on the different lengths required by the style. The first cutting line – the outer perimeter line – may be related to the nape (when starting at the back). The second cutting line – the inner perimeter line – depends on the different lengths required throughout the style.

The angle required to graduate the profile. Paul Falltrick for Matrix

Offer the razor to the hair. Paul Falltrick for Matrix

Draw down whilst holding the hair firmly. Paul Falltrick for Matrix

The graduated outline. Paul Falltrick for Matrix

REMEMBER ✔

Always ask how much the client wants cut off.

- A trim is a trim, in other words a **reshape** or reshaping cut, whereas a different or new cut is a **restyle** or restyling cut (if the client is not used to these words explain the difference).

- An inch to one person may be a centimetre to another. Don't be ambiguous, find out exactly how much needs to be cut off!

REMEMBER ✔

Far more customers are dissatisfied as a result of the stylist not listening and taking too much off than because of poor or inaccurate haircuts.

Before the cut – checklist

✓ Communicate with your client and interpret their requests.

✓ Examine the hair – its type, length, quality, quantity and condition.

✓ Explain whether requests can or cannot be carried out.

✓ After further discussion, agree with the client exactly what is to be done.

✓ Try to show the hair length to be removed.

✓ Discuss the time that will be taken and the price that you will charge.

✓ Proceed only when all checks have been made and the client has agreed to your proposals.

✓ Ensure that you choose the correct tools and techniques: scissors for club cutting, razors for tapering and texturising, castle serrations for texturising, and so on.

Step-by-step: Short hair cut – uniform layers

1 Divide the back of the hair vertically, into two even halves.

2 Now section the hair horizontally above the nape to reveal a perimeter baseline section.

3 Cut the perimeter baseline section to the required length.

4 Take a horizontal section 5 cms above this.

5 Now holding the centre section out perpendicular from the head, cut the section parallel to the contour of the head. This creates your cutting guideline which is used on the adjacent sections.

6 Continue this on the next section further up and parallel to the back of the head.

7 When the back has been completed, cross-check the layering to see that it is even from side to side.

8 Moving on to the sides, cut the perimeter baseline shape.

9 Take the next section up and horizontally through to the front hairline.

10 Join your previously created guideline from the back, with part of this new section and cut this to the same length and angle.

11 Continue these sections horizontally up the side.

12 Repeat steps 8–11 on the other side, to create a symmetrical shape. Cross-check the symmetry of the layering.

13 Lifting up the pre-cut crown section, join this cutting guideline to the top section of the head and cut to the same length. Continue forwards over the top, to the front.

14 Trim the profile hair into shape around the sides, leaving sufficient hair around the recession area, completing the shape around to the front.

Steps 1–3: Cutting the perimeter length.

Steps 4–5: Hair is held perpendicular to the head.

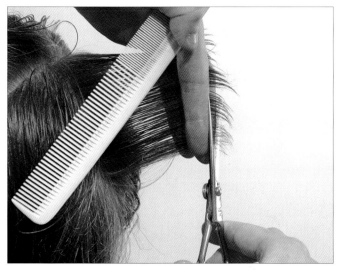

Step 6: The cutting angle is parallel to the holding angle.

Step 7: Cross-checking the layering.

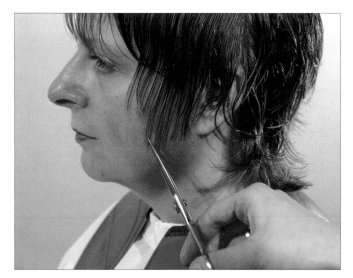

Step 8: Cutting the profile perimeter length.

Steps 9–10: Creating a new cutting guideline by blending in from the back layering.

Steps 11–12: Layering through from the top.

Step 13: Continuing forwards to the front.

Step 14: Maintaining the length of the fringe.

Final effect.

Step-by-step: Short hair cut – graduation

1 Divide the back of the hair vertically, into two even halves.

2 Now section the hair horizontally above the nape to reveal a perimeter baseline section and cut to the required length.

3 Take a horizontal section 5 cms above this.

4 Now holding the centre section out from the head, cut at an angle to the head. This creates your cutting guideline.

5 Continue this on to the adjacent sections and cut at the same angle.

6 When all of the back section has been completed, cross-check for accuracy and symmetry.

7 Moving on to the sides: take a horizontal section, above the ears forward to the hairline.

8 Cut the perimeter baseline shape.

9 Take the next section up and horizontally through to the front hairline.

10 Join your previously created guideline from the back, with part of this new section.

11 Continue the cut to the same length and angle.

12 Continue these sections horizontally up the side to the parting.

13 Repeat steps 7–12 on the other side, to create a symmetrical shape. Cross-check the symmetry of the graduation.

14 Finally, trim the fringe into the profile shape.

Before.

Steps 1–2: Cutting the perimeter length.

Steps 3–4: Hair is held with an even tension.

Step 5: The hair is held out at an angle, away from the head.

Step 5: The cutting guidelines are followed throughout the cut.

Step 6: Cross-check to maintain an even layer pattern.

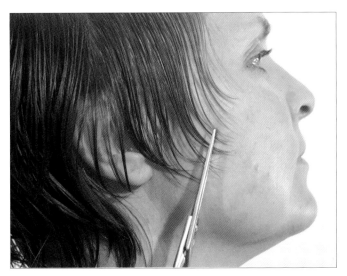

Steps 7–8: Cutting the profile perimeter length.

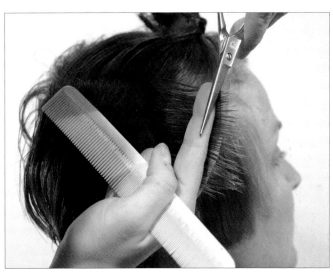

Steps 9–10: Creating a new cutting guideline by blending in from the back layering.

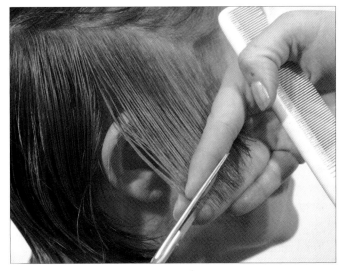

Step 11: Graduating the layers over the ears to create the shape.

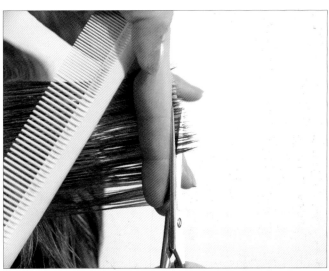

Steps 12–13: Re-check the layering to ensure an accurate finish.

Step 14: Finish off around the fringe.

Final effect.

Good practice, health and safety

It is your responsibility to ensure your client's well-being and safety at all times. First and foremost, cross-infection must be avoided: this requires that you operate hygienically and carefully at all times. All tools and materials must be clean.

- Metal tools should be cleared of all hair and debris. They should be sterilised by being placed in an autoclave for the recommended time, or disinfected by cleaning with 70 per cent alcohol wipes.
- Combs, brushes, plastic section clips and similar implements should be cleared of all hair, then washed and sterilised.
- Towels, gowns, wraps and other coverings must be freshly laundered. Only clean materials should be used on clients; they should then be discarded for washing or cleaning.
- It is important that you follow all the COSHH regulations and meet all other health and safety legislation. See the Health and Safety at Work Act 1974 and the Offices, Shops and Railways Act 1974 in Chapter 5 on Health and Safety.

Step-by-step: Long hair – reverse graduation

1 Divide the back of the hair vertically into two even halves.
2 Now section the hair horizontally above the nape to reveal a perimeter baseline section and cut to the required length.
3 Take a horizontal section 5 cms above this.
4 Comb down your next section to overfall the perimeter and cut to the same length.
5 Take a horizontal section 5 cms above this and now, holding the centre section out from the head, cut at an angle to the head. This creates your graduation guideline.
6 Continue this on to the adjacent sections and cut at the same angle.
7 Extend the section through to the front and fasten the remainder out of the way.
8 Join your previously created guideline from the back, with part of this new section and cut the perimeter shape, graduating it forwards around the face.
9 Take the next section up and horizontally through to the front hairline.
10 Join your previously created guideline from the back with part of this new section; now cut this to the same length and angle.
11 Continue these sections horizontally up the sides.
12 Repeat steps 7–11 on the other side, to create a symmetrical shape. Cross-check the symmetry and accuracy of the graduation.
13 Trim the profile hair into shape around the front and sides to complete the shape.

Before.

Steps 1–2: Cutting the perimeter length.

Steps 3–4: The next section over-falls the previously cut lengths.

Step 5: The reverse graduation showing the angle of the cut and the holding angle.

Step 6: Continue by following the guidelines.

Step 7: Extending through to the sides.

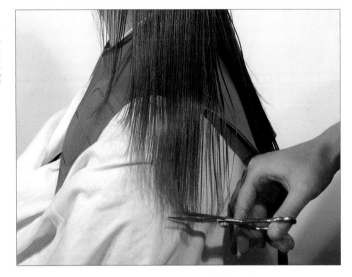

Step 8: Create the graduation around the sides.

Steps 9–10: Joining pre-cut guidelines into the sides.

Steps 11–12: Check accuracy of layering by holding up and cross-checking.

Step 13: Finishing of the profile shape.

Final effect.

During the cut – checklist

✓ To achieve precision cutting throughout, take care to check each angle at which the hair is taken and held from the head.

✓ Before you cut the hair section, be sure that it is at the angle you require.

✓ Your baselines and guideline cuts must be accurate as subsequent sections will be cut in relation to them. Think carefully before you make the first cut, and again before you follow on.

✓ When preparing baselines and guide sections, make sure that you attend to the features of your client's face and head. Use these as guides for accurate directions in the cut lines.

✓ Always check the accuracy of any layers by cross-checking (holding the hair and checking in a horizontal direction as opposed to vertical, or vice versa)

✓ Remember always that the first cuts you make often determine the finished shape of the style.

Step-by-step: Long hair – one length

1 Divide the back of the hair vertically into two even halves.

2 Now section the hair horizontally above the nape to reveal a perimeter baseline section and cut to the required length.

3 Take a horizontal section 5 cms above this.

4 Comb down your next section to overfall the perimeter and cut to the same length.

5 Extend the section through to the front and fasten the remainder out of the way.

6 Join the perimeter length from the back through to the sides to continue the profile shape.

7 Take the next section 5 cms above this to create a continuous shape.

8 Continue this on the other side and on both sides up to the parting.

9 Finally, trim the profile hair into shape around the front and sides to complete the shape.

Before.

Steps 1–2: Cutting the perimeter length.

Steps 3–4: Bringing down the next section.

Step 5: Cutting this section to the same length.

Step 6–7: Extending through to the sides.

Step 8: Comb the hair evenly into place.

Step 9: Finishing the side profile.

Final effect.

Step-by-step: Cut

1 Divide the head into three sections, one at the nape just above the occipital bone, an asymmetrical triangular section at the front and a large section in the middle.

2 Starting with the nape section, comb the hair at 0° and point cut in a v-shape starting from the middle and working outwards.

3 Visually check that you are happy with your v-shape.

4 Continuing in this section, a central vertical section is taken elevating at 90° and cutting square to create softness in the baseline. Working from left to right and right to left, the same section pattern is followed, over-directing to the centre to create heavier corners.

5 Now working into the large middle section, a central vertical section is taken and point cut following the head shape. This section pattern is pivoted around the crown so that it is curved throughout.

6 The asymmetrical triangular section starting from the right side is elevated and cut at 45° to create a layered soft line. Everything to the left of this is over-directed to this point.

7 Having dried and straightened the hair, finish using HY-PACT Protect & Style Paste.

Hair created by the International PACT art team: Chantel Marshall, Harriet White and Andy Smith; photography: Stuart Weston; make-up: Hiromi Ueda.

Before.

Step 1: Pre-sectioned cutting panels.

Step 2: Cutting the profile of the concave perimeter.

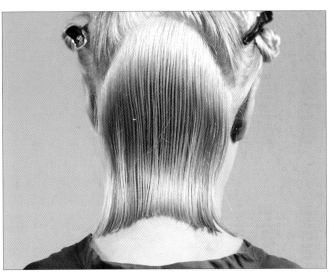

Step 3: The concave shape.

Step 4: Reverse graduation into the perimeter.

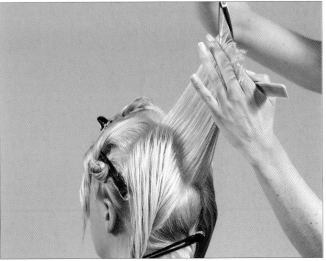

Step 5: Parallel layers up through the back.

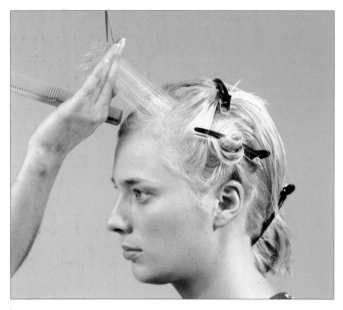

Step 6: Determine the shortest point around the front profile.

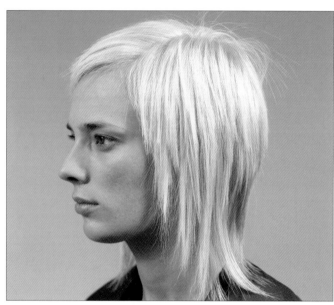

Step 7: Graduation leading up to the parting.

Final effect.

I know and understand the principles of positive communication ☐	I know why clients should be protected from loose hair clippings ☐	I can utilise a range of cutting techniques and know when to use them in my work ☐	I know how the angle at which hair is held and cut is critical to the finished effect ☐
I always carry out working practices according to the salon's policy ☐	I know why I should keep the work area hygienic and clean ☐	I know when and to whom to refer clients, in situations where external assistance is required ☐	I understand the necessity of personal hygiene and presentation ☐
I know how to work with the natural lie and fall of the hair ☐	I know that my posture and the client's seated position is important for accuracy and health and safety aspects ☐	I know how and why I should cross-check the cut during and after the service ☐	CHECKER BOARD ✓

Assessment of knowledge and understanding

The following projects, activities and assessments are directly linked to the essential knowledge and understanding for unit H6.

For each statement that is addressed wholly or in part in these activities, you will see its relevant and corresponding EKU number.

Make sure that you keep this for easier referencing and along with your work for future inclusion in your portfolio.

Project 1 (EKU H6.13, H6.21, H6.22, H6.26, H6.28)

For this project you will need to gather information from a variety of sources.

Close observation of your senior colleagues whilst they work is an invaluable means of learning. At first, cutting hair can be slow and difficult, but with practice this soon changes.

To gather together information on cutting and styling you will need to visit hairdressing demonstrations, exhibitions and competitions. Using photography and video recording is ideal. Practising first cuts, or experimenting with the various techniques, can be carried out on practice blocks, slip-ons and models.

You need to record as much as you can, including the following:

1 Carefully list the movements and techniques that you see and outline the effects produced. Try to capture the positions of the sections taken, the angles of cut, the direction of cutting lines etc.

2 Practise cutting the technique as soon as possible after seeing it.

3 Outline the plan of the cut and list the important factors to consider.

4 How do the different growth patterns affect your cutting? Describe these and try to illustrate them in your notes.

5 Try to describe the different cutting procedures and refer particularly to the different parts of the head – the fringe, sides, nape, top and back. Explain how these parts are blended or fit together.

Investigate other sources of haircutting information: magazines, DVDs, TV. The information you collect could include these items:

- how to choose suitable cutting tools
- the effects produced by the different tools
- how metal cutting tools are maintained and cleaned
- how to select the right tool for the effect required
- the difference between wet and dry cutting, and the tools used for each
- how tools should be used safely
- which razors are considered to be most hygienic.

Case study (H6.15)

Fashions change continually although the basis for haircutting, the techniques that you adopt and tools that you use, generally remain the same. It is the way in which these are applied that makes the difference. The following list encompasses all of the groupings that hairstyles fit into.

Find out what the differences are between them.

● Classic hairstyles.
● Romantic hairstyles.
● Natural hairstyles.
● Dramatic hairstyles.

Show in your portfolio several examples of each, explaining;

● what it is that is different about them.
● how they are achieved

what products, if any, are used to complete the looks.

Questions

1 How do you prepare the client for cutting services? (H6.1)
2 What is your place of work's policy in respect to service timings for different cuts? (H6.2)
3 What is your place of work's policy in respect to safe disposal of sharps? (H6.3)
4 Why do clients need protection from hair clippings? (H6.5)
5 How can you avoid posture fatigue? (H6.6)
6 What are the safety considerations that relate to cutting clients' hair? (H6.7, H6.8, H6.12)
7 What things influence the choice of style for clients? (H6.18)
8 Why are guidelines important throughout the haircut? (H6.23)
9 What is cross-checking and why is it important? (H6.25, H6.26)

Preparing for assessment checklist

Remember to:

☐ prepare clients correctly for the services you are going to carry out
☐ put on the protective wear available for styling and dressing hair
☐ listen to the client's requirements and discuss suitable courses of action
☐ adhere to the safety factors when working on clients' hair
☐ keep the work areas clean, hygienic and free from hazards
☐ promote the range of services, products and treatments with the salon
☐ clean and sterilise the tools and equipment before it is used
☐ work carefully and methodically through the processes of cutting hair whether wet or dry
☐ place, position and direct the hair appropriately to achieve the desired effect
☐ communicate what you are doing with the client as well as your fellow staff members.

chapter 7

COLOURING HAIR

Unit H13 Change hair colour using basic techniques

H13.1 **Maintain effective and safe methods of working when colouring hair**

H13.2 **Prepare for colouring**

H13.3 **Add colour to hair**

H13.4 **Permanently change hair colour**

What do I need to do?

- Take adequate precautions in preparing yourself and the client before any colouring procedure.
- Undertake the necessary tests prior to any colouring procedure.
- Prepare colouring products in readiness.
- Be able to apply a variety of colouring products.
- Be able to carry out a variety of technical procedures.

What do I need to learn?

You need to know and understand:

- why it is important to work safely and hygienically when colouring hair
- how to recognise factors that influence the way that the work is carried out
- a range of techniques and when they are applicable
- the different problems that can occur and the factors that can create them
- the range of products and equipment available for colouring hair.

Information covered in this chapter

- **The types of products used in colouring and how they work.**
- **The basic science of colour chemistry.**
- **The aspects of colouring and colour selection.**
- **A variety of techniques and applications that you will use.**
- **The variety of factors that can and will affect the colouring process.**

Contra-indication   Something that signifies that an adverse reaction has occurred.

Depth and tone   The aspects of lightness or darkness and colouration.

INTRODUCTION

Colouring is arguably the most exciting and often the most difficult aspect of hairdressing. The increasing demands and expectations of clients have made colouring and in particular special colour effects the 'must have' of hairdressing. Our clients are better informed, have a better understanding, are more aware of what's on offer and are often keen to have a go themselves. This has led to a change in salon colouring. The amount of business done by the home colouring market is huge and this has had a particular impact on salon-based work. It is now more technically demanding than ever before, but this new challenge is not a threat. It now enables all hairdressers to be more professional in their role and create the effects that people can only dream about.

REMEMBER

The removal of colour after processing is not as simple as the removal of shampoo during a general wash. If it is done badly, it can leave the hair or scalp in a chemically unbalanced state.

Photo courtesy Goldwell UK

CHECKERBOARD

At the end of this chapter the checkerboard will help to jog your memory on what you have learned and what still remains to be done. Cross off with a pencil each of the topics as you cover it (see page 234).

SAFETY AND PREPARATION

Although the health and safety chapter (Chapter 5) covers much of the general aspects that you need to know, each technical procedure has specific things that relate to that area of hairdressing alone. Hair colouring is particularly problematic as it involves the application of a variety of potentially harmful chemicals. Therefore the care that you take in handling products and preparing yourself and the client is absolutely critical to safe and successful colouring.

Records – Should be found and put ready at the beginning of the day. The appointment book identifies all the expected clients, so all their treatment history – dates of visits, who provided the services, previous chemical services, records of any tests and any addition comments – can all be collated long before the clients arrive.

Tests – Collect together the results of any tests carried out prior to the appointment. If there have been any adverse reactions or **contra-indications** no permanent chemical service can be carried out. Have you made this clear to the client and made plans for alternative services such as temporary or semi-permanent colouring? (For more information on tests see page 199.)

Materials – After the records have been found it is advisable to get all tubes, cans or bottles of colour put aside and ready along with the client's record information. Doing this earlier has several benefits. It can save valuable time later when you need to mix them, particularly if you are running on a tight schedule. But it has useful benefits for the salon's stock control systems too: when products are removed from stock you can see when certain colours are running low. These can be noted and the relevant person made aware.

Gowning – Always make sure that the client and the client's clothes are adequately protected before any process is started. Most salons have special 'colour-proof' gowns for colouring and bleaching processes. These gowns are resistant to staining and are made from finely woven synthetic fabrics that will stop colour spillages from getting through onto the client's skin or clothes. When you gown the client, make sure that the free edges are closed and fastened together. On top of this and around the shoulders you can place a plastic cape. This needs to be fastened but loose enough for the client to be comfortable throughout the service, remembering that this may be over an hour or so. Finally, take a colouring towel and secure around the shoulders, on top of the cape.

Seating position – The chair back should be protected with a plastic cover. If this is not available a colouring towel can be folded lengthwise and secured with sectioning clips at either end. The client should be sat comfortably, in an upright position, with their back flat against the cushioned chair pad.

Trolley – You should have your colouring trolley prepared and at hand with the materials you will need. Foils for highlighting should have been previously prepared to the right lengths and combs, brushes, sectioning clips etc. should be all cleaned, sterilised and ready for use.

You – Your personal hygiene and safety is particularly important. The care you take in preparing for work should be carried through in everything you do and this is made even more important when you are about to handle

Colour cards   *Photo courtesy*
Goldwell UK

REMEMBER ✓

Always follow the manufacturer's instructions when using any colouring products.

REMEMBER ✓

When mixing colouring products, never add colour or developer together by guesswork. The amounts that have to be added together are critical to a successful outcome. Don't take unnecessary risks!

Measuring tools   *Photo courtesy*
Goldwell UK

hazardous chemicals. Put on a clean colouring apron and fasten the ties in a bow. Then take a pair of disposable vinyl gloves and put them on ready for the application.

REMEMBER ✓

Dos and Don'ts

Dos	*Don'ts*
When a client's hair is developing under a Climazon, Rollerball or any other colour accelerator, do check at intervals during the processing to see that they are comfortable and that the equipment is not too hot.	Never handle electrical equipment with wet hands, always dry them first.
Do check the equipment controls so that the timing and temperature settings are correct.	Never leave colour spillages until later. Mop them up straight away while you still have your protective gloves on.
Do check manufacturer instructions before you mix any products, they will give you the recommended amounts and quantities to mix together.	Don't mix up too much product at one time, it is wasteful and expensive. If you need more you can always mix up more when you need it.
Always do a skin test on the client before any colouring process.	Never mix products up before they are needed. Colour products have a set development time and **oxidisation** will start if they are exposed or mixed too soon.
Do put screw tops and lids back on colouring products immediately. Their effectiveness will be impaired if they are exposed to the air for any longer than needed.	Never attempt to do any colouring procedure without the wearing the correct PPE.
Do make a note of low levels of stock as product is removed from storage.	Don't work in a cluttered environment, always make sure that the work area is prepared properly and ready for use.
Do make good use of your time. Always prepare your work area and the materials you will need before the client arrives; this saves valuable time later.	Don't forget to complete the client details/records after doing the service. Make sure that all aspects: dates, times, changes in materials etc. are recorded accurately.

Photo courtesy Goldwell

REMEMBER ✓

Always follow the manufacturer's instructions for mixing the correct amounts together. If the proportions are wrong the colour will be wrong.

REMEMBER ✓

Colouring materials are expensive. The profitability of the job you are about to do relates directly to the amount of colour you use. Always mix a small amount up to work with, if you do run out you can always mix up some more.

Photo courtesy Goldwell

COLOURING – THE PRINCIPLES

Seeing colour

When you look at an object, what you are actually seeing is light reflected from it. White light is really a mixture of many colours – that is why sunlight refracted through falling rain can produce a rainbow. This splitting of white

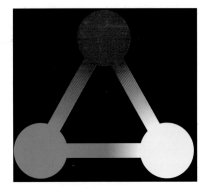

The colour triangle

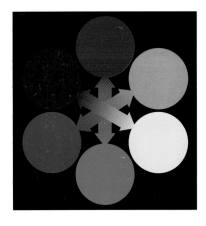

The colour circle

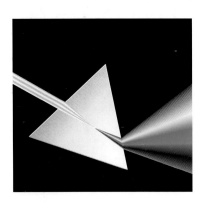

The colour spectrum

light creates what we see as seven different colours: red, orange, yellow, green, blue, indigo and violet.

A white object reflects most of the white light that falls upon it; a black object absorbs most of the light falling on it. A red object reflects the red light and absorbs everything else.

Hair colour depends chiefly on the pigments in the hair, which absorb some of the light and reflect the rest. The colour that we see is also affected by the light in which it is seen, and (to a lesser extent) by the colours of clothes worn with it.

- White light from halogen bulbs and full daylight will show the hair's natural colour.
- Yellowish light emitted from standard electric light bulbs adds warmth to hair colour, but neutralises blue ash or ashen effects.
- Bluish/green light from fluorescent tubes reduces the warmth of red/gold tones in hair.

Mixing primary colours

The colours of the pigments in paints arise from three primary colours – red, blue and yellow. Pairs of these give the secondary colours – i.e red and blue mixed together creates violet, yellow and blue creates green and yellow and red create orange. White and black can be added to vary the tone of the colour.

The primary colours in light are different – red, green and blue. (These are the three colours used in video cameras, computer screens and television.) The secondary colours are yellow, cyan and magenta.

Hair colour (pigmentation)

The natural colour of hair is determined by the colour of pigments within the hair's cortex. These are formed when the hair is in its germinating stage of growth.

Hair colour pigments – melanin – are deposited into the hair shaft at the region of the papilla and germinal matrix. The pigments responsible for black and brown hair are called 'eumelanin'; those responsible for red and yellow hair are called 'pheomelanin'. (There are in fact others, but these are the main pigments.) The hair colour you actually see is affected by the amount and proportion of the pigments present, by the light in which the hair is seen and – to a certain extent – by the colours of the clothes and make-up worn.

With age, or after periods of stress, the production of natural pigments may be reduced. The hairs already on the head will not be affected, but the new ones will. As hairs fall out and are replaced, the proportion that have the original pigmentation diminishes and the hair's overall colour changes. It may become lighter. If no pigment is produced at all, then the new hairs will be white.

The proportion of white hairs among the naturally coloured ones causes the hair to appear grey. Greyness is often referred to as a percentage; for example, '50 per cent grey' means that half of the hairs on the head are white and the rest are pigmented.

It is not uncommon for young people to exhibit some grey hairs – this does not necessarily mean that they will go grey, or completely white, at an early age.

REMEMBER

In vibrant red or bright auburn hair, nearly all the melanin is present in the form of pheomelanin; however, another alpha-amino pigment is present in a complex iron compound called trichosiderin. (In 100 g of red hair, there are 40 mg of trichosiderin.) The trichosiderin changes the colour make-up of hair, giving it the rich, attractive colour of a genetically Celtic origin.

Colouring this particular type of red hair is difficult because of this different pigmentation. Bleaching red hair to a lighter shade is especially hard as this compound is very difficult to remove.

SCIENCE BIT!
DEPTH AND TONE   **?**

We refer to hair colour in the following terms:

Depth = how light or dark it is.

Tone = the colour or hue – ashen, golden, mahogany, etc.

These terms are easier to understand if we tabulate them in the following way.

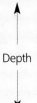

Depth				
Very light				
Light				
Medium				
Dark				
Very dark				
	Ash	Natural	Gold	Copper

Tone

Taking this principle further, the International Colour Chart (ICC) offers a way of defining hair colours systematically (although charts may vary between manufacturers). Shades of colour are divided and numbered, with black (1) at one end of the scale and lightest blonde (10) at the other. Tones of other colours (/1 /9 or also stated as .1 .9) are combined with these, producing a huge variety of colours. Charts are usually arranged with shades in rows down the side and tones in columns across the top. To use them, first identify the shade of your client's hair: that row of the chart then shows the colours you could produce with that hair.

For example, if your client has medium blonde hair (depth 7) and you colour with a copper tone (.4), the result should be a rich copper blonde (7.4). The possibilities are almost endless, as these examples indicate:

- to produce ash shades, add blue
- to produce matt shades, add green
- to produce gold shades, add yellow
- to produce warm shades, add red
- to produce purple or violet shades, add mixtures of red and blue.

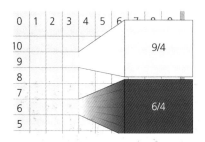

Depths and tones   Wella

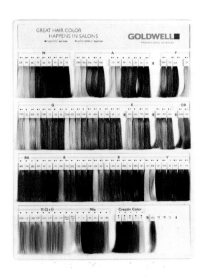

Photo courtesy Goldwell UK

ACTIVITY

Depth and tone – warm and cool shades

The natural 'depth' of hair refers to how light or dark it is, whereas 'tone' refers to colouration e.g. red, blue or green.

Task 1. With your friends and using the salon shade chart, take it in turns to select the nearest natural shade for each of them. Don't make the mistake of looking at the rest of the chart, just keep to the natural bases.

Warm tones are yellow or golden based.
Cool tones are bluish or green based.
What tones are produced from red? Well, that depends on whether the red is orange based or pink based.

Task 2. Again in a group work through your salon's shade chart and for each shade note down its shade name, number or code, then decide as a group whether it is a warm tone or a cool tone.

Save the information from both of these tasks in your portfolio for future reference.

How many warm shades were there?
How many cool shades were there?
How many were neither warm nor cool?
Did you find any surprising results?

L'Oréal – Majirel

	Natural/ Basic .0	Ash .1	Mauve ash .2	Gold .3	Copper .4	Mahogany .5	Red .6	Metallic .7
10	Lightest blonde 10							
9	Very light blonde 9	Very light ash blond 9.1						
8	Light blonde 8			Light golden blonde 8.3				
7	Medium blonde 7	Medium ash blonde 7.1			Deep copper blonde 7.44			
6	Dark blonde 6			Dark golden blonde 6.3	*Dark copper red blonde 6.46*		*Dark red iridescent blonde 6.62*	
5	Light brown 5		Truffle 5.2		Russet 5.4	*Mahogany iridescent blonde 7.52*		
4	Brown 4			Medium golden brown 4.3				
3	Dark brown 3							
2								

In the table above we see how the L'Oréal shades are positioned within the colour table. The three shades 'dark copper red blonde' (6.46), 'mahogany iridescent blonde' (7.52) and 'dark red iridescent blonde' (6.62) are defined in italic as these colours identify additional colour properties. These shades are denoted, as are many others, with having a second number after the decimal point.

Shade	Depth	Primary tone	Secondary tone
Dark copper red blonde	6	·4	6

1 The primary tone denotes the range that the shade is in.
2 Secondary tone indicates the additional colouration within the shade. This provides lots of extra colouring permutations.

Sometimes colour manufacturers want to increase a shade's intensity and vibrancy this is achieved by adding double the tone to the particular shade, doubling the tonal effect.

Shade	Depth	Primary tone	Secondary tone
Deep copper blonde	7	·4	4

Temporary colourants

Temporary colourants are available in the form of lotions, creams, mousses, gels, lacquers, sprays, crayons, paints and glitter dust. On hair in good condition these do not penetrate the hair cuticle, nor do they directly affect the natural hair colour: they simply remain on the hair until washed off.

Temporary colourants are ideal for a client who has not had colour before, as they are readily removed if not liked. They have subtle colouring effects, particularly on grey or greying hair. Hair condition, shine and control are enhanced.

If used on badly damaged or very porous hair, the temporary colourant may quickly be absorbed into the cortex, producing uneven, patchy results.

Semi-permanent colourants

Semi-permanent colourants are made in a variety of forms – some ready-mixed for immediate use, others needing to be mixed and prepared before use as necessary. Always check the manufacturer's instructions to ensure that you know which type of colourant you are going to use.

Semi-permanent colourants contain pigments which are deposited in the hair cuticle and outer cortex. The colour gradually lifts each time the hair is shampooed. Some colourants will last through six washes, others longer.

These colourants are not intended to cover large percentages of white hair – for instance, black used on white hair would not produce a pleasing result. Choose colours carefully.

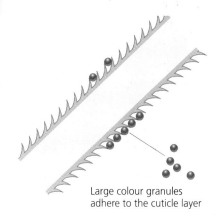

Large colour granules adhere to the cuticle layer

Temporary hair colouring

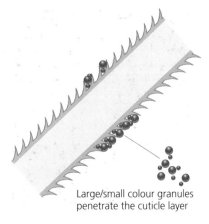

Large/small colour granules
penetrate the cuticle layer

Semi-permanent hair colouring

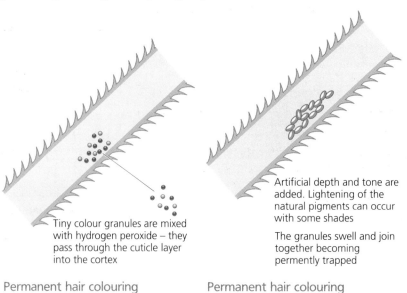

Trolley   Photo courtesy Goldwell/Olymp

Note that some permanent colourants may be diluted for use as semi-permanents. These products may contain skin sensitisers, however, so skin tests must be performed before use in this way.

Longer-lasting colourants

Now that 'frequent use' shampoos have become popular, some semi-permanent colourants are soon removed. A new generation of longer-lasting colourants has been introduced which are more practical and economical. These colourants allow for a greater coverage of white hair and last for up to 12 washes.

Quasi-permanent colourants

Quasi-permanent colourants are nearly permanent – they last for a longer period of time than semi-permanent colourants but not as long as the true permanent colourants. When using them, follow the manufacturer's instructions strictly.

Permanent colourants

Permanent colourants are made in a wide variety of shades and tones. They can cover white and natural-coloured hair to produce a range of natural, fashion and fantasy shades.

Hydrogen peroxide is mixed with permanent colourants. This oxidises the hair's natural pigments and joins the small molecules of synthetic pigment together, a process called 'polymerisation'. The hair will then retain the colour permanently in the cortex. Hair in poor condition, however, will not hold the colour and colouring could result in patchy areas and colour fading.

The use of modern permanent colourants can lighten or darken the natural hair colour, or both together in one process. This is achieved by varying the percentage strength of hydrogen peroxide.

Tiny colour granules are mixed with hydrogen peroxide – they pass through the cuticle layer into the cortex

Permanent hair colouring

Artificial depth and tone are added. Lightening of the natural pigments can occur with some shades

The granules swell and join together becoming permently trapped

Permanent hair colouring

Vegetable-based colourants

As well as being a popular source for conditioning agents, plant extracts have been used as dyeing compounds for thousands of years. These were the only sources of colourants until chemists developed synthetic alternatives. Natural henna (Lawsonia) is still used widely today in many countries and it is used for dyeing skin as well as the hair. Natural plant-based dyes do not present any problems for hairdressing treatments; however, these ingredients are sometimes added to other elements to form compounds. These are mixtures of vegetable extracts and mineral substances. One that is still available is compound henna – vegetable henna mixed with metallic salts. This penetrating colourant is incompatible with the organic chemistry (carbon hydrogen oxygen-based chemistry) items used in hairdressing salons.

Mahogany

REMEMBER

Compound henna is incompatible with hairdressing materials. It should not be confused with natural (vegetable) henna.

Metallic dyes

Metallic dyes are surface-coating colourants. They are variously known as reduction, metallic, sulphide and progressive dyes. These types of dye are also incompatible with chemical hairdressing services and are still found in men's colour restorers; such as 'Just for Men' and 'Grecian 2000'.

Mahogany

REMEMBER

Metallic and compound dyes are incompatible with hairdressing materials. Always carry out a test before using **bleach**, colour and perms on any new clients whom you do not know, or on clients who have been recently having their hair done overseas.

ACTIVITY

Solve the following problems and record your answers in your portfolio:

What could be the reasons for:

1 permanent colour fading on the ends of long hair
2 permanent colour not taking properly on the roots
3 grey/white hair resisting semi-permanent colour
4 permanent copper red colour not taking on mid-brown hair
5 blonde hair looking ashen or green?

COLOUR CONSULTATION

Before you start any colouring treatment there are a number of things that you and your client need to consider:

Colour choice

First of all

What colour would be best to suit their needs?	Should you be using temporary, semi-permanent or permanent colouring?
How can the desired effect be best achieved?	Does the colour need to be applied to the roots first, the mid-lengths and ends, or can it be applied all over? Would the effect benefit more from partial colouring such as highlights or lowlights?
How long will it last?	Will the colour fade off or does it have to grow out?
How much will it cost?	Are there any benefits to the client for changing the type of colour or process in making it last longer?
How will it affect the hair?	Will the long-term effects be what the client expects?
Is the hair suitable for colouring?	Have you tested the hair and skin beforehand to see if there are any contra-indications or hair condition issues that will affect the result?

Now consider

The client's ideas about colouring. How will the colour enhance the style and natural colour of the hair? What are the benefits?

The results of any tests. Examine the hair: does it present any limitations for what you intend to do?

What is the hair condition like? Are there any factors that will change the way in which colouring will work on the hair?

What previous information is available? What do the client's records say? Will this information influence the choice and colour process?

How will you show the effect to the client? Have you got any illustrations of the finished effect? Does the colour chart give a clearer picture of the shade the hair will go?

How long will the process take? Is there enough time to complete the effect? If the nature of the work that was booked has changed, would this now need to be rebooked or do you have the time to complete it still?

Which colour should I use?

Type, PPE and timings	Mixing	Suitability	Effects
Temporary colour PPE – wear gloves and apron. Whole head application done at workstation takes 5 mins.	No mixing required, colour applied straight from the can, bottle etc. as coloured mousses, setting lotions, hair mascara.	No skin test required. Most hair types (including coloured and permed) although it can be more difficult to remove from bleached hair. Colour control – poor, shade guide targeting can only be used as an approximation.	The colour only lasts until the next wash. Subtle toning on grey hair. Hair condition may be improved. Surface colour without chemical penetration. Does not lift natural colour, only deposits.
Semi-permanent colour PPE – wear gloves and apron. Whole head application done at workstation or at basin takes 5 mins. Left on up to 15 mins.	No mixing required, although transference to an applicator may be necessary.	Skin test may be required. Most hair types (including coloured and permed) often used as a colour refresher between permanent colour treatments. Can cover small amounts of greying hair. Colour control – poor, shade guide targeting can only be used as an approximation.	Lasts up to six shampoos. Colour fades/diffuses after each wash. Does not lift natural colour, only deposits. No regrowth, natural colour unaffected.
Quasi-permanent (longer-lasting) colour PPE – wear gloves and apron. Whole head brush application done at workstation, takes up to 25 mins. Alternatively, using an applicator bottle can save time and takes up to 15 mins. Left on up to 40 mins.	Mixed with developer or activators. These can be in liquid or crystal form. Measurement and mixing must be accurate.	Skin test required. Most hair types (including coloured and permed) often used as a colour refresher between permanent colour treatments. Will cover up to 30% grey hair. Colour control – good, will achieve shade guide targeting.	Lasts up to 12 shampoos. Colour fades a small amount after subsequent shampoos. Does affect natural colour, bonds with natural pigments. Can produce a regrowth.
Permanent colour (para dye) PPE – wear gloves and apron. Regrowth brush application done at workstation, takes up to 25 mins. Left on up to 40 mins. Whole head colouring will depend on length and order of application.	Mixed with hydrogen peroxide at either 10, 20, 30 40 volumes (3%, 6%, 9%, or 12%). Measurement and mixing must be accurate.	Skin test required. All natural hair types and most coloured and permed hair (providing hair not too porous or damaged). Will cover all grey. Can lift up to two shades – high lift colour will lift three or four shades.	Permanent colourants or para dyes are made in a wide variety of shades and tone. Long lasting and grows out. Will change natural hair pigments.

Note: All timings are approximated. Partial colouring techniques – highlights, slices, dip ends etc. – may take longer depending on the amount of colour applied and the technique used.

Mixing colour in the bowl   L'Oréal
Professionnel

Photo courtesy Goldwell

Measuring flasks and mixing bowls

Measurement of hydrogen peroxide at any strength must be accurate; the amount used in relation to colour is a critical factor to a successful outcome. Different types of colour are formulated to be used with particular developers. For example, a Wella Color Perfect should be mixed with Welloxon developer. If you use a different developer the consistency will be wrong and this will make the application difficult. All gel and cream colours, when mixed, will be stiff enough not to run drip when either on the brush or on the hair. Using unmatched, alternative developers will do the opposite and could be a potential hazard for the client.

When you measure developer into a measuring flask you must make sure that your eyeline is at the same level as the liquid in the flask. If you do put a little too much into the flask the pouring edge will allow you to put back what you don't need.

When you mix developer with colourant from tubes, you will notice that all tubes have markings on the side showing the $\frac{1}{4}$, $\frac{1}{2}$ and $\frac{3}{4}$ points. These enable you to squeeze from the bottom of the tube up to these points, knowing that your measurement will be accurate.

If you are mixing two or more shades of colour together, always mix these well in the bowl first before adding any developer. This allows the different pigments to be evenly distributed throughout the colour and also throughout the hair when it is applied!

REMEMBER

Never mix colour or put it into a bowl before you need to use it. Permanent colours will oxidise in the air; this expands the colour pigments and they will not be able to enter the hair shaft through the narrow cuticle layers, thus rendering the colour useless.

REMEMBER

- Always gown your client properly so that they are protected from spillages of chemicals.
- Always wear the PPE provided by the salon every time you apply colour.
- Always follow the manufacturer's instructions; never deviate from the tried-and-tested formulae.
- Make sure that your work position is clear and that your posture is correct.
- Make sure that the client is comfortable throughout as they will be sitting for some considerable time.

ACTIVITY

What personal health and safety aspects must you consider before undertaking any colouring treatment?
What PPE must you wear when colouring hair?
What PPE must the client wear during colouring?

Record your answers in your portfolio.

SKIN OR PATCH TESTS

The sensitivity test is used to assess the reaction of the skin to chemicals or chemical products. In the salon it is mainly used before colouring. Some people are allergic to external contact of chemicals such as PPD (found in permanent colour). This can cause dermatitis or, in even more severe cases, permanent scarring of skin tissue and hair loss. Some have allergies, such as asthma and hay fever, to irritants to which they react internally. Others may be allergic to both internal and external irritants. To find out whether a client's skin reacts to chemicals in permanent colours, carry out the following test 24 to 48 hours prior to the chemical process.

Carrying out a skin test

1 Mix a little of the colour to be used with the correct amount of hydrogen peroxide – as recommended by the manufacturer.

2 Clean an area of skin about 8 mm square, behind the ear. Use a little spirit on cotton wool to remove the grease from the skin.

3 Apply a little of the colour mixture to skin.

4 Cover the colour patch with a simple dressing to protect it. Ask your client to report any discomfort or irritation that occurs over the next 24 hours. Arrange to see your client at the end of this time so that you can check for signs of reaction.

5 If there is a positive response – a contra-indication, a skin reaction such as inflammation, soreness, swelling, irritation or discomfort do not carry out the intended service. *Never* ignore the result of a skin test. If a skin test shows a reaction and you carry on anyway, there may be a more serious reaction that could affect the whole body!

6 If there is a negative response – no reaction to the chemicals – then carry out the treatment as proposed.

7 Record the details of any tests on the client's treatment and service history.

A skin allergy test   L'Oréal Professionnel

Incompatibility test

Incompatibility test	When is it done	How is it done
This will show if there are any chemicals present, i.e. metallic salts or other mineral compounds, within the hair that will react against any new proposed services.	Prior to colouring, highlighting and perming treatments.	Place a small sample of hair in a mixture of 20 parts hydrogen peroxide (6%) and one part ammonium-based compound from perm solution. *If the mixture bubbles, heats up or discolours do not carry out the service.*

Elasticity test

Elasticity test	When is it done	How is it done
This determines the condition of the hair by seeing how much the hair will stretch and return to its original length. Overstretched hair will not return to the same length and remains permanently damaged.	Prior to chemical treatments and services. (Ideal for hair that has impaired elasticity, e.g. from bleaching or colouring)	Take a couple of strands of hair between your fingers, holding them at the roots and the ends. Gently pull the hair between the two points to see if the hair will stretch and return to its original length. (If the hair breaks easily it may indicate that the cortex is damaged and will be unable to sustain any further chemical treatment.)

Porosity test

Porosity test	When is it done	How is it done
This test also indicates the hair's current condition by assessing the hair's ability to absorb or resist moisture from liquids. (Hair in good condition has a tightly packed cuticle layer which will resist the ingress of products.) Hair that is very porous holds on to moisture; this is particularly evident when you try to blow-dry it. The hair takes a long time to dry.	Before chemical services. If the cuticle is torn or damaged, the absorption of moisture and therefore hydrogen peroxide is quicker, so the processing time will be shorter. Over-porous hair will quickly take in colour but will not necessarily be able to hold colour as the cuticle is damaged and allows the newly introduced pigments to wash away.	Rub strands of hair between your fingertips to feel how rough or smooth it is. If it feels roughened, as opposed to coarse, it is likely that the hair is porous.

Strand test

Strand test	When is it done	How is it done
Most colouring products just require the full development time recommended by the manufacturer – check their instructions. (However, some hair conditions take on the colour faster than others. A strand test will check the colour development and see if it needs to come off earlier.)	A strand test or hair strand colour test is used to assess the resultant colour on a strand or section of hair after colour has been processed and developed. A strand test is also useful prior to bleaching natural pigments from hair or prior to removing synthetic pigments (i.e. decolour or colour reducer) to see how the hair will respond.	1. Rub a strand of hair lightly with the back of a comb to remove the surplus colour. 2. Check whether the colour remaining is evenly distributed throughout the hair's length. If it is even, remove the rest of the colour. If it is uneven, allow processing to continue, if necessary applying more colour. If any of the hair on the head is not being treated, you can compare the evenness of colour in the coloured hair with that in the uncoloured hair.

Georgia Kokolis/Getty Images

COLOUR SELECTION

SCIENCE BIT!
COLOUR SELECTION

Colour selection, i.e. the process you go through in choosing the right target shade for your client's hair and the correct mixture of products to achieve that target shade, is based upon:

- customer choice (initially)
- current state of your client's hair (i.e. if it has already undergone processes such as highlights)
- current condition of your client's hair.

1 If the hair has been regularly coloured before and there is a clear regrowth, with ends that have faded, you may only need to do a straightforward regrowth application with the same colour. Then, later in the development process, the residual colour can be diluted and taken through to the rest to refresh the total effect. So in this instance a regrowth that takes 20 minutes to apply can be left for 30 minutes' development. Then, in the last 15 minutes, it can be taken through to the ends, until it is ready to be removed.

   However, if your client's hair has been coloured before, you also need to remember that it will not be possible to make the hair lighter by colouring. Permanent colour does not reduce permanent (synthetic) pigments in the hair. (If this is required you will have to use a colour remover first.)

2 If you need or want to counteract and neutralise unwanted tones in the hair, you will need to apply the principles of the colour wheel.

   If the client wants to reduce or 'calm down' unwanted red tones then you will be choosing a colour slightly darker in depth but which has the matt tones capable of neutralising that effect. Conversely, if your aim is to eliminate ashen matt tones (e.g. the colour often seen on fairer hair colours that are regularly subjected to chlorinated swimming pools) then you will be introducing warmer tones to the hair. So in this situation a 'greeny'-looking base 6 blonde will be improved by a shade depth 6 but with a tone warmth .03 (for more information see the section on depth and tone earlier in this chapter).

   If you had to reduce a tonal effect that was too yellow, say on a head that had been lightened, then (although the principle of toning bleached hair is slightly different) you would still be applying the principles of the colour wheel. Therefore a violet-based ash colour should be used to neutralise the unwanted tones.

Mahogany

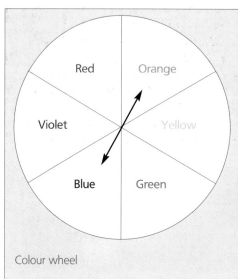

Colour wheel

The colour wheel is set out with the three primary colours: red, yellow and blue. In between these three are the secondary colours: orange, green, and violet. These are a direct result of mixing the two adjacent primary colours.

Red + Yellow = Orange

Yellow + Blue = Green

Blue + Red = Violet

However, a colour's tonal hue is neutralised if it is mixed with a colour directly opposite in the circle. Hence

Red tones are muted by Green

Orange tones are muted by Blue

Yellow tones are muted by Violet

3   If your client has never had any colour on their hair before (**virgin hair**) then colour targeting is easy. Your client will be able to choose practically any shade on the permanent shade chart, providing it is at the same depth or darker. (It is possible to lighten a shade or two with colour in certain situations. See bleaching and lightening section later in this chapter.)

4   If your client has grey or greying (i.e. white) hair then you will have to decide and agree on what reduction of grey is necessary. If the client wants to cover all the grey, then this is only achievable by using or adding base shades to the target colour, i.e. a natural shade or a natural shade plus the target shade.

The amount of base added to the target shade is directly proportional to the amount of grey. Grey hair is referred to as a percentage of the whole head; therefore a client who has about a quarter of their hair that is grey is referred to as 25 per cent grey. Similarly, a client one tenth of whose hair is grey is 10 per cent grey.

So, the formula for mixing base shades works out like this:

- If a client has 25 per cent grey/white then you need $^1/_4$ of the base shade added to $^3/_4$ of the target shade.

- If a client has 50 per cent grey/white then you need $^1/_2$ of the base shade added to $^1/_2$ of the target shade.

- If a client has 75 per cent grey/white then you need $^3/_4$ of the base shade added to $^1/_4$ of the target shade.

SCIENCE BIT!
WHITE HAIR

?

White hair is usually coarser in texture to naturally pigmented hair and this often presents a problem for colouring and styling. White hair is more resistant to colour, so a strand test is one way determining whether the colour will work. (In some situations the hair may need pre-softening before permanent colouring. See below.)

The hair is white because the melanocytes stop producing the natural pigments that give hair its depth and tone, but no one really knows why this happens. The lack of pigment is often accompanied by an overproduction in the hair's 'extrusion process'. More material is pushed up through the hair follicle and this tends to change the shape of this tube as the hair is forced through. (If you review the section on different hair types you will see that hair which has a cross-section that is circular as opposed to oval has a tendency to be straighter.)

Now, taking these factors into consideration, white or grey hair which is coarser than the naturally pigmented hair tends to stand away from the hair too. When people see these growing in areas that are more conspicuous – near the front and in the parting area – they often pluck them out and this exacerbates the problem further. When the follicle is empty it then collapses and distorts and, at the point where the new anagen growth starts again, we find the white hair now spirals away from the scalp in a frizzier texture than before!

Check it out with your own clients. If you have a client with spiralled, frizzy white hair an inch or two long standing away from beautiful darker hair, ask them if they have ever plucked their grey ones out.

Pre-softening white hair

Pre-softening is done as a preparation for colouring difficult white/greying hair.

In situations where there is a significant amount of white hair to be coloured, it is advisable that the hair be prepared by pre-softening. Resistant white hair often has a shiny or glassy look and this is due to the cuticle layer being packed down tightly in a closed, flat position. If you were to apply a permanent colour to this you would find that the colour would have a shadowed or faded look and you would still see the ashen grey underneath. To stop this from happening you need to pre-soften the hair.

How to pre-soften white hair:

1 Pour 30 cc of neat 20 volume (6 per cent) liquid hydrogen peroxide into a colour mixing bowl.
2 Apply the hydrogen peroxide to the resistant white hair with a colouring brush.
3 Place the client under a pre-heated hood drier or colour accelerator for 15 to 20 minutes.
4 Alternatively, dry in the liquid peroxide with a hand drier until the hair has dried.

Tinting brush and comb
Photo courtesy Goldwell UK

Now, after the drying has finished, the cuticle layer will have lifted sufficiently for you to be able to apply a permanent colour and it will now deposit properly into the cortex as opposed to lying at or around the cuticle's surface.

Current condition

The hair's existing condition is also a major contributing factor in the way in which it will respond when it is coloured. Hair that is too porous will absorb the colour differently. The porosity of hair is never even along the hair length, let alone across the hairs throughout the head. This is because the porosity of the hair is directly related to areas of damaged cuticle. Areas of high porosity occur at sites along the hair shaft where cuticle is torn or missing. At these points, moisture or chemicals can easily enter the inner hair without cuticle layer resistance. This changes the rate of absorption,

A healthy cuticle   L'Oréal Professionnel

A damaged cuticle   L'Oréal Professionnel

which ultimately affects the final evenness of the colour and the hair's ability to retain colour in subsequent washing etc.

During processing the only other factors that affect the achievement of an even and expected final colour result (providing your selection is correct) are:

- timing
- temperature.

Timing

The level of colour saturation is proportional to the length of time that the hair is exposed to colour. Under-processed hair will not achieve the same saturation as hair that has had full development. The longer that colour is left on, the more density the colour will have.

This can be explained in another way. Imagine that you wanted to redecorate a plain, smooth, white wall. First of all, you choose the colour and shade of paint that you want it to be. Then, after some preparation, you take a brush and start by applying the first coat. When this is dry you look at the colour, only to find that the effect is uneven and patchy. You can see that the tone you wanted is there but it is often thin and almost transparent in places. So you repaint the wall. When this extra layer of paint dries, the saturation of colour is better and more even, but still a little patchy in places. Finally you apply a third coat to the areas that are still patchy and when it dries the colour has an even density throughout. This effect is called 'saturation'; it is achieved by the evenness of the density of the colour throughout the hair.

REMEMBER

If you are in doubt about the timing of colouring always follow the manufacturer's instructions. (For more information on faults and correction see the table later in this chapter.)

Depth	Tone	Density
Lightness or darkness of colour	Range of colouration	Amount of saturation of colour

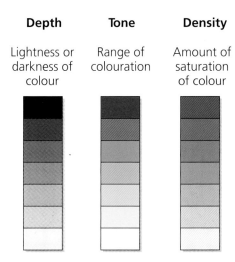

Depth, tone and density

Temperature

Temperature is also a contributing factor to colour development. The warmer the colour environment the quicker the hair will take and we know that when colour is introduced to heat it takes even more quickly. This can be localised to the client or relate to the whole salon. For instance, the salon temperature may be cool but the colour can be accelerated by putting the client under a Climazon or Rollerball.

This is not the only localised factor though: remember that the human body produces heat too. In fact up to 30 per cent of body heat is emitted through the top of your head! (This is why wearing a hat in winter keeps you warm.) This heating effect has a dramatic impact on the development of colour and even more critical when lightening or bleaching!

So with this extra heat around the scalp area, you can see there are potential problems in controlling the colour and aspects of the client's safety. To help control this process you must make sure that, when the colour is applied to the root area, the hair is lifted away from the scalp so that the air is able to

Photo courtesy Goldwell/Olymp

REMEMBER ✔

Health and safety
When the scalp becomes warm during the processing of colour and perms the skin attempts to regulate the overheating by producing sweat. At this point when the skin is moistened by sweat the colouring products become more viscous and spread more easily onto and even into the skin! This is extremely dangerous and will cause scalp burns as chemicals enter the skin through the hair follicles!

Initially, the client will not be able to distinguish between the heat from the processing and the burning sensation from the chemicals. By the time that they do, the longer-term damage is done. Chemical burns continue to act upon the skin long after the colour has been removed. You *must* avoid this happening.

If this does occur, the client must seek medical attention immediately at hospital.

circulate and ventilate the scalp evenly. This ensures that there are no 'hot spots' anywhere that might take more quickly or become a safety hazard to the client.

Colour selection checklist

✓ What is the client's target shade?

✓ What is the percentage of white/grey hair?

✓ What is the difference in depth between the natural hair and the target colour?

✓ If the target shade is lighter than the natural shade, is it achievable by colouring alone?

✓ What colouring products would be needed to achieve the effect?

✓ What developer will be needed to achieve the effect?

✓ If the hair appears porous or porous in areas, do you need to do a test cutting first?

✓ If the hair has a small percentage of white/grey, what amount of base shade will you need to add to the target shade to stabilise the effect?

ACTIVITY

You have a client who has recently been on holiday in a hot country. The hair colour that you applied to her hair beforehand has now faded off. On questioning her, you find out that she has been swimming in the pool every day. You observe that her hair colour has taken on a greenish tone.

1 Why has the hair colour changed?

2 What is your recommended course of action to rectify this problem?

Record this **case study** and your response in your portfolio.

THE EFFECTS OF COLOURING PRODUCTS ON THE HAIR

Temporary colour

REMEMBER

If the hair is very porous the colour produced by temporary colours may be uneven or difficult to remove.

Temporary colours have historically suffered from the belief that they are dated – partly because in the past they were commonly available as setting lotions and colour rinses. This has been readdressed and new products are available. The whole colour concept has been updated to accommodate those clients who only want colour for particular events. Temporary colour remains on the hair until it is washed off. The colour pigments are large and remain upon the surface of the hair unless the hair is very porous. They will not penetrate the cuticle. They are simple to apply, they need no development time and come in many forms including lotions, mousses, gels, creams sprays and colourising shampoos.

Features, benefits and points to remember about temporary colours

Feature	Benefits
Have large molecules and sit on the surface of the hair	Easy to remove as they are washed away during the next shampoo
Come in a variety of types as mousses, setting lotions, gels, creams colour sprays and colour shampoos	Easy to apply as they can either be applied during the shampoo process or alternatively as a styling or finishing product
Come in a variety of shades and colours	Can be used as a fashion statement or alternatively to enhance natural tones by either adding depth to faded hair or neutralising unwanted tones from hair

Points to remember

Only last for one wash

Often difficult to remove totally from hair that is extremely porous or bleached

You cannot lighten hair with temporary colours

You cannot target a shade in the same way as you can with longer-lasting colours

They may not give you an even coverage on the hair

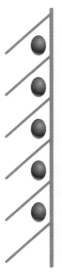

The effect of temporary colour on the hair

Application of temporary colour

1 Make sure that the client is adequately protected.

2 Colour mousses – apply by spreading the foam into a vented-type brush and brushing through the hair until the colour is dispersed evenly and then blow-dry or set the hair to style it in the normal way.

3 Setting lotions – put on a pair of latex/vinyl disposable gloves. Then apply the lotion to the hair evenly by sprinkling and combing until the colour is deposited evenly, then blow-dry or set the hair to style it in the normal way.

4 Colourising shampoos – shampoo the hair in the normal way as the tones will be added during the process. Afterwards the hair can be conditioned if needed.

5 Colour sprays are applied to the hair as a finishing product instead of using hairspray. These are particularly successful for creating a better density of colouring for fashion effects, fancy dress and stage presentations. There could be a potential chemical incompatibility hazard if metallic/glitter type colour spray is used on hair that is then subsequently (i.e. after and not before) coloured or bleached by oxidation processes.

Photo courtesy Goldwell

Photo courtesy Goldwell UK

Semi-permanent colour

Semi-permanent colours are ideal for those people who want to try colour but are not ready yet to take a big step forward into the maintenance of permanent colour effects. They last up to six or eight shampoos and do not produce any regrowth; the hair loses the colour on each subsequent shampoo so the effect fades over time. As part of the colouring package they always contain conditioning agents that add shine and improve style manageability while the colour is deposited on to the hair. They also provide an ideal solution for livening up faded mid-lengths and ends for clients who have permanent colours; this is particularly useful if the hair is not really ready yet for another treatment of peroxide-based colours.

Semi-permanents will colour white/grey hair, although the saturation of colour is relatively poor. The colour range is varied, ranging from fashion effects to many of the shades you would expect to see in a standard shade chart. They are simple to use and require no developer and hence no mixing.

Photo courtesy Goldwell UK

Features, benefits and points to remember

Feature	Benefits
Have large molecules that sit on the surface of the hair whilst other smaller ones penetrate deeper into the hair	A great way to introduce clients to colour without long-term commitment. Fairly easy to remove as they are washed away in six or eight shampoos
Come in a variety of types as mousses, liquids, gels, creams	Easy to apply, require no mixing, take a short time and leave no regrowth
Come in a variety of colours as fashion effects or as standard shade chart references	Can be used as a fashion statement or alternatively as a trial for a permanent colour regimen
Can be used in colour correction work	A simple and quick pre-filler and pre-pigmentation shade
Add tone to white/grey hair	Provides some masking/coverage for unwanted greys
Provide a different alternative to temporary colour	Can provide a colour choice for those people who because of sensitivity or allergy may not be able to have permanent colours

Points to remember

Only lasts for six or eight washes

Often difficult to remove totally from hair that is extremely porous or bleached

You can not lighten hair with semi-permanent colour

Can only colour white/grey hair will not totally cover with 100% saturation

Assimilates permanent shades with far better results than temporary colours

The effect of semi-permanent colour on the hair

Application of semi-permanent colour

1 Check the scalp for any contra-indications of cuts or abrasions.

2 Make sure that you and your client are adequately protected.

3 Shampoo the hair without conditioning, towel dry to remove excess moisture and comb the hair through ready for colouring.

4 Whilst still at the basin, starting at a lower section, secure the remainder hair out of the way and apply the colour directly from the bottle (or alternatively from a mixing bowl with a sponge) evenly to the roots, mid-lengths and ends of the hair.

5 Continue the application by working up and through the sections of the hair until all of the hair is coloured.

6 Remove any stains from around the hairlines with colour remover on a cotton wool swab.

7 Leave for the full development time.

8 Finally, rinse thoroughly without shampooing until the water runs clear.

9 Towel dry and move the client to the workstation ready for the next service.

Quasi (longer-lasting) colour

Quasi colours are used a lot in the home retail sector. They are not true permanent colours but do require the mixing of colour with a low strength developer. They last for at least 12 washes and anything up to 24 and, regardless of advertisers' claims, they do leave a regrowth. These types of colours do have a better ability to cover white/grey hair and this is the main reason why they are so popular as home colours.

Quasi colours, like all permanent colours and lighteners, do require a skin test 24–48 hours beforehand.

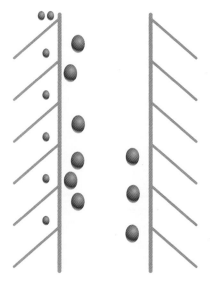

The effect of quasi colour on the hair

Features, benefits and points to remember about quasi colours

Feature	Benefits
Are processed with a developer and have similar molecules that penetrate deeper into the hair	Easy solution for all-over colouring; lasts a long time, generally up to 12–24 shampoos
Come as gels or creams	Require mixing and made easy to apply for home use. Leaves a regrowth
Come in a variety of colours as fashion effects or as standard shade chart references	Can be used as a fashion statement or as an alternative to more permanent based colour
Can be used in colour correction work	As an alternative longer-lasting pre-pigmentation shade
Add depth and tone to white/grey hair	Provide good coverage for unwanted greys
Provide a different alternative to permanent para dyes	Tend to be used regularly and more often than salon-provided treatments
Good conditioning properties, add shine and improve manageability	Useful in salon treatments particularly in partial colouring techniques for refreshing colour between foiled meshes

Points to remember

Always requires a skin test

Lasts for 12 washes, leaves a regrowth

Can only be removed by colour reduction (not removable by colour or bleach)

Often provides the basis for colour correction work if wrongly used at home

Good coverage, colours white/grey with a high saturation level up to 100%

Assimilates permanent para colours very well

Mahogany

L'Oréal Professionnel Diacolor Richesse

L'Oréal Professionnel Diacolor Gelee

Application of quasi-permanent colour

1 Check for any contra-indications from skin test.

2 Check the scalp for any contra-indications of cuts or abrasions.

3 Make sure that you and your client are adequately protected.

4 Mix the products in the applicator as directed in the manufacturer instructions.

5 On dry hair and starting at a lower section, having secured the remainder of the hair out of the way, apply the colour directly from the applicator evenly to the roots, mid-lengths and ends of the hair.

6 Continue the application by working up and through the sections of the hair until all of the hair is coloured.

7 Remove any stains from around the hairlines with colour remover on a cotton wool swab.

8 Leave for the full development time.

9 Finally, take the client to the basin, add water to emulsify and then shampoo the colour from the hair.

10 Towel dry and move the client to the workstation ready for the next service.

Permanent colour

True permanent para dyes are the only colourants that will guarantee to cover white/grey hair with 100 per cent saturation. The colours tend to come in easy-to-dispense tubes as creams or gels which are then mixed with hydrogen peroxide, as the developer, to create lasting effects that have to grow out. Even if the colour used is darker than the natural depth and deposits only, the colour effect will remain until it is either cut or grows.

Typical permanent colour composition

Hair: Desmond Murray; make-up: Xavier; photograph: Thornton Howdle; Assistant: Gemma Adams

Colour composition Ingredients	Contents
Aqua/water	
Cetearyl alcohol	
Ammonium hydroxide	≤4.6%
Oleth-30	
Hexadimethrine chloride	≤8%
Oleic acid	
Oleyl alcohol	≤7%
Pentasodium pentetate	≤3%
Ethanolamine	≤0.7%
p-Phenylenediamine	≤0.5%
Ammonium thiolactate	≤2%
2-Methyl-5-hydroxyethylaminophenol	≤0.4%
4-Amino-2-hydroxytoluene	≤0.4%
p-Aminophenol	≤1%
2-Amino-3-hydroxypyridine	≤1%
m-Aminophenol	≤0.1%
6-Hydroxyindole	≤1%
2-Oleamido-1,3-octadecanediol	≤1%
Resorcinol	≤0.1%
Parfum / fragrance	

L'Oréal Professionnel Majirel

The para dyes contain PPD (para-phenylenediamine). This is a known irritant and it is this compound that necessitates the need for conducting skin or sensitivity tests before any colouring service is carried out. There are other chemicals within para dyes and they all do different things:

- Ammonia/resorcinol is alkaline and when it comes into contact with the hair it swells the hair shaft in preparation for the pigmentation. It also acts as an **activator** for the hydrogen peroxide by releasing oxygen and starting the oxidation process.
- Conditioning agents improve the hair during the colouring process, enabling it to be smoother and shinier as a result.
- During the process hydrogen peroxide oxidises the natural pigments of the hair and this enables the synthetic pigments to bond with them, creating a permanent change within the hair's cortex.

Most permanent para dyes will only lighten hair up a few levels. However, special high lift colours are developed to obtain lift up to four levels of depth higher (although most are recommended for hair at base 6 or higher). The lift potential of colour is particularly important where clients have warm natural tones, as these can be difficult to reduce without leaving residual gold shades within the hair.

The lightening effects of hydrogen peroxide on hair

Hydrogen peroxide strength	Effect upon the hair
20 vol or (6%)	• Assists the deposit of colour into the hair making it darker
	• Enables coverage of white/grey hair
	• Will lighten two levels above base 6
	• Will lighten one level below base 4
30 vol or (9%)	• Will lighten hair three levels above base 6
	• Will lighten hair two levels below base 4
40 vol or (12%)	• Will lighten hair four levels above base 6 (with high lift colour)

Special note: When hydrogen peroxide lightens hair to any level it will reveal the natural undertone or undercoat hair colour. The undercoat colour is dictated by the amount of warm tones (pheomelanin) within the hair. These pigments are oxidised during the colouring process and can produce difficult-to-remove unwanted golden or even orange tones within the hair.

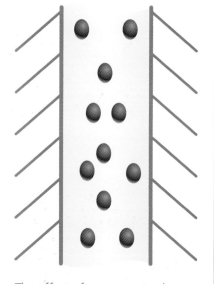

The effect of permanent colour on the hair

Level of depth	Common name	Undertone and visual appearance
10	Lightest blonde	Very pale yellow
9	Very light blonde	Pale yellow
8	Light blonde	Yellow
7	Blonde	Pale straw yellow/orange
6	Dark blonde	Orange
5	Light brown	Red/orange
4	Brown	Red
3	Dark brown	Red
2	Darkest natural brown	Red
1	Black	Red

Levels of depth and their relevant undertones

Diluting hydrogen peroxide

This illustration shows you how the strengths that you have in stock can be diluted to make lesser strength hydrogen peroxide.

The first column refers to the strength peroxide that you have, the second refers to the peroxide you want to create. The last three columns show you how many parts of the peroxide you need and how many parts of distilled water you need to add to it.

Diluting hydrogen peroxide

Strength you have	Strength you want to create	Peroxide	Add	Water
40 vol (i.e. 12%)	30 vol (i.e. 9%)	3	+	1
40 vol	20 vol (i.e. 6%)	1	+	1
40 vol	10 vol (i.e. 3%)	1	+	3
30 vol (i.e. 9%)	20 vol (i.e. 6%)	2	+	1
30 vol	10 vol (i.e. 3%)	1	+	2
20 vol (i.e. 6%)	10 vol (i.e. 3%)	1	+	1

Mahogany

Application of permanent colour

1 Check for any contra-indications from the skin test.

2 Check the scalp for any contra-indications of cuts or abrasions.

3 Make sure that you and your client are adequately protected.

4 Mix the products in the colouring bowl as directed in the manufacturer's instructions.

5 On dry hair, divide the hair in a centre parting from the front hairline to the nape and then subdivide these halves again down to each ear.

6 Secure three of the quadrants out of the way and now apply the colour with a brush to horizontal divisions about 1 cm deep. Now proceed either to number 7, full head application, or number 8, root application). (*Note*: If there are obvious areas of higher resistance e.g white hair these areas would benefit from earlier application.)

M. Balfre

Mahogany

7 Full head application: apply to the mid-lengths and ends of the hair first, allowing this to develop for the recommended time before continuing on to applying the colour at the root area.

8 Root application only: apply to each section at the root area. As you finish each quadrant move on to the next. Finally, check the application around the hairlines.

9 Remove any stains from around the hairlines with colour remover on a cotton wool swab.

10 Leave for the full development time.

11 Finally, take the client to the basin, add water to emulsify and then shampoo the colour from the hair.

12 Towel dry and move the client to the workstation ready for the next service.

Mahogany

> **REMEMBER** ✔
>
> Only work on manageable amounts of hair at any one time. Always secure the hair that you aren't working on out of the way with sectioning clips.

> **REMEMBER** ✔
>
> If you used dry heat to accelerate the development of permanent colours, don't let the heat dry out the products as this will stop the colour from developing further.

Refreshing the lengths and ends

When you are recolouring the roots on longer hair you will often find that the ends of the colour need refreshing too. This doesn't mean that a full head colour is necessary: the refreshing can be done during the application.

Appearance	1st step	2nd step	3rd step	4th step
When the colour looks the same at the ends as the target shade	Apply to regrowth	Allow to develop and then 15 minutes before full development time	Add 15–20 cc of tepid water to the mixture in the bowl then apply this to the lengths and ends	Leave for a further 5–10 minutes, to complete the development process
When the tonal quality has faded but the colour is still the same depth	Apply to regrowth	Allow to develop then 25 minutes before full development time	Add 15–20 cc of tepid water to the mixture in the bowl then apply this to the lengths and ends	Leave for a further 15–20 minutes, to complete the development process
When both the tonal quality and depth has faded on the ends	Apply to regrowth	Add 15–20 cc of tepid water to the mixture in the bowl then apply this to the lengths and ends immediately	Leave all the colour on for full development 35–40 mins	

Colouring problems and corrective measures

Problem or fault	Possible reasons why	Corrective actions
Colour patchy or uneven	Insufficient coverage by colour Poor application Poor mixing of chemicals Sectioning too large Overlapping, causing colour build-up Under-processing (colour was not given full development)	Spot colour the patchy areas
Colour too light	Incorrect colour selection Peroxide strength too high causing bleaching Peroxide strength too low Under-processed Hair in poor condition	Choose a darker shade Check strengths and recolour Check strengths Recolour Apply restructurant
Colour fades quickly	Effects of sun or swimming Harsh treatment: over-drying, ceramic straighteners etc. Hair in poor condition Under-processing	Recondition before next application Process correctly
Colour too dark	Incorrect colour selection Over-processing Hair in poor condition Metallic salts present	Senior assistance required
Colour too red	Peroxide strength too high revealing undertone colour Hair not bleached enough Under-processing	Apply matt/green tones
Discolouration	Hair in poor condition Undiluted colour repeatedly combed through Incompatibles present	Use colour wheel to correct unwanted tones Senior assistance required
White hair not covered	Resistance to peroxide/colour Lack of base shade within the mixed colours	Pre-soften Recolour with correct amount of base and tones
Hair resistant to colouring	Cuticle to tightly packed Under-processed Incorrect colour selection Poor mixing/application	Pre-soften Recolour Senior assistance required Senior assistance required
Scalp irritation or skin reaction	Chemicals not removed from hair properly after processing Peroxide strength too high Poor quality materials causing abrasions to the scalp Client allergic to chemicals	Wash hair again and condition with anti-oxidants Senior assistance required Refer to doctor/hospital

BLEACH AND BLEACHING HAIR

Bleaches are alkaline products for lightening and pre-lightening hair. Similar to para dyes, bleaching products are mixed with hydrogen peroxide to activate the oxidising process, and they are used in two main forms:

- *powder bleach* – which is used for highlighting and partial lightening techniques
- *gel/oil bleach* – which is suitable for whole head applications including the scalp

The alkaline compound acts upon the hair by swelling and opening up the cuticle, this enables the peroxide at six per cent, or nine per cent to release oxygen and oxidise the natural pigments of melanin from within the cortex. This creates oxymelanin and is seen as it reduces the natural colour through the different degrees of lift. (See the bleach toning table.)

The colour control during lightening is not the same as with colouring though. Often when full head bleaching is done the result is quite yellow. As this undertone is the last to be seen in the different levels of lift, bleach is used as a pre-lightener before a secondary process of toning takes place.

This pre-lightening phase is particularly useful for increasing the vibrancy, brightness and saturation of toning to fashion colours, which are sometimes not achievable by colouring alone.

TONING

Level of depth	Tone required	Tonal quality	Pre-lighten to
10	Silver, platinum, mauve/violet	Cool	Very pale yellow
9	Ashen blondes, light beige blonde	Cool	Pale yellow
8	Beige blonde	Cool	Yellow
8	Sandy blonde	Warm	Pale straw yellow/orange
7	Golden blonde	Warm	Pale straw yellow/orange
7	Chestnut, copper gold	Warm	Orange
6	Red copper	Warm	Red/orange
5	Mahogany	Cool	Red/orange
4	Burgundy, plum	Cool	Red/orange

Toning is the process of adding colour to previously bleached or lightened hair. A variety of pastel shades, such as silver, beige, and rose are used to produce subtle effects. Different types of toners are available; read the instructions provided by their manufacturers to find out what is possible.

Cool and warm tones

Our clients' natural skin tones, eyes and hair make a big difference to what hair colour and colour techniques are suitable for them. In the illustration above we see that the warm shade is based upon gold/orange tones whereas the cool shade is more beige or violet. Where we would normally consider red to be a hot shade we see that certain reds, i.e. mahogany and burgundy have cool hues. The reason for this is the colours' basic make-up: a red with an orange or golden yellow base remains warm whereas the same red with pink, mauve or violet base is cool. Regardless of the tonal quality desired, the table denotes the degree of lift required to deposit the tones into the hair.

Choice of bleach

Emulsion bleach

Emulsion bleach is slow acting. It is made up of two compounds that are added together and then mixed with hydrogen peroxide:

- oil or gel bleach
- activators, boosters or controllers.

This type of bleach is specially formulated for use directly onto the roots of the hair, and is suitable for contact with the scalp. It is kinder and gentler during the bleaching process and is mixed with 20 vol. hydrogen peroxide for root, mid-length and ends application. The lift through the undertone shades is aided and controlled by the addition of activators. These boost the power of the bleach whilst maintaining relatively low hydrogen peroxide strength.

Emulsion bleaches also contain additives which control the resultant colour as the bleach lightens the hair. As mentioned earlier, these tend to make hair yellow, so they have matt emulsifiers which neutralise unwanted yellow tones whilst the lifting process takes place. Heat may be used during the development of the process, but the client must be monitored closely as these types of bleach can often be more viscous and mobile and might drip!

Removing emulsion bleach
Make sure that when the bleach is removed you rinse without massaging with only tepid or warm water. The client's scalp has been subjected to chemicals and could be sensitive; the cooling action of the rinsing will stop the bleaching process and make the client more comfortable. After the emulsion has been rinsed away the hair can be shampooed with a mild colour shampoo and conditioned with an anti-oxidising treatment.

REMEMBER

Do not use powder bleach upon the scalp. It is OK for use in meshes and foils but is not recommended for direct skin application.

Mahogany

Photo courtesy Goldwell

REMEMBER

The degree of lift required in emulsion bleach is controlled by the number of activators added into the mixing bowl with the oil. It is not boosted by stronger hydrogen peroxide levels.

Always follow the manufacturer's instructions when using bleaching products.

L'Oréal Professionnel Platifiz

L'Oréal Professionnel Platine

Powder bleach

Powder bleach can be mixed with 6, 9 or 12 per cent hydrogen peroxide, depending upon the level of lift required. Powder bleaches are fast acting and are used for a variety of highlighting techniques. When they are mixed in the bowl the consistency is that of a thick, porridge-type paste. The stiffness of the consistency prevents spillages and enables the bleach to work like a poultice. As the process continues the bleach/peroxide mix will expand. This action is speeded up more if accelerated by heat, so a careful eye should be kept on the development timings.

Removing powder bleach
Again as with emulsion bleach, make sure that when the bleach is removed from the hair you rinse it without massaging, using only tepid or warm water. The removal of powder bleach can be far more problematic than that of emulsion bleach and this has more to do with the colouring technique that has been used. If highlights have been done with Easy Meche, foil, wraps, etc. these need to be removed individually as the overall colour may be affected.

Although the client's scalp has not been subjected to chemicals, it still might be sensitive from the colouring technique; again, the cooling action of the rinsing will stop the bleaching process and make the client more comfortable. Afterwards the hair can be shampooed with a mild colour shampoo and conditioned with an anti-oxidising treatment.

Bleaching service required	What you need to check for:	Technique/application	Bleach type
Whole head (on virgin hair)	Test results: • (Skin tests etc.) Natural hair depth: • Bleaches will lift five levels quite happily on hair with brown/ash pigments. However, strong red content will be difficult to remove. • Hair beyond base 5 will not lift safely beyond base 9. Suggest other colouring options. Hair length: • Lengths up to 10 cm lighten evenly, provided manufacturer's instructions are followed. • Lengths over 15 cm are not recommended, as evenness of colour will be difficult to guarantee. Hair texture: • Finer hair needs extra care and lower hydrogen peroxide strengths i.e. 6%. • Medium and coarser hair presents fewer technical problems. Hair condition: • Only consider hair in good condition for bleaching. (Bleaching removes moisture content during the process, hair that is porous or containing low moisture levels has insufficient durability for bleaching.)	Bleach mixture must be applied to mid lengths and ends first. A plastic cap should envelop the contents and can be developed with gentle heat until ready. When the bleached hair has lightened two to three levels of lift, the root application can be applied. • Always follow manufacturer's instructions	Only emulsion bleach is suggested for application to the scalp. These are used with 6% hydrogen peroxide and sachet controllers to handle levels of lift.

Bleaching service required	What you need to check for:	Technique/application	Bleach type
Full head (on previously coloured)	• Not recommended		
Root application (pre-lightened ends)	Existing client: • Yes, check previous records and current hair condition and carry out service. • No, new client: go through all the checks in the full head application table and find out the previous treatment history.	Roots only without overlapping previous lightened ends. • Always follow manufacturer's instructions	Only emulsion bleach is suggested for application to the scalp.
Highlights (fine even meshes on virgin hair) Note – The success of highlights on coloured hair is very poor in comparison. This work is often undertaken in salons, but ends seldom lighten effectively, whilst the roots lighten very quickly. (Colour should be removed with a synthetic colour remover-decolour)	Test results: • (Skin tests etc.) Natural hair depth: • Bleaches will lift five levels quite happily on hair with brown/ash pigments. However, strong red content will be difficult to remove and require stronger developer and/or additional heat. • Hair beyond base 5 will not lift safely beyond base 9. Suggest other bleaching technique. Hair length: • Hair length will have an impact on evenness of colour. However a small tolerance is acceptable, and 'visually' indistinguishable on longer hair lengths Hair texture: • Finer hair needs extra care and lower hydrogen peroxide strengths i.e. 6% • Medium and coarser hair presents fewer technical problems but generally takes longer. Hair condition: • Only consider hair in good condition for bleaching. (Bleaching removes moisture content during the process, hair that is porous or containing low moisture levels has insufficient durability for bleaching.)	• Plastic self-grip meshes (e.g. Easi-meche™ L'Oréal) • Foil meshes • Colour wraps	High lift powder bleach with suitable hydrogen peroxide developer at 6%, 9% or for highest lift 12% (providing no product is allowed to make contact with the skin/scalp).

Cap highlights

Highlight caps are a simple and popular choice for cost-effective, single-colour or bleached highlights on short layered hair. Even with the application of a single colour a multi-toned effect can be achieved. The reason for this is more to do with the cut and styling though, rather than the introduction of a solitary tone. Highlight caps can produce basic effects, whilst more complex, technically involved, multi-colour effects are achieved through woven techniques.

Step-by-step: Cap highlights

1 Check the quality of the highlight cap. A cap that has already been used for colouring hair starts to wear out. Look for enlarged holes or splits where colour/bleach can seep through on to the hair.

2 Put on your disposable gloves and apron.

3 Mix the products correctly.

4 Ask the client to take hold of the front of the cap, ensuring it is centrally positioned at the forehead. Pull the cap down smoothly, ensuring that it fits and hugs the contour of the head correctly.

5 Starting at the nape area, pull the highlights through by taking enough hair to complete each one in a single movement. Always pull through at an acute (narrow) angle to the cap.

6 Complete the pattern of repeated highlights, i.e. percentage required, all over the head.

7 Carefully apply the mixture to all of the highlights evenly. Lift the pasted hair slightly with the tail of a comb for even ventilation, so that no hair is trapped and can overheat ot overdevelop.

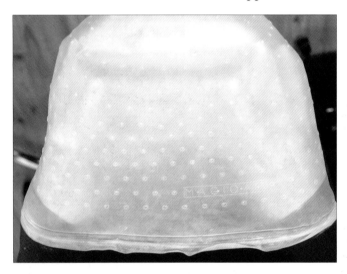

Step 1: Check the cap for worn or torn areas.

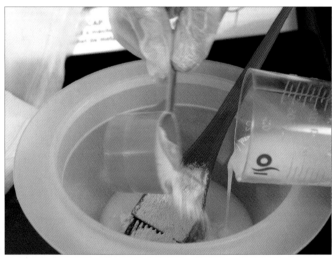

Steps 2–3: Carefully mix the bleach and developer together.

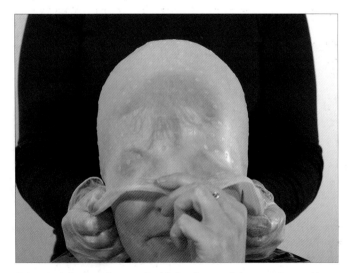

Step 4: Ask the client to hold the front of the cap in position.

Step 5: Start pulling through at the lowest part of the cap first.

Step 6: Check that the highlights are evenly distributed.

Step 7: Apply the bleach evenly to the hair.

Cap highlights

Consultation	– Find out what effect your client is trying to achieve. – How much bleached or coloured hair in relation to natural colour is expected – 5%, 10%, 25%? – How will you explain the effect to the client? – Do you have any visual aids to help? – Explain everything that you are going to do.
Prepare the client	– Make the usual protective preparations. – Brush the hair to examine the growth patterns and to remove any tangles. Look for areas where highlights would be conspicuous or unsightly. – Look for natural part/parting areas; confirm how the hair is to be worn. – If the hair has slightly longer layers or tends to tangle, apply some talcum powder to the hair and work through with your hands. This will help the hair to come through the holes, reducing any discomfort from tugging and picking the sections.
Prepare the materials	– Check the quality of the highlight cap. When a cap has previously been used for colouring it starts to wear. – Look for enlarged holes or splits where colour/bleach can seep through on to the hair. – Make sure that you have everything you need at hand. – Put on your disposable gloves and apron. – Mix the products correctly. – Ask the client to take hold of the front of the cap, ensuring it is centrally positioned at the forehead. – Pull the cap down smoothly, ensuring that the fit hugs the contour of the head correctly.
Pull the highlights through	– Start at the nape area. – Pull the highlights through by taking enough hair to complete each one in a single movement. Always pull through at an acute (narrow angle) to the cap. – Complete the pattern of repeated highlights, i.e. the percentage required, all over the head.
Apply the bleach or colour	– Carefully apply the mixture to all of the highlights evenly. – Lift the pasted hair slightly with the tail of a comb for even ventilation, so that no hair is trapped and can overheat or overdevelop.

Development	– Carefully place a clear, polyethylene cap on, and around the highlights, to stop any spillages and to aid an even development.
	– Monitor the colour development throughout the processing.
	– Apply heat if needed to speed up the development process.
	– Check with the client throughout to ensure their comfort.
Removal	– When processing is complete, rinse thoroughly until all the product is removed (a slight shampoo may be needed).
	– Lift the flanges of the cap into the basin area and remove in one smooth and even pull.
	– Shampoo and condition with an anti-oxidising agent.

Mahogany

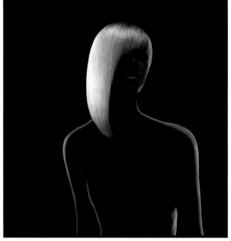

Photo courtesy Goldwell

Woven highlights

Woven highlights in foil, Easy Meche or wraps are the preferred technique for multi-toning hair. The visual effects are unlimited and new exciting colour combinations and techniques are happening each year. The application of this type of colouring is both creative and artistic, and is only limited by the vision that the stylist has.

Photo courtesy Goldwell

ACTIVITY

With your colleagues, each collect from styling magazines a selection of (say six) partial/highlight effects.

Now take it in turns to show the others each of your pictures and then explain how each effect was created, providing the technique, application and colours used.

Record these details along with the relevant pictures for use in your portfolio.

Check your assessment with your supervisor or a senior member of staff.

Step-by-step: Woven highlights

1 Brush the hair to examine the growth patterns and to remove any tangles. Look for areas where highlights would be conspicuous or unsightly. Look for the natural part/parting areas; confirm how the hair is to be worn.

2 Make sure that you have everything you need at hand including cut foils to the required length. Put on your disposable gloves and apron. Mix the products correctly.

3 Divide the hair into 2 equal sections. Start at the back of the head at the nape and divide and section and secure out of the way the remaining hair. Pick up a horizontal section of the hair and, with your pin-tail comb, weave out of the section a mesh of fine amounts of hair.

4 Place underneath the mesh, a foil long enough to protrude beyond the hair length. Apply the colour/bleach to the mesh evenly.

5 Fold in half and half again (possibly fold the edges too, if required). Continue on to next section with the alternating colour(s) or bleach.

6 Repeat up the back of the head and through the sides.

7 Monitor the colour development throughout the processing. Develop with heat if needed to speed up the development process. Check with the client throughout to ensure their comfort.

8 Each foil must be removed individually by rinsing thoroughly until all the product is removed (this ensures that the colours do not run and bleed together). Shampoo and condition with an anti-oxidising agent.

Step 1: Brush the hair to remove any tangles, and see the natural fall and partings.

Step 2: Carefully mix the selected colours and developers together.

Step 3: Divide the hair and secure the bulk out of the way.

Step 3: Weave out of the section the intended highlights.

Step 4: With the foil placed at the root and extending beyond the length of the hair, apply the colour evenly.

Step 5: Fold the foil to 'envelope' the hair so that the colour isn't squeezed out.

Step 3: Continue with the next section and colour.

Step 6: Repeat until all of the head is completed.

Step 7: Colour development under a steamer.

Step 8: Different colours are removed individually so that colours do not run together.

Step 8: Removing the alternative colour meshes.

Final effect.

Woven highlights

Consultation	– Find out what effect your client is trying to achieve. – How much bleached and/or coloured hair in relation to natural colour is expected? What percentage of each is needed 5%, 10%, 25% – How will you explain the effect to the client? – Do you have any visual aids to help? – Explain everything that you are going to do.
Prepare the client	– Make the usual protective preparations. – Brush the hair to examine the growth patterns and to remove any tangles, look for areas where highlights would be conspicuous or unsightly. – Look for natural part/parting areas; confirm how the hair is to be worn.
Prepare the materials	– Make sure that you have everything you need at hand including foils cut to the required length. – Put on your disposable gloves and apron – Mix the products correctly
Method/technique	– Divide the hair into four equal quadrants. – Start at the back of the head at the nape. – Divide the remaining hair and section and secure it out of the way. – Pick up a horizontal section of hair and, with your pin-tail comb, weave out of the section a mesh of fine amounts of hair. – Place underneath the mesh a foil long enough to protrude beyond the hair length. – Apply the colour/bleach to the mesh evenly. – Fold in half and half again (fold the edges too, if required). – Continue on to next section with the alternating colour(s) or bleach. – Repeat up the back of the head and through the sides.
Development	– Monitor the colour development throughout the processing. – Apply heat if needed to speed up the development process. – Check with the client throughout to ensure their comfort.
Removal	– When processing is complete each foil must be removed individually by rinsing thoroughly until all the product is removed (this ensures that the colours do not run and bleed together). – Shampoo and condition with an anti-oxidising agent.

Mahogany

Mahogany

Step-by-step: Regrowth application

1 After the usual protective preparations for the client brush the hair through to remove the tangles. Apply a barrier cream to the hairlines.

2 Make sure that you have everything you need at hand. Put on your disposable gloves and apron. Mix the products correctly.

3 Divide the hair into 4 equal quadrants. Start the application with a brush to the roots at the top of the head, working down and along each quadrant.

4 Pick up a horizontal section of hair within a back quadrant and with the tail of the brush. Apply the colour/bleach to the regrowth evenly.

5 Repeat down the back of the head and through the sides. Monitor the colour development throughout the processing. Apply heat if needed to speed up the development process.

Step 1: Brush the hair to remove any tangles, and see the natural fall and partings.

Step 2: Carefully squeeze out the required amount of colour.

Step 2: Now measure the correct amount of developer.

Step 3: Section the hair into four quadrants.

Step 4: Start the root application at the top of the quadrant.

Step 5: Work down and through each of the quadrants.

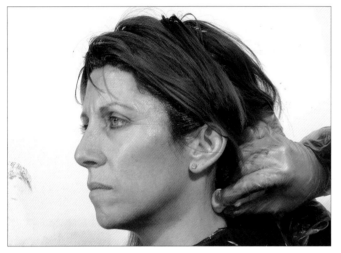

Step 5: Remove any colour from the hairline to prevent staining.

Final effect.

Regrowth application

Consultation	– Find out what needs to be done. – Are there any modifications needed to do the regrowth?
Prepare the client	– Make the usual protective preparations. – Brush the hair through to remove the tangles. – Apply a barrier cream to the hairlines.
Prepare the materials	– Make sure that you have everything you need at hand. – Put on your disposable gloves and apron. – Mix the products correctly.
Method/technique	– Divide the hair into four equal quadrants. – Start the application with a brush to the roots at the top of the head, working down and along each quadrant. – Pick up a horizontal section of hair within a back quadrant and with the tail of the brush. – Apply the colour/bleach to the regrowth evenly. – Repeat down the back of the head and through the sides.

Development	– Monitor the colour development throughout the processing.
	– Apply heat if needed to speed up the development process.
	– Check with the client throughout to ensure their comfort.
Removal	– When processing is complete, take the client to the basin and rinse the hair with tepid/warm water to emulsify the colour.
	– Rinse thoroughly until the colour is removed.
	– Shampoo and condition with an anti-oxidising agent.

Step-by-step: Full head application

1 Make sure that you have everything you need at hand. Put on your disposable gloves and apron. Mix the products correctly.

2 Divide the hair into four equal quadrants. Start the application with a brush to the mid-lengths to ends at the top of the head, working down and along each quadrant.

3 Pick up a horizontal section of hair within a back quadrant and with the tail of the brush. Apply the colour/bleach to the mid-length and ends evenly. Repeat down the back of the head and through the sides.

4 First part of development: allow the mid-length and ends to develop sufficiently first. Monitor the colour development throughout the processing. Apply heat if needed to speed up the development process. Check with the client throughout to ensure their comfort.

5 Second part of development: pick up each of the horizontal sections of hair with the tail of the brush. Apply the colour/bleach to the regrowth evenly. Repeat down the back of the head and through the sides. Monitor the colour development throughout the processing. Apply heat if needed to speed up the development process. Check with the client throughout to ensure their comfort.

Step 1: Prepare the materials.

Step 2: After brushing the hair, section off the quadrants.

Step 3: The colour is applied to mid-lengths and ends first.

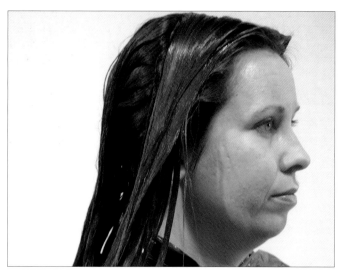

Step 4: Leave the mid-lengths and ends to develop sufficiently.

Step 5: After development the colour is applied to the roots.

Final effect.

Full head application

Consultation	– Find out what needs to be done. Are any modifications needed to the application, colour(s) or bleach?
Prepare the client	– Make the usual protective preparations. – Brush the hair through to remove the tangles. – Apply a barrier cream to the hairlines.
Prepare the materials	– Make sure that you have everything you need to hand. – Put on your disposable gloves and apron. – Mix the products correctly.

Method/technique	– Divide the hair into four equal quadrants. – Start the application with a brush to the mid-lengths and ends at the top of the head, working down and along each quadrant. – Pick up a horizontal section of hair within a back quadrant and with the tail of the brush. – Apply the colour/bleach to the mid-length and ends evenly. – Repeat down the back of the head and through the sides.
1st part of development	– Allow the mid-length and ends to develop sufficiently first. – Monitor the colour development throughout the processing. – Apply heat if needed to speed up the development process. – Check with the client throughout to ensure their comfort.
2nd part of development	– Pick up each of the horizontal sections of hair with the tail of the brush. – Apply the colour/bleach to the regrowth evenly. – Repeat down the back of the head and through the sides. – Monitor the colour development throughout the processing. – Apply heat if needed to speed up the development process. – Check with the client throughout to ensure their comfort.
Removal	– When processing is complete, take the client to the basin and rinse the hair with tepid/warm water to emulsify the colour. – Rinse thoroughly until the colour is removed. – Shampoo and condition with an anti-oxidising agent.

Mahogany

Photo courtesy Goldwell

Step-by-step: Colour

1 Create zig-zag section through right side. Then section remaining hair into four different areas: a halo section through the crown, an asymmetrical triangular section through the short graduated area at the back, a kite section above the left ear and the remaining hair is the offset triangular fringe area.

2 Starting on the zig-zag section, apply a dark colour from root to end in a colour application.

3 Apply the same technique and colour to the kite section above the left ear.

4 Apply a very light blonde colour application to the short graduated area at the back.

5 Use back-to-back blonde slices through the halo section around the crown.

6 Proceed to colour only the roots throughout the remaining hair matching the natural hair colour.

Hair created by the International PACT art team: Chantel Marshall, Harriet White and Andy Smith; photography: Stuart Weston; make-up: Hiromi Ueda.

Before.

Step 1: Section off so that the lower section is revealed.

Step 2: Apply to the zig-zag section.

Step 3: Work through to the sides.

Step 4: Apply to the other side.

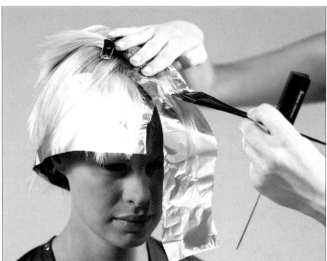

Step 5: Section off and mask with foil the halo section.

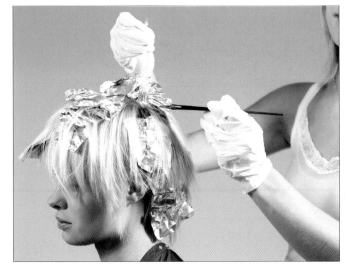

Step 6: Take back-to-back slices through the halo section.

Final effect.

I know how to prepare clients before undertaking any chemical service ☐	I know how to prepare the equipment and materials before they are used upon the client ☐	I can carry out colour consultation and understand the colour selection process ☐	I know and understand the science in respect to colouring and bleaching ☐
I always carry out tests prior to any new colouring treatment ☐	I know and understand the health, safety and hygiene risks that clients are exposed to in chemical work ☐	I know and understand the potential problems and risks of not testing hair before chemicals are introduced ☐	I know and understand the effects that colouring products have upon the hair ☐
I know when and to whom to refer clients in situations where external assistance is required ☐	I know how to recognise and implement colour correction procedures by countering unwanted tones ☐	I know and understand the ways of diluting hydrogen peroxide to make other strengths ☐	I know how to carry out a variety of full head and partial colouring techniques on a variety of hair lengths ☐
I always carry out working practices according to the salon's health and safety policy ☐			CHECKER BOARD ✓

The following projects, activities and assessments are directly linked to the essential knowledge and understanding for unit H13.

For each statement that is addressed wholly or in part in these activities, you will see its relevant and corresponding EKU number.

Make sure that you keep this for easier referencing and along with your work for future inclusion in your portfolio.

Project 1 (EKU H13.32, H13.33)

For this project you will need to collect and test a range of hair samples.

You will need to create three sets of sample batches of:

- grey/white hair
- coloured hair (with high lift colour)
- bleached hair
- coloured hair (base 6)
- natural virgin hair (base 6).

Each of the different types listed above will be coloured with

(a) a base shade 8

(b) a copper shade 8

(c) an ash/beige shade 8.

Mark each hair sample so that you know which one is which. Now mix up your three selected shades with six per cent (20 vol) hydrogen peroxide, then apply a little of each colour to each of the three collected sample batches. Allow time for the full development, then rinse each one and dry it off.

Record the changes for each sample:

- Which ones reached target shade?
- Which ones had no effect?
- Which ones have little or no coverage?
- Which ones have discoloured?

Write up the findings of your project in your portfolio. (If you have enough of each sample repeat the exercise again but now with three per cent (10 vol) hydrogen peroxide for a differing set of results.)

Case study (H13.21, H13.22, H13.23, H13.24, H13.25, H13.30)

Your salon is recommended to a client who has moved to the area. She walks into the salon with lightened hair and requests a root retouch. The hair is coarse, dry and below the shoulders.

She says that her work had tended to move her around and previous attempts by other salons have resulted in inconsistent colouring.

How would you deal with this?

List the process of events that should take place in your portfolio. Include in your responses:

- consultation aspects, questions, examination and tests
- selection of suitable products and equipment
- the precautions you would take
- the advice and conclusion you would provide.

Project 2 (EKU H13.32, H13.33)

For this project you will need to collect and test a range of hair samples.

You will need to create sample batches of:

- grey/white hair
- coloured hair (base 6)
- natural virgin hair (base 7)
- natural virgin hair (base 6)
- natural virgin hair (base 5).

Each of the different types listed above will be bleached with powder bleach to test the effects upon each prior to highlighting.

Mark each hair sample so that you know which one is which. Now mix up your bleach with nine per cent (30 vol) hydrogen peroxide, and then apply a little bleach to each of the sample batches.

Allow time for the full development, then rinse each one and dry it off.

Record the changes for each sample:

- Which ones reached a suitable shade for highlights?
- Which ones were unsuitable for highlights?
- Which ones had no effect?

Write up the findings of your project in your portfolio.

Case study

Your client recently had her hair highlighted at another salon whilst on holiday. The client did not think that the result was at all satisfactory. The resultant highlight effect was uneven, and also patchy in places that were too gold.

How would you deal with this situation?

Make notes of what you would say and do. List the questions you would ask, and the order in which you would ask them. Retain notes for your portfolio.

Here are some things you should consider:

1 Find out why the hair was not successfully treated at the other salon.

2 Find out whether the client returned there to complain and what the outcome was.

3 Record what you think might have caused the unsatisfactory results.

4 Record what you think would have been a successful course of action.

5 Find out whether the hair is in a fit state for further treatment.

6 Record the results of your discussion with your client, and what you have agreed.

Questions

1 How do you prepare the client for colouring and bleaching services? (H13.1)

2 What is your place of work's policy in respect to service timings for colouring and bleaching services? (H13.2)

3 What is your place of work's policy in respect to keeping client records of treatment history and results of tests? (H13.3)

4 What protection do clients need and why do they need it? (H13.10, H13.11, H13.12)

5 How do your work position and the positioning of equipment affect you and the client? (H13.13, H13.14, H13.16)

6 What are the safety considerations that relate to colouring and bleaching services? (H13.15, H13.17, H13.18, H13.20)

7 When is it appropriate to conduct tests on the hair prior to processing and why do you do it? (H13.24, H13.25, H13.26, H13.27, H13.28, H13.30)

8 What effects do:

(a) semi-permanent colouring

(b) permanent colouring

(c) bleaching

have upon the hair? (H13.32)

9 Why does hair pH need balancing? (H13.37)

10 What PPE must you wear when providing chemical services? (H13.12)

11 Why is it necessary to follow the manufacturer's instruction at all times? (H13.42, H13.43, H13.44)

12 What factors influence colour selection for a client? (H13.31)

13 What sorts of problems might occur when (a) colouring and (b) bleaching? How might you resolve them? (H13.48–56 inclusive)

14 Why is it important to use products economically? (H13.47)

15 What would constitute a contra-indication for colouring and bleaching services? (H13.21, H13.29, H13.40)

Preparing for assessment checklist

Remember to:

- prepare clients correctly for the services you are going to carry out
- check the results of any tests that have been undertaken
- put on the protective wear available for colouring and bleaching
- listen to the client's requirements and discuss suitable courses of action
- adhere to the safety factors when working on clients' hair
- keep the work areas clean, hygienic and free from hazards
- promote the range of services, products and treatments with the salon
- clean and sterilise the tools and equipment before they are used
- apply the science aspects you have learnt relating to colouring and bleaching
- work carefully and methodically through the chemical processes
- time the development of any chemical processes carefully
- communicate what you are doing with the client as well as your fellow staff members
- record the processes in the client's treatment history.

chapter 8

STYLING HAIR

What do I need to do?

- Take adequate precautions in preparing yourself and the client before any styling or dressing procedure.
- Be able to use a variety of styling equipment.
- Be able to use a variety of styling products.
- Be able to carry out a range of technical styling procedures.
- Be able to put long hair up in a pleat.
- Be able to plait hair and add hair in to plaits.

What do I need to learn?

You need to know and understand:

- why it is important to work safely and hygienically when styling or dressing hair
- how to recognise factors that influence the way that the work is carried out
- a range of styling and dressing techniques and when they are applicable
- the methods of handling and manipulating different lengths of hair when styling or dressing hair
- the ways of fixing the hair into different finished looks.

Information covered in this chapter

- **The types of products used when styling hair and how they work.**
- **The types of equipment used when styling hair and how they are used.**
- **How to blow-dry, set and dress hair into a style.**
- **A variety of styling techniques that you will use.**
- **The basic science of how heat and humidity effect hairdressing.**
- **The advice you should give to clients in order to maintain their own hair.**

KEY WORDS

Temporary bonds   The hydrogen bonds within the hair that are modified and fix the style into shape.

Alpha and beta keratin   The different states of hair that take place during setting and blow-drying.

REMEMBER

Always look after your brushes and combs. Make sure they are washed, dried and hygienically clean before you start your work.

INTRODUCTION

'Styling' and 'dressing' are two short words that cover a wide variety of methods, techniques and skills used during blow-drying and setting to produce wonderful creative effects. This chapter looks at the basic principles, the methods and the applications of those fundamental, everyday hairdressing operations.

CHECKERBOARD

At the end of this chapter the checkerboard will help to jog your memory on what you have learned and what still remains to be done. Cross off with a pencil each of the topics as you cover it (see page 280).

SAFETY AND PREPARATION

Photo courtesy Goldwell

Although Chapter 5 covers much of the general aspects that you need to know about health, safety and hygiene within the salon environment, each technical procedure you carry out has particular things that are relevant to health and safety. Styling and dressing hair are always carried out at the styling units and therefore the main health and safety concerns should relate to the client's comfort, positioning and protection as well as your posture, accessibility and care.

Client comfort

Setting and blow-drying always follow other services, even if the earlier service was only shampooing. There is one thing that is common to all previous services and that is that your client is left with wet hair. You need to make sure that if the towel is taken away the client's hair will not drip. This is not a safety issue but a measure of your care and attention. It's bad enough when saturated short hair drips down on to the gown and soaks the client's clothes, but this becomes even worse and far more uncomfortable if the client has long hair.

You might find that it is easier to cut hair when it is wet. In fact many stylists will use a water spray in order to keep the hair wet, but this can be quite unpleasant for the client. Wet hair soon feels cold.

Think back and remember what it feels like when you get out of the shower or the bath. Even in a warm environment you grab a towel to dry yourself, as the warm water quickly turns cool and the body feels cold. This is exactly the same feeling that the client has if they sit with wet hair!

If you can, the best way to tackle any service is with the client's hair in a slightly damp i.e. semi-dry state and this goes for cutting, perming or setting. Working with damp hair is far more comfortable for the client and is the preferred option for busy stylists with little time to spare.

REMEMBER
Always dry the client's hair well to remove the excess water before combing, cutting, setting or curling.

Why work with damp/semi-dried hair?

- During cutting it enables the natural tendencies of the hair to be seen. This is extremely important for cutting hair, with the wave, movement and hair growth patterns all being considered as the style is developed.
- In setting and blow-drying it cuts down the time of drying and maximises the work efficiency and amount of time spent on each client. Hair that is saturated still has to be dried and using the dryer on maximum heat and top speed, scorching the hair dry, is definitely not the solution!
- In perming, semi-dried hair eliminates the possibility of failure. Resistant hair will always need a perm that has the strength to do its job; so any additional moisture will dilute this action and the perm will not work in those areas.

M. Balfre

Client positioning

Client positioning has a lot to do with your safety too. If a client is slouched in the chair, they are a danger not only to themselves but to you too. Client comfort should extend to the point where it makes the salon visit a welcome and pleasurable experience. But that's where it ends. The salon is not an extension of the client's own front room! They should not clutter the floor around the styling chair with bags, magazines and shopping. Anything that can safely be stored away should be: it is not only a distraction, it's a safety hazard too!

M. Balfre

Salon chairs are designed with comfort and safety in mind; your client should be seated with their back flat against the back of the chair, their legs uncrossed and the chair at a height at which it is comfortable for you to work. You need to be able to get to all parts of the head, so the chair's height should be adjusted to suit the particular height of the client. Don't be afraid of asking the client to sit up: it is in their best interest too!

Client protection

Make sure that the gown is on properly and fastened around the neck. It should cover their clothes and come up high enough to cover collars and necklines. Don't make the fastening too tight, but it should be close enough at least to stop things going down the back of the neck.

If you can style and dry hair with a towel around the client shoulders, do so. But in some situations this is not possible as the length of the hair can get in the way of the styling or drying technique. Remember, the towel and gown are the main pieces of personal protective equipment for the client and these are the only things guarding them from the things that you do.

> **REMEMBER** ✓
>
> Look out for ways and things that can make your client's visit more comfortable and pleasurable. This is the first step in providing a better customer service.

STYLING EQUIPMENT AND PRODUCTS

Make sure that you have prepared the area. Get everything that you need together beforehand and this includes equipment as well as the products. You should have your trolley prepared with all the materials you will need. Rollers for setting should have been previously prepared by thorough washing and combs, brushes, sectioning clips etc. should be all cleaned, sterilised and made ready for use. (For more information on cleaning, sterilisation and general hygiene see Chapter 5.)

Styling products and their applications

Application → Product ↓	Short hair	Medium-length layered	Medium to long, one-length	Long layers
Mousse (styling product) 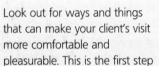 L'Oréal Professionnel Techni.Art Volume Lift	Apply a blob the size of a golf ball evenly to the roots and ends on damp hair to give volume and texture	Apply a blob the size of a small orange evenly to the roots and ends on damp hair to give volume and texture	Apply a blob the size of a small orange evenly to the ends for styling hold	Apply a blob the size of an orange evenly to the ends for styling hold

Application → Product ↓	Short hair	Medium-length layered	Medium to long, one-length	Long layers
Setting lotion (styling product)  L'Oréal Professionnel Valence Setting Lotion	Apply half the contents of the bottle all over evenly for volume and styling hold	Apply the contents of a bottle all over evenly for volume and styling hold		
Styling gel/glaze (styling product) L'Oréal Professionnel Techni.Art a-head glue	Apply a small amount all over evenly for firmer styling hold	Apply a moderate amount all over evenly for firmer styling hold		
Dressing cream (setting and finishing product) L'Oréal Professionnel Techni.Art Curl Memory Down Cream	Apply a small amount to your fingertips. Work through before combing out to give control, reduce static and calm down strays	Apply a small amount to your fingertips. Work through before combing out to give control, reduce static and calm down strays		
Serum (setting/blow-drying finishing product) L'Oréal Professionnel Techni.Art Liss Control	Apply a small amount to your fingertips. Work through to flatten and add shine	Apply a small amount to your fingertips. Work through to flatten and add shine	Apply a small amount to different areas with your fingertips. Work through to flatten and add shine	Apply a small amount to different areas with your fingertips. Work through to flatten and add shine
Wax (setting/blow-drying finishing product) L'Oréal Professionnel Techni.Art a-head web	Apply a small amount to your fingertips. Work through to define and hold	Apply a small amount to your fingertips. Work through to define and hold	Apply a small amount to different areas with your fingertips. Work through to define and hold	

Application → Product ↓	Short hair	Medium-length layered	Medium to long, one-length	Long layers
Hairspray (setting/blow-drying finishing prod)	Apply mist to hair from about 30–40 cm away from the hair for a 'fixed' hold	Apply mist to hair from about 30–40 cm away from the hair for a 'fixed' hold	Apply mist to hair from about 30–40 cm away from the hair for a 'fixed' hold	Apply mist to hair from about 30–40 cm away from the hair for a 'fixed' hold

L'Oréal Professionnel Techni.Art Airfix

Heat protection		Apply to lengths after drying to provide protection from intense heat when using straightening irons	Apply to lengths after drying to provide protection from intense heat when using straightening irons	Apply to lengths after drying to provide protection from intense heat when using straightening irons

L'Oréal Professionnel Techni.Art Hot Style Iron Finish

Styling equipment and their applications

Application → Equipment ↓	Short hair	Medium-length layered	Medium to long, one-length	Long layers
Setting rollers	Wet setting with firmer root and end movement	Wet setting with firmer root and end movement		Wet setting with firmer end movement
Velcro rollers	Dry setting with softer root and end movement	Dry setting with softer root and end movement	Dry setting with softer end movement	Dry setting with softer end movement
Heated rollers	Dry setting with firmer root and end movement	Dry setting with firmer root and end movement	Dry setting with firmer end movement	Dry setting with firmer end movement
Tail or pin comb	Setting/dressing, perming and highlights	Setting/dressing, perming and highlights	Setting/dressing, perming and highlights	Setting/dressing, perming and highlights
Straight combs	Dressing, cutting and waving	Dressing, cutting and waving	Dressing, cutting and waving	Dressing, cutting and waving

Denman

Denman

Application → / Equipment ↓	Short hair	Medium-length layered	Medium to long, one-length	Long layers
Lift pick comb	Dressing/backcombing	Dressing/backcombing	Dressing/backcombing	Dressing/backcombing
'Jumbo' wide-tooth combs	Conditioning, detangling and dressing	Conditioning, detangling and dressing	Conditioning, detangling and dressing	Conditioning, detangling and dressing
Denman Classic Styling brush	General brushing Pre-dressing and blow-drying straight	General brushing Pre-dressing and blow-drying straight	General brushing Blow-drying straight	General brushing Blow-drying straight
Vented brush	Disentangling and blow-drying straight	Disentangling and blow-drying straight	Disentangling, pre-dressing and blow-drying straight	Disentangling, pre-dressing and blow-drying straight
Paddle brush	General brushing disentangling and pre-dressing	General brushing disentangling and pre-dressing	General brushing disentangling	General brushing disentangling and pre-dressing
Radial brushes	Blow-drying with firm wave, volume or curl	Blow-drying with firm wave, volume or curl	Blow-drying with firm wave	Blow-drying with firm wave, volume or curl
Diffuser	Scrunch drying with movement or texture	Scrunch drying with movement or texture		Scrunch drying with movement or texture
Pin curl clips	Wet or dry setting with firmer end movement/curl	Wet or dry setting with firmer end movement/curl		

> **REMEMBER** ✔
>
> Root direction will determine hair flow within a style.

> **REMEMBER** ✔
>
> Scrunch drying is a way of drying hair more naturally with a diffuser. It uses the natural body or movement within the hair to create tousled and casual effects.

> **REMEMBER** ✔
>
> All items of electrical equipment have to be tested and certified fit for use by a competent person each year. The items are tested, labelled and recorded and a compiled list is made available for inspection.

> **REMEMBER**
>
> The cool-shot switch on a dryer is really useful for fixing in stronger volume or end movement into hair. After the hair has been heated, with the brush still in position, the cool shot immediately cools the hair fixing the 'set' hair into position (just as allowing set hair to cool down after the rollers have been carefully removed makes the set last longer).

Blow dryers

The blow dryer is one of the most commonly used items of equipment in the salon. There is a huge range of models available; with a variety of power outputs, speeds and heat settings. The latest ionic dryers can even reduce the 'flyaway' effect that is produced by static electricity when hair is heated in a colder environment.

A well-designed professional dryer needs to have a number of special features and you should bear this in mind when you buy one. The dryer should have both hot and cold (cool-shot) settings and it should have at least two speeds as well as different nozzles to focus the generated temperatures.

There is no real value in choosing a dryer that is too powerful, as this will easily burn or scorch the client's hair. The dryer should be well balanced – so that when it's held it doesn't protrude too far forwards and becomes heavy to hold. You need to be able to work comfortably too and this means at a height and distance that doesn't impede correct posture or cause shoulder fatigue. The dryer's lead should be long enough to work with comfortably around either side of the client so tht you don't trail the lead over their lap!

When a dryer is not in use there should be a safe position to store it. In daily salon use this could be a dryer holder attached to the side of the workstation; in the evening this could be in a storeroom or cupboard upon a shelf.

Denman Classic Styling brush
Denman

Paddle brush   Denman

Brushes

Brushes come in a wider variety than dryers and they are a vitally important as each has different applications and uses. Good-quality, general-purpose brushes should have flexible and comfortable bristles. The handles should be designed to fit comfortably in the hand enabling you to get a good grip. The typical salon brushes like this are either vented, to allow good airflow when drying hair, or similar to Denman brushes, which have cushioned removable teeth.

Although the majority of brushes are plastic, the handles are often made from a different material and there is a special reason for this. Blow-drying involves a lot of twisting and rotating of brushes quickly; this speed stops the blast from the dryer from creating hot spots at any point along the hair. Because of this, the brush needs to be easy to grip and use in any temperature and conditions, wet or dry. Therefore handles may be made of 'soft touch' materials like cork, rubber and wood; this is particularly applicable to circular radial brush types.

The shape and curvature of the brush denotes the amount of movement it will create: a curved Denman brush used in blow-drying creates smooth curved shapes with little volume, whereas a small radial brush can create firm or tight curls.

Vented brush   Denman

Radial or curling brush   Denman

ACTIVITY

Collect information on the range of different styling products available in the salon. Now set out a table to describe:

1 each product by name
2 how it is used
3 what it does
4 which hair type it is for.

Photo courtesy Goldwell UK

Styling products

There is an ever-growing range of styling and finishing products available to the profession. As this has been the major growth area, careful market research and product development have ensured that each one is specifically designed to do a particular job. As a result the huge range is confusing and is driven by successful advertising and brand awareness. If you look closely at each manufacturer's range you will find that the brand leaders all have similar and competing products. The more these numbers of similar products increase, the more confused the purchaser becomes. At this stage the only factor that can help someone to make a choice between one product and another is a reputable and recognisable name.

Styling products contain plasticisers as a fixative to hold and support the hair in its shape. Apart from hold, they often have other agents and additives within the products that can retain or repel moisture, provide protective sun-screens, add shine and lustre or add definition and shape.

Photo courtesy Goldwell UK

- *Blow-drying* products – Such as mousses protect the hair from excessive heat. They increase the time that the hair is held in shape and the volume and/or movement created, all whilst being exposed to the blast from the dryer's nozzle. They can be in a variety of different strengths for differing hair types and holds.

- *Dressing aids* – Are products that enhance the hair by adding shine or gloss and improve handling and control by removing static or fluffiness from the hair. Certain finishing products like waxes will define the movement in hair, giving texture or spikiness that could not otherwise be achieved.

- *Protection* – Many products provide protection from heat styling. Regular use of straightening irons could damage the hair so there are a number of products that can be applied to eliminate any long-term effects. Other products provide protection from harsh UVA in sunlight in a variety of 'leave-in' treatments that can be used at any time. They are put on before exposure to harsh sunlight and can be removed after by washing. This is particularly useful for clients who have coloured hair, as the bleaching effects of sunlight will quickly remove tint. Other products have the ability to resist or remove the effects of minerals on the hair such as chlorine from swimming pools. This is particularly useful as blonde hair that is regularly subjected to chlorine tends to look green!

Photo courtesy Goldwell UK

● *A variety of other products* – Can enhance or increase curl, whilst others can flatten or smooth out unwanted wave or frizziness in hair. Some have moist or wet looks. Others, for those people who like their hair to look cleaner, can achieve similar styling effects but with a dryer look.

Photo courtesy Goldwell

THE PRINCIPLES OF STYLING HAIR

Blow-drying and setting are methods of forming wet or damp hair into a dried finished shape. These methods of styling and dressing hair are used to produce the variety of temporary looks that can be either classic or contemporary. You can make hair straighter, curlier, fuller, flatter or wavier.

Blow-drying involves drying damp hair into position using brushes, combs and a hand dryer only. In addition to this a variety of other techniques have evolved as finishing techniques:

● scrunch drying, a technique using the hands as the tools for manipulating the roots and ends of the hair to increase lift, body and overall movement;

● natural drying, a variant on leaving hair to dry by itself, achieved by using diffusers as an attachment to hand dryers so that the drying process is speeded up and the overall effect is assisted by some manual manipulation.

Setting involves placing and positioning wet hair in to selected positions, and fixing it there while it dries into shape. You may roll the hair round curlers, secure it with clips or pins, or simply use your fingers. Once dry, you complete the process by dressing the hair with brushes and combs.

Hair must be manipulated in a planned and controlled way if you are going to achieve the desired effect. This dexterity – the skilled, competent hand and finger movements – are only achieved with practice. They enable you to attain both effective control and variety of shapes.

Photo courtesy Goldwell UK

SCIENCE BIT!
THE EFFECTS OF HUMIDITY ON THE HAIR

As with other techniques, setting produces only a temporary change in hair structure (and this is covered below). The fixed or set effect is soon lost if moisture is absorbed or introduced to the hair. You have probably already discovered this yourself: if, after having your hair done, you take a bath in a steamy bathroom, what happens to the hairstyle?

Moisture is all around us though and, in more extremes of humidity, is seen as mist and fog. To help prevent style deterioration from happening, a wide variety of setting aids are available to slow down the 'collapsing' process and therefore hold the shape longer.

Different effects can be produced by different techniques:

- *increasing volume* – Adding height, width and fullness, by lifting and positioning 'on base' when rollering or curling
- *decreasing volume* – Producing a close, smooth, contained or flat style by pincurl stem direction, or by dragged or angled rollering 'off base'
- *movement* – Variation of line waves and curls, produced by using differently sized rollers, pincurls or finger waving.

Relaxed hair effects can be produced by wrapping hair or by using large rollers. Different techniques are used for hair of different lengths:

- Longer hair (below the shoulders) requires large rollers, or alternating large and small rollers, depending on the amount of movement required.
- Shorter hair (above the shoulders) requires smaller rollers to achieve movement for full or sleek effects.
- Hair of one length is ideal for smooth, bob effects.
- Hair of layered lengths is ideal for full, bouncy, curly effects achieved by, say, barrel or clockspring curls.

Different techniques can also be used to improve the appearance of hair of different textures:

- Fine, lifeless hair can be given increased body and movement. Lank hair can be given increased volume and movement.
- Coarse thick hair requires firmer control.
- Very curly hair can be made smoother and its direction changed.

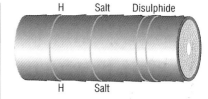

Normal unstretched hair bonds

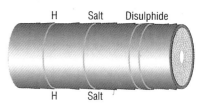

Stretched broken bonds

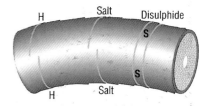

Water/moisture returns links to normal

SCIENCE BIT!
THE PHYSICAL CHANGES THAT TAKE PLACE WITHIN THE HAIR

Hair in good condition is flexible and elastic. As hair is curled or waved, it is bent under tension into curved shapes. The hair is stretched on the outer side of the curve and compressed on the inner side. If it is dried in this new position, the curl will be retained. This happens because when hair is set the hydrogen bonds and salt bonds between the keratin chains of the hair are broken. The linking system is moved into a new temporary position. (The stronger disulphide links remain unbroken.)

Hair, however, is 'hygroscopic' – it is able to absorb and retain moisture. It does so by capillary action: water spreads through minute spaces in the hair structure, like ink spreading in blotting paper. Wet hair expands and contracts more than dry hair does, because water acts as a lubricant and allows the link structure to be repositioned more easily. So the amount of moisture in hair affects the curl's durability. As the hair picks up moisture the rearranged beta keratin chains loosen or relax into their previous alpha keratin shape and position. This is why the humidity – the moisture content of air – determines how long the curled shape is retained.

The condition and the porosity of hair affect its elasticity. If the cuticle is damaged, or open, the hair will retain little moisture, because of normal evaporation. The hair will therefore have poor elasticity. If too much tension is applied when curling hair of this type it may become limp, overstretched and lacking in spring. Very dry hair is likely to break.

REMEMBER

The **temporary bonds** within the hair are only formed when the hair is completely dry. However, they will revert to their former shape if moisture or water is introduced to the hair.

Photo courtesy Goldwell

ACTIVITY

Write down in your portfolio how each of the following items are made safe and hygienic in preparation for salon use:

Setting rollers

Pin clips

Ceramic straighteners

Radial brushes

Combs

Heated rollers

Photo courtesy Goldwell

REMEMBER

Safe use of electrical equipment – the Dos and Don'ts

Do	*Don't*
Do check the plugs and leads to make sure they are not loose or damaged before they are used.	Do not use electrical equipment with wet hands.
Do replace equipment after every time it is used.	Do not use any piece of equipment for any purpose other than that for which it was intended.
Do unravel and straighten the leads properly before use.	Do not ravel up leads tightly around the equipment, it could work the connection loose.
Do switch off electrical items when they are not in use.	

Before styling checklist

✓ Prepare the client by carefully gowning them and making sure that they are comfortable.

✓ Remove any damp towels and loose clippings, then replace towel with a fresh dry one.

✓ Look at the hair you are working with. Would the hair benefit from any styling aids? Are there any other limiting factors that need to be considered: physical features, growth patterns or density for example?

✓ Confirm the style, its purpose and what you are about to do next. If further explanation is required use pictures or style magazines as a visual aid.

✓ After further discussion, agree with the client exactly what is to be done.

During styling checklist

✓ Is the heat from the dryer comfortable?

✓ Is the body or volume OK?

✓ Is the parting or division of hair in the right place?

✓ Is the finished hairstyle ok? If not what aspect needs to be changed?

BLOW-DRYING HAIR

Blow-drying is a technique that is suitable for either men or women. It involves good coordination between both hands irrespective of whether you are left or right handed. If you find this difficult at first, regular practice will enable you to gain the equal manual dexterity needed to use a brush or dryer in either hand.

A checklist for the principles of blow drying

This is what you do	*This is why you do it*
1 The hair is always dried from root to point	This smoothes the layers of cuticle, making the hair lie flatter and increases the hair's ability to shine.
2 The nozzle of the dryer should point away from the client's head	This will avoid any discomfort from burning the scalp or neck.
3 The section or mesh of hair taken should be no deeper than the bristle or teeth section of the brush and no wider than the width of the brush	Matching the amount of hair to be dried with the bristle or teeth 'footprint' of the brush will always guarantee that you are not trying to handle too much hair.
4 The flat jet of warm air from the nozzle should be parallel with the section being dried.	This ensures that all the hair dries at an even rate.
5 The drier *must* be kept moving in relation to the lengths of the sections of hair.	This will avoid hot spots and hair damage as a consequence.
6 The hair is dried with an even tension without pulling; the movement, volume or curl is achieved by curving the hair in the direction required.	This ensures that the movement that you create in the hair will be even throughout the hairstyle and will last.
7 Extra curl or movement is achieved by quickly cooling a previously dried section whilst the brush is still in place (i.e. cool-shot drying: most professional hand dryers have this facility).	The cooling action fixes the hair from alpha to beta keratin state, whereas warm hair can still revert back from beta to its original alpha state.

Photo courtesy Goldwell

ACTIVITY

Collect information on the range of styling equipment available in the salon.

Now set out a table to describe:

1 each item of equipment by name
2 what it is mainly used for
3 how it should be maintained on a daily basis.

REMEMBER

Hairdryers only blow out what they suck in from the other end.

Always make sure that the filter is attached to the back of the dryer, as this will prevent your client's hair from getting sucked in. This is not only embarrassing for you, it is dangerous and unpleasant for the client too.

Photo courtesy Goldwell

Blow dry styling dos and don'ts

Dos	Don'ts
Do dry off the hair well so that it's moist but not wet before starting the blow-dry.	Don't leave damp towels around the client's shoulders.
Do take small enough sections that you can control and dry evenly throughout.	Don't leave the dryer running whilst you resection the hair.
Do try to direct the flow of air away from the client.	Don't use the top heat setting unless its really necessary.
Do adjust the chair height so you can reach the top of the client's head without overstretching.	Don't pass the brushes to the client for them to hold in between sectioning.
Do ask the client to adjust their head position if you need to.	Don't try to use the same hand for brush work on both sides of the head.
Do clip out of the way any sections that are not yet being worked on.	Don't over-dry the hair as this will cause permanent damage.

Techniques for blow-drying hair

Step-by-step: Blow-drying short hair

1 Apply a small amount of styling mousse to the hair evenly, then divide the hair at the back so that the blow-dry can be started at the nape.

2 Work up the back, dropping one side whilst the other remains secured.

3 Continue up the back until all of the hair is completed.

4 Section off the sides and start at the lower section again.

5 Complete both sides in the same way.

6 Finally work forward from the crown towards the frontal/fringe area.

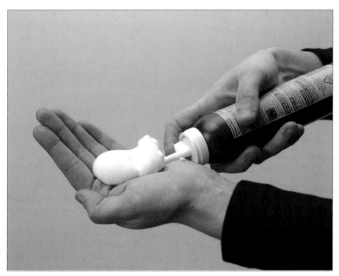

Step 1: Squeeze out sufficient mousse to blow-dry with.

Step 1: Sectioning to start.

Step 2: Creating lift and direction.

Step 3: Creating lift under the crown.

Step 4: Directing the hair back from the sides.

Final effect.

Step-by-step: Blow-drying long hair

1 Apply a small amount of styling mousse to the hair.
2 Divide the hair at the back so that the nape can be blow-dried first.
3 Work up the back, finishing and drying each section before moving on to the next.
4 Continue up the back until all of the hair is completed. Section off the sides and start at the lower section again.
6 Finally work forward from the crown towards the frontal/fringe area.

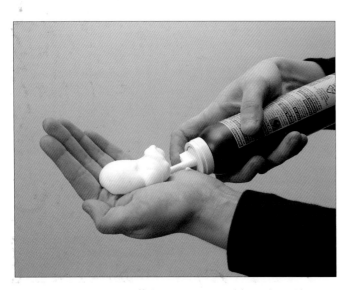

Step 1: Squeeze out sufficient mousse to blow-dry with.

Step 2: Sectioning to start.

Step 3: Smooth even tension.

Step 3: Directing the flow of air in line with the hair fall.

Step 4: Back complete, move on to the sides.

Step 5: Finishing around the face.

HEATED TONGS, BRUSHES, STRAIGHTENING AND CRIMPING IRONS

BaByliss

Electric curling tongs, heated brushes and straightening irons are a popular way of applying finish to a hairstyle. They are particularly useful in situations where:

- blow-drying alone will not achieve the desired look
- the hair is not in a suitable condition to be dried into shape.

Sometimes blow-drying will not achieve the result that the client is expecting. When extra volume, movement or curl is needed on hair that lacks natural body, or is very fine, additional help is needed to create a lasting effect. Heated tongs and/or brushes provide a quick solution to do this. They can be bought in a variety of different sizes (i.e. diameters), which give different levels of movement and are usually preheated whilst the blow dry is in progress.

After the blow dry, the hair is resectioned in a similar way; i.e. clipping the large amounts out of the way, until you are ready to work with them. Each section is then taken and the tongs wound in the direction that you want the hair to move. The same amount of time is given to each section with the hair wound around, then, after a few moments, the tongs are released and the hair left in position for later combing out and finishing.

When the hair is not really in a condition to be blow-dried – too porous or bleached – you should provide the client with an alternative styling solution. Dry setting or heated rollers would be a good alternative, but if the client insists that they want more of a blow-dried effect, you may find that heated tongs or straighteners are the only realistic solution.

Step-by-step using Ceramic Dial a Heat Tong by Patrick Cameron

1 Starting at the nape, place tongs in the first section, about 3 cm from the scalp. Place the tongs straight across the section, close the clasp and wind hair halfway around the barrel. Make sure the tongs are clasp side up. Remove from hair.

2 Turn the tongs up the other way and place across the hair, directly under the last tonged section. This process creates a perfect wave. Clasp side up creates the valley and clasp side down the crest.

3 Repeat this process with the tongs clasp side up. The porcelain dial a heat's offer a perfect surface for creating this style – smooth and durable. The tongs don't snag or pull the hair and provide a beautiful, glossy finish.

4 Continue this process through the sections of hair. Make sure your sections are about 1 cm in depth and no more than 4 cm wide.

5 Continue the process throughout all the hair.

6 Make sure that you use smaller tongs as open-ended curls/waves always drop by half.

7 To add a new look at the front of the style braid from a low parting at the side, across the front of the brow and tuck under on the opposite side.

Ceramic straighteners, ghd salon styler

Hair: Patrick Cameron for BaByliss Pro; photography: Thornton Howdle; make-up: Alison Chesterton; styling: Sharon Brigden.

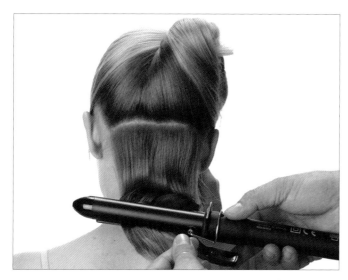

Step 1: Start underneath at the back.

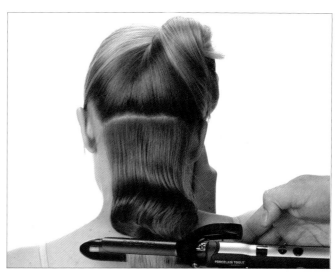

Step 2: Reversing the wave.

Step 3: Continuing the 'S' shape.

Step 4: Working up through the next section.

Step 5: Repeating the wave reversal.

Step 6: Continue the rest in the same way.

Step 7: A little braiding keeps the hair away from the face.

Final effect.

Step-by-step using BaByliss Pro Curl Press® by Patrick Cameron

1 Divide the hair and take individual sections of about $\frac{1}{4}$ inch, twist the hair slightly to keep together. Secure the end of the section under the level and then wind the rest of the hair upwards around the barrel of the Curl Press®. For larger, softer curls simply select bigger sections of hair.

2 Push the press switch on the handle to activate the moving spiral and hold for no longer than five seconds to create a very pressed, defined curl. Then unwind.

3 Repeat this process through the sections.

4 As you get to the top of the style weave sections with your fingers so as to avoid a predictable curl line.

5 Continue throughout all the hair.

Step 1: Start underneath at the back.

Step 2: Working up through the back.

Step 3: Activate the moving spiral to fix the curl into place.

Step 4: A woven section reduces any tell-tale curl marks.

Step 5: Curling the woven pieces.

Final effect.

Tip – For a softer look you could first pull all hair in to a ponytail, curling only sections made from the tail and removing the band for the finished look. Another version is to split the hair via a middle parting, create two pigtails and repeat.

Hair: Patrick Cameron for BaByliss Pro; photography: Thornton Howdle; make-up: Alison Chesterton; clothes: Accent, Leeds.

Straightening irons and particularly ceramic straightening irons have been a very popular way of calming unruly hair. They work by electrically heating two parallel plates so that the hair can be run between them in one movement from roots to ends, smoothing out the unwanted wave or frizz in the process.

Photo courtesy Goldwell

Ceramic straighteners have been particularly successful as they heat up in just a few moments and have a higher operating temperature than metal irons (150°C). This alarmingly high temperature would initially be considered as damaging to hair but, because they have the ability to transfer heat quickly and smoothly to the hair without grabbing, they are very effective in creating smoother effects.

When straightening is needed to complement the look on longer hair, it is often better to straighten each section as the blow-dry proceeds. If you start underneath, each section is completely finished before you move on up the head. The hair will stay flatter from the outset and each section is totally dry, stopping the hair from reverting to its previous state (i.e. reverting to alpha keratin).

The use of crimping irons tends to go through phases of popularity every ten years or so. They too have parallel fixed plates but these are wavy and produce flat 'S' waves on longer hair. They are a great styling accessory for competition and stage work as crimped effects are visually striking and very unusual. In staged hairdressing shows models with crimped hair will often accompany the look with strong fashion colours.

Unlike tongs and straightening irons, crimpers are not turned, twisted or drawn through the hair.

1 Each mesh of hair is started near the head and works down to the points of the hair.

2 The meshes should be no wider than the crimping irons and are crimped across the width of the plates.

3 After a few moments of heating each section of the mesh the crimpers are moved to the last wave crest created and pressed again.

4 This is repeated down the lengths of the hair until all of the hair is crimped.

5 The final look is not combed out or brushed, but allowed to fall in waved sections.

Crimping is not advisable on shorter, layered hair unless a frizzy, fluffy look is wanted. The most successful results are on longer, one-length hair.

> ### REMEMBER ✔
>
> **Care for tongs, straighteners and crimpers**
> When hairspray or styling products have been used on hair they can cause a build-up on the surface of electric tongs and straighteners. Over time, this will cause tacky or sticky points to develop upon the surface of the equipment when it is hot. Hair will stick to these areas and will cause damage. Sticky prints on tongs and straighteners stop the equipment from gliding smoothly over the hair.

Electrical accessories health and safety checklist

✓ Never get too close to the client's head with hot styling equipment

✓ Never leave the styling equipment on one area of hair for more than a few moments

✓ Always replace the styling tools into their holder at the workstation when not in use

✓ Always check the filters on the back of hand dryers to make sure that they are not blocked (this will cause the dryer to overheat and possibly ignite)

✓ Look out for trailing flexes across the floor or around the back of styling chairs

✓ Let tools cool down before putting them back into storage

✓ Always check for deterioration in flexes or equipment damages

✓ Never use damaged equipment under any circumstances

How hair types and lengths respond

Length	Texture	Tools	Techniques	Effect
Short layers	Tight/very curly/fine/ medium or coarse	Radial brushes, straighteners, tongs	Blow-drying and styling	Smoother or straight; controlled curl
Short one length	Curly/fine/medium or coarse	Curved brushes, radials, straighteners	Blow-drying and styling	Smoother or straight
Medium layered	Curly/fine/medium or coarse	Flat/paddle brushes, curved brushes, radials, straighteners, tongs	Blow-drying and styling	Smooth, wavy or curls; straightened; controlled wave
Medium one length	Curly/fine/medium or coarse	Flat/paddle brushes, curved brushes, radials, straighteners	Blow-drying and styling	Smooth, wavy or curls; straightened
Long layers	Curly/fine/medium or coarse	Flat/paddle brushes, curved brushes, radials, straighteners	Blow-drying and styling	Smooth, wavy or curls; straightened
Long one length	Curly/fine/medium or coarse	Flat/paddle brushes, curved brushes, straighteners	Blow-drying and styling	Smooth; straightened

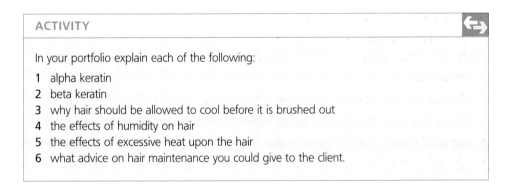

ACTIVITY

In your portfolio explain each of the following:

1 alpha keratin
2 beta keratin
3 why hair should be allowed to cool before it is brushed out
4 the effects of humidity on hair
5 the effects of excessive heat upon the hair
6 what advice on hair maintenance you could give to the client.

SETTING HAIR

Curling techniques

Curls are series of shapes or movements in the hair. They may occur naturally, or be created by hairdressing – this could be chemically by perming or physically by setting. Curls add 'bounce' or lift to the hair, and determine the direction in which the hair lies.

Each curl has a root, a stem, a body and a point. The curl base – the foundation shape produced between parted sections of hair – may be oblong, square, triangular and so on. The shape depends on the size of the

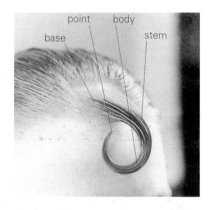

point body

base stem

Curl parts

Photo courtesy Goldwell

Securing rollers

curl, the stem direction and the curl type. Different curl types produce
different movements.

You can choose the shape, size and direction of the individual curls: your
choice will affect how satisfying the finished effect is and how long it lasts.
The type of curl you choose depends on the style you're aiming for – a high,
lifted movement needs a raised curl stem; a low, smooth shape needs a flat
curl. You may need to use a combination of curl types and curling methods
to achieve the desired style – for example, you might lift the hair on top of
the head using large rollers, but keep the sides flatter using pincurls.

Rollering

There are various sizes and shapes of roller. In using rollers you need to
decide on the size and shape, how you will curl the hair on to them and
the position in which you will attach them to the base.

- Small rollers produce tight curls, giving hair more movement. Large
  rollers produce loose curls making hair wavy as opposed to curly.
- Rollers pinned on or above their bases so that the roots are upright,
  produce more volume than rollers placed below their bases.
- The direction of the hair wound on the roller will affect the final style.

Step-by-step: Rollering

1 Comb through to remove any tangles and apply the setting lotion evenly
   to the hair.

2 Start by taking a clean, smooth section of hair – that is no longer or wider
   than the 'footprint' of the roller being used – straight out, but slightly
   forwards from the head.

3 Place the hair points centrally on to the roller. Use both hands to retain
   the hair section angle and keep the hair points in position.

4 As you turn the roller 'lock' the hair points against the body of the roller.
   Then continue winding down with an even tension until you reach the
   base of the section.

5 As you work make sure that any shorter or wispy flyaway ends are
   included in the wound roller.

6 Place the wound roller centrally on to the sectioned base (i.e. 'on base')
   to achieve full height/volume from the set.

7 Secure the roller by pinning through to stop it unravelling. Make sure that
   the pins are comfortable and link through to other rollers and not on to
   the client's scalp.

Common rollering problems

- Rollers not secured properly on base either dragged or flattened will not produce lift and volume in the final style.
- Too large a hair section will produce reduced movement in the final effect.
- Too small a hair section will produce increased movement or curl in the final effect.
- Longer hair requires larger rollers unless tighter effects are wanted.
- Poorly positioned hair over-falling the sides of the roller will have reduced/impaired movement in the final effect.
- Incorrectly wound hair around the roller will create 'fish hooks' and/or split ends.
- Twisted hair around the roller will distort the final movement of the style.

Pinning rollers

Pincurling

Pincurling is the technique of winding hair into a series of curls or flat waves, which are pinned in place while drying. The two most common types of curl produced in this way are the barrel curl and the clockspring.

- The barrelspring curl has an open centre and produces a soft effect. When formed, each loop is the same size as the previous one. It produces an even wave shape and may be used for reverse curling, which forms waves in modern hairstyles. In this, one row of pincurls lies in one direction, the next in the opposite direction. When dry and dressed, this produces a wave shape. When used in just the perimeter outline of a short hair style they can control the shape and stop the ends (that could be otherwise be set on rollers) from buckling.
- The clockspring curl has a closed centre and produces a tight, springy effect. When formed each loop is slightly smaller than the previous one. It produces an uneven wave shape throughout its length. It can be suitable for hair that is difficult to hold in place.

Clockspring curl

Barrelspring curl

Step-by-step: Pincurling

1 Neatly section the hair and comb through any setting lotion – the size of the section will relate to the degree of movement achieved.

2 Hold the hair in the direction it will lie after drying.

3 Hold the hair at the midpoint in one hand using the thumb and first finger, with the thumb uppermost. Using the thumb and first finger of your other hand and thumb underneath, hold the hair a little way down from the hair points.

4 Turn the second hand to form the first curl loop. The hand should turn right round at the wrist.

5 On completion of the first loop, transfer the hair to the finger and thumb of the other hand.

Stand-up pin curls

6 Form a series of loops until the curl base is reached. The last loop is formed by turning the curl body into the curl base. The rounded curl body should fit into the curl base.

7 Secure the curl with a clip without disturbing the curl formed in the process.

REMEMBER ✓

Common pincurl faults

- Tangled hair is difficult to control. Comb well before starting.
- If the base is too large curling will be difficult.
- If you hold the curl stem in one direction but place it in another the curl will be misshapen and lift.
- If you don't turn your hand far enough it will be difficult to form concentric loops.

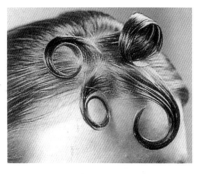

Curl body directions

Curl body directions

A flat curl may turn either clockwise or anti-clockwise. The clockwise curl has a body that moves around to the right and the anti-clockwise a body that moves around to the left. Stand-up pincurls, like rollers, have a body that lifts away from the scalp.

Reverse curls are rows of alternating clockwise and anti-clockwise pincurls; these will produce a finish that has continuous 's' waves, similar to the effect of finger waves throughout the style.

REMEMBER ✓

- Never place grips or pins in your mouth – this is unhygienic and could cross-infect.
- Never place tailcombs in your pocket – you could injure yourself and pierce your body.
- Never work on wet slippery floors and always clear up loose clippings of hair.
- Never use any items of personal equipment that have not been cleaned or sterilised.

Step-by-step: Finger waving

Finger waving is a technique of moulding wet hair into 'S'-shaped movements using the hands, the fingers and a comb. It is sometimes called water waving or water setting. The technique is often used as part of an overall finished style. To form the wave:

1 Use one finger of one hand to control the hair and to determine the position of the wave. Comb the hair into the first part of the crest, and continue along the head.

2 Place the second finger immediately below the crest formed, and comb the hair in the opposite direction.

3 Form the second crest similarly, to complete the final wave shape.

REMEMBER ✓

The elbow and arm should be held above the hand when it is placed on the head. Only the index finger should touch the head. This gives the required control and pressure. A comb with both widely and closely spaced teeth is the most suitable for this.

Finger waving: first crest

Finger waving: second crest

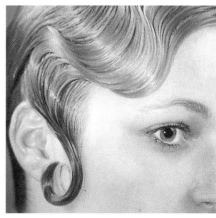

Finger waving: third crest

REMEMBER ✔

Finger waves

- Finger waving is most successful on medium or fine hair that is about 10 cm long. Coarse or lank hair can be difficult.
- Setting lotion, gel, mousse or emulsion will be needed to hold the waves.
- Keep your forearm level with or slightly higher than the wrist, to control the hair and your hand during waving. Hold the comb upright and don't use too much pressure when combing, to avoid tearing the scalp.
- Keep the waves the same size and depth. About 3 cm (the tips of two fingers) between crests is usually best.
- Pinching or forcing the crests will distort the waves. Correct control and angling will produce the best waves.
- Positioning is important. Comb the hair to make it lie evenly, and return it to this position after each wave movement is complete.
- Keep the hair wet (but not dripping) during waving. If you find that it is drying out, dampen it while you work and apply more setting lotion if necessary.
- Dry the completed shape under a hood dryer, preventing movement or slip.
- Dressing out should not disturb the waves. The hair is not normally brushed.

Toni & Guy at the 50th Anniversary L'Oréal Colour Trophy, London, May 2005

Step-by-step: Drying the set

Wet setting is normally dried under a fixed or manoeuverable hood dryer. You need to do the following:

1 Make sure that the client is comfortable.

2 Set the dryer to a temperature that suits the client. Most dryers have an adjustment for the client so that if the dryer becomes too hot they can turn it down themselves.

3 Set the timer for drying. You should allow around 15 minutes for short fine hair, and up to 45 minutes for long thick hair. The average is around 25–30 minutes.

4 Always check the client from time to time during the process.

Toni&Guy at the 50th Anniversary L'Oréal Colour Trophy, London, May 2005

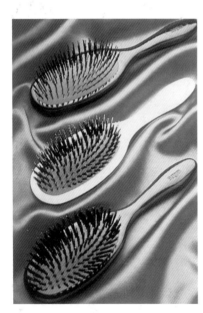

Brushes for dressing hair   Denman

5 After drying has finished, remove the hood dryer and let the hair cool down for a short while.

6 Then check to see if the hair is dry by carefully removing one roller from the crown area, one from the nape and one from the front; if they are all dry carry on carefully removing all the pins and rollers, leaving the set curl carefully in its position without dragging or distorting the formed curl.

Dressing out

Dressing is the process of applying finish to previously set hair. Setting gives movement to hair in the form of curls or waves. Dressing blends and binds these movements into an overall flowing shape, the style you set out to achieve. It produces an overall form that flows, lightening the head and face and removing dull, flat or odd shapes.

Dressing uses brushing and combing techniques, and dressing aids such as hairspray to keep the hair in place. If you have constructed the set carefully and accurately only the minimum of dressing will be required.

Step-by-step: Brushing

Brushing blends the waves or curls, removes the partings left at the curl bases during rollering and gets rid of any stiffness caused by setting aids.

1 One way of achieving the finished dressing is with a brush and your hand. The thicker the hair, the stiffer the brush bristles need to be. Choose a brush that will flow through the hair comfortably.

2 Apply the brush to the hair ends. Use firm but gentle strokes.

3 Work up the head, starting from the back of the neck.

4 Brush through the waves or curls you have set, gradually moulding the hair into shape.

5 As you brush, pat the hair with your hand to guide the hair into shape. Remember, though, that overdressing and overhandling can ruin the set.

The technique of double brushing uses two brushes, applied one after the other in a rolling action.

Backbrushing

Backbrushing is a technique used to give more height and volume to hair. By brushing backwards from the points to the roots, you roughen the cuticle of the hair. Hairs will now tangle slightly and bind together to hold a fuller shape. The amount of hair backbrushed determines the fullness of the finished style.

Tapered hair, with shorter lengths distributed throughout, is more easily pushed back by brushing. Most textures of hair can be backbrushed; because it adds bulk, the technique is especially useful with fine hair.

Step-by-step: Backbrushing

1 Hold a section of hair out from the head; for maximum lift, hold the section straight out from the head and apply the backbrushing close to the roots.

2 Place the brush on the top of the held section at an angle slightly dipping in to the held section of hair.

3 Now, with a slight turn outwards with the wrist, turn and push down a small amount of hair towards the scalp.

4 Repeat this in a few adjacent sections of hair.

5 Smooth out the longer lengths in the direction required, covering the tangled backbrushed hair beneath.

Note: The more the hair is backbrushed the greater the volume and support will be.

Mahogany

Backcombing

This technique is similar to backbrushing above; however, in this situation a comb is used rather than a brush to turn back the shorter hairs within a section to provide support and volume. Backcombing is applied deeper toward the scalp than backbrushing and therefore provides a stronger result.

REMEMBER

Backcombing is applied to the underside of the hair section. Don't let the comb penetrate too deeply otherwise the final dressing and smoothing out will remove the support you have put in.

ACTIVITY

Answer these questions in your portfolio:

1 What difference would there be from setting with rollers on base as opposed to off base?

2 What type of effect do you get from clockspring pin curls?

3 Why do you need to brush the hair first when combing out?

4 Why is the direction of airflow important in blow-drying?

5 What difference to styling or dressing out is there between backcombing and backbrushing?

Backcombing

Use the styling mirror

As you work keep using the mirror to check the shape that you are creating. If you find that the outer contour is misshapen or lacking volume, don't be afraid to go back to resection and backbrush/comb again.

When you have finished the look hold a back mirror at an angle to maximise what the client can see of their hairstyle.

All these styling aspects create the basis for creating a variety of effects. The next part of this chapter looks at how this is applied to long hair dressings.

M. Balfre

DRESSING LONG HAIR

Many people find long 'hair-ups' daunting, but they needn't be. The main reason why someone would find any part of hairdressing difficult is because they are not doing that aspect on a regular basis. It really is that simple.

The most important things to remember with long hair-ups are:

- assessing whether a particular look or effect is going to suit the client
- agreeing the effect before you start
- having a plan of what you are trying to achieve
- building enough structure to support the look.

It may seem like this list states the obvious, but each one is vital and this is why:

Assessing the suitability

This is the first aspect that you should consider. In most cases, hair-up is a special situation. It's not a quick, casual throw-up that the client does to get their hair out of the way. They come to the salon for the things that they can't achieve themselves: that's what hairstyles for special occasions are.

The problem from a suitability point of view is, how will the client know if they are going to like their hair up if they seldom have it styled that way? For people who don't normally wear their hair up there is always underlying reasons and these could be:

- their hair is too thick
- they don't like the shape of their ears
- it makes their nose bigger
- they prefer their hair to have volume so they don't like it scraped back
- their hair isn't really long enough.

The table below provides a quick look up for the physical limiting factors.

Physical features – suitability

Physical features / Hair style	◯	◯	Head shapes ♡	▽	☐	Protruding ears	Prominent nose	Short neck
Vertical roll/pleat	✓	With height to compensate	✓	With height to compensate	With height and width to compensate	Volume at the sides to cover	Volume at the sides	Needs to be sleek
Barrel curls	✓	✓	✓	✓	✓	Volume at the sides to cover (not triangular)	Volume at the sides	Needs to be sleek

Physical features / Hair style	Head shapes (oval)	Head shapes (round)	Head shapes (heart)	Head shapes (triangle)	Head shapes (square)	Protruding ears	Prominent nose	Short neck
Low knot or chignon	✓	With height	✓	✗	With height	Volume at the sides to cover (not triangular)	✗	✗
High knot or chignon	✓	✓	✓	✓	✓	Volume at the sides to cover (not triangular)	✗	Needs to be sleek
Plaiting or braiding	✓	With height	✓	✓	✗	Volume at the sides to cover (not triangular)	✓	Needs to be sleek

Agreeing the effect before you start

When you have selected a suitable look you need to find examples of how this would look on the client. Visualisation and, more importantly, self-visualisation from the client's point of view is very difficult. You need to try to rearrange the hair loosely, so they can get an idea of the weight distribution, height and width. If you can convey to them roughly what it will look like when their face is exposed, and they like what they see, you are halfway there. It will save lots of time later and save you having to unpick everything that you have done.

Hair by American Dream

Having a plan

If the client likes the effect in principle then you can set out a plan of how you will achieve it. You need to work out where you need to start, the midpoint in the styling and what the final touches will be. The starting point will be a position that you will be unlikely to get at and change later on, so it's a bit like making a cake.

- You start with a recipe – the style you want to create.
- You gather the ingredients – all the pins, grips, bands, and accessories.
- Get out tools – get all the equipment you need together.
- Start preparing the mix – start the process.
- Place in the oven – mould and spray.
- Take out and ice the cake – finish off with the decoration/accessories.

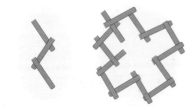

Interlocking grips

Build the structure

The style needs support; it cannot be durable without it. It needs to be secure as well as creative in its effect. It can only be secure if you use backcombing, grips, bands etc. Do not be afraid to backcomb the hair. It may look as if the whole thing is getting too big, but don't forget you can take out as much as you like within the dressing. Backcombing provides you with a solid base that you can grip without the fear of the grips dropping out. As you become more experienced in handling long hair, you will find that you won't need to use much spray in the styling stage, but only later in the finishing off.

The other main tool for giving structure and support is grips. Kirby grips have one leg with a serrated profile; this helps them to stay in the hair much better.

Wherever possible ensure that you interlock your grips; whether the patterning is in a straight line (e.g. in supporting and fixing a pleat), or whether it is placed in a complete interlocking circlet (e.g. in hair dressed in knots, chignons or any other centrally positioned dressings).

Vertical roll (French pleat)

The vertical roll is a formal classic dressing that suits many special occasions. The hair can be enhanced further by the additions of accessories or fresh flowers. If you review the planning stages for putting hair up you will see under 'building the support' that backcombing is an essential aspect for creating a solid foundation. This should be your starting point for the step-by-step procedure.

Step-by-step: Vertical roll (French pleat)

1 Section and backbrush the bulk of the hair.
2 After smoothing the hair, interlock a row of grips to secure the base of the pleat.
3 Sweep the hair over and tuck the free edges inwards.
4 Secure the smooth pleat with fine pins.
5 Style and finish the remainder into position.

Step 1: Apply a little backbrushing.

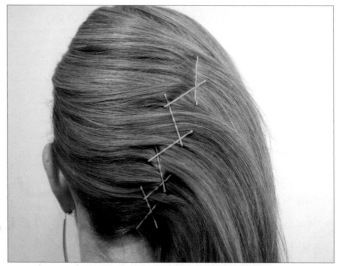

Step 2: Interlock the grips to provide a secure base.

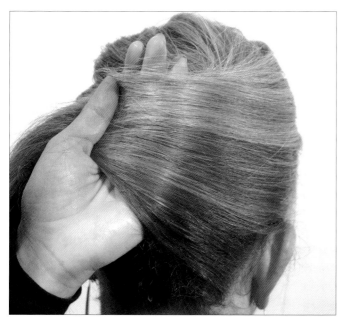

Step 3: Take across smoothly.

Step 4: Fold ends in and secure into place.

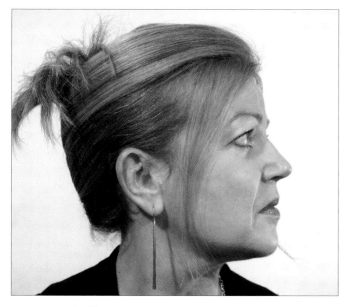

Step 5: Final effect.

Step-by-step: Asymmetric chignon (courtesy Patrick Cameron)

This simple but very effective hair-up is an ideal quick option for either party or formal wear.

1 Brush through well and smooth down the side opposite to where the chignon will be.

2 Divide the hair down to the ear. Fix one section with a band low to the hairline at the nape behind the ear.

3 Twist the remainder down to meet the hair secured with the band.

4 Now twist the hair in the covered band too.

5 Twist this section underneath the other and continue through to the ends with both sections.

6 Secure the sections together with a band at the ends.

7 Now feather the effect by pulling out some loose ends.

8 Loop around and fix in position.

9 Continue to twist and secure with grips.

10 Finally smooth out the front area and fix down into position.

Extracted from *Dressing Long Hair 4* by Patrick Cameron
www.patrick-cameron.com tel: 020 7923 0599

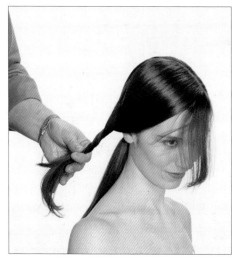

Step 1: Lightly mist the hair to provide extra control.

Step 2: Creating the division.

Step 3: Twisting down the sections towards the ends.

Step 4: Repeating the twist on the other sections of hair.

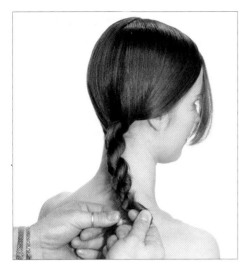

Step 5: Now join both by twisting together.

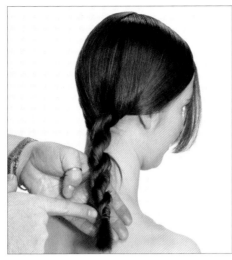

Step 6: Secure with a covered band.

Step 7: Tease out looser hair to soften the effect.

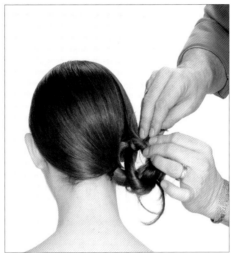

Step 8: Form a loop with the twisted hair.

Step 9: Secure the chignon into place.

Step 10: Finish off by smoothing into place.

Plaits and braids

Plaiting is a method of intertwining three or more strands of hair to create a variety of woven hairstyles. When this work is done for specific occasions, it is often accompanied by ornamentation: fresh flowers, glass or plastic beads, coloured silks and added hair are also popular.

The numerous options for plaited effects are determined by the following factors:

- number of plaits or braids used
- positioning of the plait or braid across the scalp or around the head
- way in which the plaits are made (under or over)
- any ornamentation/decoration or added hair applied.

'Plaits' usually refers to a free-hanging stem(s) of hair that is left to show hair length. This length can be natural or can be extended by adding hair during the plaiting process; an example is the 'French' or 'fish tail' plait.

Conversely, the term 'braids' traditionally referred to plaits that were secured close to the scalp, to create head-hugging designs, e.g. corn rows or cane rows.

Step-by-step: Three-stem plait

The three-stem plait is easily achieved and demonstrates the basic principle of plaiting hair.

1 Divide the hair to be plaited into three equal sections.
2 Hold the hair with both hands, using your fingers to separate the sections.
3 Starting from either the left or the right, place the outside section over the centre one. Repeat this from the other side.
4 Continue placing the outside sections of hair over the centre ones until you reach the ends of the stems.
5 Secure the free ends with ribbon, thread or covered band.

Step-by-step: Three-stem 'French' plaiting

1 Brush the hair to remove all tangles.
2 With the hair tilted backwards, divide the foremost hair into three equal sections.
3 Starting from either the left or the right, cross an outside stem over the centre stem. Repeat this action with the opposite outer stem.
4 Section a fourth stem (smaller in thickness than the initial three stems) and incorporate this with the next outside stem you are going to cross.
5 Cross this thickened stem over the centre, and repeat this step with the opposite outer stem.
6 Continue this sequence of adding hair to the outer stem before crossing it over the centre.
7 When there is no more hair to be added, continue plaiting down to the ends and secure them.

> **REMEMBER** ✓
>
> The tension used in plaiting can exert exceptional pressure on the hair follicle. Scalp-type braids create more vulnerability than free-hanging plaits. In extreme cases hair loss may be caused by this pulling action and thinning areas may be result.
>
> This condition is called 'traction alopecia' and is often seen at the temples of young girls with long hair who regularly attend dancing classes and have to wear their hair up.

Step 1: Section the hair from the hairline into three stems.

Step 2: Plait the sections in with the main stem.

Step 3: Continue to plait.

The completed plait.

Hair by American Dream

Hair by American Dream

Three-stem braids 'cane rows'

'Cane rows' otherwise known as 'corn rows' are a technique that originated in Africa. Its ethnic origins have been a unique way of displaying hair art and design and have often incorporated complex patterns that historically indicated status or tribal connection. In fact, as this art form has been passed down by subsequent generations for thousands of years, it is quite probable that the very first hairdressers worked on these elaborate techniques, as it is unlikely that people could do these themselves.

Cane rows create design patterns across the scalp by working along predefined channels of hair. These channels are secured to the scalp by interlocking each of the three subdivided stems as the plaiting technique progresses.

Short or even layered hair can be made to look longer still if hair is added, via extensions, during the process. The added hair is plaited into the style along each of the sections that create the braided effect.

When cane rows have been applied to the hair the effect can last for up to ten weeks before they should be removed. Advice should be given on handling and maintaining the hair although regular shampooing can still be carefully achieved.

Step-by-step: Cane rowing

1 Wash, condition and dry the hair straight.

2 Section out a channel of hair with a tail comb to create the direction of the design required.

3 Use a sectioning clip to secure the other parts of the remaining hair out of the way.

4 For cane rows without added hair, subdivide the client's hair from the front of the channelled section into three stems.

5 Hold the front, first section between the middle and third finger of the left hand and the next, middle section between the index finger and thumb. Now take the last or third section between the middle and third finger of the right hand.

6 Pass the middle section with the index finger of the left hand under the last outer section of the right hand and pass the new middle section under the outer section of the left hand.

7 Pick up a little hair along the channel with the fourth finger and incorporate into the outer third stem.

8 Repeat 6 and 7 until you have worked along the complete channel of hair until the point where the plait leaves the scalp to hang freely.

9 Then continue plaiting the single, three stems down the hair section's length until all of the hair is complete.

10 Secure the ends with a covered professional band and start the process from 2 to 10 again on the next cane row.

Steps 1 and 2: Brush hair to remove tangles.

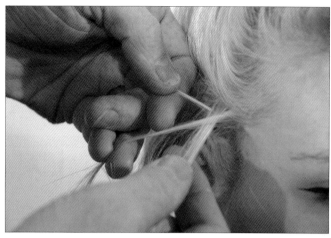

Steps 3–4: Create a channel for the braid to travel along.

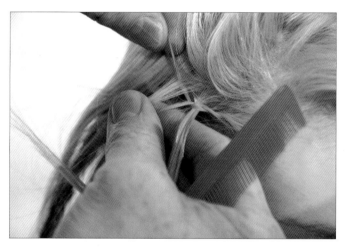

Step 5: Working backwards pick a little hair from the head and add it to the third stem, locking the braid to the head.

Steps 6–7: Carry on plaiting the stems until you have completed the corn row.

Step 9–10: Secure the ends.

Final effect.

Method for adding hair into the cane row

To add or extend the hair take narrow strands of hair extensions and add them to take the place of the two outer sections: you loop them across the client's natural hair to create the first and third stem of the braid. Then, each time the outer braid introduces part of the client's hair, the added hair is secured down to the scalp.

Added hair or extension hair can be made from a variety of materials, natural or synthetic. They come in a variety of different textures, types and colours and can be added to the client's natural hair for a variety of different styling reasons. Subtle, harmonising tones and textures can be added to make the client's own hair appear longer than it is. Conversely, bright fashion colour extensions can be added to create dramatic, contrasting effects.

Weaving

Hair weaving is a process of interlacing strands of hair to produce a wide variety of effects. A small area of woven hair can be very effective by itself, or used to highlight a particular part of a style. Hair weaving is also used to place and hold lengths of hair.

At its simplest, hair weaving may be used to hold long hair back from the face. This may be done by taking strands of hair from each side, sweeping them over the hair lengths and intertwining them at the back.

More intricate is the basket weave which uses a combination of plaiting, twisting and placing to form many shapes and patterns. It is important to wet or gel the hair before starting to weave. Weave tightly or loosely according to the effect you are aiming for.

Step-by-step: Weaving

1 Use six meshes of hair, three in the left hand and three in the right.

2 Start with the furthest right-hand mesh. Pass this over the inner two meshes.

3 From the left, pass the outside mesh under the next two and over one.

4 Continue to the ends of the hair.

5 Tuck in the hair ends and secure them in position.

Note: Practise on colleagues or models and experiment with different woven shapes before you attempt to weave hair for clients.

AFTER-CARE ADVICE

Good service is supported through good advice. The work that you do in the salon needs to be cared for at home by the client too. What would be the point of creating something if the client doesn't know how to achieve and maintain the same effects at home?

Home-care checklist

✓ Talk through the style as you work; that way the client sees how you handle different aspects of the look.

✓ Show the client the products that you use, explain why you use them, let them see how much is needed.

✓ Show the client how you use the equipment, so that they can benefit from your knowledge and experience.

✓ Demonstrate the techniques that you use so they can achieve that salon hair look too.

✓ Recommend the products/equipment that you use so that the client gets the right things to enable them to get the same effects.

I know and understand the health, safety and hygiene aspects of styling, dressing and finishing hair ☐	I understand the physical properties and changes within the hair that take place during styling and dressing ☐	I always recognise the critical influencing factors when I analyse the client's hair ☐	I know how the effects of excessive heat can damage hair ☐
I know the ranges of products available and how they should be used on the hair ☐	I know how to create a range of blow-dried effects on short, medium and longer hair ☐	I know the principles of setting and how they are applied to achieve a variety of different looks ☐	I can carry out a variety of styling techniques on different lengths of hair ☐
I provide clients with home care advice about style maintenance and product use ☐	I know how the ranges of equipment should be used on the hair to achieve different effects ☐	I know how to achieve a French pleat on longer hair ☐	I know how to achieve different plaiting effects on longer hair ☐
			CHECKER BOARD ✓

Assessment of knowledge and understanding

The following projects, activities and assessments are directly linked to the essential knowledge and understanding for unit H10.

For each statement that is addressed wholly or in part in these activities, you will see its relevant and corresponding EKU number.

Make sure that you keep this for easier referencing and along with your work for future inclusion in your portfolio.

Project (EKU H10.20, H10.21, H10.22, H10.24, H10.25, H10.27)

For this project you will need to gather information from a variety of sources.

Collect together photographs, digital images and magazine clippings about styling, blow-drying, setting and dressing techniques.

Include styles for long hair as well as short; for weddings, special occasions and casual wear.

In your portfolio describe:

- how the styles were achieved
- why each is suitable for its purpose
- the equipment (with examples) that was used to create the effects
- the products (with examples) used to help hold or define the effects.

Case study (H6.15)

A regular client asks you to change from blow-drying to setting their hair. How do you deal with the request? Work through the following and record your answers in your portfolio:

- What factors should you consider first?
- How would you respond?
- How do you cover the different aspects of maintenance and new products?
- How would you cover the negative and positive aspects of changing to something completely different?

Questions

1 How do you prepare the client for styling services? (H10.1)

2 What is your place of work's policy in respect to service timings for setting and blow-drying different hair lengths? (H10.2)

3 What is your place of work's policy in respect to the COSHH regulations? (H10.3)

4 What protection do clients need and why do they need it? (H10.5, H10.7)

5 How does work position and positioning of equipment affect you and the client? (H10.6, H10.8)

6 What are the safety considerations that relate to styling and dressing client's hair? (H10.7, H10.8, H6.10, H10.12, H10.13)

7 Why should products be used economically? (H10.14)

8 What are the effects of humidity on hair? (H10.15)

9 Why is the angle and direction of winding rollers important when setting? (H10.28, H10.26)

10 Why is the angle and direction of airflow important when blow-drying hair? (H10.30)

Preparing for assessment checklist

Remember to:

- prepare clients correctly for the services you are going to carry out
- put on the protective wear available for styling and dressing hair
- listen to the client's requirements and discuss suitable courses of action
- adhere to the safety factors when working on clients' hair
- keep the work areas clean, hygienic and free from hazards
- promote the range of services, products and treatments with the salon
- clean and sterilise the tools and equipment before they are used
- work carefully and methodically through the processes of setting and blow-drying hair
- place, position and direct the hair appropriately to the achieve desired effect
- communicate what you are doing to the client as well as your fellow staff members.

chapter 9

PERMING, RELAXING AND NEUTRALISING HAIR

NVQ/SVQ reference, unit title and main outcome

Unit H12/15/16 Perm, relax and neutralise hair

H12/15/16.1	**Maintain effective and safe methods of working when perming, relaxing and neutralising hair**
H12/15/16.2	**Prepare for perming, relaxing and neutralising**
H12/15/16.3	**Perm and neutralise hair**
H15/16.4	**Relax hair**

What do I need to do?

- Take adequate precautions in preparing yourself and the client before any perming, relaxing or neutralising procedure.
- Be able to use a variety of perming, relaxing and neutralising equipment.
- Be able to use a variety of perming, relaxing and neutralising products.
- Conduct a variety of tests on the hair before and during chemical processing.
- Be able to add wave and/or curl to hair by using a variety of perm wind techniques.
- Be able to reduce wave or curl from hair by using relaxing treatments.
- Be able to neutralise hair after perming and relaxing.

What do I need to learn?

- The factors which can affect the processing of perms, relaxers and neutralising.
- Why it is important to work safely and hygienically when perming, relaxing and neutralising hair.
- How to recognise factors that influence the course of action to be taken.

- How the different chemicals affect the hair.
- The methods of handling different lengths, densities, types and textures of hair.

Information covered in this chapter

- The types of products used for perming, relaxing and neutralising hair and how they work.
- The types of equipment used when perming, relaxing and neutralising hair and how they are used.
- How to prepare the client and yourself before chemical processing.
- A variety of perming techniques that you can use to create different effects.
- The basic science of how perming, relaxing and neutralisers work.
- The advice you should give to clients in order to maintain their own hair.

KEY WORDS

Disulphide bonds The bonds within the hair that are permanently rearranged during perming, relaxing and neutralising.

Lye and no-lye The chemical composition of relaxing treatments.

Softening/reduction The alkaline chemical process which breaks the disulphide bridges within the polypeptide chains by introducing hydrogen.

Curl rearranger Changing the amount and position of natural curl by a chemical process.

Moulding The process of forming shape by using tension e.g. (a) with rods to create waves or curls and (b) with larger rollers to smooth out or reduce unwanted curl.

Fixing/oxidation The acidic chemical process which reforms the disulphide bridges within the polypeptide chains by introducing oxygen.

INTRODUCTION

REMEMBER ✔

Make sure that you always follow the manufacturer's instructions when chemically processing hair.

Perming and colouring are complex technical operations; they rely heavily upon wide-ranging, theoretical background knowledge. Without this knowledge the only thing that can be guaranteed is failure. But like many things in life it is easy when you know how. This chapter provides you with all the essential information you need to get it right every time.

CHECKERBOARD

At the end of this chapter the checkerboard will help to jog your memory on what you have learned and what still remains to be done. Cross off with a pencil each of the topics as you cover it (see page 321).

In perming, as in many other hairdressing services, hair condition is the main consideration. If the client's expectations are matched to the right chemicals and carefully processed, no loss of condition will occur. The quality of the hair – the condition – is directly linked to actions of these chemicals upon the hair. *Moisture is the key*. If the hair retains its natural moisture levels after perming or **relaxing**, the signs of its health are obvious: the shine, the strength, easy 'combability' and great flexibility. Together these features indicate a style that can easily be managed. Lose these qualities and the hair will be dull, lifeless, tangled and difficult to manage. So bearing this principle in mind, let's see how you get everything else right too.

Hair: Patrick Cameron; photography: Thornton Howdle; make-up: Alison Chesterton

HOW PERMS AND RELAXERS WORK

SCIENCE BIT!
THE PHYSICAL CHANGES THAT TAKE PLACE WITHIN THE HAIR ?

'Perming' is the term given to the physical and chemical processing of hair, changing it into waves or curls. 'Relaxing' is the term for chemically reducing wave or curl from hair. Unlike the movement and curl or smoothness produced by blow-drying or setting, the adding or reduction of movement to hair produced by perming and relaxing is permanent: the hair does not return to its previous state when it is dampened. However, hair continues to grow and the new hair retains its natural tendency. So, the waves and curls produced by perming, or the smoothness produced from relaxing, gradually gets further and further away from the scalp as the hair grows. To keep the same style the hair will, at some point, need to be permed or relaxed again.

Because perming really does make a permanent change to the hair, you cannot easily correct mistakes (as you can with blow-styling, for example). The process also involves a variety of chemicals. It is therefore important that you make sure you understand what you are doing.

Changing the keratin
Before going ahead with this section, refer to 'the chemical properties of hair' in chapter 1 on consultation (page 13).

Of the cross-links between the polypeptide chains of hair keratin, the strongest are the disulphide bridges that give hair its strength. Each disulphide bridge is a chemical bond linking two sulphur atoms, one in each of two polypeptide chains lying alongside each other. Each sulphur atom forms part of an amino acid unit called cysteine; the pair of linked units is called cystine.

During perming some of these bridges are chemically broken, converting each cystine into two cysteine units. The breaking of the bridges makes the hair softer and more pliable, allowing it to be moved into a new position of wave or curl.

Only 10–30 per cent (depending on lotion strength) of the disulphide bridges are broken during the action of perming. If too many are broken, the hair will be damaged beyond

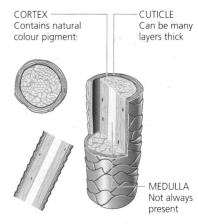

CORTEX
Contains natural colour pigment

CUTICLE
Can be many layers thick

MEDULLA
Not always present

Cross-section of hair

Photo courtesy Goldwell UK

L'Oréal Professionnel

repair. You need to keep a check on the progress of the perm and stop it at the right time. You do this by rinsing away the perm lotion and neutralising the hair. During neutralising, pairs of cysteine units join up again to form new cystine groups at different sites along the hair. The new cross-links thus formed hold the permed hair firmly into its new shape.

Changing the bonds

The hair is first wound with tension on to some kind of former, such as a curler or rod. This is the moulding stage. Then you apply perm lotion to the hair, which makes it swell. The lotion flows under the cuticle and into the cortex. Here it reacts with the keratin, breaking some of the cross-links within and between the polypeptide chains. This softening stage allows the tensioned hair to take up the shape of the former: you then rinse away the perm lotion and neutralise the hair. This fixing stage permanently rearranges the disulphide bonds into the new shape.

This process can also be described in chemical terms. The softening part that breaks some of the cross-links is a process of **reduction**. The disulphide bridges are split by the addition of hydrogen from the perm lotion. (The chemical in the perm lotion that supplies the hydrogen is called a 'reducing agent'.) The keratin is now stretched: it is in a beta-keratin state.

The final part of the process, the fixing stage, makes new cross-links. It occurs by an oxidation reaction. New disulphide bridges form and the hydrogen that was previously added is chemically changed. The hydrogen reacts with the oxygen in the neutraliser, forming water. (The chemical in the neutraliser that supplies the oxygen is called an 'oxidising agent' or 'oxidant'.) The keratin is now in a new, unstretched form: it is alpha-keratin state again.

Disulphide bridges

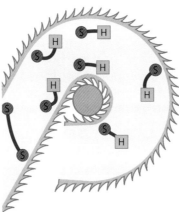

Reduction: breaking the disulphide bridges

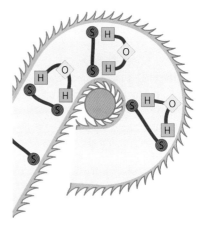

Oxidation: forming new disulphide bridges

PREPARING AND PLANNING THE PERM

Gowning the client

Photo courtesy Goldwell UK

Because of the way that perms are generally applied to hair – by *post damping* (where the lotion is applied and easily absorbed into previously wound sections of hair) – the solutions tend to be very watery and mobile. This, potentially, could be a hazard to the client unless you take adequate precautions. The majority of perm lotions and relaxers are alkaline. If they drip or soak into textiles they will be held against the skin like a poultice. This could cause irritation, swelling and even cause burns; this is bad enough in the areas that you see around the hairlines where you would normally apply cotton wool. But this problem is exacerbated further if it does go onto the client's clothes. It may even discolour the fabrics too!

Make sure that you protect your client well so that this never happens. Put on a chemical-proof gown and secure into place, a clean, fresh towel around their shoulders. On top of this you should fix a plastic cape, ensuring that it is comfortable around the neck.

Protecting yourself

Your salon provides all the personal protective equipment (PPE) that you may need in routine daily practices. Perming involves the handling and application of chemicals, so this is one of those special occasions where you must protect yourself from their caustic effects. Always read the manufacturer's instructions and follow the methods of practice that they specify. You have an obligation by law to wear and use the PPE provided for you, these being vinyl gloves, a waterproof apron and barrier cream.

The Control of Substances Hazardous to Health Regulations (COSHH) 2003 lay out the potential risks that hairdressing chemicals can have. You need to make yourself aware of the information provided by the manufacturers about their handling, storage and safe disposal. Generally, though, perm solutions should be stored in an upright position, in a cool, dry place away from strong sunlight. When they are used they should be applied in a well-ventilated area and if there is any waste (materials that cannot be saved and used another time) it should be disposed of by flushing down the basin with plenty of cold water.

Photo courtesy Goldwell

REMEMBER

Disposable gloves
Your salon will provide disposable gloves for your personal safety when you are handling any chemicals in the workplace. It is recommended that these are of the vinyl variety and only used once and then be discarded. If your gloves tear or stretch during use change them immediately as their protection will be impaired.

Working effectively

Experienced hairdressers work in a way that makes the most out of the time available: they optimise the way in which they work. You need to learn the ways in which you can optimise your time and effort so that your work is both productive and effective. There are a number of ways that you can make this happen:

Minimise waste – get into the habit of eliminating waste. All the resources that you use cost money and the only way that you can be more effective is to maximise your time and effort whilst minimising the cost of carrying out your work. This can be illustrated further by thinking about what goes down the sink. Water is the first thing that comes to mind; cold water is a costly but essential part of hairdressing. All business premises have metered water so, in principle, every shampoo and conditioning rinse can be a calculated cost. But sometimes people rinse far longer than they need to or leave taps running between shampoos and that's where the additional cost is incurred. This is made even worse if the water is hot! We know that cold water is metered, now we've got the additional cost of heating it too!

We should apply the *maximise the resources by minimising the cost* principle to everything we do. Is it necessary to throw away what's left in the perm bottle? Not necessarily, we can use the cold wave type perms another time. Should we mix more colour than we need? Should electrical equipment be left on when not in use? The answer is always no.

Hair: Pat Wood; photography: Thornton Howdle; make-up: Alison Chesterton

Hair: American Dream

Maximise your time: always make good use of your time. There are always things to do in a hairdressing salon and most of them relate to preparation.

- Prepare the salon by cleaning work areas so that it is ready to receive the clients.
- Prepare the materials, look out for stock shortages and report them.
- Prepare the equipment, cleaning and washing the brushes, combs and curlers.
- Prepare client records, updating information and getting things ready for when they arrive.
- Prepare the trolleys, get the right curlers ready, make sure that the rubbers haven't perished and the end papers are at hand.

The list goes on.

ACTIVITY

Minimising waste

How can you minimise wastage?

Have a look around your salon and see what things you can do to reduce the waste of resources.

Create a table for the information, recording what things you can find and how they could be used in the most effective way.

Hair: Sacha New, Wickham Hair Studio

Types of perm

For the client a perm is a major step – they will have to live with the result for several months. They may not be familiar with the range of perming solutions available so you will need to explain what the differences are and what is involved in each.

- Cold, permanent wave solutions, such as Wella's Perform Carnitin or Innowave, are mild alkaline perms. These types of perm are most widely available and simplest to use with applications for all hair types and tendencies and most conditions. These solutions tend to have a pH at around 9.5 so they are a fairly strong alkali that will swell the hair and affect around 20 per cent of the disulphide bridges. They reduce the natural moisture levels within the hair and are therefore better on normal to greasy hair types. They are particularly good for achieving strong, pronounced movement and curl and therefore create lasting effects that can withstand the high maintenance of regular blow-drying, setting etc.
- Acid wave solutions – such as Zotos's Acclaim and 7th Dimension – provide alternatives for perming when the hair is particularly delicate and needs to retain higher moisture levels or requires softer, gentler movement. They have lower pH values at around 6–7 and are therefore much gentler in the way that they work. They are suited to drier, more porous hair types too. Acid perms are two-part solutions and require the components to be mixed together just before application so that the perm is self-activated. Any residual lotion left over after application will not last and is always discarded.

- Exothermic perming systems – such as Zotos's Warm and Gentle – tend to be similar to acid waves in their chemical composition and therefore can have similar benefits. The only difference is that these perms need heat to be activated and will therefore self-generate their heat during processing when the two chemical parts (reagents) are added together, without the need for accelerators or hood driers.

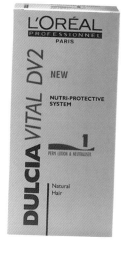

L'Oréal Professionnel Dulcia Vital DV2

> **REMEMBER** ✔
>
> **Contra-indications for perming/relaxing**
> The following list indicates situations when perming should *not* be undertaken
>
> - when the hair is particularly porous (possibly over-bleached)
> - when the scalp has abrasions or sensitive areas
> - when the hair is weakened, broken or damaged
> - when the hair is inelastic (does not have any ability to stretch and return to same length)
> - when incompatibles have been used on the hair (Just for Men, Grecian 2000, compound henna etc.)
> - when the hair has varying levels of porosity throughout the lengths (poorly coloured or bleached)
> - when there is any evidence of physical or chemical changes on the hair or scalp and the client is unable to provide you with a full, satisfactory account of what actions have been taken
> - any evidence of scalp disease or disorder.

L'Oréal Professionnel

> **REMEMBER** ✔
>
> Acid and exothermic perms require the mixing of part A and B together before the perms are applied to the curlers. This starts a chemical reaction, enabling the perm to work on the hair. Make sure that you protect your client by applying moistened cotton wool around the hairlines, so that any drips do not cause any irritation or burning of the skin.
>
> It is advisable to check that the client is comfortable during processing and, if necessary, change the cotton wool again with more moistened cotton wool.

Consultation for perming/relaxing

Find out your client's requirements – what they expect from perming – and determine whether this is the best solution bearing in mind the added maintenance, care and attention needed to achieve the desired effect.

- Consider the style and cut, together with your client's age and lifestyle.
- Examine the hair and scalp closely. If there are signs of inflammation, diseases or cut or grazed skin, do *not* carry out a perm. If there is excessive grease or a coating of chemicals or lacquer you will need to remove these by washing with a pre-perm shampoo first. Previously treated hair will need special consideration.
- Analyse the hair texture. Carry out the necessary tests to select the correct perm lotion.

- Always read manufacturer's instructions carefully.
- Determine the types of curl needed to achieve the chosen style.
- If this is a regular client, refer to the records for details of previous work done on their hair.
- Advise your client of the time and costs involved. Summarise what has been decided, to be sure there aren't any misunderstandings.
- Minimise combing and brushing, to avoid scratching the scalp before the perm.

Analysis/examination

It is important to make sure you choose the most suitable perm lotion, the correct processing time and the right type of curl for the chosen style. Consider the following factors.

- *Hair texture* – For hair of medium texture, use perm lotion of normal strength. Fine hair curls more easily and requires weaker lotion; coarser hair can often be more difficult to wave and may require a stronger lotion for resistant hair. (Although this is not true for oriental hair types.)
- *Hair porosity* – The porosity of the hair determines how quickly the perm lotion is absorbed. Porous hair in poor condition is likely to process more quickly than would hair with a resistant, smooth cuticle. See the section on pre-perming treatments later in this chapter.
- *Previous treatment history* – 'Virgin' hair – hair that has not previously been treated with chemicals – is likely to be more resistant to perming than hair that has been treated. It will require a stronger lotion and possibly a longer processing time.
- *Length and density of hair* – Long heavy hair requires more perming than short hair because the hair's weight will pull on the curls. Short, fine hair may become too tightly curled if given the normal processing time.
- *Style* – Does the style you have chosen require firm curls or soft, loose waves? Do you simply wish to add body and bounce?
- *Size of rod, curler or other former* – Larger rods produce larger curls or waves; smaller rods produce tighter curls. Longer hair generally requires larger rods. If you use very small rods in fine, easy-to-perm hair, the hair may frizz; if you use rods that are too large you may not add enough curl. To check, make a test curl before you start. (See hair tests on opposite page.)
- *Incompatibility* – Perm lotions and other chemicals used on the hair may react with chemicals that have already been used – for example, in home-use products. Hair that looks dull may have been treated with such chemicals. Ask your client what products are used at home, and test for incompatibility.

REMEMBER

Always record the details of the consultation/service for future reference.

REMEMBER

Some medical conditions affect the way that hair responds. For example, clients with thyroid problems will find that perms don't seem to last.

REMEMBER

Clients that have been taking health supplements such as cod liver oil over long periods of time will notice that they affect the way that the perm takes in the hair. (When cod liver oil supplements are taken, increased levels of moisture are deposited into the hair which, ultimately, slackens the hair and results in limp curls.)

HAIR TESTS

- *Elasticity test* – This tests the tensile strength of the hair. Hair in good condition has the ability to stretch and return to its original length, whereas hair in poor or damaged condition will stretch and will not return to original length. This lack of elasticity will make the hair difficult to manage and maintain. A clear indication for this would be to ask the client how long their set or blow-dry lasts after it has been done. When the styling drops or can't be sustained in the hair, it is a clear indication that the hair has lost this vital attribute of elasticity. Take a single hair strand and hold firmly at either end then stretch between your fingers. If it breaks easily the cortex may be damaged, and perming could be harmful.

- *Porosity test* – The purpose of this test is to find out how well protected the inner cortex is by the cuticle layers. Porous hair has a damaged cuticle layer and readily absorbs moisture; this presents a problem when drying, as this hair takes longer to dry and often lacks an ability to hold a style well. This can be done by taking a small section of hair and sliding from the root, through to the points, between your fingertips. From this you can feel how rough or smooth it is. Rougher hair (as opposed to coarse hair) is likely to be more porous, and will therefore process more quickly.

- *Incompatibility test* – Hairdressing products are based upon organic chemistry formulations. These are incompatible with inorganic chemistry compositions and will cause damage to the client's hair. This test will identify whether metallic salts are present within the hair, a clear contra-indication that the perm may be carried out. Protect your hands by wearing gloves. Place a small cutting of hair in a mixture of hydrogen peroxide and ammonium hydroxide. Watch for signs of bubbling, heating or discolouration: these indicate that the hair already contains incompatible chemicals. The hair should not be permed, nor should it be coloured or bleached. Perming treatment might discolour or break the hair, and might burn the skin.

- *Pre-perm test curl* – If you are unsure about how your client's hair will react under processing you could conduct a pre-perm test curl. Sometimes this can be done on the head and in other situations where there isn't sufficient time etc. you will need to cut your sample for testing. Wind, process and neutralise one or more small sections of hair. The results will be a guide to the optimum rod size, the processing time and the strength of lotion to be used. Remember, though, that the hair will not all be of the same porosity.

- *Development test curl* – This test is always carried out after the hair has been damped with perm solution and during the processing time. It will determine the stage of curl development so that the processing is not allowed to continue beyond the optimum. Unwind – and then rewind – rods during processing, to see how the curl is developing. If the salon is very hot or cold this will affect the progress of the perm: heat will accelerate it, cold will slow it down. When you have achieved the 'S' shape you want, stop the perm by rinsing and then neutralising the hair.

REMEMBER
Temperature has a major impact on perming. This could be general salon temperature or by added heat from a hood dryer. In either case remember that processing times will be *reduced* considerably.

Hair: Sacha New, Wickham Hair Studio

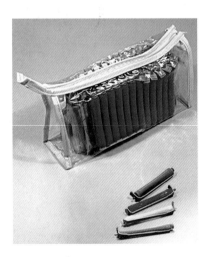

L'Oréal Professionnel

Comby

Pre-perming and post-perming treatments

Matching the correct perm lotion to hair type is an essential part of the hair analysis. However, many perming solutions come in only a tinted, normal or resistant formula and this alone will not cater for all hair conditions. Dry, porous hair will absorb perming solutions more readily; therefore special attention needs to be given in these situations. Pre-perming treatments are a way to combat these conditioning issues. Porous hair that is suitable for perming will have an uneven porosity throughout the lengths. Hair that is nearer the root will have a different porosity level to that at mid-length hair, or that of the ends. Therefore the hair's porosity levels will need to be evened out, i.e. balanced before the perm lotion is applied. This enables the hair to absorb perm lotion at the same rate, evening out the development process and ensuring that the perm doesn't over-process in certain areas. A pre-perming treatment is applied before winding on damp hair and combed through to the ends. Any excess is removed and the hair is wound as normal.

After perming and neutralising it is also necessary to rebalance the hair's pH value back to that of 5.5. Post-perm treatments do this by removing any traces of residual oxygen from the neutralising process; these treatments are also known as 'anti-oxidants'.

Protect the client

After gowning your client as described at the beginning of the chapter, you should now apply the barrier cream to the hairline.

REMEMBER	

Barrier cream is a thick protective cream, ideally suited for wearing on your hands as an invisible coating to help prevent the action of chemicals causing you any harm.

It is equally important for the client too. Barrier cream applied around the hairline will also help prevent the action of chemicals harming them during processing.

REMEMBER	

Vinyl gloves provide you with a guaranteed barrier against the action of harsh chemicals upon the skin.

PERM PREPARATION AND TECHNIQUE

Step-by-step: Perm preparation

1 Protect your client with a gown and towels.
2 Shampoo the hair to remove grease or dirt with a pre-perming, soapless shampoo (failure to remove build-up of styling products could otherwise block the action of the perm lotion).

3 Towel-dry the hair. (Excess water dilutes the lotion, but if the hair is too dry the perm lotion won't spread evenly through the hair.)

4 Some perm lotions contain chemicals to treat porosity. If you are going to use a pre-perm lotion to help even out porosity apply it now. Make sure you have read the instructions carefully. Too much pre-perm lotion may block the action of the perm itself.

5 Prepare your trolley. You will need:
   • rods or curlers of the chosen sizes
   • end papers, for use while winding
   • a tail comb and clips, for sectioning and dividing
   • cotton wool strips, to protect your client
   • vinyl gloves, to protect your hands
   • perm lotion and a suitable neutraliser/normaliser (read the instructions carefully)
   • a water spray, to keep the hair damp
   • a plastic cap and a timer for the processing stage.

6 Check that your client's skin and clothing are adequately protected.

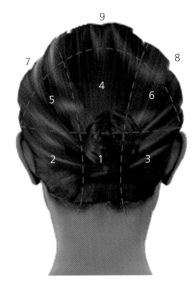

Sectioning: nine-section wind

Sectioning/sequence of winding

First of all divide the hair into workable sections. This makes the hair tidier and easier to control. Done properly, sectioning makes the rest of the process simple and quick. If it's not done well, you will have to resection the hair during the perm, and this may spoil the overall result.

Step-by-step: Nine-section perm wind

1 Following shampooing and towel drying; comb the hair to remove any tangles.

2 Make sure you have the tools you will need, including a curler to check the width of the section size.

3 Now divide the hair into nine sections, as follows (use clips to secure the hair as you work):
   • divide the hair from ear to ear to give front hair and back hair
   • divide the back hair into lower, nape hair and upper top back hair
   • divide the front hair, approximately above mid-eyebrow to give a middle and two sides
   • divide the top section along the same lines, to give a middle and two sides
   • divide the nape section likewise, to give a middle and two sides.

Sub-sectioning

Once the hair has been divided into the nine sections and firmly secured with clips you can start to wind in the perm rods. The diagram on sectioning shows these sections, the numbering refers to the order in which the sections are wound. You start winding at the occipital area down the back of the head in a organised and controlled way.

Note. The sectioning techniques for perming can be adapted and used for many other techniques. For more information on directional and brick-type winds see the section on winding techniques below.

Winding: taking a hair section

REMEMBER ✓

Note that the tension of the held section is even throughout. There is no slack or pulling from one side to the other.

Six-section wind

The National Occupational Standards for hairdressing S/NVQ Level 2 require the learner to demonstrate the nine-section wind technique. There is another, quicker version of this that is more commonly used in salons and that is the six-section wind.

In the diagram on the previous page – the six-section winding technique amalgamates the zones 5 and 2, 4 and 1, and 6 and 3, to form only three rear panels at the back of the head. This means that the wind is started centrally, at the top rather than halfway down the back. This is easier to manage than the nine-section wind, although it will take a little more care in sectioning accurately.

WINDING

Winding is the process of placing sectioned hair onto a variety of rods or curlers. There are various winding techniques, designed to produce different effects, but the method is basically the same in each case. In modern perming systems you need to wind the hair finely and evenly, but without stretching the hair or leaving it in tension.

ACTIVITY

First practise winding wet hair on a block. It should be dampened with water rather than perm lotion, as this gives you more time. When you can wind a block in 60 minutes, move on to a live model. When you can do this in under 30 minutes, you can try 'live perming' with perm lotion.

Step-by-step: Winding

1 Divide off a section of hair, of a length and thickness to match the curler being used (see the diagram on the previous page).
2 Comb the hair firmly, directly away from the head. Keep the hair together, so that it doesn't slip.
3 Place the hair points at the centre of the curler. Make sure the hair isn't bunched at one side and loose at the other.
4 Hold the hair directly away from the head. If you let the hair slope downwards, the curler won't sit centrally on the base section: hair will overlap, and the curler will rest on the skin.
5 Before winding, make sure the curler is at an angle suited to the part of the head against which it will rest when wound.
6 Hold the hair points with the finger and thumb of one hand. The thumb should be uppermost.
7 Direct the hair points round and under the curler. Turn your wrist to achieve this. The aim is to lock the points under the curler and against the main body of hair – if they don't lock, they may become bucked or 'fish-hooked'. Don't turn the thumb too far round or the hair will be pushed away from the curler and won't lock the points.

Winding: depth of section

Winding: width of section

8 After making the first turn of the curler; pass it to the other hand to make the next turn. The hands need to be in complete control: uncontrolled movement, or rocking from side to side, may cause the ends to slip, the hair to bunch or the firmness to slacken.

9 After two or three turns the points will be securely locked. Wind the curler down to the head. Keep the curler level – if it wobbles from side to side, the hair may slip off or the result may look uneven.

10 At the end, the curler should be in the centre of the section. If it isn't, unwind it and start gain,

11 Secure the curler. Don't let the rubber fastener press into the hair – it might damage it.

Before.

Make sure you have everything to hand.

Step 1: Divide the hair into nine secured sections or more conveniently, into six sections.

Step 3: Start at the top, take a section no wider or deeper than the curler being put in.

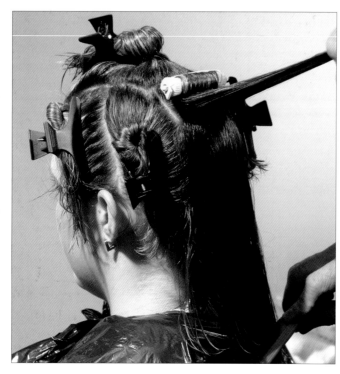

Step 4: Wind down the curler with even tension.

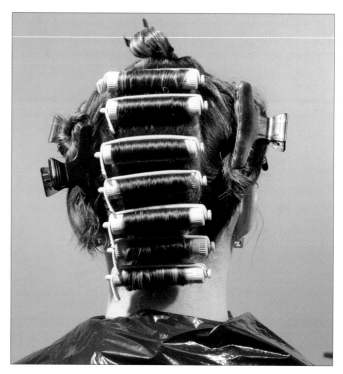

Step 5: Position the curler so that it sits upon its own base and doesn't impede the next curler's positioning.

Step 6: Continue down the back until all of the curlers have been placed, then move on to the sides.

Step 7: With the first back section wound, start the sides ensuring that the remainder hair on the top is no wider than the width of a curler.

Step 8: With the sides and back completed and bridging strips in place, finish off the top working forwards from the crown.

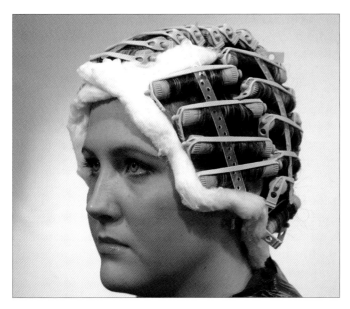

Step 9: Apply lightly dampened cotton wool around the hairline and then apply the perm lotion to each curler.

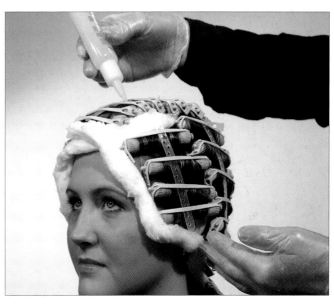

Step 10: Apply just enough lotion to each curler so that it is moisturised but not saturated. Then a plastic cap can be placed around all of the curlers for the devlopment process.

Finished effect.

Winding techniques

There are various winding techniques, used to produce varied effects. The following are the most commonly used.

Directional winding – The hair is wound in the direction in which it is to be finally worn. This technique is suitable for enhancing well-cut shapes. The hair can be wound in any direction required, and the technique is ideal for shorter hairstyles.

L'Oréal Professionnel

REMEMBER	
Wear gloves from the beginning. It is inconvenient to have to put them on later.	

Directional winding   L'Oréal

Staggered or brick winding

Spiral winding

Weave winding   Wella

Brick winding – The wound curlers are placed in a pattern resembling brickwork. By staggering the partings of the curlers, you avoid obvious gaps in the hair. This technique is suitable for short hairstyles.

Spiral winding – The hair is wound from roots to points around one of a variety of objects: sticks, shapers, hair moulders or curlers of one shape or another. Triangular and square shapers have been used. The effects produced are mainly in the lengths of the hair, the root ends being less affected. This is probably the oldest form of winding. It is most effective, and most practical, when used on long hair.

Weave winding – The normal size section is divided into two and then the hair is woven. A large curler is used to wind the upper subsection, and a smaller one is used for the lower subsection. This produces two different curl sizes, giving volume without tight curls. Alternatively, one sub-section is wound and the other left unwound. If the hair is cut after perming, on shorter hairstyles this could produce spiky effects.

Double winding – This technique consists of winding a section of hair halfway down on a large curler, then placing a smaller curler underneath and winding both curlers down to the head. This produces a varied curl effect.

Piggyback winding – This is winding using a small and a large curler. The normal-size section is wound from the middle on to a large curler, down to the head. The ends are then wound from the points on to a smaller curler, which is placed on top of the large curler. This produces softly waved roots and curly points. Alternatively this technique can be used to produce root movement only if you do not wind the point ends.

Stack winding – This is used where fullness is required in long hair, with little curl movement on top – it is ideal for bobbed hair lengths. The sections are wound close to the head in the lower parts; the upper sections are part wound only, at the points. This allows the curlers to stack one upon another.

To appreciate the effects of different techniques of winding you need to experiment with them.

ACTIVITY

Using blocks, practise the different winding techniques. Process them as well, so that you are familiar with their effects before live perming.

Winding aids

- The pin-tail comb is useful for directing small pieces of hair onto the curler. The pin-tail comb is narrower than a plastic tail comb so you can guide the wound hair around the wound section to make sure that all the hair has an even tension.

- End papers or wraps are specially made for winding perms. Very few hairdressers would consider winding without them as they ensure control of the hair when it is wound. Fold them neatly over the hair points (never bundle them). The wrap overlaps the hair points and prevents fish-hooks. For smaller or shorter sections of hair, half an end wrap is sufficient – a full one would cause unevenness. Other types of tissue may absorb the perm lotion and interfere with processing, and these are best avoided.

- Many kinds of curler are suitable for perm winding. Plastic, wood and PVC foam are amongst the commonest materials used. The manufacturer uses different colours to indicate size. The greater the diameter or the fatter the curler, the bigger the wave or curl produced. The smallest curlers are used for short nape hair or for producing tight curls. Most curlers are of smaller diameter at the centre: this enables the thinner, gathered hair points to fill the concave part evenly and neatly as the hair is wound, widening out to the shoulder of the curler as you wind closer to the head.

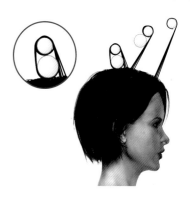

Weave winding

ACTIVITY

Try out different curlers, rods and winding shapes. Note the varied effects they produce. Practise the different curler positions for perming. Try these out on blocks or models to appreciate the differences.

On a practice block of sample hair cuttings, experiment with the effects produced by different incorrect forms of winding. This will help you to recognise and avoid these effects.

Processing and development

Perm lotion may be applied before winding (**pre-damping**) or when winding is complete (post-damping). Pre-damping is often used on long hair to ensure the solution penetrates evenly through the hair length. When pre-damping, you have to work quickly to avoid over-processing the hair. Your work should be complete within 35 minutes. Follow the manufacturer's instructions on the type of application to use. Post-damping is perhaps more convenient as you can wind the hair without wearing gloves and the time taken in winding doesn't affect the overall processing time.

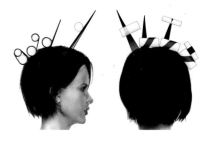

Double winding

Applying the perm lotion

Most modern perming systems come in individually packed perm lotions, ready for application. Others may need to be dispensed from a litre-size bottle to a bowl, before applying to the wound head using cotton wool, a sponge or a brush.

- Underlying hair is often more resistant to perming (e.g. at the nape of the neck), so you could apply lotion to those areas first (see the diagram on sectioning on pages 297 and 301).

- Keep lotion away from the scalp. Apply it to the hair section, about 12 mm from the roots.

- If post-damping, apply a small amount of the perm lotion to each rod; do not over-saturate as the lotion will flood onto the scalp and will drip on to the client. This could cause either irritation or burning on the scalp or skin.

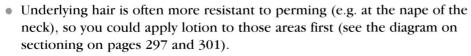

Piggyback winding

REMEMBER ✔

Always read the instructions carefully before applying.

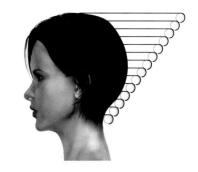

Stack winding

L'Oréal Professionnel

Hair: Pat Wood; photography: Thornton Howdle;
make-up: Alison Chesterton

- It is better to apply the lotion again once the first application has started to absorb into the hair.
- Don't overload the applicator, and apply the lotion gently. You will be less likely then to splash your client.
- If you do splash the skin, quickly rinse the lotion away with water.

Processing time

Processing begins as soon as the perm lotion is in contact with the hair. The time needed for processing is critical. Processing time is affected by the hair texture and condition, the salon temperature and whether heat is applied, the size and number of curlers used and the type of winding used.

Hair texture and condition   Fine hair processes more quickly than coarse hair and dry hair than greasy hair. Hair that has been processed previously will perm faster than virgin hair.

Temperature   A warm salon cuts down processing time; in a cold salon it will take longer. Even a draught will affect the time required. Usually the heat from the head itself is enough to activate perming systems. Wrap your client's head with plastic tissue or a cap to keep in the heat. Don't wrap the hair in towels: these will absorb the lotion and slow down the processing.

Some perm lotions require additional heat from computerised accelerators, roller balls or dryers. Don't apply heat unless the manufacturer's instructions tell you to – you might damage both the hair and the scalp. And don't apply heat unless the hair is wrapped; the heat could evaporate the lotion or speed up the processing too much.

Curlers   Processing will be quicker with a lot of small sections on small curlers than with large sections on large curlers. (The large sections will also give looser results.)

Winding   The type of winding used, and the tension applied, can also affect processing time. Hair wound firmly processes faster than hair wound slackly – in fact, if the winding is too slack it will not process at all. Hair wound too tightly may break close to the scalp. The optimum is a firm winding without tension.

Development test curl   This involves testing the curl during processing. As processing time is so critical, you need to use a timer. You also need to check the perm at intervals to see how it's progressing. If you used the pre-damping technique, check the first and last curlers that you wound. If you applied the lotion after winding, check curlers from the front, sides, crown and nape.

- Unwind the hair from a curler. Is the 's' shape produced correct for the size of curler used?
- If the curl is too loose, rewind the hair and allow more processing time. (But if the test curl is too loose because the curler was too large, extra processing time will damage the hair and won't make the curl tighter.)
- If the curl is correct, stop the processing by rinsing.

Step-by-step: Synchrone application

Pre-treatment

1 Before every synchrone application. Apply presifon 1 carefully before sectioning the hair.

2 Apply presifon 2 where hair is highlighted and/or very sensitised. Choose the appropriate winding technique and tools for the desired hair and look.

Application

3 Always wear disposable gloves. Select the synchrone wave lotion according to the hair type. Prepare 80 ml of the chosen synchrone wave lotion in the synchrone applicator (silver top). Apply the wave lotion slowly over each wound section three times to ensure the lotion penetrates the hair.

4 Wrap the sections in clingfilm. Develop at toom temperature – Red: 15 minutes, Blue: 10 minutes, Green: 10 minutes. Rinse thoroughly for five minutes and blot dry.

5 Prepare 100 ml of synchrone neutralising lotion in the second synchrone applicator (white top). Apply to each wound section. Leave for five minutes.

6 Unwind, gently massaging the hair and applying any remaining neutralising lotion. Leave for three minutes. Rinse thoroughly. If required apply an instant série expert powerdose curl. Style as required using tecni.art.

Step 1: Applying presifon 1.   L'Oréal Professionnel

Step 2: Applying presifon 2.   L'Oréal Professionnel

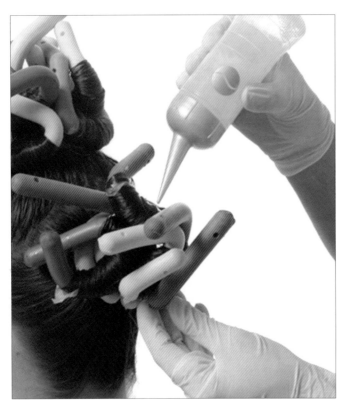

Step 3: Apply sinchrone wave lotion.   L'Oréal Professionnel

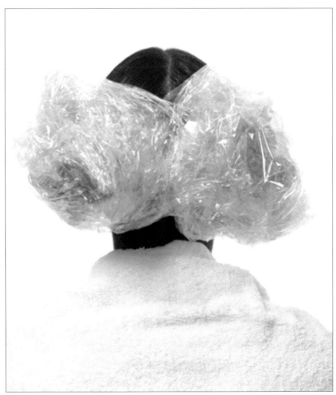

Step 4: Wrap sections in clingfilm and leave to develop at room temperature.   L'Oréal Professionnel

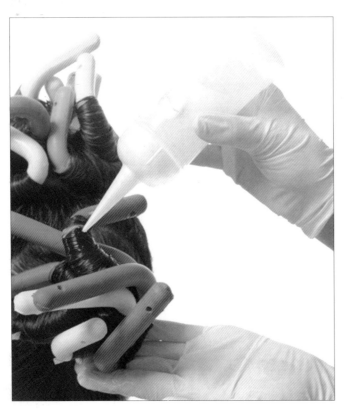

Step 5: Apply neutralising lotion.   L'Oréal Professionnel

Step-by-step: Sultry wave

1 Divide the hair into 12–16 vertical sections. If required use end paper to hold hair together.

2 Without elevating the root, wind the section onto the synchrone shaper. Fix with the clip.

3 Continue to wind each section following a vertical pattern. Tip: For a more natural result leave out a couple of inches of hair at the root.

Step 1   L'Oréal Professionnel

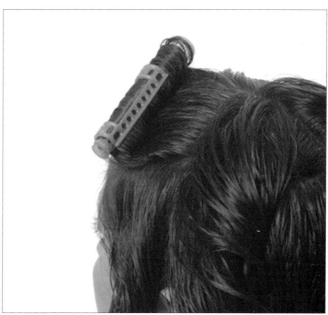

Step 2   L'Oréal Professionnel

Step 3   L'Oréal Professionnel

L'Oréal Professionnel

Step-by-step: Beach wave

1 Divide the hair into two ponytails. Use synchrone bendies to secure each section.

2 From each ponytail, wind sections of hair into synchrone bendies. If required use end paper to hold hair together.

3 Continue to wind each section in a random pattern.

4 Tip: This variation on the ponytail is very useful when the hair has different degrees of sensitivity.

Step 1   L'Oréal Professionnel

Step 2   L'Oréal Professionnel

Step 3   L'Oréal Professionnel

L'Oréal Professionnel

NEUTRALISING

Introduction

The successful outcome of a perm or a relaxing treatment is dependant on the correct processing of the hair during perming/relaxing and the way the hair is rebalanced during the action of neutralising. The principles for neutralising are similar in both perming/relaxing services, although the technique used in each does vary. Therefore this section is about neutralising following a perm. Information on neutralising following relaxing services can be found later in the chapter.

In this section we will look at:

- the principles of neutralising perms
- how neutralising works
- choosing a neutraliser
- neutralising techniques
- what to do after perming.

L'Oréal Professionnel

> **REMEMBER**
>
> Read labels and check contents of boxes – before use.

The principles

Neutralising is the process of reconditioning or rebalancing the hair after perming. An industry term, 'neutralising' is a little misleading. In chemistry, a 'neutral' chemical condition is neither acidic nor alkaline (pH 7.0). Conversely, during the hairdressing treatment of 'neutralising', the previously processed hair is returned to the skin's healthy, slightly acidic natural state of pH 4.5–5.5.

How neutralising works

As described earlier, perm lotion acts on the keratin in the hair. The strongest bonds between the polypeptides are the disulphide bridges. Perm lotion breaks some of these, allowing the keratin to take up a new shape. This is how new curls can form.

What neutralising does is to make new disulphide bridges. If you didn't neutralise the hair it would be weak and likely to break, and the new curls would soon fall out. Neutralising is an oxidation process – a process that uses oxidising agents such as hydrogen peroxide, sodium bromate and sodium perborate.

Choosing a neutraliser

Manufacturers of perm lotions usually produce matching neutralisers. These are designed to work together. If possible, always use the neutraliser that matches the perm lotion you've used. As most perms are individually packed you will find a perm lotion and its matched neutraliser in the box.

Photo courtesy Goldwell UK

Photo courtesy Goldwell UK

L'Oréal Professionnel Dulcia Tonica

A neutraliser may be supplied as an emulsion cream, a foam or a liquid. Always follow the manufacturer's instructions. Some can be applied directly from the container, others are applied with a sponge or a brush.

ACTIVITY

Try perm processing with one type of perm lotion on two or more hair samples or practice blocks. Use a different neutraliser for each. Record the differences that you find between them.

Neutralising technique

Neutralising follows directly on from perming. Imagine that you have shampooed, dried and wound the hair. The hair is now perming, and you are timing the perm carefully and making tests to check whether it is complete. You will also be reassuring the client that they have not been forgotten! As soon as the perm is finished, you need to be ready to stop the process immediately.

Preparation

1 Gather together the materials you will need.
2 Make sure there is a back basin free. (This makes it easier for you to keep chemicals away from the client's eyes.)

First rinsing

1 As soon as the perm is complete, move your client immediately to the back wash. Make sure they are comfortable.
2 Carefully remove the cap. The hair is in a soft and weak stage at this point, so don't put unnecessary tension on it. Leave the curlers in place.
3 Run the water. You need an even supply of warm water. The water must be neither hot nor cold as this will be uncomfortable for the client. Hot water will also irritate the scalp and could burn. Check the pressure and temperature against the back of your hand. Remember that your client's head may be sensitive after the perming process.

4   Rinse the hair thoroughly with the warm water. This may take about five minutes or longer if the hair is long. It is this rinsing that stops the perm process – until you rinse away the lotion, the hair will still be processing. Direct the water away from the eyes and the face. Make sure you rinse *all* the hair, including the nape curlers. If a curler slips out, gently wind the hair back onto it immediately.

Applying neutraliser

1   Make sure your client is in a comfortable sitting position.

2   Blot the hair thoroughly, using a towel (you may need more than one). It may help if you pack the curlers with cotton wool.

3   When no surplus water remains, apply the neutraliser. Follow the manufacturer's instructions. These may tell you to pour the neutraliser through the hair, or apply it with a brush or sponge, or use the spiked applicator bottle. Some foam neutralisers need to be pushed briskly into the hair. Make sure that neutraliser comes into contact with all of the hair on the curlers.

4   When all the hair has been covered, time the process according to the instructions. The usual time is five to ten minutes. You may wrap the hair in a towel or leave it open to the air – follow the manufacturer's instructions.

5   Gently and carefully remove the curlers. Don't pull or stretch the hair. It may still be soft, especially towards the ends, and you don't want to disturb the curl formation.

6   Apply the neutraliser to the hair again, covering all the hair. Arrange the hair so that the neutraliser does not run over the face. Leave for the time recommended, perhaps another five to ten minutes.

Second rinsing

1   Run the water, again checking temperature and pressure.

2   Rinse the hair thoroughly to remove the neutraliser.

3   You can now treat the hair with an after-perm (anti-oxidant) or conditioner. Use the one recommended by the manufacturer of the perm and neutraliser, to be sure that the chemicals are compatible.

Perm aids or conditioner and balanced conditioners (anti-oxidants) help neutralise the effect of the chemical process by helping to restore the pH balance of the hair to pH 4.4–5.5 and smooth down the hair cuticle improving the hair's look, feel, combability and handling.

> **REMEMBER**
>
> When applying a conditioner apply to the palms of the hands first and gently work the conditioner through the hair. Do not massage the scalp or pull the hair as it may soften the newly formed curl.

> **ACTIVITY**
>
> Wind several curlers and perm process them. Neutralise in the normal way. When unwinding, make a point of stretching some of them. Compare the result with others that were more carefully undone. Record the differences in your portfolio when the hair is dry.
>
> Collect together several hair samples. Wind and process each with perm lotion. Follow the manufacturer's instructions. Apply neutraliser to each sample. Process the neutraliser allowing 5, 10, 15 and 20 minutes and longer. Compare the results. Record the effects produced by the different neutralising times.

Step-by-step: Neutralising

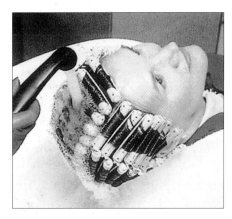

Neutralising: first rinse.
L'Oréal Professionnel

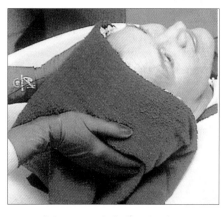

Neutralising: towel drying the hair.
L'Oréal Professionnel

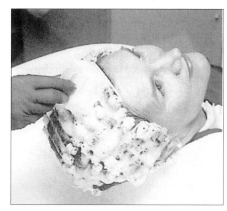

Neutralising: first application.
L'Oréal Professionnel

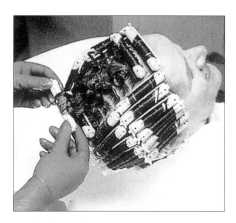

Removing curlers.   L'Oréal Professionnel

Second application of neutraliser.
L'Oréal Professionnel

Hair: Desmond Murray; make-up: Xavier;
photography: Thornon Howdle; assistant:
Gemma Adams

At the end of the neutralising process, you will have returned the hair to a normal, stable state.

- The reduction and oxidation processes will have been completed.
- The hair will now be slightly weaker – fewer bonds will have formed than were broken by the perm.
- Record any hair or perm faults on the client's record card. Correct faults as appropriate.
- Under-neutralising – not leaving neutraliser on for long enough – results in a slack curls or waves.
- Over-oxidising – leaving the neutraliser on too long or using oxidants that are too strong – results in weak hair and poor curl.

The hair should be ready for shaping, blow-drying or setting.

After the perm

- Check the results of perming.
  – Has the scalp been irritated by the perm lotion?
  – Is the hair in good condition?
  – Is the curl even?

- Dry the hair into style.
  - Depending on the effect you want, you may now use finger drying, hood drying or blow-drying.
  - Treat the hair gently as the hair may take a few washes to settle in. If you handle it too firmly the perm may relax again.
- Advise the client on how to manage the perm at home.
  - The hair should not be shampooed for a day or two.
  - The manufacturer of the perm lotion may have supplied information to be passed to the client.
  - Discuss general hair care with your client.
- Clean all tools thoroughly so that they are ready for the next client.
- Complete the client's record card.
  - Note details of the type of perm, the strength of the lotion, the processing time, the curler sizes and the winding technique.
  - Record any problems you have had. This information will be useful if the hair is permed again.

Hair: Desmond Murray; make-up: Xavier; photography: Thornon Howdle; assistant: Gemma Adams

RELAXING HAIR

Relaxing processes have always, in one form or another, been applied to hair. Throughout hairdressing history, people with very tightly curled hair have wanted less curly or smoother looks. Most early relaxing processes were physically based and temporary in their effects, but today's chemical techniques can produce effective and permanent results.

Photo courtesy Rush London for Goldwell Styling

SCIENCE BIT! THE PRINCIPLES OF RELAXING HAIR	?

Two-step process

The chemistry of hair relaxing with a thioglycollate derivative is a two-step process, similar to permanent waving. The disulphide bridges in the cystine links between the keratin chains of the hair are reduced (broken) by the action of the ammonium thioglycollate in the relaxing cream/gel/lotion. This softens the hair, which can then be moulded into its new relaxed shape. This is followed by neutralisation, which is an oxidation process (a reaction with oxygen). Cysteine groups pair up again to form cystines, and the disulphide bridges reform in new positions. (See the section on neutralising earlier in this chapter.)

(One-step process)

Other chemicals, such as sodium hydroxide, can also be used. Sodium hydroxide breaks down the disulphide bonds in hair by 'hydrolysis' – that is, the breakdown of a substance by, and with, water. Cystine groups are separated into cysteines, and sulphuric acid is also formed; continued processing produces lanthionine – another amino acid – and other single sulphur links. The hair softens and relaxes, tight curls are loosened, and the hair can be moulded into a more relaxed shape. When a sufficient degree of relaxation is reached the hair is shampooed with an acid-balancing neutralising shampoo, which returns to its normal acid state. No oxidising neutraliser is used.

This one-step chemical process differs from the relaxing and perming processes using ammonium thioglycollate reduction followed by oxidation. It is very important to vet closely the subsequent use of other chemical processes on the chemically relaxed hair because the basic nature of the hair has been changed. Fewer disulphide bridges are now present, so further reduction processes should not be used.

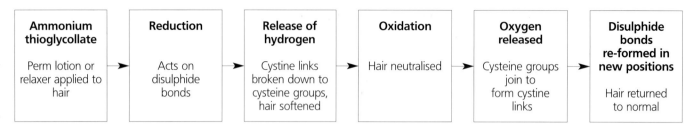

Ammonium thioglycollate	**Reduction**	**Release of hydrogen**	**Oxidation**	**Oxygen released**	**Disulphide bonds re-formed in new positions**
Perm lotion or relaxer applied to hair	Acts on disulphide bonds	Cystine links broken down to cysteine groups, hair softened	Hair neutralised	Cysteine groups join to form cystine links	Hair returned to normal

Relaxing hair: Two-stage reduction and oxidation

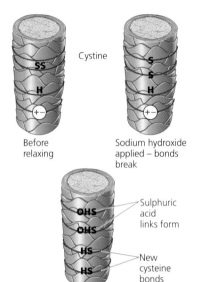

Before relaxing

Cystine

Sodium hydroxide applied – bonds break

Sulphuric acid links form

New cysteine bonds

Sulphuric acid and cysteine links form

Lanthionine links

Further reaction produces lanthionine, a single sulphur amino acid link

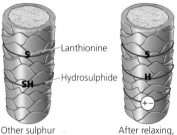

Lanthionine

Hydrosulphide

Other sulphur combines with water to form hydrosulphide

After relaxing, mostly single sulphur lanthionine left, and hydrogen and salt links reformed

Relaxing hair: a continuous one-stage process (simplified)

In this section we will look at the application of permanent methods currently used in salons to reduce or remove curl from the hair.

Relaxing hair is a process of removing curl or wave, wholly or in part. Clients with naturally very curly, kinky or frizzy hair may want it looser, softly curled or straight. After a total head treatment the regrowth will need treating from time to time.

> **REMEMBER** ✓
>
> Once the hair has been relaxed with sodium or non-sodium compounds, the structure of hair is permanently changed. With only one sulphur bond the hair can never be permed.

Preparation

In addition to carrying out the normal preparation of your client (see the beginning of this chapter) and covering their hair, as well as ensuring you have all the tools/materials required, you should double-check the following for this service:

● client's needs

● your client's hair type (curly or wavy) and hair texture (fine, medium or coarse)

M. Balfre

M. Balfre

- whether your client's hair is 'virgin' (chemically untreated) hair; if so, it may be more resistant to relaxing
- the condition of the hair if it has previously been chemically treated e.g. coloured
- the hair and scalp for signs of poor condition, sensitivity or disease
- contra-indications are present, then refer to your seniors so a decision can be made
- with your client, exactly what is to be done, about how long it will take and what it will cost
- that the client is comfortable and that they remain so throughout the service.

REMEMBER

Health and safety
In all relaxing processes you must take great care to prevent damage to your client's hair or skin. You must ensure that the client is adequately protected throughout.

Relaxing products (lye and no-lye)

Like perms, relaxing products are alkaline in their composition, although most tend to be chemically stronger than perms and therefore have a higher pH value at above pH 10. If these products are used incorrectly the hair could be easily and permanently damaged. One-step relaxing products contain sodium hydroxide which is also referred to as **lye**. These products are imported from outside the UK and its standards for usage and compliance; they are stronger than perms and likely to cause irritation and some discomfort. Alternatives to products based on lye, **no-lye** products, are also available. These are just as strong and tend to be caustic potassium or calcium-based compounds.

In two-step treatments where ammonium thioglycollate-based products are used to modify the hair structure, the neutralisers are similar to those used in perming. The oxidising agents may be hydrogen peroxide-based, but, for kinder, gentler use on African-Caribbean hair, use an agent derived from sodium bromate, although this does tend to lead to longer processing times.

Test the hair

Always make tests on your client's hair to ensure that it is in a suitable state for relaxing, particularly when dryness, brittleness or breakage of the hair are evident. The following tests are recommended (see page 291 on testing hair):

- a test cutting, to check the likely result of the intended process
- elasticity check, to determine the hair condition
- porosity check, to determine the rate of absorption
- testing a strand, to check on process development
- incompatibility test, to detect the presence of metallic compounds.

M. Balfre

M. Balfre

Factors affecting product choice and application

Product knowledge is essential. Whatever you decide to use, you must be familiar with it. You must study the manufacturer's instructions for use before your client arrives or before you attempt to apply the product. (This also applies to your tools and equipment.) You should only decide on the most suitable strength of chemical product after doing the following:

- The consultation with your client, and making sure you know exactly what your client requires.
- Checking to determine whether your client is taking any prescribed medication, and if they have any allergies.
- Examining the hair and scalp condition.
- Finding out the results of the relevant tests.
- Checking with a salon senior or specialist (proceed only after agreement is reached).
- Ensuring products are in stock to avoid disappointing your client.
- Deciding whether the hair is fine, medium, coarse, thick, thin, porous or resistant (coarse hair requires the longest processing time and fine hair the shortest; grease or heavy chemical build-up on hair can block the relaxer product; hair that has been previously bleached, permed, straightened or relaxed can be very receptive and may process very fast).
- Noting any other helpful information.

You can begin the relaxation process once you have considered the following factors:

- Whether the hair is in a suitable condition for processing (for instance, a rough cuticle could indicate uneven porosity; which would be likely to affect the result).
- The salon temperature – a hot salon could speed processing, a cold one could delay it.
- The hairstyle required after the hair has been relaxed, taking into account your client's head and face shape and hair growth patterns. If the client's hair is to change from very curly to very straight, they may need guidance from you about managing it afterwards and about home maintenance products.

Relaxing methods and procedures

The permanent methods are chemical ones. These involve the use of strong chemicals which must be used with care. The types of chemical relaxers currently available include:

- ammonium thioglycollate-based lotions, made for looser-curled hair, such as Caucasian-type hair
- specially made creams, also ammonium thioglycollate-based, intended specifically for African-Caribbean hair
- creams or gels based on sodium hydroxide – lye – or caustic soda, made for African-Caribbean clients

- creams or gels based on potassium/calcium hydroxide, called non-lye products, made for tightly curled hair and a wide range of hair textures
- creams based on ammonium and sodium bisulphites, which are slower acting and kinder to the hair; also suitable for a range of hair textures.

Important differences between these products are:

- *the strengths* – how much of the active chemical is present: this varies considerably and affects the process speed
- *the pH* – the degree of alkalinity; the higher the alkalinity the stronger the product
- *the contact time* – length of processing required.

In general, do not apply any heat that that would accelerate the chemical process, causing damage to the hair and irritation to the skin. Some newer products, however, specifically recommend a certain amount of applied heat.

Note: Protective gels or creams should always be applied to the skin and around the hairline and ears before the relaxing process commences. Relaxing products tend to swell whilst the hair is processing and if the application has been made quite close to the skin it will prevent these chemicals making contact with it and causing any irritation or discomfort.

L'Oréal Professionnel

Photo courtesy Goldwell UK

Step-by-step: A relaxing method used for Caucasian-type hair

The following is an outline of suggested application method using ammonium thioglycollate derivatives, *but this should not be used in place of the manufacturer's instructions*.

1 Section the hair into four: centrally, from forehead to nape, and laterally, from ear to ear (see diagram).
2 Apply the basing product.
3 Subdivide the nape sections into smaller ones.
4 Apply the relaxer cream, gel or lotion, avoiding the skin. Do not go closer than 12 mm from the scalp.
5 Comb the hair gently. Use a comb with widely spaced teeth. Some manufacturers advise you to wait till the hair has softened before combing.
6 Do not continually comb the hair when it is soft. Treat it gently at this stage – it can easily break. Leave the hair as straight as the client requires.
7 Processing time depends on the product and the hair. Softly curled hair relaxes quickly. Kinky hair takes longer. It is safest to monitor continuously throughout the process. Do not exceed the manufacturer's recommended time for processing.
8 When processing is complete, you may apply neutralisers. Neutralisers vary; some are based on hydrogen peroxide. Whichever product is used, it must thoroughly cover the area treated.
9 After final rinsing and conditioning with moisturisers or other products, the hair may be styled.

Sectioning hair

Relaxer has been applied and is allowed to process

The hair has been cut and styled for the finished effect

Step-by-step: A relaxing method for African-Caribbean type hair

The following is an outline of a suggested application method for a head of virgin hair, using a relaxer that is sodium or non-sodium-based, but this should not be used in place of the manufacturer's instructions.

1 Apply a pre-relaxer treatment if the hair condition is dry or porous.

2 Apply a protective barrier cream to protect the skin.

3 Divide the hair into four: centrally, from forehead to nape, and laterally, from ear to ear (see previous diagram).

4 Apply the relaxer to the mid-lengths and ends first. Start from the nape area or the most resistant part of the head towards the crown; leave the front hairline until last as this is usually the weakest area. Use small sub-sections of hair, smoothing and combing the hair as you work.

5 Once you have applied the relaxer to the mid-lengths and ends go back and apply to the roots.

6 Comb the hair from roots to ends and smooth the hair with your fingers until the required degree of straightness has been achieved. To check if the hair has been relaxed enough, take a strand of hair and remove the product with cotton wool. If the strand of hair stays straight and does not revert to its original curl then you can remove the relaxer.

7 Rinse the hair thoroughly, using tepid water as the scalp will be sensitive. The force of the water and gentle finger movements will remove the product from the hair. Check to make sure all traces of the relaxer have been removed from the hair and scalp.

8 Apply a neutralising shampoo to the hair. Shampoo gently and rinse thoroughly. Reapply the neutralising shampoo at least once more to ensure that all the relaxer has been removed.

9   Post-perm treatments can be used after a relaxer. These are acidic and will help to bring the hair back to its natural pH level of 4.5–5.5, close the cuticle and return the hair to a stable condition.

10 Gently towel dry the hair and comb through. You can now apply styling products and style the hair.

Dealing with regrowth

As hair grows approximately 12 mm ($^1/_2$ inch) each month, within a few weeks of relaxing very curly hair will begin to show itself above the scalp. This will need to be processed if the client wishes to continue with relaxed hair. When applying a process to the regrowth – called 'retouching' – you must take care to avoid the scalp; make sure it is based well (i.e. forms some sort of barrier) where required.

Step-by-step: Applying a regrowth application

1   Apply a pre-relaxer treatment to the hair that has already been relaxed.

2   Apply a protective barrier to protect the skin.

3   Always use the same product type that has been used previously, either sodium or non-sodium-based, as the two different types are not compatible.

4   Section the hair in the same way as a virgin application. When applying the relaxer it is best to work across two sections to keep the application even instead of applying the relaxer and completing one section first before moving onto another.

5   Use small sub-sections and, starting in the nape area or most resistant area, first apply the relaxer to the roots of the hair about 6 mm away from the scalp using the back of a comb. This will allow the relaxer to expand and creep up the hair to the scalp without it actually touching the scalp.

Relaxed hair Splinters Academy   **Relaxed hair** Splinters Academy

Do not apply to the hair that has previously been relaxed as it will damage the hair or cause the hair to break.

6 Once you have applied the relaxer to the whole head go back to the beginning and start combing the product through the hair and smoothing it with your fingers. Make sure that you do not comb beyond the regrowth area and that you do not scrape the scalp: it is kinder on the scalp to smooth with your fingers.

7 Take a strand test to make sure the hair has been relaxed enough before rinsing and neutralising. This is done in the same way as in the virgin application described above.

Curly perms

A curly perm is a two-step hair-smoothing process designed to reduce very tight curly hair of African-Caribbean texture to a softer, looser curl or wave. This makes the fashioning of hair styles more practical. It may also be successfully applied to excessively tight curly hair of Caucasian and other types where curl softening is required and recommended.

The curly perm is chemical similar to perming processes where the active ingredients are based on ammonium thioglycollate. It includes the reduction and oxidation processes of permanent waving – although the hair is uncurled instead of being curled. The procedure includes the straightening of the hair with a 'curl rearranger' – an ammonium thioglycollate-based cream or gel. This is available in different strengths – mild for fine hair, regular for normal hair, super for coarse hair, maximum for coarse, resistant hair – the choice depending on the condition of the hair, previous chemical treatments and the amount of curl reduction required.

Once the curl rearranger has been applied, the hair is smoothed with the fingers and back of the comb until the hair softens and straightens. The curl rearranger is then rinsed from the hair. Surplus moisture is removed by blotting and gently patting the hair with tissue or a towel.

The next stage is to apply a 'curl booster', either by pre-damping or post-damping. A curl booster is similar to an ammonium thioglycollate-based permanent waving lotion, usually of a strength weaker than the curl arranger. The hair is then wound onto rods or curlers in the same way as other perms.

When the hair has reached its required straightness, determined by the amount of curl remaining, it is rinsed and mopped or blotted. The hair is then thoroughly neutralised. Oxidising agents such as hydrogen peroxide or sodium perborate are commonly used.

Other products, such as skin-protecting creams, pre-straightening protective hair lotions, moisturisers to retain resilience and after-care conditioners may also be recommended. It is important to follow the manufacturer's directions to achieve safe and successful treatments – this includes instructions for pre-treatment tests, application of all chemical products, amounts to use, timing of processes, use of heat (if applicable) and caring for the clients' hair and skin. Do remember that you will need to know these differences from checking instruction sheets before making any application.

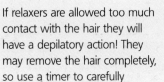

REMEMBER

If relaxers are allowed too much contact with the hair they will have a depilatory action! They may remove the hair completely, so use a timer to carefully monitor the chemical processes.

REMEMBER

Never mix different chemical relaxers when retouching.

Splinters Academy

Courtesy Namasté Laboratories LLC

Regrowth treatments

It is necessary to carry out the service again once the new root hair has grown. It is better to keep to the same curl-rearranging products previously applied to the lengths of the hair for matched results. Always make a note of the materials and the processes applied.

> **REMEMBER** ✔
>
> Avoid overlapping previously chemically treated areas. This could cause breakage or permanent damage.

PERMING FAULTS AND WHAT TO DO ABOUT THEM

Fault	Action now	Possible cause	Action in future
The perm is slow to process	Increase warmth but do not dry out; check the winding tension and the number of curlers	Winding was too loose	Wind more firmly or use smaller curlers
		The curlers were large, or too few were used	Use smaller curlers and more of them
		The wrong lotion was used	Double-check labels on bottles
		The sections were too large	Take smaller sections
		The salon is too cold	The temperature should be comfortable
		Lotion was absorbed from the hair	Don't leave cotton wool on the hair
		Too little lotion was used	Don't skimp on the lotion or miss sections

Fault	Action now	Possible cause	Action in future
The scalp is tender, sore or broken	Seek advice from a qualified first aider	The curlers were too tight	Don't apply too much tension when winding
		The wound curlers rested on the skin	Curlers should rest on the hair
		Lotion was spilt on the scalp	Keep lotion away from the scalp
		There was cotton wool padding soaked with perm lotion between the curlers	Renew the cotton wool as necessary or don't use it
		The hair was pulled tightly	Don't overstretch it
		The perm was over-processed	Time perms accurately
There are straight ends or pieces	Re-perm, if the hair condition permits*	The curlers or sections were too large	Take sections no longer or wider than the curler used
		Sections were overlooked	Check that all hair has been wound
		Too few curlers were used	Put curlers closer together
		The winding was too loose	Be a little firmer next time
		Lotion was applied unevenly	Take care to apply it evenly
There are fish-hooks	Remove by trimming the ends	The hair points were not cleanly wound	Comb the hair cleanly
		The hair points were bent or buckled	Place hair sections evenly on to the curlers
		The hair was wrapped unevenly in the end papers	Curl from the hair points
		Winding aids were used incorrectly	Take more care; practise winding
Hair is broken	Nothing can be done about the broken hair. After discussion with your senior or trainer, condition the remaining hair	The hair was wound too tightly	Wind more loosely next time
		The curlers were secured too tightly	Secure them more loosely next time
		The curler band cut into the hair base	Keep it away from the hair base
		The hair was over-processed	Follow the instructions more carefully
		Chemicals in the hair reacted with the lotion	Test for incompatibility beforehand

Fault	Action now	Possible cause	Action in future
The hair is straight	Re-perm, if the hair condition permits*	The wrong lotion was used for hair of this texture	Choose the lotion more carefully
		The hair was under-processed	Time perms accurately
		The curlers were too large for the hair length	Measure the curlers beforehand
		The neutralising was incorrectly done	Follow the instructions more carefully
		Rinsing was inadequate	Rinse more thoroughly
		Conditioners used before perming were still on the hair	Prepare the hair more carefully
		The hair was coated and resistant to the lotion	Check for substances that block the action of perm lotion: shampoo if necessary
The hair is frizzy	Cut the ends to reduce the frizziness	The lotion was to strong for hair of this texture	Assess texture correctly; select suitable lotions; read manufacturer's instructions
		The winding was too tight	Practise and experiment to avoid this
		The curlers were too small	Choose more suitable curlers
		The hair was over-processed	Time perms accurately
		The neutralising was incorrectly done	Follow the instructions more carefully
		There are fish-hooks	Avoid bending hair points when winding
The perm is weak and drops**	Re-perm, if the hair condition permits*	Lotion was applied unevenly	Apply lotion more evenly
		The neutraliser was dilute	Follow the instructions more carefully
		Neutralising was poorly done	Be more careful
		The hair was stretched while soft	Handle the hair gently
		The curlers or sections were too large	Use more curlers
Some hair sections are straight	Re-perm if the hair condition permits*	The curler angle was wrong	Wind correctly
		The curlers were placed incorrectly	Wind correctly
		The curlers were to large	Use smaller curlers
		Sectioning or winding was done carelessly	Practise before perming again
		Perm lotion or neutraliser was not applied correctly	Make sure that all curlers get the correct application of chemicals
The hair is discoloured	Tone the hair to correct this	Metallic elements or compounds present	Test for incompatibility

* Don't re-perm the hair unless its condition is suitable. For example, you should not re-perm if the hair is over-processed. Conditioning treatments and/or cutting may help. Discuss the problem with a senior or your trainer.

** Before attempting to correct this fault make sure that the hair is not over-processed. Dampen the hair to see how much perm there is.

RELAXING FAULTS AND WHAT TO DO ABOUT THEM

Problems	Possible cause	What to do
Hair breakage before relaxing	Poor dressing or the results of previous relaxing methods; poor condition	Do not relax hair, wait until improved; refer to your senior/trainer
Hair breakage after relaxing	Over-processing, relaxers too strong or poor neutralising	Condition if possible; refer to your senior/trainer
Bald areas	Traction baldness due to poor relaxing or over-processing	Do not relax hair; avoid tension and treat gently
Sore scalp	Harsh treatment (e.g. combing) or sign of disease, or relaxers too strong or left too long	Do not relax hair, wait till improved; refer to your senior/trainer
Discolouration or pink colour	Metals present, wrong relaxer used or over-processing	Test and check, recondition, colour rinse, avoid using further chemicals
Hair too curly	Not relaxed enough, wrong method chosen or not normalising sufficiently	Condition the hair, choose the correct method and relax again after two weeks if the condition permits

I know and understand the principles of perming, relaxing and neutralising hair ☐	I know and understand the health and safety aspects that must be considered before carrying out any chemical process ☐	I know why, when and how I conduct tests on the hair for perming ☐	I always recognise contra-indications when I analyse the client's hair ☐
I am familiar with a range of perming equipment and winding techniques and know when to apply them ☐	I know the basic science of how perming, relaxing and neutralising chemicals affect the hair during processing ☐	I always carry out working practices according to the salon's policy ☐	I know the effects of lye and no-lye products upon the hair during relaxing ☐
I understand the science of perming and know the effects of heat and chemicals upon the hair ☐	I know when and to whom to refer clients in situations where external assistance is required ☐	I know the effects of using different size rods and curlers on the hair ☐	I know the reasons for always following manufacturer's instructions ☐
I know why pre- and post-perm treatments are used upon the hair ☐			CHECKER BOARD ✓

Assessment of knowledge and understanding

The following projects, activities and assessments are directly linked to the essential knowledge and understanding for units H12,15 and 16.

For each statement that is addressed wholly or in part in these activities, you will see its relevant and corresponding EKU number.

Make sure that you keep this for easier referencing and along with your work for future inclusion in your portfolio.

Project 1 (EKU H12, 15, 16.30, 16.31, 16.35)

For this project you will need collect and test a range of hair samples.

Over a period of time, collect and fix together a variety of different hair samples.

You will need to create three batches of:

- grey/white hair
- coloured hair
- double processed hair
- bleached hair
- previously permed hair
- natural virgin hair.

For each type, record the differences in tendency texture and condition.

Use a little perm lotion in each scenario.

1 Perm your first batch of samples with the correct/matched lotion for the correct length of development time with a medium size curler.

   After you have rinsed and neutralised each one, note any changes in tendency, texture and condition in your portfolio.

2 Repeat the process again with a second batch of samples using:
   - tinted lotion on the grey/white hair
   - normal lotion on the tinted, bleached and double processed hair
   - resistant lotion on the previously permed and virgin hair.

   Now record your findings again after over-processing the samples and see the differences.

Note: Keep your third batch for a later project with neutralising.

Case study 1 (Hx.21)

A new client requests a perm. Their hair is fine, oily and below the shoulders. Previous attempts at other salons have been unsatisfactory. How would you deal with this?

List the process of events that should take place in your portfolio, include in your responses:

- consultation aspects, questions, examination and tests
- selection of suitable products and equipment
- the precautions you would take
- the advice and conclusion you would provide.

Project 2 (EKU H12, 15, 16.30, 16.31, 16.35)

Use the remainder of your hair samples from project 1. Perm them and prepare them, ready for neutralising.

Try out different ways of neutralising. Note the different effects produced and record them for your portfolio. Carry out this project in the following ways:

1 Without rinsing the hair sample, apply the neutraliser and time as directed by the instructions. What are the effects produced when the hair is still wet and the effects when it has been dried?

2 Using another permed hair sample, rinse the hair but do not apply any neutraliser. What are the effects produced when the hair is still wet and the effects when it has been dried?

3 On the third sample, leave out both rinsing and neutralising phases. What are the effects produced when the hair is still wet and the effects when it has been dried?

4 Rinse and neutralise the fourth sample as directed by the perm manufacturer. What are the effects produced when the hair is still wet and the effects when it has been dried?

5 Retain these samples and compare the results when the hair has dried out. Then check again after 12, 24 and 48 hours.

6 List and try out different types of neutraliser, with varying times of application. Compare the results.

7 Repeat these experiments using hair of different textures. Make sure that you have a correctly permed and neutralised sample with which to compare your results.

Case study 2

Your client recently had a perm at another salon. The client did not think that the result was satisfactory. The hair was slightly curly or wavy in parts but mostly straight otherwise.

How would you deal with this situation?

Make notes of what you would say and do. List the questions you would ask, and the order in which you would ask them. Retain notes for your portfolio.

Here are some things you should consider:

1 Find out why the hair was not successfully treated at the other salon.

2 Find out whether the client returned there to complain and what the outcome was.

3 Record what you think might have caused the unsatisfactory results.

4 Record what you think would have been a successful course of action.

5 Find out whether the hair is in a fit state for further treatment.

6 Record the results of your discussion with your client, and what you have agreed.

Questions

1 How do you prepare the client for perming and relaxing services? (H15/16.1)

2 What is your place of work's policy in respect to service timings for perming, relaxing and neutralising hair? (H15/16.2)

3 What is your place of work's policy in respect to keeping client records of treatment history and results of tests? (H15/16.3)

4 What protection do clients need and why do they need it? (H15/16.10, H15/16.11)

5 How does work position and positioning of equipment affect you and the client? (H15/16.12, H15/16.13, H15/16.16)

6 What are the safety considerations that relate to perming, neutralising and relaxing client's hair? (H15/16.14, H15/16.15, H15/16.17, H15/16.20)

7 When is it appropriate to conduct tests on the hair prior to processing? (H15/16.25, H15/1626, H15/16.27)

8 What effects do:
(a) perming
(b) neutralising
(c) relaxing

have upon the hair? (H15/16.30)

9 What is a neutralising shampoo? (H15/16.37)

10 What PPE must you wear when providing chemical services? (H15/16.14)

11 Why is it necessary to follow the manufacturer's instruction at all times? (H15/16.45)

12 What factors influence your choice of curler when perming? (H15/16.51)

13 What sorts of problems might occur when perming, neutralising and relaxing? How might you resolve them? (H15/16.54, H15/16.55)

14 When would you use
(a) pre-perm and
(b) post-perming treatment? (H15/16.47)

15 What would constitute a contra-indication for perming or relaxing hair? (H15/16.43)

Preparing for assessment checklist

Remember to:

- prepare clients correctly for the services you are going to carry out
- check the results of any tests that have been undertaken
- put on the protective wear available for perming or relaxing and neutralising
- listen to the client's requirements and discuss suitable courses of action
- adhere to the safety factors when working on client's hair
- keep the work areas clean, hygienic and free from hazards
- promote the range of services, products and treatments within the salon
- clean and sterilise the tools and equipment before they are used
- apply the science aspects you have learnt relating to perming, relaxing and neutralising hair
- work carefully and methodically through the chemical processes
- time the development of any chemical processes carefully
- communicate what you are doing with the client as well as your fellow staff members
- record the processes in the client's treatment history.

chapter 10

MEN'S STYLING

NVQ/SVQ reference, unit title and main outcome

Unit H7   Cut hair using basic barbering techniques

H7.1 **Maintain effective and safe methods of working when cutting hair**

H7.2 **Cut hair to achieve a variety of looks**

What do I need to do?

- **Take adequate precautions in preparing yourself and the client before cutting hair.**
- **Work safely at all times.**
- **Be able to cut a range of different hairstyles, types and lengths.**
- **Be able to apply a variety of cutting techniques in different styling situations.**

What do I need to learn?

You need to know and understand:

- **why it is important to take adequate measures in protecting and preparing your client before cutting the hair**
- **how to recognise whether a style is suitable for a client, as well as how to carry out the appropriate techniques to achieve it**
- **how to recognise the factors that influence suitable styling choices**
- **the design aspects of shape, balance and form**
- **why checking and rechecking shape, balance and form are important.**

Information covered in this chapter

- **The principles that influence styling choice and suitability.**
- **The range of hairstyles and techniques that you will need to be able to do.**
- **The principles and design aspects of balance, shape and form.**
- **The range of cutting tools available and the ways in which they are used.**
- **The safe working practices that you must adhere to.**

KEY WORDS

Club cut or clubbing hair or blunt cutting   The most basic and most popular way of cutting sections of hair straight across, parallel to the index and middle finger.

Scissor over comb   A technique of cutting hair with scissors, using the back of the comb as a guide, especially when the hair is at a length that cannot be held between the fingers.

Clipper over comb   A technique of cutting hair with electric clippers, using the back of the comb as a guide, especially on very short hair and hairline profiles.

INTRODUCTION

Men's hairdressing tends to be based on a variety of different layered looks. The perimeter lengths vary considerably but the overall principles that apply to style selection, suitability and execution are similar to those of women's styling. So, in order to achieve these layered effects, a regimen of precise movements and accurate cutting angles is essential.

There are subtle differences between women's and men's styles. This is largely dictated by the differences in hair distribution, neckline patterns, facial hair and physical features. Remember, when working with shorter styles, that the hair is too short to hide mistakes, so great care is necessary. As masculine and feminine looks often overlap, it is the small details that really make the difference. This area of hairdressing needn't be difficult if you bear in mind that it's your client consultation process that is central to getting this right.

REMEMBER

Cutting men's hair uses many of the principles of cutting women's hair. Review Chapter 6, on cutting, for more information.

CHECKERBOARD

At the end of this chapter the checkerboard will help to jog your memory on what you have learned and what still remains to be done. Cross off with a pencil each of the topics as you cover it (see page 343).

HAIR-STYLING CONSIDERATIONS

Decide, with the help of your client, what needs to be done, which techniques you are going to use and in particular, whether you will cut the hair wet or dry. Prepare your client so that they will be comfortable and well protected throughout the cutting process. Cutting short layered styles, particularly on dry hair, often involves a lot of small, sharp, spiky hairs which need to be kept constantly cleared for the client's comfort, personal hygiene and safety. Be careful not to expose yourself to flying hairs as these can easily enter the eye and be potentially harmful.

Hair: Stella Lambrou, The Crib, Lytham; make-up: Lynsey Alexander; photography: Emma Hughes; styling: Stuart Weil

Paul Falltrick for Matrix

Preparation checklist

✓ Make sure that the client is well protected with a clean fresh gown and a snugly fitting cutting collar.

✓ Find out what the client wants. Men can often be more difficult during consultation as they are often reluctant to use technical terms or express themselves clearly to people they don't know.

✓ Style books/files provide lots of male looks as well as women's hairstyles.

✓ Make sure you consider the reasons for and the purpose of the style. Hairstyles required for professional purposes have more restrictions on freedom and expression than fashionable, trendy looks or more general wear.

✓ Assess the styling limitations – hair and skin problems or physical features.

✓ Avoid technical jargon or style names. If you or the client do use jargon, always clarify in simple terms what it means to avoid confusion.

✓ Don't just do the style if you think that it's wrong. If there are reasons why you think it will be unsuitable, you will be doing the client a big favour in the longer term if you tackle the issue straight away.

✓ Always give them some advice on how to handle the style themselves. Men often need products to help them achieve the style themselves, so make sure you show them how they can use and apply any new products.

✓ Give them an idea of how long it will take to do.

Hair: The Company Hairdressing, Surrey; photography: Thornton Howdle; assistant: Gemma Adams

General styling considerations

Square and oblong facial shapes	Square and oblong face shapes are typically masculine and provide a perfect base for classic well-groomed looks.
Round faces	If shorter, more classic styles are required the round face is improved by the introduction of angular or linear perimeters. Conversely, if the hair is to be worn longer, the roundness of the face will be diminished, as more will be covered.
Square angular features: jaw, forehead etc.	Again, these facial attributes are traditionally accepted as a feature of masculinity. They do not really pose any limitations for classic work. They also work well with longer hair too.

Hair: The Company Hairdressing, Surrey;
photography: Thornton Howdle; assistant:
Gemma Adams

Hair: The Company Hairdressing, Surrey;
photography: Thornton Howdle; assistant:
Gemma Adams

Flatter heads at the back	Are improved by tailored graduation. This creates a contour and shape that is missing from heads with a flatter occipital bone.
Thinning hair/baldness	Younger men can be quite sensitive about thinning hair. Be tactful and try to find solutions that are realistic and sympathetic to the problem. When dealing with male pattern baldness most men will opt for shorter hairstyles than long.

Physical feature considerations

Physical feature	How best to work with it
Prominent nose	Hair taken back away from the face accentuates this feature, whilst hair around the face and forehead tends to diminish the feature.
Protruding ears	Are better left covered rather than exposed. Sufficient hair should be left to cover and extend beyond their length if at all possible.
Narrow foreheads	Are disguised by softer fringes and side partings, while they are made more obvious by hair taken back away form the face.
Bushy, thick eyebrows	If the eyebrows are a different colour to the natural hair, the feature will be even more prominent. The hairstyle will be improved with some form of light trimming and grooming.
Large faces	Are augmented by classical, short cropped or sculpted hairstyles.
Shapes of glasses	Generally people will have had assistance in the selection and suitability of their frames. Therefore they should not work against the hairstyle that you want to create as they will already suit the shape and size of the face.
Long sideburns	Are made more prominent with shorter hairstyles. Make sure that this is acceptable to your client first as they might be rather attached to their facial hair feature.
Beards	Make sure that the client's beard is still going to be balanced with the amount of hair on top of the head in the finished effect. If an imbalance is going to occur, mention it first and give them the option of taking the beard shorter to compensate.

REMEMBER

The health, safety and personal hygiene factors that affect women's hairdressing are the same in men's hairdressing. To save duplication review Chapter 5 on health and safety for more information.

Examination of hair and scalp

While you are looking at your client's hair and scalp, be particularly aware of the texture of the hair. If it is coarse and tightly curled, you will need stronger combs to stretch the hair out from the head before cutting, and firmer movements will need to be applied. The density of the hair is important too: if it is thick, then styles with varied hair lengths are possible. Conversely, sparse hair and particularly fine hair require a great deal of attention and expertise. If finely textured hair has to cover a sparsely haired area of the head, it will have to be longer than hair of coarser texture. The amount, type and distribution pattern of hair are all important too. Younger men may have distinctly higher forehead hairlines than women of similar age. Thinning crowns and decreasing density of hair mark many male patterns, though these are not usually seen in women until much later in life. Take this into consideration when designing and cutting hairstyles specifically for men and women. Hair growth, at a rate of about 12 mm each month, is more noticeable with shorter layered styles. To keep them tidy, regular trimming is essential.

Interpret your client's wishes

Understanding the wishes and requirements of your clients is important. Creatively interpreting their needs and desires is a major part of hairstyle design. Clients of different age groups, careers, lifestyles and social positions require separate consideration. Factors such as practicality, suitability and the client's ability to cope with his hair are matters which you must not overlook. The final effects will be influenced by other considerations too – the amount of hair, its distribution, its texture etc. – and unless you do take all these factors into consideration, you will have an unhappy, disgruntled client on your hands.

However, if you carefully and sympathetically interpret your client's requirements, you will be able to achieve a positive and professional result.

Men can wear longer hair as well as short: a whole range of modern contemporary styling effects has developed since the basic and traditional short back and sides. The general acceptance and application of men's hair products 'dress up' the otherwise professional or classic-looking hairstyle into something with a more distinctive look for social or special occasions.

Now and again a named men's style becomes fashionable. Some of these names, such as 'crew cut', the 'mullet', the wedge and the Mohawk, have passed into the general vocabulary. Always make sure that you know what your client means if they use a name to describe a style. It may be completely different from your idea of that style! Discuss with your client in detail what shape they want, and apply it as agreed.

REMEMBER	✔

Heavy fringes used with the intention of hiding bald areas can do the opposite and make them more obvious. Careful angling and placement of hair is usually more effective.

Photo courtesy Goldwell

ACTIVITY	⇆

With your colleagues, take it in turns at acting as a stylist or a client and go through the consultation process. Notice how different stylists adopt different approaches.

SAFE PRACTICE FOR CUTTING HAIR AND CUTTING EQUIPMENT

Like all other practical services in hairdressing, it is essential that you work safely when cutting hair. In doing this you must take the time to prepare and protect the client adequately.

This means that you have:

- pre-selected all the equipment that you are going to use: gowns, towels, combs, scissors, razor and clippers etc.
- checked that they are prepared for use i.e. new blades for the razor; freshly laundered towels and gowns; washed cutting collars; cleaned and sterilised combs, brushes, clipper blades and scissors
- got them all at hand and ready for use
- ensured that the client is comfortable and in a position where you can work safely.

Client gowning

Gowning	Gowning can take place before or after consultation, it really depends upon the salon's policy. However, gowning must always take place before a dry cut is started or, if the service is a wet cut, then before the client is shampooed.
For dry cutting	Use a clean fresh cutting gown and put it on your client whilst they are sitting at the styling location. Make sure that the back is fastened and that any open, free edges are closed together, keeping any loose clippings away from the client's clothes. Place a cutting collar around the neck to ensure that any bumps or lumps in the client's clothing don't present any false, physical baselines for the haircut and ensure that the collar edges fit snugly against the neck, so that there are no irritating hair fragments that will leave the client itching until they get home.
For wet cutting	Do the same as the gowning above but, when your client is at the basin, place a clean fresh towel around their shoulders before positioning them back carefully and comfortably. Make sure that the client's neck is supported by the basin properly and that the flanged edges of the basin nestle comfortably on to the client's shoulders (which are protected from any moisture by the towel).

Seat positioning

The positioning of the client at the workstation is just as important as at the backwash. Both areas have implications for personal safety, quality of service and good customer care.

From a working point of view, any angle of the client's head other than perpendicular to the mirror, combined with the angle of the client's head to their seated position, will affect the line, quality and balance of the haircut.

Salon workstations have built-in foot rests and there are good reasons for this. The foot rest:

1 is there to improve the comfort for the seated client at any cutting height

2 helps balance the client and encourages them to sit squarely in front of the mirror

3 should discourage the client from sitting cross-legged

4 promotes better posture by making the client sit back properly with their back flat against the back of the chair.

All of the above factors are critical for you and the client in ensuring that they are comfortable throughout and that you are not hindered in doing your task. For example, if your client sits with crossed legs, it will alter the horizontal plane of their shoulders and this will make your job more difficult in trying to get even and level base and guidelines.

Photo courtesy Goldwell

Your work position

The position of the client and their height from the floor have a direct effect on your posture too. You must be able to work in a position where you do not have to bend 'doubled up' to do your work. Cutting involves a lot of arm and hand movements and you need to be able to get your hands and fingers into positions where you can cut the hair without having a bad posture.

1 You should adjust the seated client's chair height to a position where you can work upright without having to over-reach on the top sections of their head.

2 You should clear trolleys or equipment out of the way so that you get good all-round access (300°) around the client.

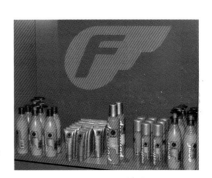

M. Balfre

<table>
<tr><td colspan="2">**REMEMBER** ✔</td></tr>
<tr><td colspan="2">Health and safety when cutting</td></tr>
<tr><td>**Spillages**
Take care when moving trolleys around in the salon, or when you place products, drinks etc. on the shelves in front of clients</td><td>**What do I do?**
If you do spill anything on to the floor, mop it up straight away. If the spillage is chemical make sure you know how to handle it. If you don't tell someone in charge</td></tr>
<tr><td>**Slippery floors**
Other than spillages the hair clippings are also a potential hazard as people could easily slip on them</td><td>Sweep clippings up immediately and put them into a lined and covered bin</td></tr>
<tr><td>**Tools and equipment**
Clippers, driers, tongs and straighteners can also be a hazard to clients and staff alike</td><td>Always unplug them and ravel up the trailing leads so that they can be stored safely for next time</td></tr>
<tr><td>**Obstructions**
Trolleys and moveable equipment. i.e. Rollerballs, Climazones, hood dryers and steamers, are potential hazards</td><td>Equipment should always be removed from the work area as soon as it is finished with and put back into its storage areas</td></tr>
</table>

Rounded neckline

Tapered neckline

Square neckline

Hair outlines – round, tapered, square

Scissors, clippers combs and brushes

Good care and regular maintenance of your tools are an essential part of hairdressing and barbering. For more information on looking after these items see Chapter 6 on cutting hair.

OUTLINE SHAPES

Many short, layered cuts are graduated at the sides and into the nape sometimes by clipper over comb or, when left slightly longer, by scissor over comb techniques. On shorter hairstyles the neck and hairlines become the main focal perimeters of the hairstyle and emphasising these requires careful attention.

The natural necklines of both men and women lack consistency. The growth is often uneven, intermittent or sparse. Therefore the outline shapes for men wearing shorter hair need to be defined. The more natural the nape line, the softer and less severe will be the look. The higher the cuts made into the hairline, the harsher and starker the look becomes.

The nape line can be of a variety of shapes: rounded, tapered or square. These shapes can be achieved by shaping with the electric clippers or shaving the outlines. Traditionally shaving was carried out with open-bladed razors; now electric shavers or safety razors can be used. Often outlining is done with the points of the scissors. Softer, graduated lines are to be preferred to blocky, blunt effects. The precise outline is determined by the style required.

The shaping of front hair into a fringe can produce variety of facial frames and the focal point it creates changes the overall effect dramatically. The front hairline of many men recedes and this is often a sign of male pattern baldness, which influences the choice and positioning of perimeter fringe shapes. Always give this some thought before cutting the hair.

In men, the side hairlines, sideburns or sideboards bridge the hairstyle and beard shape. These need to fit, and care must be taken in shaping them. Lining the hair above the ears and along the sides of the nape is usually carried out with the scissor points or with inverted clippers.

Cutting with or without partings

Positioning and placement of partings in a hairstyle will produce variation in the final visual effect. Central partings divide the hair mass and can help to make a heavy head of hair look more balanced. If the hair is distributed evenly and symmetrically, it becomes more manageable. Side partings can be used to divert attention from a prominent point, such as a large nose or uneven ears; they can carry the eye of the viewer away from the unwanted look. Changing hair fashions affect the way in which partings are used, and many styles have no partings at all.

Before attempting to cut, experiment by combing the hair to see if has tendencies to lie in specific directions. Part the hair in several ways, diagonally, short or long, straight or angled, to see the how the overall effect is changed.

Photo courtesy Goldwell

Ears

Nature does not guarantee symmetry, and this is particularly true with faces. One side of the face is not exactly the same as the other and this applies to ears too. They may be larger or smaller, irregular in shape as well as at different heights. You need to make sure that you have considered this before you start. Unevenness on long hair doesn't matter, but when short hair is uneven every imperfection will be clear to see.

You need to find out how your client feels about their facial features. Sometimes these natural imperfections are not a concern for the client, who views them as merely a characteristic of their personality. Don't forget to check on whether your client wears glasses or a hearing aid. Take all of these factors into your assessment.

Finally you and your client you will be able to agree exactly what look is required, and you will then have a basis on which to decide how the work is to be carried out.

Photo courtesy Goldwell UK

Hair type

If your client's hair is very curly, do remember that it will coil back after stretching and cutting. Similarly, wavy hair, when cut too close to the wave crest, can be awkward to style as it tends to spring out from the head. Very fine straight hair will easily show cutting marks or can disclose unwanted lines from clippering if the sections taken are too large. Make sure that the sections you take are accurately divided.

Wet and dry cutting: a special note

If the hair is dirty, then for hygienic reasons it must be washed before you cut it. Wet hair is a necessity for blow-shaping and finishing, but some scissor tapering movements have to be restricted on wet hair. Clean, dry hair should not be cut with a razor because of the discomfort to your client and the tearing and dragging of the hair.

REMEMBER

Tapering and thinning encourage the hair to curl at the ends, whilst club cutting increases density and reduces that tendency.

Feathering and texturising can produce extra lift and bounce.

REMEMBER

Wet hair stretches by anything from a third to half its length. Allow for this if you cut stretched hair, so that when it reverts to its original length it is not too short.

If you wish to dry cut, then wash and dry the hair first. Explain this to your client so that he can express his wishes and needs.

Other influencing factors

Hair and scalp problems – Men and women's hair are similar in many ways. The aspects that you must consider in consultation with women still apply when styling men's hair. Therefore you should review the section on hair and scalp problems, disorders and diseases in Chapter 1 on consultation.

Hair growth patterns – The movement and direction of hair is particularly problematic on shorter hairstyles. Make sure that you take this into consideration during your consultation with your client.

Male pattern baldness – Look for signs of thinning, sparse and balding areas everywhere, not just on the top or at the front hairline. The amount of hair does affect what you can do. Make sure you know before you have started!

ADDITIONAL CUTTING TECHNIQUES

As well as the techniques featured in Chapter 6 on cutting you may find the following particularly helpful when you are dealing with short, layered styles.

Club-cutting or clubbing (blunt cutting) is more often required for shorter styles. Clubbing can be done 'over the comb'; continuous clubbing over the comb with scissors is often used for short graduations, such as that at the nape or the lower sides. In an 'over the fingers' technique the hair is combed out, transferred to the fingers, and then cut straight across. Angles are determined by the amount of graduation required and the size of the section taken.

Thinning techniques, using special thinning scissors with serrated blades, may be required but you must take great care with short hair. The hair could become spiky, particularly when it begins to grow again.

Razoring, on wet hair, is easier and quicker than scissor tapering. Take short, gentle strokes with the razor, to ensure evenness.

Clippering over comb or fingers is ideal for clubbing level lengths on short styles. It can also be used on its own; it is an invaluable technique for graduation. Clipper grades (the attachments that provide uniform cutting lengths) are made in a range of sizes for different purposes, and are numbered accordingly.

Clipper attachment size	Length of cut hair
No attachment	Very close to skin, almost like shaving.
1 = 3 mm ($\frac{1}{8}$")	Very short, on darker hair it will leave a shadowing effect over the scalp.
2 = 6 mm ($\frac{1}{4}$")	Close cut, will see some skin on finer hair.
3 = 9 mm ($\frac{3}{8}$")	Typically cuts to short scissor over comb lengths.
4 = 13 mm ($\frac{1}{2}$")	Longer scissor over comb types of effects.
8 = 25 mm (1")	Not particularly popular for hair cutting, often used as a cutting guide for beard shaping.

Note There are no set standard sizes for clipper attachment combs/grades. You will need to adapt the hair length required by your client in light of the make and model of clippers that you have or your salon provides.

Summary of cutting techniques

Club cutting	Over the fingers with either scissors or electric clippers.
Tapering	Scissors – Backcomb the hair first and remove hair in a slithering movement along the section.
	Razor – Lightly remove hair throughout the section, in a movement away from the head out to the points.
	Thinning scissors – Remove hair along the section working outwards to the hair points.
Graduation	Clippers – By varying the cutting length throughout the sides or back with grades working down from the largest to smaller shorter lengths. Each phase finishes lower than the previous grade.
	Scissor over comb – A technique of cutting with scissors while using the comb as the cutting guide when the hair is often too short to be held between the fingers.
	Clipper over comb – Same as scissor over comb but using clippers.
Freehand cutting	Scissors – Ideal for personalising profile hair and accurate cutting of fringe lengths.

Layering

Layering is achieved by holding sections of hair away from the head and cutting them at varying angles to it. The aim is to achieve an unbroken outline shape from series of tiny, imperceptible lines or layers. Layering is a method of shaping and controlling a head of hair. If you cut the layers that follow the underlying contours of the head and face, you can achieve attractive and satisfying results. Of course, as usual, you have to take into consideration the limitations of the hair, growth patterns, head and face shape, wearing of spectacles or hearing aids and so on. Make allowance too for any varying face shapes, such as bumps and hollows that need to be disguised or hidden by the overlying hairstyle.

Procedure

- Prepare your client for cutting and styling.
- Fully discuss your client's requirements with them.
- Examine their hair and note its length, quantity and texture, their face and head shape, and any abnormal or unusual features.
- Determine what needs to be done, with the agreement of your client.
- Decide which cutting techniques are likely to achieve the desired results.
- Make sure you have all the tools and equipment to hand.
- Position your client's head carefully so that you can carry out your chosen techniques efficiently.
- Where to start the cut is an individual choice, but bear in mind that all cutting is systematic in its approach and therefore has a start, a middle and an end.

Cutting method

- Accurate sectioning and graduation produce fine layering. This is partly determined by how much hair there is to cut. Longer lengths can be sectioned with the comb and taken between the fingers, whilst short lengths are best tackled either by clipper over comb or scissor over comb techniques (also known as 'barbering').
- With short layered styles, clippers must be used to tidy the neckline, graduating from the natural line out from the head. How far up the head and how short this cut needs to be is determined by the style and shape agreed with your client. If longer lengths are required higher in the back hair, then the clippers need to graduate away from the head sharply.
- Cross-checking is an essential part of cutting. It is your way of including a quality control. As you progress through the cut, you obviously need to change your stance, holding position and holding angle. These factors can lead you to go wrong. Typical mistakes are the back section doesn't integrate with the sides properly, or the top doesn't blend with the sides or the fringe doesn't fit with the top. Whatever the potential problem the easiest way to compensate for this is to cross-check to make sure that the cut works well in different planes.

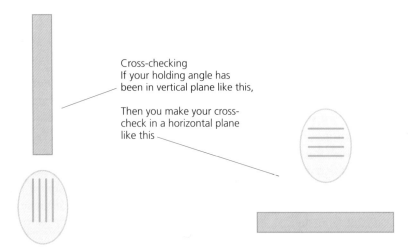

Cross-checking
If your holding angle has been in vertical plane like this,

Then you make your cross-check in a horizontal plane like this

Cross-checking your cut

Step-by-step: Men's graduation and classic layered cut

Step 1: Secure any hair that overfalls the nape out of the way. Put on the selected clipper attached and in a scooping movement remove the hair.

Step 2: Continue until all of the lower section is complete, then tidy the outline perimeter neckline.

Step 3: Working further up towards the crown blend the clippered graduation into the longer lengths.

Step 4: When the back has been completed, cross-check the layering to see that it is even from side to side.

Step 5: Moving on to the sides blend the graduation into the top. Then trim the perimeter shape.

Step 6: After repeating the process on the other side, finish off the top section moving forwards to the forehead.

Step 7: When the top is completed, finish the cut by trimming the profile hair into shape around the sides, leaving sufficient hair around the recession area and completing the shape around to the front.

Final effect.

Before.

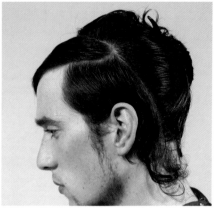

Step 1: Section the head into four areas, working one section at a time using different techniques.

Step 2: Starting from the left section around the ear, use slightly diagonal sections, elevating and cutting at 90°. When this is complete, clip away.

Step 3: Take the large section around the crown and point-cut following the head shape.

Step 4: On the right section behind the ear into the nape, elevate at 90° and scoop out creating a tail.

Step 5: Elevate and point-cut the final section, elevating everything over to the right.

Step 6: Apply HY-PACT Protect & Style Paste into wet hair. Finger dry and straighten.

Step 7: Back-cutting, slicing and deep point-cutting texturising techniques are used to personalise. Finish using HY-PACT Moulding Material to create matte textured finish.

Final effect.

Hair created by the International PACT art team: Chantel Marshall, Harriet White and
Andy Smith; photography: Stuart Weston; make-up: Hiromi Ueda

Before.

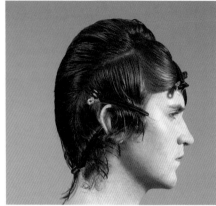

Step 1: Divide the hair into four sections – two symmetrical sections starting from the nape, a triangular section through the fringe and a large middle section consisting of the remaining hair.

Step 2: Clip away the two symmetrical sections and the triangular section. Now working on the middle section, apply a pivoting technique from the crown using orange segment sections and cutting a curve to follow the head shape.

Step 3: On completing the top, comb it away, now working on the two symmetrical side sections. Stating from the hairline, elevate vertical sections at 90° and scoop away.

Step 4: Continue this through both sides.

Step 5: Split the front triangular section into a parting and over-direct 'T to the part' elevating at 90° and cutting 'T to the part' creating a curved shape around the eye.

Step 6: Rough dry the hair and straighten using 'Silver Bullet' straighteners.

Step 7: Personalise the hair by deep point-cutting and back-cutting.

Step 8: Slicing techniques are also used. Finish with HY-PACT Moulding Material.

Final effect.

Hair created by the International PACT art team: Chantel Marshall, Harriet White and Andy Smith; photography: Stuart Weston; make-up: Hiromi Ueda

ADVICE AND HOME MAINTENANCE

No service is complete unless the client leaves in the knowledge that they can achieve the same result at home as that done in the salon. If they can't achieve a similar effect they are unlikely to return. You can make sure that they do. You have gone through a lot of training and have worked hard to get this far. The real sign of success is your client booking their next visit before they leave salon. You can achieve this easily by:

- making sure that you tell them how long the effect will last and when they need to come back
- explaining which products and equipment you have used and how they might benefit the client at home
- telling them what they need to do in order to achieve the same effect when they next wash their hair.

I know and understand the principles of positive communication ☐	I know why clients should be protected from loose hair clippings ☐	I always recognise the critical influencing factors when I carry out consultation ☐	I can utilise a range of barbering techniques and know when to use them in my work ☐
I know how the angle at which hair is held and cut is critical to the finished effect ☐	I know why I should keep the work area hygienic and clean ☐	I always explain technical terms eliminating ambiguity and false beliefs ☐	I know how to achieve club cut effects by using scissor and clippers over combs ☐
I know how to work with the natural lie and fall of the hair ☐	I know that my posture and the client's seated position are important for accuracy and health and safety aspects ☐	I know how and why I should cross-check the cut during and after the service ☐	I know when and to whom to refer clients, in situations where external assistance is required ☐
			CHECKER BOARD ✔

Assessment of knowledge and understanding

The following projects, activities and assessments are directly linked to the essential knowledge and understanding for unit H7.

For each statement that is addressed wholly or in part in these activities, you will see its relevant and corresponding EKU number.

Make sure that you keep this for easier referencing and along with your work for future inclusion in your portfolio.

Project 1 (EKU H7.16, H7.17, H7.20, H7.21, H7.22)

For this project you will need to gather information from a variety of sources.

Men's styles involve much the same techniques and methods as those used in ladies' cutting; however, there are some differences.

1 Write down in your portfolio the aspects of women's hairdressing that tend to be unique to them.

2 Now write down those aspects that tend to be unique to men's work.

From the information that you have collected, illustrate your project with as much visual material as you can. What conclusions can you draw from doing this exercise?

Case study

Men can have their hair cut in either in barber's salons or in joint ladies' and gents' salons, but the two type of business are quite different.

What is different between the two types of business?

You will need to collect information about each type of salon before you can make your evaluation. When you have collected the information, answer the following questions in your portfolio.

1 What is the general difference between the two appointment systems?

2 What is the difference between the ranges of services offered between the salon types?

3 What is the difference between the ranges of products offered between the salon types?

4 What is the difference between the salon environments?

5 What similarities do both types of salon share?

Questions

1 How do you prepare the client for cutting services? (H7.1)

2 What is your place of work's policy in respect to service timings for different cuts? (H7.2)

3 What is your place of work's policy in respect to safe disposal of sharps? (H7.3)

4 Why do clients need protection from hair clippings? (H7.6)

5 How can you avoid cross-infection/infestation? (H7.9)

6 What are the safety considerations that relate to cutting clients' hair? (H7.5, H7.7, H7.8, H7.9, H7.10, H7.11, H7.13)

7 What things influence the choice of style for clients? (H7.17)

8 Why should hair product be removed from the hair before cutting? (H7.18)

9 Why are guidelines important throughout the haircut? (H7.27, H7.28)

10 What is cross-checking and why is it important? (H7.29, H7.30)

11 What ways are common for controlling the accuracy throughout all haircuts? (H7.25, H7.32)

12 Why is it important to cut to the natural hairline in men's hairdressing? (H7.33)

Preparing for assessment checklist

Remember to:

- prepare clients correctly for the services you are going to carry out
- put on the protective wear available for styling and dressing hair
- listen to the client's requirements and discuss suitable courses of action
- adhere to the safety factors when working on clients' hair
- keep the work areas clean, hygienic and free from hazards
- promote the range of services, products and treatments with the salon
- clean and sterilise the tools and equipment before they are used
- work carefully and methodically through the processes of cutting hair whether wet or dry
- place, position and direct the hair appropriately to achieve the desired effect
- communicate what you are doing with the client as well as your fellow staff members.

TONI & GUY AT THE 50TH ANNIVERSARY
L'ORÉAL COLOUR TROPHY, LONDON, MAY 2005.

ANTOINETTE BEENDERS AT THE 50TH ANNIVERSARY
L'ORÉAL COLOUR TROPHY, LONDON, MAY 2005.

TREVOR SORBIE AT THE 50TH ANNIVERSARY
L'ORÉAL COLOUR TROPHY, LONDON, MAY 2005.

CHARLES WORTHINGTON AT THE 50TH ANNIVERSARY
L'ORÉAL COLOUR TROPHY, LONDON, MAY 2005.

M. BALFRE AT THE ALTERNATIVE HAIR SHOW, 2005.

part three

chapter 11

WORKING EFFECTIVELY

NVQ/SVQ reference, unit title and main outcome

Unit G8 Develop and maintain your effectiveness at work

G8.1 **Improve your personal performance at work**

G8.2 **Work effectively as part of a team**

What do I need to do?

- Be able to identify your own strengths and weaknesses.
- Take opportunities to learn new things.
- Listen and respond to the needs of your fellow staff members.
- Work together harmoniously as a team.
- Avoid conflicts and the situations when they could arise.

What do I need to learn?

- How to communicate positively and effectively.
- Your job roles and your responsibilities.
- The limits of your authority and your responsibilities.
- The salon's work expectations and personal targets.
- Ways of developing yourself further within your job.

Information covered in this chapter

- Identifying personal strengths and weaknesses.
- Appraisals and setting targets.
- Working together effectively as a team.

KEY WORDS

Appraisal   The system of reviewing your past and planning your future work objectives.

Strengths and weaknesses   The difference between personal skill areas that you excel in and those that need to work on.

Harmony   Maintaining a good working relationship and atmosphere with your fellow staff.

Personal development   Recognising the opportunities that arise at work when you get the chance to learn new things.

INTRODUCTION

This chapter is about you at work and how you get along with your colleagues. It has particular reference in how you take responsibility for improving yourself as well as your work performances. Working towards pre-set, known targets is the baseline or benchmark in the world of work; without them we wouldn't know if we got things right. Sometimes these targets will be set by others, perhaps following appraisals or training reviews. But what if you could learn to set your own goals? Work independently of others? And what if you had the confidence to take on tasks that you never thought you could do on your own before?

Alan Edwards at the 50th Anniversary L'Oréal Colour Trophy, London, May 2005

CHECKERBOARD

At the end of this chapter the checkerboard will help to jog your memory on what you have learned and what still remains to be done. Cross off with a pencil each of the topics as you cover it (see page 361).

This chapter is about taking responsibility for your work by constantly trying to improve your performance at work and also working well with your colleagues to ensure the salon and your contribution is effective.

REMEMBER ✔

The National Occupational Standards (NOS) can be obtained from the Hairdressing and Beauty Therapy Industry Authority (Habia).

DEVELOPING AND IMPROVING PERFORMANCE

Your ability to meet the expected standards at work is referred to as 'personal effectiveness'. These standards refer to:

- *personal standards* – That is the care that you take about your appearance and personal hygiene (see Chapter 5 on health and safety) as well as the overall image that you portray to fellow staff members and, most importantly, the customers

- *occupational standards* – That is the levels of skill and knowledge that you apply to the individual activities that make up the NVQ Level 2

- *professionalism* – That is your ability to conduct yourself in a way that communicates the image of a positive and supportive professional person to clients and fellow staff members

You should have a clear understanding of what you should be doing and what you are aiming to achieve at work. If you don't know this how can you tell whether you are getting it right? Most of what you do will depend on others: the way that your colleagues do their work, and how you help them and the ways they help you to achieve your own working objectives is dependent on this teamwork.

If you find yourself wandering around aimlessly at work it is probably because you don't know what you should be doing. Just think how your colleagues will see this; they might view you as lazy or deliberately trying to avoid working as a team player. If you are unclear about what you should be doing at work, ask your manager or a senior member of staff.

The Level 2 standards cover all the jobs that you should be doing at work. They give a specification, a sort of framework, for the correct methods of working, the techniques that you need to use when working and the order or sequence in which hairdressing tasks are done.

If you don't follow these pre-set procedures and try to do things your own way, these things will happen:

1 The result of what you are attempting to do will be wrong.

2 You will be not only letting yourself down, but all your other colleagues with whom you work too.

3 You will find yourself in the manager's office explaining why you thought your way was a better idea.

In many hairdressing procedures there are other ways of doing things, but you must know what the expected result is, before you can work out other ways of doing tasks. This is why the National Occupational Standards exist: they provide you with the simplest correct ways of doing things so that you know you are doing things right.

The periodical process of evaluation and review is called 'appraisal'. It can be undertaken in two ways: by yourself, that is self-appraisal (you measure your own strengths and weaknesses against set standards) or in conjunction with your manager on a more formal basis.

REMEMBER

'Continuing professional development' (CPD) is the term used by professionals who continually update their skills. Your trainer and assessor will undertake CPD activities.

ACTIVITY

A skill is the combination of knowledge applied to a method. A method is a process or sequence of events that, if done correctly, will have successful conclusion. However, if the sequence is done in the wrong order it can have a disastrous result.

In this activity there are four simple statements that relate to colouring. Only one sequence is correct, but which one is it? (Can you see that by doing this in another sequence the result will be wrong?)

1 Apply the colour with a brush carefully, to cover the mid-lengths and ends, and leave for 15 minutes.

2 Apply the conditioner to the hair and leave for five minutes.

3 Apply the barrier cream around the client's hairline and put a colouring towel around the shoulders.

4 Apply the colour with a brush carefully, to cover all the grey roots, and leave for 30 minutes.

Performance Appraisal	
Name:	*Jane Manners*
Job Title:	*Trainee stylist*
Date of Appraisal:	*5/6/2006*
Objectives:	*To obtain competence within: Cutting hair layering techniques across the range. Blow-drying hair on a variety of hair types and lengths.*
Notes on Achievement:	*Competence has been achieved across the range for all the cutting requirements.* *Competence has been achieved for most blow-drying range requirements.*
Training Requirements:	*Further training and practice is needed within the area of blow-drying longer length effects.*
Any other comments on performance by Appraiser:	*Jane has achieved most of the objectives set out during the last appraisal.*
Any comments on the Appraisal by the staff Appraised:1	*I feel that this has been a fair appraisal of my progress although I did not achieve all of my performance targets.* *J. Manners*
Action Plan:	*To achieve occupational competence across the range for blow-drying (i.e. longer length hair).* *To undergo training and practice in perming methods and techniques.* *To take assessment for perming.*
Date of Next Appraisal:	*4/12/2006*

An appraisal form

However, you should not wait for a formal review or appraisal. If you are having problems with any aspect of your training or your job you should ask for support or assistance from a senior stylist, your trainer or manager. If you have completed the objectives set out in your training or appraisal before the due target date, ask for more objectives to be set. This will help to keep you more motivated by completing your training earlier and increasing your knowledge of the job, enabling you to do higher-skilled work.

MEASURING EFFECTIVENESS

To be able to measure progress towards training targets as well as overall work contributions, there need to be clear, stated expectations of the performance required of you. For both training and work activities, this is the standard to which you will need to demonstrate competence.

In training situations, your personal programme will state the:

- training activities that will take place
- tasks which need to be performed
- standards and the levels of performance expected
- types of assessment that should be expected
- review of your progress towards these agreed targets and when it is to take place.

In normal work situations, performance appraisal will be based on the following factors:

- results achieved against set objectives and job requirements
- any additional accomplishments and contributions
- contributions made by the individual as compared with those of other staff members.

The job requirements will be outlined in your employee's job description. A job description is a list of the functions and roles expected within the job. The job descriptions should include details of the following:

- the job title
- the work location(s)
- responsibility (to whom and for what)
- the job purpose
- main functions (listed)
- standards expected
- any other special conditions.

The standards expected from the job holder will often be produced in the staff handbook. They would normally include:

- standards of behaviour and appearance
- the salon's code of conduct

Job description – Stylist

Location:	Based at salon as advised
Main purpose of job:	To ensure customer care is provided at all times
	To maintain a good standard of technical and client care, ensuring that up-to-date methods and techniques are used following the salon training practices and procedures
Responsible to:	Salon manager
Requirements:	To maintain the company's standards in respect of hairdressing/beauty services
	To ensure that all clients receive service of the best possible quality
	To advise clients on services and treatments
	To advise clients on products and after-care
	To achieve designated performance targets
	To participate in self-development or to assist with the development of others
	To maintain company policy in respect of:
	● personal standards of health/hygiene
	● personal standards of appearance/conduct
	● operating safety whilst at work
	● public promotion
	● corporate image
	as laid out in employee handbook
	To carry out client consultation in accordance with company policy
	To maintain company security practices and procedures
	To assist your manager in the provision of salon services
	To undertake additional tasks and duties required by your manager from time to time.

Job description

● the grievance procedure

● employee legal entitlements and responsibilities

● health and safety requirements.

If these have been stated from the outset, at least the employee knows what is expected. If you do not have a job description ask your employer or manager if you can have one, so that you know precisely what is expected of you and how your job role fits into or alongside those of your colleagues. You will have a clear guide on your **limits of authority**. Some large salons will have a staff structure chart that explains everyone's role in the salon and the reporting structure.

The appraisal process

At the beginning of the appraisal period, the manager and the employee discuss jointly, develop and mutually agree the objectives and performance measures (targets) for that period. An action plan will then be drafted, outlining the expected outcomes.

During the appraisal period, should there be any significant changes in factors such as objectives or performance measures, these will be discussed between the manager and employee and any amendments will be added to the action plan.

At the end of the appraisal period, the results are discussed by the employee and the manager, and both manager and employee sign the appraisal. A copy is prepared for the employee and the original is kept on file.

An appraisal of performance will contain the following information:

- employee's name
- appraisal period
- appraiser's name and title
- performance objectives
- job title
- work location
- results achieved
- identified areas of strengths and weaknesses
- an ongoing action plan
- an (optional) overall performance grading.

IDENTIFYING YOUR OWN STRENGTHS AND WEAKNESSES

Being able to spot your own mistakes is a starting point. We all know that if we do things the right way, we gain the personal satisfaction of getting it right. Conversely, if we keep making mistakes and get it wrong more times than right, we feel wretched. This low self-esteem needs to be avoided; it is negative and does nothing for our self-motivation.

One way of measuring personal strengths and weaknesses is self-appraisal. The important aspect of self-appraisal is having the ability to make an honest evaluation and review of your own progress. Try the activity below as an example of how you could do this for yourself.

After you have completed the activity of putting the letters A–Q in the appropriate box, you may have other additional statements that you want to add to your list. Does your supervisor agree with your responses? Hand this to your supervisor and ask to have your responses checked. Lastly, your supervisor can fill in the last column in the same way. Now see if both columns match.

ACTIVITY

Fill in the middle column with the letters A, B, C, etc. for the statements that best apply to you (here is an example):

I can do this very well	A
	G
	H
	P

A   I neutralise perms on short to medium-length hair
B   I neutralise perms on long hair
C   I handle payments by cards at reception
D   I make appointments for all services
E   I help, assist and communicate with clients on a routine basis
F   I prepare the chemicals carefully for the stylists
G   I recommend products to clients, encouraging them to buy
H   I recommend treatments to clients, encouraging them to buy
I   I conduct salon business over the phone
J   I blow-dry clients' hair to help out the stylists
K   I apply colour for stylists
L   I am always punctual for work
M   I am particular about my appearance
N   I thoroughly clean and prepare the working surfaces
O   I monitor the usage of stock and materials
P   I notice when things need doing
Q   I recognise situations where there may be a potential hazard

Level of Ability	Employee fills in this column	Supervisor fills in this column
I can do this very well		
I can do this OK		
I think I'm getting there		
I find this a bit tricky		
I can't do this at all		

WORKING AS A TEAM

Creating and maintaining good working relationships with your fellow staff members is essential. Only a harmonious working team can be productive and effective. The relationships that must be built and maintained at work are very different to those that exist outside of that environment. Hairdressing businesses rely solely upon providing a repeat service to its customers at a price that is profitable for the firm and that its clients are happy to pay.

The formula may seem simple: unfortunately it isn't. There are so many factors that affect this delicate balance. Unlike other businesses, personal services rely solely upon people and the communication between them.

M. Balfe

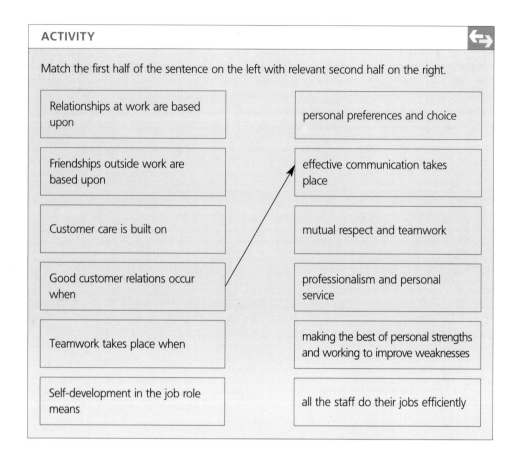

ACTIVITY

Match the first half of the sentence on the left with relevant second half on the right.

Relationships at work are based upon	personal preferences and choice
Friendships outside work are based upon	effective communication takes place
Customer care is built on	mutual respect and teamwork
Good customer relations occur when	professionalism and personal service
Teamwork takes place when	making the best of personal strengths and working to improve weaknesses
Self-development in the job role means	all the staff do their jobs efficiently

Hairdressing is not just about selling. Why is that? Well, when a product is sold, more often than not, the purchaser has made a conscious decision to buy. The standard or quality is defined by the product's composition. The only factors affecting the sale are competing products and their price, availability, features and benefits.

In hairdressing, the standard and quality of hairdressing skills provided by stylists of the same level of expertise might only vary slightly between salons. So another, far more important variable comes into play: what matters is not so much what is provided but how it is provided. Here communication becomes the vital link: not to sell products, but to sell a complete service.

Be an effective team member

When you work in a salon, regardless whether it is a large company chain, or a small independent salon, you will be an important part of their team. You will be working with other people whom you don't know, yet you will have to get on with them. As a team member you will need to know:

- the other members of the team
- who is responsible for different things
- to whom you need to go if you need any help.

Teamwork is about making an active contribution, seeking to assist others even if it is only holding brushes whilst the stylist is blow-drying. Don't expect to be asked to do things all the time; think ahead and see if you can anticipate what others will need.

REMEMBER ✔

There is a huge difference between the friendships that you build out of choice and the others that you have to accept and work with in the professional world.

M. Balfe

Anticipating the needs of others is a follow-on from providing support by cleaning and preparing the work areas ready for use, locating and preparing products as and when they are required.

Respond to requests willingly

Cooperate with your colleagues. Make a positive contribution to your team. When a colleague asks you for help you should respond willingly and politely to the request. Remember, working in a public place is like being on show all the time, clients will see, hear and *feel* any tension within the salon. How others see you in your work role will have a huge impact on your professionalism: you would rather be thought of as a willing, helpful trainee than a quiet, moody one!

Maintain harmony and always try to minimise conflicts. Most good working relationships develop easily; others, however, will need to be worked at. Whatever your personal feelings are about your colleagues or the boss, clients must never sense a bad atmosphere. You will spend a lot of time in the company of people you work with, but you will not always like everyone you meet. People at work are different, so in order for you to work as a team player you must develop a mutual respect for others, even if they would *never* get on your personal friends list.

Speak to people in the way that you would expect others to speak to you; and remember this goes for the clients too. They will be making up their mind about what they think of you in the first few moments of contact. Be positive and maintain eye contact; always make a point of helping them where and when you can.

Make effective use of your working day

Always make good use of your time. In a busy salon there is always something that needs doing, so sometimes you will have to juggle between two or three things at the same time!

- Keep a list of the different tasks you have been asked to do (that way you won't get into trouble for trying to remember them all).
- Find out which ones take priority. Some jobs are more important or urgent and they will need to be done first.
- If you don't understand what has been asked of you, ask someone before it's too late!
- Remember, if you do have to leave something halfway through, make sure that you get back to complete it at the earliest convenient moment.

Report problems to relevant people

Within any organisational structure there is a hierarchy and this is important for you to know to whom you should go if you need any help.

REMEMBER
Treat other people as you would wish to be treated yourself.

REMEMBER
You should only try to do the things that you have been shown and trained to do. Never attempt to do anything new without the assistance of a senior member of staff.

REMEMBER
- Treat others with respect.
- Be sensitive and responsive to the needs of others.
- Show concern and care for others.
- Avoid actions that may offend others.

ACTIVITY

Look at the following organisational diagram and first of all; answer the questions. Then, in the space provided complete the structure for your own workplace environment.

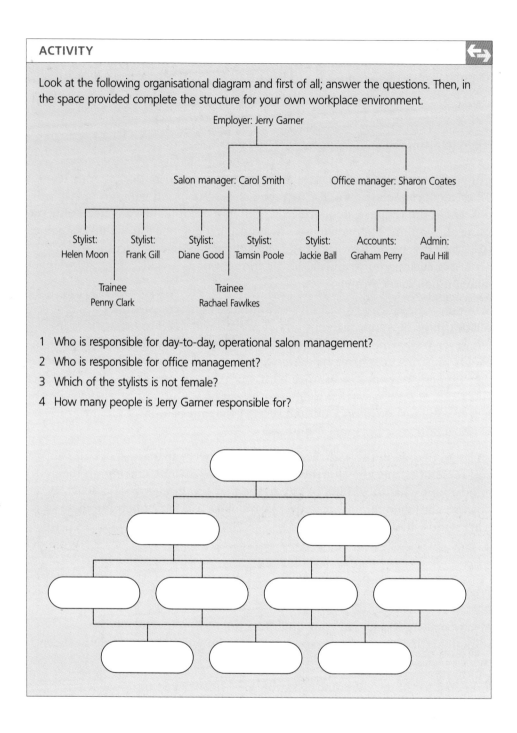

1 Who is responsible for day-to-day, operational salon management?
2 Who is responsible for office management?
3 Which of the stylists is not female?
4 How many people is Jerry Garner responsible for?

As you can see from the example above, different people do different jobs. For example, you would need to know who to contact if you were ill and couldn't get into work. Conversely, if you had a query about your wages you might need to contact somebody else.

In another situation, imagine that a client has returned to the salon with a complaint about her hair and she is demanding her money back. You won't have the authority to deal with this; you will have to get someone to handle the complaint.

M. Balfe

Resolving problems with other members of the team

If you do have a problem with another member of the team, you need to approach them privately about it first. You should think carefully about what you are going to say and make sure that your time and place is suitable.

If you cannot sort it out yourselves, you should report it to your manager who will want to resolve the situation quickly and fairly. Make sure that you cover all the relevant facts and provide any other supporting information. Remember there are always two sides to a story, so your manager will want to hear the other side as well before taking any action.

M. Balfe

Grievance and disciplinary procedures

There are times when disputes cannot be sorted out easily. In these situations a formal salon procedure comes into play. Your salon will have its own way of implementing grievance or disciplinary procedures, and you should receive this information during your induction. The procedure will cover the following issues:

- conflict at work between staff
- unfair or presumed unfair treatment at work (e.g. being asked to do tasks beyond your abilities or unsafe practices)
- discrimination in any situation or scenario.

Where staff members fail to meet the required standards, they can expect disciplinary action to be taken against them. Although this can vary between salons, the following indicates the formal steps involved:

> **REMEMBER**
>
> Never carry out any task at work if you are unsure what has been asked of you. Ask a senior colleague to explain what the task involves.

> **REMEMBER**
>
> There are a number of actions that fall outside of this disciplinary procedure.
>
> Acts of gross misconduct if proven will always incur summary dismissal.

Standard disciplinary procedure

Step 1	Issue a statement of grounds for action	The employer writes to the employee detailing the conduct, capability or circumstances that may result in dismissal or disciplinary action
Step 2	Arrange a meeting	A meeting must be arranged with the employee to discuss the issue. After the meeting the employer must tell the employee what the decision is and offer the employee a right of appeal
Step 3	Arrange an appeal	The employee must tell the employer if they wish to appeal. The employer must invite the employee to a second meeting and the employee should try to attend. The final decision must be communicated to the employee

ACTS OF GROSS MISCONDUCT/GROSS INCOMPETENCE

Your salon will have its own standards and expectations relating to conduct and behaviour and the team are happier in their work if they know what is expected of them. These rules and working conditions and disciplinary procedures are generally clarified and displayed through job descriptions and organisational policy. However, there are certain actions that will, *if proven* effect an instant dismissal. The following is a list of some of these acts of gross misconduct:

- carrying or taking illicit drugs on the work premises
- theft from the salon or fellow staff members
- drinking alcohol on the premises
- wilful damage to company property
- endangering yourself, fellow staff members or salon clients and visitors
- disclosure of private company information and data.

Acts of gross incompetence will have the same summary dismissal as gross misconduct. These actions of negligence can occur during normal work activities and will put the salon's good name and reputation in jeopardy. Typical examples of this would be:

- careless use of chemicals on clients, e.g. spillages causing bodily harm incurring hospitalisation
- careless timing of chemical treatments, e.g. causing scalp burns, hair damage or loss
- careless use of equipment, e.g. tampering with electrical items causing harm to others, incorrect timings of processes causing harm or damage.

REMEMBER

If you are unsure of what constitutes an act of gross misconduct or an act of gross incompetence/negligence, ask your supervisor.

I understand my job position and how it fits in with the work team ☐	I know why I should always get permission before doing things off my own back ☐	I always follow the salon's policy in respect to client care and customer service ☐	I know to whom I can turn if I have any difficulties at work ☐
I know what is expected at work in relation to conduct, attendance and punctuality ☐	I understand the salon's grievance procedures ☐	I know the salon's procedures for progress review and performance appraisal ☐	I know how to communicate effectively with staff and customers ☐
I understand the implications of poor staff communications ☐	I know how the appraisal system works and that I must achieve my work targets ☐	I understand principles for identifying my own strengths and weaknesses ☐	I know who can help me with furthering my professional development and training ☐
I know how to make the best use of my time at work ☐	I know how to anticipate the needs of other team members ☐		CHECKER BOARD ✔

Assessment of knowledge and understanding

The following projects, activities and assessments are directly linked to the essential knowledge and understanding for unit G8.

For each statement that is addressed wholly or in part in these activities, you will see its relevant and corresponding EKU number.

Make sure that you keep this for easier referencing and along with your work for future inclusion in your portfolio.

Project (EKU G8.12)

For this project you will need to gather information from other people with whom you work.

There is a simple tried-and-tested method for self-assessing one's own current position: the SWOT analysis. This helps you think through your:

- strengths
- weaknesses
- opportunities
- threats

in relation to where you are now and where you need to be.

For each of the titles – strengths, weaknesses, opportunities and threats – write a small summary of your attributes, and then show this to your supervisor to see if they agree.

The completed SWOT analysis can be recorded in your portfolio and will provide a basis for your future action plan.

Case study

After completing your SWOT analysis, look carefully at the positive and negative aspects.

Choosing the positive aspects first. How can you develop these attributes further?

Now select the negative aspects. What do you need to do in order to change these into positives too?

This exercise will help you form the basis of your next action plan: discuss your SWOT analysis and your suggested routes for further development with your supervisor.

Keep copies of all the information for use in your portfolio.

Questions

1 How do the National Occupational Standards help you to identify your training needs? (G8.15)

2 How do you keep abreast of changing fashions? (G8.17)

3 What is meant by the term 'continuing professional development'? (G8.13)

4 What information does your job description contain? (G8.1, G8.2)

5 How and when do you know if you are working to the required standards set by the salon? (G8.6, G8.9, G8.10)

6 Why is it important to work together harmoniously? (G8.19)

7 What would constitute as positive feedback from (a) your reviewer (b) you in your training review or appraisal? (G8.20)

8 How would you describe good time management in reference to what you do in your work? (G8.22)

Preparing for assessment checklist

Remember to:

- communicate positively and effectively in the salon at all times
- develop yourself in those activities that provide further progress in your career
- work together harmoniously as a team player
- recognise the occasions when others need assistance
- work at maintaining professional relationships with fellow staff members
- use your time efficiently and effectively
- work towards personal targets and know why they should be achieved.

chapter 12

PROMOTING THE BUSINESS

What do I need to do?

- Be able to identify opportunities to promote services and products to clients.
- Take opportunities to promote new things to clients.
- Find different ways to inform clients of services and products.
- Choose the most appropriate time to inform clients about services and products.

What do I need to learn?

- The techniques of selling to clients.
- How to communicate positively and effectively.
- How to gauge a client's interest.

Information covered in this chapter

- How to identify client needs.
- How to promote yourself and the salon.
- The selling process.
- Customer complaints.

Promotion   The ways of communicating products or services to clients that lead to sales.

Marketing   The strategy and planning that takes place before the promotion of products or services.

Features   Refers to the different functions of a product.

Benefits   Refers to the results or outcomes of those functions.

INTRODUCTION

This chapter is about promoting the business. Without its sales and marketing aspects, the business would cease to exist. We find that we are being sold to every time we go into town, when we turn the TV on, when we pick up the post and often when we answer the phone. Clever marketing gets the message over by making sure that we know what they are trying to sell. We are so used to being sold to, that we *expect* to see 'new and improved', 'latest version' and 'just in'. The secret is that people like new things and this is the simplest marketing ploy of all. More often than not, many of those new things are old things, they just happen to be put in a new light with a different slant.

CHECKERBOARD

At the end of this chapter the checkerboard will help to jog your memory on what you have learned and what still remains to be done. Cross off with a pencil each of the topics as you cover it (see page 377).

The hairdressing industry exists by providing a service to customers that they expect and are happy to pay for. But it doesn't end there. Hairdressing is a constantly changing environment, with new fashions, techniques, products and services. Unless we continue to provide these new options to clients, we will stop moving forwards and fall backwards into decline. Therefore it is essential that we build on experience and continue to develop the necessary skills. In this chapter we look closely at the ways and techniques that you can use to promote the services and products that are available in your salon.

M. Balfre

Photo courtesy Goldwell UK

Photo courtesy Goldwell UK

PROMOTING BUSINESS

The services and treatments provided by salons to clients form the basis of the business. This particular business model is built on two specific factors:

- maintaining client satisfaction
- retaining client loyalty.

In 99 per cent of salons these two factors are directly linked and are essential for a business to succeed. It is possible to make a really good job of satisfying our clients, but unless they return reasonably soon their annual contribution to the salon will be drastically reduced. So we need to stimulate the client's loyalty by encouraging them to:

- return on a regular basis
- buy into other services, products and treatments
- share their experiences with their family, friends and work associates.

We should bear in mind that the bond built between the client and stylist is purely a business arrangement. Hairdressing may be a very social occupation but the clients are not your friends.

So how do we serve that target group? We serve them by promoting:

- ourselves
- hairdressing services, products and treatments
- the sales environment.

PROMOTING OURSELVES

There is one thing that we should cover first of all about hairdressers and hairdressing. Believe it or not, good communication far outweighs technical excellence when it comes to success. In order to be a successful, busy, popular stylist you don't have to be a brilliant technical hairdresser.

Hairdressing is changing very quickly, and not just because of changing fashions and trends. Customers expect more: they have a right to do so. People's expectations in respect to accountability, reliability, responsibility and recourse have changed greatly in the last few years. People have learned not to take second best and therefore competition between salons is fierce. Our customers want to *see* these aspects demonstrated in the salon, and the quicker they develop, the sooner a respect and loyalty for you and the team will be gained.

Good customer service is being customer focused. It is centred upon the needs of the client and is reflected within all of the aspects that are involved within routine salon operations: the telephone response times, salon refreshments and magazines, visually pleasing interiors and the polite and friendly staff.

Why do clients come to our salon? They come because they want to feel better in themselves and also want to look good. Have you ever considered what the client thinks and feels before you start the service? Your client's hair is vitally important and they are passing on that responsibility on to you and, they hope, a safe pair of hands!

Photo courtesy Goldwell

REMEMBER

Put yourself in the client's position. How would you like and expect to be dealt with?

Mahogany

ACTIVITY

The easiest way to practise your technique of selling or promoting products and services is to try it out with people you know first.

Role-play is an ideal way of finding out how people respond in different ways when they are being offered new or different products or services.

When you have a quiet moment, take it in turns with your colleagues to play the client and the stylist. Watch how others tackle situations, answer questions and respond to information.

PROMOTING HAIRDRESSING SERVICES, PRODUCTS AND TREATMENTS

The clients to whom we have been recommended are from a particularly special group. They have found us through the network of already satisfied customers. The quality of our workmanship, the ways that we communicate and our personality have all preceded us. Our satisfied customers feel confident enough in our technical expertise to promote and recommend us to their friends and colleagues.

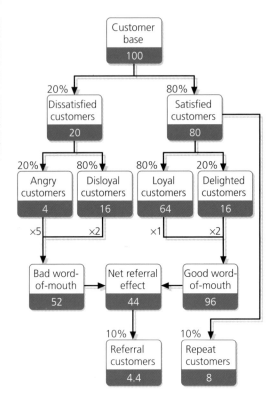

```
                    ┌──────────┐
                    │ Customer │
                    │   base   │
                    │   100    │
                    └──────────┘
           20%                        80%
    ┌──────────────┐          ┌──────────────┐
    │ Dissatisfied │          │  Satisfied   │
    │  customers   │          │  customers   │
    │      20      │          │      80      │
    └──────────────┘          └──────────────┘
   20%         80%          80%          20%
┌────────┐ ┌──────────┐ ┌────────┐ ┌──────────┐
│ Angry  │ │ Disloyal │ │ Loyal  │ │ Delighted│
│customers│ │customers │ │customers│ │ customers│
│   4    │ │    16    │ │   64   │ │    16    │
└────────┘ └──────────┘ └────────┘ └──────────┘
   ×5        ×2           ×1          ×2
┌────────┐ ┌──────────┐           ┌──────────┐
│  Bad   │ │   Net    │           │Good word-│
│ word-  │ │ referral │           │ of-mouth │
│of-mouth│ │  effect  │           │          │
│   52   │ │    44    │           │    96    │
└────────┘ └──────────┘           └──────────┘
              10%          10%
          ┌──────────┐ ┌──────────┐
          │ Referral │ │  Repeat  │
          │customers │ │customers │
          │   4.4    │ │    8     │
          └──────────┘ └──────────┘
```

Mahogany

If recommendation is such a powerful channel of communication, why don't we use it more often? Well we can. The perfect time to talk about the variety of services and treatments available in the salon is when the client is in the chair in front of us or sitting back at the basin. Recommendation and professional advice are the simplest way of making clients aware of the range of services, products and treatments that the salon has to offer.

Not all the salon's services or treatments are suitable for every client though. A client may want their hair to last longer between washes and you might suggest that they have a perm. Will they still be happy if when they get home their hair takes a lot longer to do, or is more difficult to style than it was before?

Sometimes our clients want more than they are capable of handling; they might not have the skills to achieve the same effect as you and this is where your advice and support are needed.

Routine, continual use of the same products is another trap to fall into. You might have some favourites in your salon's styling ranges and enjoy using them a lot. But are they really suitable for every client's hair?

Your client may see one of the photos of hairstyles that you show them and really like the finished effect and the definition provided by the heavy moulding waxes used within it but has never liked the feel of products on their hair.

- Are they really going to be satisfied with the final effect?
- Would they continue to use it at home if they bought some?

Perhaps in a situation like this a halfway house is a better option. Your client likes the finished look and you want to introduce the benefits of using styling products. The answer here is to get the client used to the handling and the feel of the hair with newly introduced products, so choose something that will give definition but doesn't overload the hair. When they have got used to this, they might want to take another step next time.

REMEMBER	

Listen to your client, identify their needs, ask them questions and then you will be able to advise and recommend.

REMEMBER	

Good hairdressers need to be good communicators and that means good at listening too! You need to know how to ask the right questions, listen carefully to the client's response and build on the information they have given you.

The selling process

1	Find out the client's needs	Listen to your clients; find out how well they manage their hair. Ask questions about the products they already use.
2	Give your advice	Keep it simple, don't use technical words. Explain what the product etc. does, how the client will benefit.
3a	Look for client interest	Is the client interested in what you are saying? Provide answers to the client's questions. If it's a product let them handle it and smell it. Tell them how much it costs.
3b	Recognise when a client isn't interested	Are they trying to change the subject? Are they distracted by other activity in the salon? Watch their body language: what is it telling you?
4	Gain agreement	Ask them, 'Would you like to take some home with you today?' Have it prepared at reception ready for when they leave.

In order for you to promote your salon's services, treatments and products you need to recognise how they are viewed by the clients. To do this you need to consider each service in terms of its features and its benefits:

- 'Features' are the functions – what the service, treatment or product does.
- 'Benefits' are the results of the functions – what the service etc. achieves.

For example, suppose you hope to persuade a client to spend £30 on a cut and blow-dry. Why should she do so? What are the benefits of the service?

The feature is a precision cut.

The benefits are keeping shape and easier home styling. The client must decide whether the payment of £30 is justified by these benefits.

Consider a second example: application of a semi-permanent colour. In this case the features are that the colour is not permanent and is applied in a conditioning base. The benefits are that it will wash out after six to eight shampoos and meanwhile it will create shine.

Knowledge of service and product features enables you to sell your clients the benefits. You thereby create a need, and once the client has accepted the need, you are in a good position to make the sale.

The first step is therefore for you to gain a thorough knowledge of each service and product available in the salon, and to convert this knowledge into an understanding of the features and benefits for each one.

ACTIVITY

Create a table with three columns. In the first column list all of the services and retail products that your salon has on offer.

Then, in the second column, next to each one listed write down what features they have.

Then in the last column list what benefits to the customer they have.

Photo courtesy Goldwell

Photo courtesy Goldwell UK

RETAILING TIPS: GOOD AND BAD SELLING

Fierce competition and the rise of professional home hair-care products have meant that retailing is a major contributor to the salon's income. Innovative, forward-thinking stylists, salons and suppliers have led this important turnaround.

What is retailing? Retailing is the selling of home-care products to clients. This can be in single or bulk, professional-size quantities. If it is done well, retailing enhances the image of both hairdresser and the salon and, most importantly, the clients enjoy it – people like to shop! It meets needs, fulfils desires and makes them feel good.

REMEMBER

Good practice: good selling skills

- Listening, asking questions, showing interest.
- Using the client's name.
- Empathising (putting yourself in the client's place); establishing a bond.
- Recognising non-verbal cues (dilated pupils 'I approve'; ear-rubbing = 'I've heard enough').
- Identifying needs; helping clients reach buying decisions.
- Knowing your products/services.

REMEMBER

Bad selling

- Doing all the talking.
- Not listening; not 'hearing' unspoken thoughts; arguing.
- Interrupting, but never letting the client interrupt you, thus losing an open opportunity for giving extra information.
- Hard selling; 'spieling' (working to a script).
- Threatening: 'You won't get it cheaper anywhere else'; knocking the opposition.
- Manipulating – 'Oh dear, I'll miss my sales target.'
- Knowing nothing about the product.
- Treating 'No thanks' as personal rejection.
- Blinding clients with science.
- Staying mainly silent, waiting for an order.
- Insisting the client should buy the product.

REMEMBER

The 'bad' list is longer because bad selling still persists in retailing.

Promoting other services to clients

Good business is repeated business and the best time to recommend other services to clients is when they are sitting at the styling section having their hair done.

With your colleagues, select five of the services provided by your salon that would be suitable to recommend to clients. Then discuss how you would introduce these new services to the client. Make a record of the collective opinions and keep this within your portfolio for future reference.

PROMOTING SALES: THE ENVIRONMENT

'Closing' a sale isn't just the final notes, it's the whole process from the moment a client walks in: the friendly welcome, the relaxing ambience, your focused attention and pleasant and friendly manner. You should always try to address their inner concerns and suggest solutions or alternatives, e.g. 'We should be able to help you' or 'Have you thought about…?'

Experienced stylists call it 'setting the scene' or creating the right 'selling atmosphere' – and that is one that encourages clients to buy. Our main drivers for buying are centred on health, security, pride, prestige, status, ego and even greed. These emotions are strong motivators and that is why simply selling on technical aspects doesn't work! 'Clients don't buy formulas – they buy solutions.' This clever marketing strap-line created by Paul Mitchell only goes to prove that people aren't switched by jargon – they just want results.

In-salon promotion and presentation of product is helped by:

- point-of-sale merchandising – e.g. a central 'island', an open cabinet, shelf displays
- 'shelf-talkers' – printed promotional slips/cards fixed to/dangling from shelves; 'mobile' ones that bob or bounce deliver best results
- eye-catching displays that are instantly informative; they should be located where they'll be seen – at reception or centrally in treatment areas
- arrangement of popular lines at eye level with price details; use 'price watch' stickers
- linking displays with money-off and other special offers – first visit, loyalty, recommend-a-friend discounts, and promotional tie-ins with major local stores.

The salon image is an immensely important sales environment, it communicates to our clients through their senses of sight, hearing, touch, taste and smell. These senses quickly convey an overall impression which, if positive, will enhance what we try to do as individuals. But if it's negative it will erode the benefit of the service we aim to provide.

Photo courtesy Goldwell UK

Photo courtesy Goldwell UK

What do they see?

Is the salon in a basement or hidden upstairs? Is it on the main high street or on a housing estate? What colour schemes have been used inside? Is this carried through in printed stationery (price lists, cards, service information)?

What do they hear?

How are they spoken to on the telephone? How are they greeted when they enter the salon? How are they received, directed and consulted afterwards? What background noises can they hear?

What do they feel?

Can they feel the quality of fresh gowns and towels? Can they feel the level of professional contact in the way that services and treatments are carried out?

What can they smell?

What is the salon atmosphere like? What do the products used smell like? Do the staff smell clean and hygienic? Does the fragrance of fresh ground coffee linger in the air?

What can they taste?

What beverages or food is available? What is the quality of these drinks or food? What does it say to our clients?

Photo courtesy Goldwell

ACTIVITY

Features and benefits
With your colleagues, select six of the services provided by your salon and jointly consider what are the features and benefits to the client, in each case. Make a record of the collective opinions and keep this within your portfolio for future reference.

HANDLING COMPLAINTS

It would be impossible not to get complaints. Even if the percentage of complaints against the number of clients the salon dealt with a fraction of one per cent, there will still be complaints sometimes. Unfortunately, a trainee or newly qualified stylist will get more than most. This is because:

- experience in handling people and different situations takes time
- good communication between new staff and clients takes time to develop
- aspects of client consultation are missed or overlooked through lack of time.

There is one common denominator for all of the above: time. One way or another it becomes a part of all the problems that can occur.

Your salon will have its own policy for handling complaints and, as a matter of reference, the table below covers the main types.

In any average salon there tend to be four main types of complaint:

Types of complaint

Scenario 1	The client has got what they asked and paid for, but after a few days decide that their partner hates it. It's all your fault as far as they are concerned.
Scenario 2	A customer who had a body wave perm finds their scalp becomes sore and the hair breaks off at the ends. You forgot to do a strand test. *You* are at fault.
Scenario 3	A customer who had a body wave perm finds that their scalp becomes sore and the hair breaks off at the ends. You provided advice and did a strand test. The day after the salon visit they begin taking medication which caused the reaction. Nevertheless, they still blame you!!
Scenario 4	You've had an off day and your work with the client was not as good as usual.

So what happens when you are faced with angry clients? In all these scenarios, it's vital that, no matter how abusive the client is being, you receive them pleasantly and politely, move them to a quieter part of the salon and get a senior member of staff to attend to them.

Mahogany

Scenario 1 complaint

Scenario 1 is the most likely to happen and this is because different people have their hair done for different reasons.

Every client has their hair done to enhance or change their appearance.

● Is it to please themselves?	Most clients fall into this category.
● Is it because they want approval from others?	Many clients fall into this category.
● Is it because they need approval from others?	Some clients fall into this category.
● Is it to spite someone else?	Few clients fall into this category.

Experienced consultation will identify which group the client falls into.

Scenario 2 complaint

In the case of scenario 2, it might be too late to correct the damage. More worrying still, it's one of those cases that these days with so many law firms offering 'no win no fee' will probably end up in court. In cases like this there are several important issues that need to be addressed:

1 The salon cannot admit liability.

2 The manager must be consulted immediately.

3 The salon's insurers will be notified immediately that there is the possibility of a claim arising.

4 All subsequent correspondence is passed on unanswered to the insurers.

Scenario 3 complaint

In the case of scenario 3, the person handling the complaint should establish any changes in the customer's lifestyle since they left the salon to find out possible causes for these events and also to exonerate the salon.

Again, all matters relating to the case should be dealt with by the salon's insurers.

Scenario 4 complaint

In the case of scenario 4 complaints, unfortunately they happen all too often. You are at fault, but in most cases and particularly if the client is a regular the complaint can be easily rectified.

REMEMBER

The all-important body language!

Don't . . .

When you get to the point where you handle simple complaints, remember that the loss or profit and reputation caused by one unhappy customer may require ten new customers to make up for it. You might do better to take a deep breath and put on your most sympathetic face when faced with an angry client.

- Don't fold your arms. It looks defensive.
- Don't lean too far forward. It can look aggressive.
- Don't clench your teeth or tense your muscles. You might be doing so to try and mask your own tension but it looks like you are defending your own patch and, at worst, can look as if you're merely trying to control your temper.
- Don't interrupt. Instead, look interested and listen.
- Don't make body contact. Keep a respectable physical distance from your client.

CONSUMER LEGISLATION

The Consumer Protection Act (1987)

This Act follows European laws to protect the buyer in the following areas:

- product liability
- general safety requirements
- misleading prices.

The Act is designed to help safeguard the consumer from products that do not reach reasonable levels of safety. Your salon will take adequate precautions in procuring, using and supplying reputable products and maintaining them so that they remain in good condition.

Cosmetic Products (Safety) Regulations 1996

These regulations are all part of consumer protection. European laws lay down stringent regulations about the chemical composition of products, their labelling of these ingredients and how the product is described and marketed. This clear labelling policy helps people who are sensitive or allergic to certain chemicals to find out what a product contains before they buy.

The Prices Act (1974)

The price of products has to be displayed in order to prevent a false impression to the buyer.

The Trades Descriptions Act (1968 and 1972)

Products must not be falsely or misleadingly described in relation to their quality, fitness, price or purpose, by advertisements, orally, displays or descriptions. And since 1972 it has also been a requirement to label a product clearly, so that the buyer can see where the product was made.

Briefly, a retailer cannot:

- mislead consumers by making false statements about previous and present product pricing
- offer sale products at half price unless they have been offered at the actual price for a minimum of 28 days.

The Resale Prices Act (1964 and 1976)

The manufacturers can supply a recommended price (MRRP or manufacturers' recommended retail price), but the seller is not obliged to sell at the recommended price.

The Sale and Supply of Goods Act (1994)

This Act encompasses the following laws:

- the Supply of Goods and Services Act 1982
- the Supply of Goods (Implied Terms) Act 1973
- the Unfair Contract Terms Act 1977.

The vendor must ensure that the goods they sell are of 'satisfactory quality' which is defined as of a standard that would be regarded by a reasonable person as satisfactory, having taken into account the description of the goods, the price and other relevant circumstances. The goods must also be 'reasonably fit': the vendor must ensure that the goods can fulfil the purpose they claim they can.

Briefly the Act requires the vendor to:

- be responsible in only selling goods at the very best quality and condition
- refund the purchaser if a product is found to be defective or at least offer an exchange
- make the supplier aware of the complaint.

The Supply of Goods and Services Act 1982

The law has relevance to:

- *Goods* – This enables the consumer to claim back some or the entire purchase price paid for the goods if they are not in merchantable condition
- *Services* – This ensures that services paid for by consumer are provided at a reasonable price, with reasonable care and attention and in an acceptable timescale.

Consumer Protection (Distance Selling) Regulations 2000

These are derived from a European Directive and cover the supply of goods and/or services from suppliers acting in a commercial capacity to consumers i.e. individuals acting outside a trade business or profession. The regulations should be of concern to any individual purchasing goods or services by telephone, using the internet, digital TV or mail order catalogues and conversely be of concern to any suppliers dealing with consumers through these media.

Started it ☐	I know and understand the principles of selling services and products to clients ☐	I can communicate positively and professionally with the clients ☐	I know the limits of my own authority in dealing with clients ☐
I am aware of the legislation that protects clients from unlawful selling ☐	I know the rights that clients/consumers have ☐	I always carry out working practices according to the salon's policy ☐	I know the range of services and products that the salon offers ☐
I always explain technical terms eliminating ambiguity and false beliefs ☐	I know the factors that influence clients in making purchasing decisions ☐	I know how to advise, promote and sell other services and products to clients ☐	I know and respect the clients' rights, data protection, consumer legislation ☐
Done it all! ☐			CHECKER BOARD ✔

Assessment of knowledge and understanding

The following projects, activities and assessments are directly linked to the essential knowledge and understanding for unit G6.

For each statement that is addressed wholly or in part in these activities, you will see its relevant and corresponding EKU number.

Make sure that you keep this for easier referencing and along with your work for future inclusion in your portfolio.

Project (EKU G6.1 and G5.1 part)

For this project you will need to gather information from a variety of sources.

For the following legislation find out how:

(a) the Health and Safety at Work Act

(b) the Data Protection Act

affect the way that services can be provided to clients.

In your project pay particular attention to the aspects that would have impact on a business and the implications if this legislation were not considered.

Case study (G6.9, G6.10, G6.11, G6.12, G6.13, G6.14, G6.15)

On Thursday morning Stephen got to work a little late. His first client, Mary, was waiting so Joanne had provided Mary with a coffee and a magazine. Stephen made his apologies and confirmed with Mary that the appointment was for a trim and blow-dry.

Mary had been looking through the magazine and had seen a picture that she thought looked really good. She asked Stephen what he thought. Stephen said, 'We'll talk about it whilst I do the trim and blow-dry.'

When Mary was being shampooed, Stephen was called to reception to help the receptionist recommend a suitable product for a guy who had just walked in. The man said 'I've not seen this salon before. It looks really cool; can you recommend something to make my hair look a bit more defined?'

'Yes', said Stephen.

'Jenny, can you get a greasy hair shampoo down for the gent; his hair needs body because it's lank?'

Stephen returned to Mary and as he started trimming her hair he relayed the events that had just happened in the reception. Stephen finished off Mary's hair in the usual way and then she paid and left the salon.

Stephen went to the staff room, made himself a strong black coffee and started to tell his workmates about the nightclub he went to last night.

What do you think of Stephens's customer service?

What mistakes has he made?

What are the implications to the salon?

Questions

1 How does the consumer legislation affect the way that retail products are handled and sold to clients? (G6.1 part)

2 What is your job role and what are the conditions applying to it in your job specification? (G6.4)

3 What is your place of work's policy in respect to the achievement of targets? (G6.5)

4 What rights do clients have and what are their service expectations? (G6.7)

5 How would you introduce new services and products to clients? (G6.12 and G6.14)

Preparing for assessment checklist

Remember to:

> communicate effectively in the salon
>
> maintain confidentiality and be mindful of the consequences of failing to keep things private
>
> listen to clients and show them that you care
>
> use positive body language and the reasons why it plays such an important part in good customer service
>
> acknowledge the legal rights of clients and what might happen if they were breached
>
> promote the range of services, products and treatments with the salon
>
> use your time efficiently and effectively
>
> work towards personal targets and know why they should be achieved.

assessment

Quick Quiz: A selection of different types of questions to check your knowledge.

Q1   The three stages of hair growth are anagen, _____ and telogen.
Fill in the blank.

Q2   The cortex is the outermost layer of the hair – true or false?

☐ True   ☐ False

Q3   Which of the following are infectious diseases? (select all that apply)

☐ 1 Impetigo

☐ 2 Scalp ringworm

☐ 3 Alopecia

☐ 4 Head lice

☐ 5 Psoriasis

☐ 6 Eczema

Q4   The natural colour of hair depends on the amount of melanin within it – true or false?

☐ True   ☐ False

Q5   Which of the following is commonly known as split ends?

☐ a Trichorrhexis nodosa

☐ b Monilethrix

☐ c Tinea capitis

☐ d Fragilitas crinium

Q6   Dandruff is a condition of the scalp usually caused by fungal infection – true or false?

☐ True   ☐ False

Q7 Which of the following tests are carried out *during* technical services?
(select all that apply)

☐ 1. Skin test

☐ 2. Strand test

☐ 3. Development test curl

☐ 4. Imcompatibility test

☐ 5. Porosity test

☐ 6. Test cutting

Q8 The lower layers of the skin are called the _____ . Fill in the blank.

Q9 Which face shape suits most hairstyles and lengths?

☐ a. Square

☐ b. Oblong

☐ c. Oval

☐ d. Triangular

Q10 During consulation and hair analysis, a contra-indication will not allow the planned service to be carried out – true or false?

☐ True   ☐ False

Chapter 2: Client care and communication questions

Quick Quiz: A selection of different types of questions to check your knowledge.

Q1 Good personal _____ is essential in a personal service industry. Fill in the blank.

Q2 Poor posture leads to physical fatigue – true or false?

☐ True   ☐ False

Q3 Which of the following are essential PPE for the clients?

☐ 1. Towels

☐ 2. Barrier creams

☐ 3. Aprons

☐ 4. Gowns

☐ 5. Plastic capes

☐ 6. Latex gloves

Q4 Poor-quality combs are uncomfortable and can scratch the client's scalp – true or false?

☐ True   ☐ False

Q5 Which of the following is an example of poor customer service?

☐ 1. Checking that the towels and gowns are clean

☐ 2. Cleaning the work surfaces

☐ 3. Sweeping up loose hair clippings

☐ 4. Forgetting to offer the client a drink

Q6 Talking and listening to your client is one of the most important parts of good communication – true or false?

☐ True   ☐ False

Q7 What information should you remember to get when taking messages?

☐ 1. Address of contact

☐ 2. Time and place of call

☐ 3. Purpose of call

☐ 4. Details and instructions

☐ 5. Client treatment history

☐ 6. Client service details

Q8 Non-verbal communication is another name for _____ language. Fill in the blank.

Q9 Which of the following is poor body language?

☐ 1. Maintaining eye contact with the client

☐ 2. Moving into someone's personal space

☐ 3. Smiling when you greet someone

☐ 4. Maintaining the same eye level as the client

Q10 Hands at waist height, with palms upward, indicates that the person has nothing to hide – true or false?

☐ True   ☐ False

Chapter 3: Salon reception questions

Quick Quiz: A selection of different types of questions to check your knowledge.

Q1   Visa and MasterCard are both forms of _____ card. Fill in the blank.

Q2   A charge card is the same as a debit card – true or false?

☐ True   ☐ False

Q3   Which of the following card types are debit cards?

☐ 1. Loyalty card

☐ 2. Switch card

☐ 3. American Express card

☐ 4. MasterCard

☐ 5. Maestro card

☐ 6. Store card

Q4   The VAT within a selling price is calculated by deducting 17.5 per cent – true or false?

☐ True   ☐ False

Q5   The inclusive VAT figure for an item selling for £10.00 is?

☐ a. £0.175

☐ b. £1.75

☐ c. £1.49

☐ d. £8.51

Q6   You should always take a contact number when making appointments – true or false?

☐ True   ☐ False

Q7   Which of the following are examples of ineffective use of resources?

☐ 1. Explaining services and costs to clients on the telephone

☐ 2. Discarding excess product after application

☐ 3. Overrunning on appointments

☐ 4. Turning the lights off in corridors and staff areas

☐ 5. Washing up in the dispensary

☐ 6. Ordering stock over the telephone

Q8   _____ retail products are for maintaining hair between visits. Fill in the blank.

Q9   Which of the following procedures monitors the usage of products within salons?

☐ a. Stock control

☐ b. Monitoring wastage

☐ c. Retail product and display cleaning

☐ d. Stock rotation

Q10   A job description is a document containing the employee's terms and conditions of employment – true or false?

☐ True   ☐ False

Chapter 4: Shampooing and conditioning hair questions

Quick Quiz: A selection of different types of questions to check your knowledge.

Q1   Coarser, _____ hair takes longer to dampen than finer, oilier hair during shampooing. Fill in the blank.

Q2   Petrissage is commonly used during shampooing – true or false?

☐ True   ☐ False

Q3   What factors should you consider during shampooing and conditioning? (select all that apply)

☐ 1. Water hardness

☐ 2. Water pressure

☐ 3. Water softness

☐ 4. Water temperature

☐ 5. Water wastage

☐ 6. Water wetness

Q4   Effleurage is a massage movement of circulatory movements – true or false?

☐ True   ☐ False

Q5   The pH value of pH-balanced shampoos and conditioners is:

☐ a. 3.5–4.5

☐ b. 4.5–6.0

☐ c. 5.5–6.5

☐ d. 7.0–7.5

Q6   Dandruff is a condition of the scalp usually treated by shampoo – true or false?

☐ True   ☐ False

Q7   Select all that apply: Which of the following would take place after chemical processing? (select all that apply)

☐   1. Pre-perm shampoo

☐   2. Anti-oxidant conditioning

☐   3. Medicated treatment

☐   4. Conditioning rinse

☐   5. Anti-dandruff shampoo

☐   6. Pre-perm treatment

Q8   When conditioning long hair it is important to apply to the mid-lengths and _____ . Fill in the blank.

Q9   A shampoo for dry hair would typically contain:

☐   a. Citric acids

☐   b. Oils

☐   c. Medicating agents

☐   d. Anti-dandruff agents

Q10   During conditioning it is always necessary to leave the treatment on – true or false?

☐ True   ☐ False

Chapter 5: Health and safety in the salon questions

Quick Quiz: A selection of different types of questions to check your knowledge.

Q1   A _____ is something with potential to cause harm. Fill in the blank.

Q2   Risk assessment is a process of evaluation to ensure safe working practices – true or false?

☐ True   ☐ False

Q3 Which of the following are environmental hazards? (select all that apply)

☐ 1. Boxes of stock left in the reception area

☐ 2. Stock upon shelves in the store room

☐ 3. Wet or slippery floors

☐ 4. Shampoo backwash positions

☐ 5. Salon work stations

☐ 6. Trailing flexes from electrical equipment

Q4 First-aid boxes should contain paracetamol tablets – true or false?

☐ True   ☐ False

Q5 Which of the following regulations relates to the safe handling of chemicals?

☐ a. PPE

☐ b. RIDDOR

☐ c. COSHH

☐ d. OSRPA

Q6 All salons must have a written health and safety policy – true or false?

☐ True   ☐ False

Q7 Which of the following records must a salon keep up to date by law?

☐ 1. Telephone book

☐ 2. Accident book

☐ 3. Appointment book

☐ 4. Electrical equipment annual test records

☐ 5. Health and safety at work checklist

☐ 6. Fire drill records

Q8 The _____ _____ regulations require employers to provide adequate equipment and facilities in case of an accident occurring. Fill in the blank.

Q9 What colour is the label on a dry powder-filled fire extinguisher?

☐ a. Red

☐ b. Cream

☐ c. Black

☐ d. Blue

Q10 A dry powder filled fire extinguisher can be used on all classes of fire – true or false?

☐ True   ☐ False

Chapter 6: Cutting hair questions

Quick Quiz: A selection of different types of questions to check your knowledge.

Q1 Accuracy is achieved by _____ and cutting the hair at the correct angle. Fill in the blank.

Q2 A razor should be used on wet hair – true or false?

☐ True ☐ False

Q3 Select from the following list those that are *not* texturising techniques:

☐ 1. Club cutting

☐ 2. Graduation

☐ 3. Slice cutting

☐ 4. Layering

☐ 5. Point cutting

☐ 6. Chipping

Q4 Symmetrical shapes produce equally balanced hairstyles – true or false?

☐ True ☐ False

Q5 Which of the following is not a cutting term?

☐ a. Cross-checking

☐ b. Thinning

☐ c. Free hand

☐ d. Free style

Q6 Precision cutting is dependent upon cutting angles and even tension – true or false?

☐ True ☐ False

Q7 Which of the following hair growth patterns will effect the natural fall and way that a fringe lies after it is cut?

☐ 1. Nape whorl

☐ 2. Double crown

☐ 3. Widow's peak

☐ 4. Low hairline

☐ 5. Cow lick

☐ 6. High hairline

Q8 A _____ is the perimeter shape produced by cutting. Fill in the blank.

Q9 Which of the following cuts would easily describe a disconnection? (select all that apply)

☐ a. Graduation in a long hair style

☐ b. Reverse graduation in a long hair style

☐ c. A fringe in a shoulder length bob style

☐ d. Texturising in a short cropped style

Q10 'Personalising' is the term that refers to any technique that is used to complete a style, tailoring it to the client's specific needs – true or false?

☐ True   ☐ False

Chapter 7: Colouring hair questions

Quick Quiz: A selection of different types of questions to check your knowledge.

Q1   A _____ test will identify a client's sensitivity to colour products. Fill in the blank.

Q2   A quasi-permanent colour lasts longer than semi-permanent colour – true or false?

☐ True   ☐ False

Q3   Which of the following products are likely to be incompatible with other treatments? (select all that apply)

☐ 1. Permanent colour containing PPD

☐ 2. Retail permanent tint containing PPD

☐ 3. Vegetable henna

☐ 4. Compound henna

☐ 5. Single-step applications for covering grey i.e. Just for Men

☐ 6. Single-step toners for application to bleached hair

Q4   Bleaches and high lift colours are the same – true or false?

☐ True   ☐ False

Q5   Which of the following tests do not apply to colouring services?

☐ a. Skin test

☐ b. Incompatibility test

☐ c. Porosity test

☐ d. Development test curl

Permanent colours alter the pigmentation of hair within the cuticle – true or false?

☐ True   ☐ False

Which of the following colour products do not require the addition of hydrogen peroxide as a developer?

☐   1. Powder bleach

☐   2. Semi-permanent colour

☐   3. Quasi-permanent colour

☐   4. Temporary colour

☐   5. Vegetable henna

☐   6. High lift colour

Green tones within hair are neutralised by adding _____ tones. Fill in the blank.

Hair lightened from natural base 7 should be capable of maximum lift to?

☐   a. Red

☐   b. Pale yellow

☐   c. Yellow

☐   d. Yellow/orange

Lightened hair that appears too yellow can be neutralised by adding mauve – true or false?

☐ True   ☐ False

Chapter 8: Styling hair questions

Quick Quiz: A selection of different types of questions to check your knowledge.

Q1   Self-cling rollers are commonly known as _____ rollers. Fill in the blank.

Q2   Humidity in the atmosphere will help to retain set hairstyles – true or false?

☐ True   ☐ False

Q3 Which of the following dressings are traditionally long 'hair-up' styles?
(Select all that apply)

☐ 1. Plaits

☐ 2. Knots

☐ 3. Weaves

☐ 4. Rolls

☐ 5. Braids

☐ 6. Pleats

Q4 The keratin bonds of stretched hair are said to be in the beta state – true or false?

☐ True ☐ False

Q5 Which chemical bonds within the hair are *not* affected during setting?

☐ a. Hydrogen bonds

☐ b. Disulphide bonds

☐ c. Salt bonds

☐ d. Oxygen bonds

Q6 Heated rollers are a quick way of setting wet or dry hair into style – true or false?

☐ True ☐ False

Q7 Hair set on rollers produces which of the following results and effects?

☐ 1. Increased body at the roots

☐ 2. No body at the roots

☐ 3. No movement at the ends

☐ 4. Straighter effects

☐ 5. Wavy effects

☐ 6. Same as blow dried effects

Q8 The common name for a centrally positioned, vertically folded effect, worn on the back of the head, on long hair is a _____ . Fill in the blank.

Q9 Which item of equipment would smooth and flatten frizzy, unruly hair best?

☐ a. Curling tongs

☐ a. Ceramic straighteners

☐ a. Crimping irons

☐ a. Blow-dryer

Q10 'Hair-ups' are easier to perform on hair that has just been washed, conditioned and dried off – true or false?

☐ True ☐ False

Chapter 9: Perming, relaxing and neutralising hair questions

Quick Quiz: A selection of different types of questions to check your knowledge.

Q1   A development test _____ will identify when optimum movement is achieved. Fill in the blank.

Q2   Cold wave perms are usually post-damped – true or false?

☐ True   ☐ False

Q3   Which of the following factors are likely to be affected by perming?

☐   1. Elasticity

☐   2. Natural colour

☐   3. Thickness

☐   4. Texture

☐   5. Porosity

☐   6. Abundance

Q4   Neutralisers contain hydrogen peroxide – true or false?

☐ True   ☐ False

Q5   Which of the following chemical bonds are permanently rearranged during perming?

☐   a. Salt bonds

☐   b. Hydrogen bonds

☐   c. Disulphide bonds

☐   d. Oxygen bonds

Q6   Time and temperature have a direct impact upon perm development – true or false?

☐ True   ☐ False

Q7   Which of the following tests are *not* applicable to perming?

☐   1. Strand test

☐   2. Incompatibility test

☐   3. Peroxide test

☐   4. Porosity test

☐   5. Elasticity test

☐   6. Skin test

Q8   The rearrangement of chemical bonds takes place within the _____ . Fill in the blank.

Q9   The chemical compound responsible for modifying the hair's structure during perming is:

☐ a. Hydrogen peroxide

☐ b. Ammonium hydroxide

☐ c. Ammonium thioglycolate

☐ d. Sodium perborate

Q10   Smaller perming rods produce tighter curl effects – true or false?

☐ True   ☐ False

Chapter 10: Men's styling questions

Quick Quiz: A selection of different types of questions to check your knowledge.

Q1   Club cutting is also known as _____ cutting. Fill in the blank.

Q2   Clubbing is a cutting technique – true or false?

☐ True   ☐ False

Q3   Select from the following list those which are the texturising techniques: (Select all that apply)

☐ 1. Club cutting

☐ 2. Graduation

☐ 3. Slice cutting

☐ 4. Layering

☐ 5. Point cutting

☐ 6. Chipping

Q4   Men's hair cutting is similar to women's hair cutting – true or false?

☐ True   ☐ False

Q5   Which of the following techniques is not suitable for thinning hair?

☐ a. Tapering

☐ b. Blunt cutting

☐ c. Clubbing

☐ d. Layering

Q6   The recession area will normally be near a side parting – true or false?

☐ True   ☐ False

Q7   Which of the following are typical outlines for men's hairline perimeters? (select all that apply)

☐   1. V shape

☐   2. U Shape

☐   3. T shape

☐   4. Rounded

☐   5. Square

☐   6. Oval

Q8   The range of attachment combs for clippers are commonly known as
_____ . Fill in the blank.

Q9   Which of the following techniques is not done with scissors?

☐   a. Clippering

☐   b. Clubbing

☐   c. Chipping

☐   d. Chopping

Q10   Men's hair grows faster than women's hair – true or false?

☐ True   ☐ False

Chapter 11: Working effectively questions

Quick Quiz: A selection of different types of questions to check your knowledge.

Q1   Working in _____ minimises conflict between staff members. Fill in the blank.

Q2   Relationships at work are different to those outside of work – true or false?

☐ True   ☐ False

Q3   Which of the following are examples of good teamwork?

☐   1. Sitting in the staff room exchanging jokes

☐   2. Preparing trolleys with curlers

☐   3. Sitting at the reception desk

☐   4. Recognising the needs of others

☐   5. Collecting cakes at breaktime

☐   6. Passing up materials to the stylists

Q4 Personal development is about getting your own way – true or false?

☐ True ☐ False

Q5 Which of the following is part of SWOT analysis?

☐ a. Diluting peroxide strengths

☐ b. Identifying personal opportunities

☐ c. Threatening others

☐ d. Feeling weak

Q6 Talking and listening to your seniors is an important part of good team communications – true or false?

☐ True ☐ False

Q7 What takes place in an appraisal?

☐ 1. A review of your aspirations

☐ 2. A review of your current position

☐ 3. A review of your future conduct

☐ 4. A review of your past conduct

☐ 5. A review of client's treatment history

☐ 6. An informal chat about your fellow staff

Q8 Your non-verbal communication will say more about what you are _____ than your mouth. Fill in the blank.

Q9 Which of the following is contained in a job description?

☐ a. Records of your conduct

☐ b. Terms and conditions of employment

☐ c. Roles and responsibilities

☐ d. Records of your training

Q10 Your effectiveness at work is also linked to your efficiency – true or false?

☐ True ☐ False

Chapter 12: Promoting the business questions

Quick Quiz: A selection of different types of questions to check your knowledge.

Q1   Selling opportunities occur when the features and _____ are explained.
Fill in the blank.

Q2   Business develops without promotion or advertising – true or false?

    ☐ True   ☐ False

Q3   Which of the following are types of in-salon promotion? (select all that apply)

    ☐ 1. Radio advertising

    ☐ 2. Hairdressing competitions

    ☐ 3. Hairdressing demonstrations

    ☐ 4. Point of sale material

    ☐ 5. Reception displays

    ☐ 6. Merchandising

Q4   PR is a term which refers to professional media handling – true or false?

    ☐ True   ☐ False

Q5   What is the most cost effective way of selling services to clients?

    ☐ a. External demonstrations

    ☐ b. Internal promotions

    ☐ c. Client consultation and advice

    ☐ d. Point-of-sale material

Q6   Merchandising is a retailing strategy – true or false?

    ☐ True   ☐ False

Q7   Which of the following are laws protecting consumer purchases?

    ☐ 1. The Consumer Protection Act

    ☐ 2. COSHH

    ☐ 3. Trades Descriptions Act

    ☐ 4. RIDDOR

    ☐ 5. The Prices Act

    ☐ 6. The Data Protection Act

Q8   The vendor must ensure that goods they sell are of _____ quality. Fill in the blank.

Q9   When handling complaints avoid:

    ☐ a. Maintaining eye contact with the client

    ☐ b. A discussion in a quieter area of the salon

    ☐ c. Telling the manager about the event

    ☐ d. Folding your arms and being defensive

Q10   A prospective client bases their first impressions of salon staff in less than ten seconds – true or false?

    ☐ True   ☐ False

Hair and skin multiple choice questions

Quick Quiz: A selection of different types of questions to check your knowledge.

Q1   In which layer of the hair does permanent colouring and bleaching react with the natural pigments?

    ☐ a. cortex

    ☐ b. cuticle

    ☐ c. dermal papilla

    ☐ d. medulla

Q2   How do nutrients reach the root of the hair?

    ☐ a. by osmosis

    ☐ b. by the blood capillary network

    ☐ c. via the nerve endings

    ☐ d. by absorption

Q3   What is the name of the tube within the skin from where the hair grows?

    ☐ a. arrector pilli

    ☐ b. follicle

    ☐ c. sebaceous

    ☐ d. cortex

Q4   What does the arrector pili do?

☐   a. senses temperature

☐   b. makes a hair stand up

☐   c. creates sweat

☐   d. produces sebum

Q5   In the hair's growth cycle, what is the name of the active phase called?

☐   a. anagen

☐   b. catagen

☐   c. telogen

☐   d. oxygen

Q6   In the hair's growth cycle, what is the resting phase called?

☐   a. anagen

☐   b. catagen

☐   c. telogen

☐   d. oxygen

Q7   Which is the odd one out?

☐   a. anagen

☐   b. catagen

☐   c. telogen

☐   d. oxygen

Q8   Which is the odd one out?

☐   a. hydrogen

☐   b. sulphur

☐   c. salt

☐   d. pepper

Q9   What is the hair made up of?

☐   a. amino acids

☐   b. citric acids

☐   c. nitric acids

☐   d. sulphuric acids

Q10 Which ethnic hair type is the most cylindrical in cross-section?

☐ a. African-Caribbean

☐ b. Alien

☐ c. Asian

☐ d. European

Q11 If you have very long hair, you are likely to have a longer lasting _____ growth stage.

☐ a. anagen

☐ b. adult

☐ c. catagen

☐ d. telogen

Q12 Which part of the hair is made up of overlapping layers?

☐ a. cortex

☐ b. cuticle

☐ c. dermal papilla

☐ d. medulla

Q13 Hair in its natural state is called:

☐ a. alpha keratin

☐ b. beta keratin

☐ c. delta keratin

☐ d. omega keratin

Q14 Hair in its stretched state is called:

☐ a. alpha keratin

☐ b. beta keratin

☐ c. delta keratin

☐ d. omega keratin

Q15 Which bonds in the hair are broken down during shampooing?

☐ a. hydrogen bonds

☐ b. disulphide bonds

☐ c. keratin bonds

☐ d. polypeptide chains

Q16   The strong permanent cross links made up of amino acids are called:

☐   a. hydrogen bonds

☐   b. disulphide bonds

☐   c. keratin bonds

☐   d. polypeptide chains

Q17   Which one denotes neutral on the pH scale?

☐   a. 4.5–5.5

☐   b. 5.5–6.5

☐   c. 7

☐   d. 7.5–9

Q18   Which one denotes the skin's natural state?

☐   a. 4.5–5.5

☐   b. 5.5–6.5

☐   c. 7

☐   d. 7.5–9

Q19   Which one denotes the strongest acid pH range?

☐   a. 4.5–5.5

☐   b. 6.5–7.5

☐   c. 7

☐   d. 7.5–9

Q20   Which one denotes the strongest alkali pH range?

☐   a. 4.5–5.5

☐   b. 6.5–7.5

☐   c. 7

☐   d. 7.5–9

Q21   Which one will turn pink litmus paper blue?

☐   a. 4.5–5.5

☐   b. 6.5–7.5

☐   c. 7

☐   d. 7.5–9

Q22 Which one will turn blue litmus paper pink?

☐ a. 4.5–5.5

☐ b. 6.5–7.5

☐ c. 7

☐ d. 7.5–9

Q23 Which one will have no effect on litmus paper?

☐ a. 4.5–5.5

☐ b. 6.5–7.5

☐ c. 7

☐ d. 7.5–9

Q24 What shape would the tip of an uncut hair take?

☐ a. grooved

☐ b. tapered

☐ c. rounded

☐ d. square

Q25 What shape would the tip of scissor cut hair take?

☐ a. grooved

☐ b. tapered

☐ c. rounded

☐ d. square

Q26 What does the structure of the cortex look like?

☐ a. cotton wool

☐ b. plastic straws

☐ c. rope-like fibres

☐ d. rubber bands

Q27 The texture of hair is proportional to its _____.

☐ a. abundance

☐ b. individual thickness

☐ c. length

☐ d. mass

Q28 What is the uppermost layer of the skin called?

☐ a. cornified

☐ b. dermis

☐ c. epidermis

☐ d. subcutaneous

Q29 What gland helps to cool the body?

☐ a. alpha

☐ b. beta

☐ c. sebaceous

☐ d. sweat

Q30 Sebum is a _____.

☐ a. form of sweat

☐ b. hair spray

☐ c. hair wax

☐ d. natural oil

Answers

Chapter 1: Client consulation

Q1	Catagen	Q6	True
Q2	False	Q7	2, 3
Q3	1, 2, 4	Q8	Dermis
Q4	True	Q9	C
Q5	D	Q10	True

Chapter 2: Client care and communication

Q1	Hygiene	Q6	True
Q2	True	Q7	3, 4
Q3	1, 4, 5	Q8	Body
Q4	True	Q9	B
Q5	D	Q10	True

Chapter 3: Reception

Q1	Credit		Q6	True
Q2	False		Q7	2, 3
Q3	2, 5		Q8	Home care
Q4	False		Q9	A
Q5	C		Q10	False

Chapter 4: Shampooing and conditioning hair

Q1	Dry		Q6	True
Q2	False		Q7	2, 4
Q3	2, 4, 5		Q8	Ends
Q4	False		Q9	B
Q5	C		Q10	False

Chapter 5: Health and safety in the salon

Q1	Hazard		Q6	False
Q2	True		Q7	2, 4
Q3	1, 3, 6		Q8	First aid
Q4	False		Q9	D
Q5	C		Q10	True

Chapter 6: Cutting hair questions

Q1	Holding			
Q2	True		Q6	True
Q3	1, 2, 4		Q7	3, 5
Q4	True		Q8	Baseline
Q5	D		Q9	C
			Q10	True

Chapter 7: Colouring hair

Q1	Skin			
Q2	True		Q7	2, 4, 5
Q3	4, 5		Q8	Red
Q4	False		Q9	B
Q5	D		Q10	True
Q6	False			

Chapter 8: Styling hair

Q1	Velcro		Q6	False
Q2	False		Q7	1, 5
Q3	2, 4, 6		Q8	Pleat
Q4	True		Q9	B
Q5	B		Q10	False

Chapter 9: Perming, relaxing and neutralising hair

Q1	Curl		Q6	True
Q2	True		Q7	1, 3
Q3	1, 5		Q8	Cortex
Q4	True		Q9	C
Q5	C		Q10	True

Chapter 10: Men's styling

Q1	Blunt		Q6	True
Q2	True		Q7	2, 4, 5
Q3	3, 5, 6		Q8	Grades
Q4	True		Q9	A
Q5	A		Q10	False

Chapter 11: Working effectively

Q1	Harmony		Q6	True
Q2	True		Q7	2, 4
Q3	2, 4, 6		Q8	Thinking
Q4	False		Q9	C
Q5	B		Q10	True

Chapter 12: Promoting the business

Q1	Benefits		Q6	True
Q2	False		Q7	1, 3, 5
Q3	4, 5, 6		Q8	Satisfactory
Q4	True		Q9	D
Q5	C		Q10	True

Hair and skin multiple choice

Q1	A		Q16	B
Q2	B		Q17	C
Q3	B		Q18	B
Q4	B		Q19	A
Q5	A		Q20	D
Q6	C		Q21	D
Q7	D		Q22	A
Q8	D		Q23	C
Q9	A		Q24	B
Q10	C		Q25	D
Q11	A		Q26	C
Q12	B		Q27	B
Q13	A		Q28	C
Q14	B		Q29	C
Q15	A		Q30	D

useful addresses and websites

Arbitration, Conciliation and Advisory Service (ACAS)

Head Office
Brandon House
180 Borough High Street
London, SE1 1LW

T: 020 7210 3613

www.acas.org.uk

Helpline 08457 47 47 47

Association of Hairdressing Teachers (AHT)

5 Viscount Gardens
Byfleet
Surrey, KT14 6HE

Black Beauty and Hair

Culvert House
Culvert Road
London, SW11

T: 020 7720 2108

www.blackbeauty.co.uk

British Association of Beauty Therapy and Cosmetology Limited (BABTAC)

Meteor Court
Barnett Way
Barnwood
Goucester, GL4 3GG

Caribbean and Afro Society of Hairdressers (CASH)

42 North Cross Road
East Dulwich
London, SE22 8PY

T: 020 8299 2859

City and Guilds (C&G)

1 Giltspur Street
London, EC1A 9DD

T: 020 7294 2800

www.city-and-guilds.co.uk

Commission for Racial Equality

Elliot House
10–12 Allington Street
London, SW1E 5EH

T: 020 7828 7022

www.cre.gov.uk

Cosmetic, Toiletry and Perfumery Association (CTPA)

Josaron House
5–7 John Princes Street
London, W1G 0JN

T: 020 7491 8891

www.ctpa.org.uk

Department for Education and Skills

www.dfes.gov.uk

Lifelong Learning

www.lifelonglearning.co.uk

Equal Opportunities Commission

Arndale House
Arndale Centre
Manchester, M4 3EQ

T: 0161 833 9244

Fellowship for British Hairdressing

Bloxham Mill
Barford Road
Bloxham
Banbury
Oxon

T: 01295 724579

Freelance Hair and Beauty Federation

6 Warleigh Road
Brighton
East Sussex, BN1 4TN

T: 01273 604556

www.fhbf.org.uk

Guild of Hairdressers (GUILD)

Unit 1E
Redbrook Business Park
Wilthorpe Road
Barnsley, S75 1JN

T: 01226 730112

Hairdressers Journal International (HJ)

Quadrant House
The Quadrant, Sutton
Surrey, SM2 5AS

T: 020 8652 3500

www.reedbusiness.com

Hairdressing and Beauty Industry Authority (HABIA)

Oxford House
Sixth Avenue
Sky Business Park
Robin Hood
Airport
Doncaster, DN9 3GG

T: 08452 306080

www.habia.org

Hairdressing and Beauty Suppliers' Assocation (HBSA)

Bedford Chambers
The Piazza,
Covent Garden
London, WC2E 8HA

T: 020 7836 4008

Hairdressing and Beauty Suppliers Association

1st Floor, Manfield House
1 Southampton Street
Covent Garden
London, WC2R OLR

Hairdressing Council (HC)

12 David House
45 High Street
South Norwood
London, SE25 6HJ

T: 020 8771 6205

www.haircouncil.org.uk

Hairdressing Employers Association (HEA)

10 Coldbath Square
London, EC1R 5HL

T: 020 7833 0633

Health and Beauty Employers Federation (part of the Federation of Holistic Therapists)

18 Shakespeare Business Centre
Hathaway Close
Eastleigh
Hampshire, SO50 4SR

www.fht.org.uk

Health and Safety Executive

Publications
PO Box 1999
Sudbury
Suffolk, CO10 6FS

(HSE) Infoline
T: 0845 345 0055

www.hse.gov.uk

Incorporated Guild of Hairdressers, Wigmakers and Perfumers

Unit 8, Vulcan Road
M1
Distribution Centre
Meadowhall
Sheffield, S9 1EW

The Institute of Trichologists

Ground Floor office
24 Langroyd Road
London, SW17 7PL

T: 08706 070602

www.trichologists.org.uk

National Hairdressers' Federation (NHF)

One Abbey Court
Fraser Road
Priory Business Park
Bedford, MK44 3WH

www.the-nhf.org

Qualifications and Curriculum Authority (QCA)

83 Piccadilly
London, W1J 8QA

T: 020 7509 3097

www.qca.org.uk

Union of Shop, Distributive and Allied Workers (USDAW)

188 Wilmslow Road
Fallowfield
Manchester, M14 6LJ

T: 0161 224 2804

Vocational Training Charitable Trust (VTCT)

46 Aldwick Road
Bognor Regis
West Sussex, PO21 2PN

www.vtct.org.uk

World Federation of Hairdressing and Beauty Schools

PO Box 367
Coulsdon
Surrey, CR5 2TP

T: 01737 551355

World Federation of Hairdressing Schools

73 Marlpit Lane
Coulsdon
Surrey, CR5 2HF

key skills: information

Key skills are the fundamental skills that are most commonly needed to succeed in a range of work- or training-related activities. Key skills are for everyone under the age of 19 years. If you have already achieved these skills prior to your vocational training, e.g. at school within a GNVQ, you will not be required to do them again.

However, if you haven't covered these before you will be working towards the achievement of these during your training towards Hairdressing S/NVQ Level 2.

Don't panic, this is your lecturer's responsibility. Whilst you are training, your lecturer will recognise the opportunities that provide potential evidence. These will be during the everyday tasks that arise during your work and will be linked to your personal training programme.

Key skill and qualification level	These key skills enable people to:
Application of Number L.1	Use numbers with confidence
Communication L.2	Communicate effectively with others
Information Technology L.1	Use computers at work
Working with Others L.2	Work together well with others
Problem Solving L.2	Make informed decisions
Improving own Learning and Performance L.2	Develop themselves further

The following key skills provide summary information of what is needed and the references to the individual standards. (Credit: Qualification Curriculum Authority; QCA 2004)

APPLICATION OF NUMBER AT LEVEL 1

To achieve this, you must be able to apply your number skills to suit different purposes. You will show that you can:

1 interpret information from two sources

2 carry out and check calculations

3 interpret the results of your calculations and present your findings.

Interpret information

- Read and understand tables, charts, graphs and diagrams.
- Read and understand numbers used in different ways (e.g. large numbers in figures or words, simple fractions, decimals, percentages).
- Read scales on familiar measuring equipment (e.g. watch, tape measure, measuring jug, weighing scales, thermometer) using everyday units (e.g. minutes, millimetres, litres, grams, degrees).
- Make accurate observations (e.g. count number of people or items).
- Identify suitable calculations to get the results you need for your task.

N1.1 Interpret information from two different sources. *At least one source must include a table, chart, graph or diagram.*

1.1.1   Obtain the information you need to meet the purpose of your task

1.1.2   Identify suitable calculations to get the results you need.

Carry out calculations

- Add and subtract, with whole numbers and simple decimals with or without a calculator (e.g. using money or length).
- Work to the level of accuracy you have been told to use (e.g. round to the nearest whole unit, nearest 10, two decimal places).
- Multiply and divide a simple decimal by a whole number with and without a calculator (e.g. using money or length).
- Understand and find simple fractions and percentages (e.g. $\frac{2}{3}$ of £15 is £10, 75 per cent of 400 is 300).
- Work out areas of rectangular spaces (e.g. floor area).
- Work out volumes of rectangular-based shapes (e.g. a box).
- Use scales on diagrams such as 20 mm to 1 m (e.g. finding distances from maps).
- Use ratios and proportion (e.g. three parts to one part).
- Find the average (mean) of up to 10 items (e.g. temperatures, prices, time).
- Find the range for up to 10 items (e.g. temperature range from highest to lowest was 16°C).
- Make sure your answers make sense and use different methods to check your calculations (e.g. estimate to reject impossible answers, check a subtraction by 'adding back').

N1.2 Carry out and check calculations to do with:
   (a) amounts or sizes
   (b) scales or proportion
   (c) handling statistics.

1.2.1   Carry out calculations to the levels of accuracy you have been given

1.2.2   Check your results make sense.

Interpret results and present your findings

- Use suitable ways of presenting information, including a chart or diagram.
- Use the correct units (e.g. for area, volume, weight, time, temperature).
- Label your work correctly (e.g. use a title or key).
- Describe what your results tell you.

N1.3 Interpret the results of your calculations and present your findings – *in two different ways using charts or diagrams.*

1.3.1   Choose suitable ways to present your findings

1.3.2   Use more than one way of presenting your findings

1.3.3   Present your findings clearly using a chart or diagram

1.3.4   Describe what your results tell you.

COMMUNICATION AT LEVEL 2

To achieve this, you must be able to apply your communication skills to suit different purposes. You will show that you can:

1   take part in a group discussion

2   read and summarise at least two documents

3   give a short talk

4   write two types of document, each giving different information.

Discuss

- Use varied vocabulary and expressions to suit your purpose.
- Adapt what you say to suit different situations.
- Listen carefully to what others say.
- Identify the speaker's intentions.
- Move the discussion forward.

C2.1a Take part in a group discussion.

C2.1a.1 Make clear and relevant in a way that suits your purpose and situation.

C2.1a.2 Respond appropriately to others.

C2.1a.3 Help to move the discussion forward.

Give a short talk

- Prepare for the talk.
- Adapt your language to suit your subject, purpose and situation.
- Structure what you say to help listeners follow a line of thought or series of events.
- Use a variety of ways to support the main points of your talk including using images.

C2.1b Give a talk of at least four minutes.

2.1b.1 Speak clearly in a way that suits your subject, purpose and situation.

2.1b.2 Keep to the subject and structure your talk to help listeners follow what you are saying.

2.1b.3 Use appropriate ways to support your main points.

Read and summarise information

- Select and use different types of documents to obtain relevant information.
- Skim documents to gain a general idea of content.
- Scan documents to identify the information you need.
- Recognise the writer's intentions.
- Identify the main points, ideas and lines of reasoning from text and images.
- Summarise information for a purpose.

C2.2 Read and summarise information from at least two documents about the same subject. Each document must be a minimum of 500 words long.

2.2.1 Select and read relevant documents.

2.2.2 Identify accurately the main points, ideas and lines of reasoning.

2.2.3 Summarise the information to suit your purpose.

Write documents

- Use different formats for presenting information, including essays, reports and articles.
- Structure your writing to help readers follow and understand your main points.
- Use different styles of writing to suit different purposes.
- Proof-read and where necessary redraft your documents so that:
  - spelling is accurate including familiar technical words
  - sentences are formed correctly with accurate use of conjunctions
  - punctuation is accurate including use of commas, apostrophes and inverted commas.

C2.3 Write two different types of documents each one giving different information. One document must be at least 500 words long.

2.3.1 Present relevant information in a format that suits your purpose.

2.3.2 Use a structure and style of writing to suit your purpose.

2.3.3 Spell, punctuate and use grammar accurately.

2.3.4 Make your meaning clear.

INFORMATION AND COMMUNICATION TECHNOLOGY AT LEVEL 1

You need to know how to use ICT to help you in different tasks:

- save information so it can be found easily
- minimise health risks
- know how to get help when dealing with errors
- send and receive e-mail.

To achieve this level, you must be able to apply your ICT skills to suit different purposes. You will show that you can:

1 find, enter, explore and develop relevant information
2 present information, including text, images and numbers, using appropriate layouts and save information.

Find information

- Find different types of information from ICT sources (e.g. files, CD-ROMs, the internet) and non ICT sources (e.g. written notes, price lists, diagrams).
- Select information relevant to your purpose.

ICT1.1 Find and select relevant information.

1.1.1   Choose information that is relevant to your tasks.

Develop information

- Enter information (e.g. copy and paste text, import images) using formats that help development (e.g. tabs, tables, format of numbers).
- Develop information in the form of text, image and numbers (e.g. structure information, carry out calculations using suitable software, move and resize images).

ICT1.2 Enter and develop information to suit the task.

1.2.1   Enter information using formats that help development.
1.2.2   Save information so it can be found easily.

Present information

- Use layouts and techniques to suit different purposes (e.g. select page layouts for different types of document such as letters or invoices, organise the presentation by moving, copying, deleting or inserting information).

- Present information in a consistent way (e.g. fonts, bulleted lists, alignment) making sure it is accurate and clear (e.g. Ask others, proof-read, use a spell-checker, highlight information to improve its clarity).

ICT1.3 Develop the presentation so that the final output is accurate and fit for purpose.

1.3.1   Use appropriate layouts for presenting information in a consistent way.

WORKING WITH OTHERS AT LEVEL 2

To achieve this, you must be able to apply your skills to suit different purposes. You will show that you can:

1 identify what you need to achieve together

2 organise and carry out tasks to meet your responsibilities

3 identify your role in helping to achieve things together.

Plan work with others

- Make sure you understand what makes groups or teams effective.
- Identify what you need to achieve together (from the objectives suggested by your supervisor, tutor, yourself or others).
- Contribute and use relevant information to identify tasks, resources (materials, equipment and/or tools) and timescales.
- Suggest ways you could help and find out what others would like to do.
- Identify individual responsibilities:
  – who will be responsible for organising and carrying out each task
  – the ground rules for working together (ways of behaving that show respect for each other's rights, feelings, ideas and contributions, what you and others should and should not do).
- confirm the arrangements for working together:
  – who you will be working with, where and when
  – health and safety procedures
  – the appropriate people to go to for advice and support when needed.

WO2.1 Plan work with others.

2.1.1   Identify what you need to achieve together.

2.1.2   Share relevant information to identify what needs to be done and individual responsibilities.

2.1.3   Confirm the arrangements for working together.

Work cooperatively towards achieving the identified objectives:

- Organise and carry out tasks so you can meet your responsibilities.
- Get and make the best use of resources.
- Pace your work to meet deadlines.
- Work safely to avoid accidents, health risks, offending others or disrupting their work.
- Use correct techniques and approaches to help you produce the quality of work required.
- Support cooperative ways of working.
- Anticipate the needs of others for information and support.
- Avoid actions that offend or discriminate against others.
- Act assertively, when needed, to protect your own rights.
- Show willingness to sort out disagreements or other problems.
- Check progress towards the objectives, seeking advice from an appropriate person to help resolve any conflicts or other problems.

WO2.2 Work cooperatively towards achieving the identified objectives.

2.2.1 Organise and carry out tasks safely using appropriate methods, to meet your responsibilities.

2.2.2 Support cooperative ways of working to help achieve the objectives for working together.

2.2.3 Check progress, seeking advice from an appropriate person when needed.

Review your contributions and agree ways to improve work with others:

- Contribute information and listen to others on what went well and less well, including tasks and working relationships.
- Identify and describe your role in helping to achieve things together.
- Agree ways of improving your work with others, including interpersonal skills.

WO2.3 Review your contributions and agree ways to improve work with others.

2.3.1 Share relevant information on what went well and less well in working with others.

2.3.2 Identify *your* role in helping to achieve things together.

2.3.3 Agree ways of improving your work with others.

PROBLEM SOLVING AT LEVEL 2

To achieve this, you must be able to apply your skills to suit different purposes. You will show that you can:

1 accurately describe the problem

2 plan what you need to do to solve the problem

3 identify way of improving your problem-solving skills.

Help identify a problem and identify different ways of tackling it:

- Work with an appropriate person, such as your tutor or supervisor, to help identify a problem, by providing an accurate description of its main features:
  - what is known and not known about the problem
  - how it affects you and other people.
- Identify how you will know the problem has been solved:
  - find out the results people expect from tackling the problem
  - find out about methods you could use to check it has been solved.
- Come up with different ways of tackling the problem:
  - learn about different methods for solving problems and how similar problems have been solved
  - find out about the risks (the likelihood of things going wrong) and other factors that might affect the way you tackle the problem (time and expertise needed, health and safety rules)
  - decide what could help to solve your problem.

PS2.1 Identify a problem, with help from an appropriate person, and identify different ways of tackling it.

2.1.1 Provide information to help identify a problem, accurately describing its main features.

2.1.2 Identify how you will know the problem has been solved.

2.1.3 Come up with different ways of tackling the problem.

Plan and try out a way of solving the problem

- Confirm with an appropriate person, such as your tutor, supervisor or other person in authority, how you will try to solve the problem, adapting your ideas if necessary to meet rules and regulations.
- Plan what you need to do, identifying:
  - resources you will use (materials, tools, equipment, information and support from others)
  - the methods, steps and timeline for working through the problem, including ways of overcoming difficulties
  - health and safety procedures.

- Use your plan effectively, taking responsibility, when needed, for:
  - health and safety
  - getting support from your supervisor or other person with relevant expertise
  - keeping track of the steps taken in tackling the problem and revising your plan to deal with unexpected events.

PS2.2 Plan and try out at least one way of solving the problem.

2.2.1   Confirm with an appropriate person how you will try to solve the problem.

2.2.2   Plan what you need to do, identifying the methods and resources you will use.

2.2.3   Use your plan effectively, getting support and revising your plan when needed to help tackle the problem.

Check if the problem has been solved and identify ways to improve problem solving

- Learn how to use the methods you have been given for checking if the problem has been solved and use these accurately.
- Describe clearly the results of your checking, including the strengths and weaknesses of how you tackled the problem at each stage.
- Identify ways of improving your problem-solving skills.

PS2.3 Check if the problem has been solved and identify ways to improve problem-solving skills.

2.3.1   Check if the problem has been solved by accurately using the methods you have been given.

2.3.2   Describe clearly the results, including the strengths and weaknesses of how you tackled the problem.

2.3.3   Identify ways of improving your problem-solving skills.

IMPROVING OWN LEARNING AND PERFORMANCE AT LEVEL 2

To achieve this, you must be able to apply your skills to suit different purposes. You will show that you can:

1   plan your time well to meet your targets

2   identify when you need support to help you meet targets

3   identify ways you learn best and how to improve your performance.

Help set targets and plan how these will be met

- Work with an appropriate person, such as your tutor, supervisor or adviser, to make sure you understand how planning and reviewing your learning can help to improve your performance and what is meant by learning styles and evidence of achievement.

- Develop an individual learning plan that includes:
  - targets that say exactly what you want to achieve and how you will prove you have met them;
  - provide information to make sure they are realistic, including what might affect your chances of success
  - the action you will take (action points) for each target and dates (deadlines) to help you manage your time
  - how to get the support you need, including who will review your progress, and where and when this will take place.

LP2.1 Help set targets with an appropriate person and plan how these will be met.

2.1.1   Provide information to help set real targets for what you want to achieve.

2.1.2   Identify clear action points for each target and how you will manage your time.

2.1.3   Identify how to get the support you need and arrangements for reviewing your progress.

Take responsibility for some decisions about your learning

- Work through your action points to complete these on time, revising your plan when needed to overcome unexpected events or problems.

- Choose different ways of learning (learning styles) and decide on the methods that best suit you (e.g. pictures/diagrams, reading/talking/writing, listening to others, watching or doing something practical).

- Work for short periods without close supervision so you have to take some decisions about your learning.

- Identify when you need support and use this effectively to help meet your targets.

LP2.2 Take responsibility for some decisions about your learning, using your plan to help meet targets and improve your performance.

2.2.1   Use your action points to help manage your time well; revising your plan when needed.

2.2.2   Choose ways of learning to improve your performance, working for short periods without close supervision.

2.2.3   Identify when you need support and use this effectively to help you meet targets.

Review progress and provide evidence of achievements

- Work with an appropriate person, such as your tutor, supervisor or adviser, to:
  - identify what you learned and how you used learning from one task to meet the demands of another task
  - identify the targets you have met, by checking your plan to see if you have done what you set out to do
  - identify evidence of your achievements
  - identify ways you learn best (your preferred learning style/s and methods of learning) and how to improve your performance (the quality of your work, the way you work).

LP2.3 Review progress with an appropriate person and provide evidence of your achievements.

2.3.1 Identify what you learned, and how you have used your learning in another task.

2.3.2 Identify targets you have met and evidence of your achievements.

2.3.3 Identify ways you learn best and how to further improve your performance.

glossary and key terms

Access and egress   The ways of getting into and out of the building. See *evacuation procedures*.

Activators   Products used to maintain curl in permed or naturally curly hair.

Adverse skin and scalp conditions   Limiting factors that have an effect on what and how services are delivered to clients, e.g. head lice, psoriasis, alopecia, cysts, impetigo, scars, moles etc.

Alpha keratin   The normal, coiled form of keratin.

Appointment system   The system which organises the volume of work (client services or treatments) undertaken by a salon. This may be manual or computerised.

Assessment   An evaluation or judgement of input, value and/or attainment.

Assignment   A personal account or allocation of work, written, pictorial or practical, based around clearly set objectives.

Basic uniform layer cut   This type of haircut has sections that are equal i.e. the same length throughout.

Beta keratin   The form keratin takes when it has been stretched, set and dried.

BD   Appointment abbreviation for blow dry.

Bleach   A hairdressing product that dissolves/removes natural colour pigments from hair.

Body language   A non-verbal form of communication that reveals the way a person is thinking or feeling.

Brick cutting   A cutting technique that uses the points of the scissors to remove fine chunks of hair from within the mid-sections.

Case study   A study, examination or evaluation of specific event(s) either factual or hypothetical.

CBD   Appointment abbreviation for cut and blow dry

Chemically treated hair   Hair that has been previously permed, coloured, bleached or relaxed.

Client care   Providing service to salon customers in a way that promotes goodwill, comfort, satisfaction and interest, which ultimately results in regular return visits from clients.

Client consultation   A service which is usually provided before the client has anything done to their hair. Consultation will find out what the client wants, identify any styling limitations, provide advice and maintenance information and formulate a plan of action.

Clipper over comb   A technique of cutting hair with electric clippers, using the back of the comb as a guide, especially on very short hair and hairline profiles.

Club cutting or clubbing hair   The most basic and most popular way of cutting sections of hair straight across, parallel to the index and middle finger.

Col (Rt or Fh)   Appointment abbreviation for colouring, either root application or full head.

Communication   Listening, hearing and responding to the client.

Confidential information   May include personal aspects of conversations with clients or colleagues, contents of client records, client and staff personal details (e.g. address, telephone numbers etc.) financial aspects of the business, hearsay/gossip.

Consumer and Retail Legislation   **The Consumer Protection Act (1987)**: This Act follows European directives to protect the buyer from unsafe products. The Act is designed to help safeguard the consumer from products that do not reach reasonable levels of safety. **The Consumer Safety Act (1978)**: There is a requirement to reduce the possible risk to consumers from any product that may be potentially dangerous. **The Prices Act (1974)**: The price of products has to be displayed in order to prevent a false impression to the buyer. **The Trades Descriptions Act (1968 and 1972)**: Products must not be falsely or misleadingly described in relation to its quality, fitness, price or purpose, by advertisements, orally, displays or descriptions. And since 1972 it is also a requirement to label a product clearly, so that the buyer can see where the product was made. **The Resale Prices Act (1964 and 1976)**: The manufacturers can supply a recommended retail price (MRRP), but the seller is not obliged to sell at the recommended price. **The Sale and Supply of Goods Act (1994)**: The vendor must ensure that the goods they sell are of satisfactory quality (defined as the standard that would be regarded by a reasonable person as satisfactory having taken into account the description of the goods, the price and other relevant circumstances) and reasonably fit (ensuring as a vendor that the goods can meet the purpose they are claimed to do). **Consumer Protection (Distance Selling) Regulations 2000**: These are derived from a European Directive and cover the supply of goods and/or services made between suppliers acting in a commercial capacity and consumers, i.e. an individual acting outside a trade business or profession. The regulations should be of concern to any individual purchasing goods or services by telephone, using the Internet, digital TV or mail order catalogues and conversely be of concern to any suppliers dealing with consumers through these media.

Contra-indication Something that signifies that an adverse reaction has occurred.

Cortex The inner part of the hair where permanent colour is deposited and where perms make physical changes to the hair.

Critical influencing factors Anything which could affect the hairdressing service.

Cross-infection The passing on of disease from one person to another, either by contact or proximity, caused by poor hygiene and sanitation.

Cuticle The outer protective layers of the hair shaft.

Database An archive of information, usually held on computer, relating to business records: clients, staff, sales, products etc.

Data Protection Act Under this Act, you must not pass on any client- or salon-related information without the permission of the person involved. You have a duty of care to keep any such information safe and secure.

Depth The lightness or darkness of a hair.

Dermis The lower layers of newer skin below the outer epidermis.

Dermatitis A skin condition which results in a red, sore, hot and itchy rash, usually between the fingers. This is sometimes caused by contact with hairdressing chemicals and solutions.

Disulphide bonds The bonds within the hair that are permanently rearranged during perming, relaxing and neutralising.

Double booking An error in the appointment system where client's bookings overlap.

Dry hair A condition (usually the result of chemical treatments) in which the hair loses natural moisture levels, affecting the handling, maintenance and style durability.

Effleurage A gentle stroking movement used in shampooing.

Epidermis The older, upper, protective layers of skin at the surface.

Evacuation procedures The arrangements made by the salon, i.e. exit route, assembly point etc., for emergency purposes.

Follicle A tube-like indentation within the skin, from which the hair grows.

Freehand cutting A cutting technique carried out without holding the hair, usually to compensate for the natural fall of hair.

Friction (massage technique) A vigorous rubbing movement used when shampooing on the scalp areas.

Full head application of colour or bleach A colouring technique that requires a sequence of applications to the mid-lengths, ends and regrowth area.

Graduation A cutting technique that joins together longer hair that over falls shorter hair in one continuous cutting angle.

Greasy hair A condition caused by the over-production of natural oils, i.e. sebum, which exudes from glands within the scalp on to the surface and eventually the hair. Thus affecting the handling, maintenance and style durability.

Hair colour The resultant effect from two colour aspects: *depth*, the lightness or darkness of a colour and *tone*, the degree of red, gold, ash etc. within the hair.

Hair texture Texture refers to the 'thickness or thinness' of individual hairs: coarse, medium or fine.

Hair tendency The hair's straightness, wave, body, curl or frizziness.

Hazard Something with a potential to cause harm.

HL or H/L Appointment abbreviation for highlighting.

HL T sect Appointment abbreviation for highlight, top and sides only.

Layering (layered cut) A cutting technique carried out on either short or long hair to produce a multi-length effect.

Legal requirements This refers to laws affecting the way businesses are operated, how the salon or workplace is set up and maintained, people in employment and the systems of working which must be maintained.

Limits of your authority The extent of your responsibility at work.

Long graduation cut A cut when the inner/upper layers of a haircut are shorter than the lengths of the outline, perimeter hair.

Lye and no-lye A term referring to the chemical composition of relaxing treatments (i.e. sodium hydroxide-based or not).

Manufacturer's instructions Explicit guidance issued by manufacturers or suppliers of products or equipment, concerning their safe and efficient use.

Neutraliser The second chemical (rebonding) phase for perming or relaxing hair. See *permanent wave*; *relaxing*.

No-lye See *lye*.

Oblong facial shape An outline perimeter facial shape that has proportions that roughly resembles an oblong shape.

One-length cut A cutting technique where the hair is cut *with* the natural hair fall to produce a one-length effect.

Outlines The shapes created by the perimeter of nape and front hairlines.

Oval facial shape An outline perimeter facial shape that has proportions that roughly resembles an oval or elipsed shape.

Overbooking See *double booking*.

Oxidation The acidic chemical process which reforms the disulphide bridges within the polypeptide chains by introducing oxygen.

Perm (permanent wave) A two-part system for adding movement to hair by chemical means.

Perm solution The first part of a permanent wave system which chemically modifies the hair's inner structure.

Permanent tint (permanent colour) A penetrating colour product that adds synthetic pigments to natural hair until it grows out.

Personal presentation This includes personal hygiene and the use of personal protective equipment, clothing and accessories suitable to the particular workplace.

Personal protective equipment (PPE) You are required to use and wear the appropriate protective equipment during perming, colouring and relaxing services or in any situation where personal harm may be encountered.

Personalising   A variety of cutting techniques that are used to achieve different effects within the cutting scheme of a hairstyle.

Personalising hair   A variety of cutting techniques that are used to achieve different effects within the cutting scheme of a hairstyle.

Petrissage (massage technique)   A slower circulatory kneading movement generally used for scalp massage when applying conditioner.

Point cutting (pointing)   A cutting technique where the cutting angle is changed to remove hair bulk from the ends of each cutting section.

Post-damping   Application of perming lotion to previously wound curlers.

Potentially infectious condition   A medical condition or state of health which may be transmitted to others (see *cross-infection*).

Porous hair   Hair that has lost surface protection, therefore having a greater absorption and less resistance to chemicals and products. This affects the hair's manageability, handling and ability to hold in a style (see *dry hair*).

Portfolio   A system for recording experiences, case studies, personal accounts, results from tests/assessments and the findings from projects and assignments.

Pre-damping   Application of perming lotion prior to winding in the curlers.

Pre-perm treatment   A product applied to the hair before perming to balance out uneven porosity.

Professional advice   Providing information based upon experience and knowledge.

Project   Similar to an *assignment*.

PU   Appointment abbreviation for 'put up' – longer hair dressed up for party, ball or bridal occasions.

PW   Appointment abbreviation for permanent wave (perm).

Quasi-permanent colours   Colour products which should be treated as permanent colours in terms of application, testing and future services.

Rearranger   Ammonium thioglycollate-based product used to pre-soften tight/curly hair prior to winding a perm.

Reduction   The alkaline chemical process which breaks the disulphide bridges within the polypeptide chains by introducing hydrogen.

Relaxing   A chemical process (usually in two parts) which removes natural movement/curl from hair.

Reshape (reshaping)   Cutting hair back into style (a six-weekly reshape cut will maintain a hairstyle).

Restyle   Cutting hair into a new hairstyle.

Resources   Anything used to enable the delivery and completion of service to the client (e.g. people, equipment stock).

Responsible persons   A term used particularly in health and safety to mean the person(s) at work to whom you should report any issues, problems or hazards. This could be a supervisor, line manager or your employer.

Reverse graduation   A cutting technique that joins together shorter hair down to longer hair in one continuous cutting angle.

Risk   The likelihood of the hazard's potential actually occurring.

Role play   A way of exploring different scenarios by simulation.

Rotary massage   A quicker and firmer circular movement used in shampooing.

Round facial shape   An outline perimeter facial shape that has proportions that roughly resembles a circular or round shape.

Salon requirements   Any hairdressing procedures or work rules issued by the salon management.

Salon services   The extent and variety of all the services offered in your workplace.

Scalp   The skin covering the top of the head.

Scalp plaits   Also known as a French plait, a cane row or corn row.

Scissor over comb   A technique of cutting hair with scissors, using the back of the comb as a guide, especially when the hair is at a length that cannot be held between the fingers.

Shape, form and balance   The physical and notional aspects that control hair design and hair styling.

Sharps   A Health and Safety Executive term to describe sharp objects e.g. razors and razor blades, scissors.

Short graduation cut   A short graduation cut is when the inner/upper layers of a hair cut are longer than the lengths of the outline, perimeter hair.

Slice or slider cutting   A technique used with very sharp scissors assimilating the action and effect produced by razoring to create a tapering effect.

Square facial shape   An outline perimeter facial shape that has proportions that roughly resembles a square shape.

Stock check (stock taking)   An accounting process for monitoring and controlling the movements and usage of stock.

Strand test   A test carried out upon hair prior to chemical services to determine the effects of processing.

Style line   The directions in which the hair is positioned or appears to flow.

Tapered Necklines   Tapered necklines have soft outlines that follow the natural hairline shape so that the nape outline appears to fade out with no harsh lines visible.

Temporary bonds   The hydrogen bonds within the hair that are modified and fix the style into shape.

Temporary colourant   Colour added to hair that lasts until the next wash.

Texturising   A variety of cutting techniques that are used to achieve different effects within the cutting scheme of a hairstyle.

Tint and tinting   The professional term for colour and colouring (see *hair colour*).

Tone   The aspects of colouration of the hair, normally grouped into similar tints i.e. copper tones, red tones, ash tones.

Trichologist   A 'hair and scalp doctor' or qualified person who specialises in hair and scalp problems. A trichologist diagnoses hair and scalp dysfunctions or conditions and prescribes remedial treatments or suitable courses of action for them.

Trimming hair   See *reshape*.

Uniform layer cut   This type of haircut has sections that are equal i.e. the same length throughout.

Virgin hair Hair that has not been chemically treated.

Verify (Verifier) A person responsible for quality assurance within a training scheme, who makes sure that candidates and staff are working to the correct standards.

Workplace policies This covers the documentation prepared by your employer on the procedures to be followed in your workplace.

Workplace practices Any activities, procedures, use of materials or equipment and working techniques used in carrying out your job.

WC Appointment abbreviation for wet cutting.

index